JOURNAL FOR THE STUDY OF THE OLD TESTAMENT
SUPPLEMENT SERIES
294

Sheffield Academic Press

The Emergence of Yehud in the Persian Period

A Social and Demographic Study

Charles E. Carter

Journal for the Study of the Old Testament
Supplement Series 294

To Irving Goodman Lubich

יצחק בייר אברהם סענדער

Of Blessed Memory

9 May 1923–2 October 1998

Copyright © 1999 Sheffield Academic Press

Published by
Sheffield Academic Press Ltd
Mansion House
19 Kingfield Road
Sheffield S11 9AS
England

Typeset by Sheffield Academic Press
and
Printed on acid-free paper in Great Britain
by Bookcraft Ltd
Midsomer Norton, Bath

British Library Cataloguing in Publication Data

A catalogue record for this book is available
from the British Library

ISBN 1-84127-012-1

CONTENTS

LIST OF FIGURES

LIST OF TABLES

LIST OF CHARTS

ACKNOWLEDGMENTS

Scholarship is in many respects a communal enterprise, for the best scholarship results from creative interaction with others—interaction that stimulates personal and academic growth. I have been fortunate to have spent the last 12 years in settings with just this type of creative atmosphere. Therefore, much of the credit for whatever contribution this study may make goes to those who have invested themselves in my life and academic career.

This work stems from my dissertation, 'A Social and Demographic Study of Post-Exilic Judah', completed at Duke University (Durham, NC) in December 1991. Writing a dissertation is demanding not only for the student but also for his or her mentors. My heartfelt gratitude, then, goes out to each member of my committee: Professors Eric Meyers, Carol Meyers, Gerhard Lenski, James Crenshaw and Melvin Peters. Each contributed not only to this project but also to my development as a scholar. Special thanks goes to Eric Meyers, who directed my dissertation. At each stage of my initial research Eric was available to give me prompt and honest appraisals of my work. He proved to be a patient and careful listener, took my work seriously, and pushed me to consider the implications of my research.

Many other scholars have contributed to this work. Israel Finkelstein and Avi Ofer provided me with invaluable data on Persian period settlements in the biblical territory of Benjamin and the hill country of Judah, respectively. Israel Finkelstein and Magen Broshi shared with me insights on the methodology of population estimates and the use of survey data for social reconstructions of antiquity. Donald Ariel gave me access to his forthcoming report on the seal impressions from the City of David excavations. Jane Cahill provided me with a draft of her forthcoming study on the pottery and other finds of Area G of the City of David excavations, and read a draft of my own report on Jerusalem. Amos Kloner, Yonatan Nadelman and Shimon Gibson graciously shared with me results of the ongoing survey of Jerusalem.

Several institutions have provided financial support throughout my graduate studies, dissertation research and my career at Seton Hall University (South Orange, NJ). After graduating from Gordon-Conwell Theological Seminary (South Hamilton, MA), I was granted the Parsonage Graduate Fellowship for Study Abroad, which funded a year of research at the Hebrew University in Jerusalem. The Duke Center for Judaic Studies awarded me a Rabbi Nathan Perilman Fellowship in 1989–90. The American Schools of Oriental Research awarded me two grants: an Endowment for Biblical Research Travel Grant in the summer of 1989 and the Samuel H. Kress Fellowship that funded research in the summers of 1989 and 1990. I am particularly indebted to Seymour Gitin, Edna Sachar, and the rest of the staff of the W.F. Albright Institute for Archaeological Research in Jerusalem for helping to make my two summers of residency as the Kress Fellow so productive. The Graduate School of Duke University awarded me a Dissertation Travel Grant in 1990 and the William H. Poteat Instructorship in Religion in 1990–91. Seton Hall University awarded me a University Research Grant in 1994 that allowed me to travel to London and Jerusalem to conduct further research that contributed to the revision of this study.

Kenneth Hoglund and I have had many fruitful discussions on the archaeology of the Persian period. He has read the draft of this reworking of my dissertation in its entirety, and has made several useful critiques and suggestions along the way. Carol Meyers, Tamara Eskenazi, William Glanzmann and Daniel Fleming also read portions of this work in various stages, and also made numerous helpful comments. I also wish to thank many of my colleagues here at Seton Hall, whose friendship and collegiality have enriched my time here. Gisela Webb, Peter Ahr, Judith Stark, Martin Finkelstein, David Abalos and Donald Wimmer have invested in my work as teacher and scholar. Gerald Pire and Paul Holmes have both been very supportive of my work through their service as department chair. Special thanks go to Ms Penny Akin for her assistance in creating the biblical and author indexes, and to Ms Stacey Colter—secretary of the Religious Studies department— for careful reading of the manuscript proofs. I have also benefited from the support of former Dean Jerry Hirsch and current Associate Dean Steven House and Dean of the College of Arts and Sciences, James VanOosting.

A work such as this would not have come to fruition without the patience and supoort of the editorial staff of Sheffield Academic Press. I am truly indebted to Philip Davies for bearing with the many missed deadlines and for accepting my penchant for making things just right. I am certain that he would have liked this study to have been completed long ago, but he has understood that my teaching and administrative duties at Seton Hall have made the rewriting of my book a much longer process than either of us would have liked. Thanks also go to John Jarick, David Clines, managing editor Steve Barganski, and my desk editor, Vicky Acklam.

I have saved for last the thanks that is most important and most heartfelt, that which goes to my family. My parents, Harriet and Floyd Carter, instilled within me from an early age a love for God and for scripture that ultimately led me to pursue graduate studies in Hebrew Bible. Both helped in practical ways in this study as well, proofing my penultimate draft and finding numerous typographical errors. My in-laws, Irving and Ida Lubich, have also been unwavering in their love and support. It is to Irving Goodman Lubich, whom we lost after a lengthy but courageous battle with cancer, that this book is dedicated.

I can never, however, say enough to thank my wife, Elyse, my daughter, Alanna, and my son, Ezra, for their love, encouragement and understanding as I have given birth to this project not once, but twice. Elyse created the maps and figures in this study, but more importantly created an environment in which I could grow and thrive as a husband, a father, a scholar and a teacher. You have all understood my preoccupation with my work and have helped me to stay focused and to persevere. I love you all more than words can say.

ABBREVIATIONS

AA	*American Antiquity*
AAASH	Acta Antiqua Academiae Scientiarum Hungariae
AASOR	Annual of the American Schools of Oriental Research
AB	Anchor Bible
ABD	David Noel Freedman (ed.), *The Anchor Bible Dictionary* (New York: Doubleday, 1992)
ADAJ	*Annual of the Department of Antiquities of Jordan*
AJA	*American Journal of Archaeology*
AJBA	*Australian Journal of Biblical Archaeology*
AJR	H. Geva (ed.), *Ancient Jerusalem Revealed* (Jerusalem: Israel Exploration Society, 1994)
ANET	James B. Pritchard (ed.), *Ancient Near Eastern Texts Relating to the Old Testament* (Princeton, NJ: Princeton University Press, 1950)
AO	*Archéologie Orientale*
ARA	*Annual Review of Anthropology*
ASHCB	I. Magen and I. Finkelstein (eds.), *Archaeological Survey of the Hill Country of Benjamin* (Jerusalem: Israel Antiquities Authority, 1993)
AT	*Anthropology Tomorrow*
BA	*Biblical Archaeologist*
BAIAS	*Bulletin of the Anglo-Israel Archaeological Society*
BAR	*British Archaeological Reports*
BARev	*Biblical Archaeology Review*
BASOR	*Bulletin of the American Schools of Oriental Research*
BAT 1990	A. Biran and J. Aviram (eds.), *Biblical Archaeology Today, 1990: Proceedings of the Second International Congress on Biblical Archaeology* (Jerusalem: Israel Exploration Society, 1993)
BPES	*Bulletin of the Palestine Economic Society*
BSO(A)S	*Bulletin of the School of Oriental (and African) Studies*
BWANT	Beiträge zur Wissenschaft vom Alten und Neuen Testament
CA	*Current Anthropology*
CAH	Cambridge Ancient History
CBQ	*Catholic Biblical Quarterly*

CBZ	O.R. Sellers, *The Citadel at Beth-Zur* (Philadelphia: Westminster Press, 1933)
CHJ	W.D. Davies and L. Finkelstein (eds.), *The Cambridge History of Judaism* (2 vols.; Cambridge: Cambridge University Press, 1984–)
CIS	*Corpus inscriptionum semiticarum*
EAEHL	*Encyclopedia of Archaeological Excavations in the Holy Land*
EI	*Eretz Israel*
ESI	*Excavations and Surveys in Israel*
HA	*Hadashot Archaeologiot*
HSM	Harvard Semitic Monographs
HTR	*Harvard Theological Review*
HUCA	*Hebrew Union College Annual*
IDB	George Arthur Buttrick (ed.), *The Interpreter's Dictionary of the Bible* (4 vols.; Nashville: Abingdon Press, 1962)
IDBSup	*IDB*, Supplementary Volume
IEJ	*Israel Exploration Journal*
INJ	*Israel Numismatic Journal*
Int	*Interpretation*
JAR	*Journal of Anthropological Research*
JAAR	*Journal of the American Academy of Religion*
JAOS	*Journal of the American Oriental Society*
JBL	*Journal of Biblical Literature*
JJS	*Journal of Jewish Studies*
JNES	*Journal of Near Eastern Studies*
JPES	*Journal of the Palestine Economic Society*
JPMS	*Journal of Political and Military Sociology*
JPOS	*Journal of the Palestine Oriental Society*
JRAS	*Journal of the Royal Asiatic Society*
JSG	M. Kokhavi (ed.), *Judea, Samaria and the Golan: Archaeological Survey 1967–1968* (Jerusalem: The Archaeological Survey of Israel, 1972 [Heb.])
JSOT	*Journal for the Study of the Old Testament*
LRS	*Lectures on the Religion of the Semites*
NEAEHL	*New Encyclopedia of Archaeological Excavations in the Holy Land*
OEANE	Eric M. Meyers (ed.), *The Oxford Encyclopedia of Archaeology in the Near East* (5 vols.; Oxford: Oxford University Press, 1997)
OLP	*Orientalia lovaniensia periodica*
OOIA	D. Eitam and M. Heltzer (eds.), *Olive Oil in Antiquity: Israel and Neighboring Countries from Neolith to Early Arab Period* (Haifa: University of Haifa, 1987)
OTL	Old Testament Library

PCC	P.W. Lapp. *Palestine Ceramic Chronology: 200 B.C.–A.D. 70* (Publications of the Jerusalem School, Archaeology, 3; New Haven: American Schools of Oriental Research, 1961)
PEFA	*Palestine Exploration Fund Annual*
PEFQS	*Palestine Exploration Fund, Quarterly Statement*
PEQ	*Palestine Exploration Quarterly*
PTMS	Pittsburgh Theological Monograph Series
QJE	*The Quarterly Journal of Economics*
RB	*Revue Biblique*
RHPR	*Revue d'histoire et de philosophie religieuses*
RSR	*Religious Studies Review*
SJA	*Southwestern Journal of Anthropology*
SJOT	*Scandinavian Journal of the Old Testament*
SUNT	Studien zur Umwelt des Neuen Testaments
SWP	C.R. Conder and H.H. Kitchener, *The Survey of Western Palestine: Memoirs of the Topography, Orography, Hydrography, and Archaeology*, III (London: Palestine Exploration Fund, 1883)
TA	*Tel Aviv*
TN	C.C. McCown (ed.), *Tell en-Nasbeh*. I. *Archaeological and Historical Results* (Berkeley and New Haven: The Palestine Institute of Religion and the American Schools of Oriental Research, 1947)
VT	*Vetus Testamentum*
VTSup	*Vetus Testamentum*, Supplements
WA	*World Archaeology*
WBC	Word Biblical Commentary
ZA	*Zeitschrift für Assyriologie und vorderasiatische Archäologie*
ZAW	*Zeitschrift für die alttestamentliche Wissenschaft*
ZDPV	*Zeitschrift des deutschen Palästina-Vereins*

INTRODUCTION

> [The historian] must of necessity relax the stringent claim of 'what the evidence obliges us to believe' and substitute for it a modest 'what the evidence makes it reasonable for us to believe', for it is only by taking account of evidence which is suggestive, when the suggestion is in itself reasonable, rather than compelling evidence, that he will be able to integrate his data in a consistent and meaningful presentation.[1]

The biblical scholar wishing to reconstruct any aspect of life in Israel during the exilic and postexilic periods will find that he or she suffers from a decided lack of reliable sources. The biblical texts are ideological in nature[2] and the archaeological record is sparse and inconclusive. Frequently, the type of data the biblical writers were interested in was different from that of modern scholars. They sought to validate their positions of power, to comfort or cajole a populace unsure of its place in the Persian empire or its deity's involvement in their affairs, to impose a particular religious perspective on the inhabitants of the province, or to challenge the status quo. But they had little—if any—interest in preserving a detailed portrait of either socio-political or socio-economic setting of their territory for posterity. Under these circumstances, to use Jacobsen's categories, one can at best hope to make 'reasonable'

---

1. T. Jacobsen, 'Early Political Development in Mesopotamia', *ZA* 52 (1957), pp. 91-140 (95). While Jacobsen is speaking of the difficulties Mesopotamian scholars encounter when attempting to reconstruct the history of that region in the mid-third millennium BCE, the parallels with the Persian period will soon become apparent to the reader.

2. Compare, for example, the the population of Yehud estimated below (Chapter 4) with the biblical number of 42,360 given in the lists of Ezra 2.64//Neh. 7.66. See also the treatment of the borders of the province (Chapter 2). Here, one should also keep in mind the difficulties in using a text with concerns other than 'history' to reconstruct an historical reality. The recent work edited by L.L. Grabbe, *Can a 'History of Israel' Be Written?* (JSOTSup, 245; Sheffield: Sheffield Academic Press, 1997), addresses the complex issues of historiography and the appropriate methodologies for historical reconstruction.

presentation of the evidence of the social, political and economic setting of the province of Yehud.

This study, like most, has had its own history and is now somewhat
removed from its original problem. I began intending to attempt a socio-
economic reconstruction of a particular biblical institution, the tithe, and
in one particular period, the Persian (or early Second Temple) period. I
soon realized that in order to reconstruct the tithe I would have first to
understand the workings of the economy of the postexilic province of
Judah (known as Yehud in the epigraphic sources). This would involve
examining excavation and survey reports of sites that existed in that
period, addressing such questions as the autonomy and size of the province, and how the province functioned in the larger Persian administrative unit known as Eber Nāri (Aramaic: *eber nahara*). Having looked
at these issues, I would still be no closer to an understanding of either
the tithe or the economy of Yehud. After all, neither the biblical texts
nor the archaeological *realia* are exactly transparent concerning economic issues. For example, the tithing texts that are more or less contemporaneous with the Persian period, those in the books of Nehemiah
and Malachi, speak only descriptively, and then from a particular theological standpoint.[3] Nehemiah records that Levites were sent out among

---

3.   I am consciously avoiding Pentateuchal texts here, as the question of the
date of any of the sources of the Pentateuch is beyond the scope of this study. The
various positions regarding these dates are well known and need not be discussed in
detail here. The majority of scholars of the Hebrew Bible followed the traditional
Wellhausenian dating of the Priestly Source in the sixth-fourth centuries BCE for
nearly a century, with Yehezkel Kaufman arguing instead for a pre-exilic date for
that source (See *The Religion of Israel: From its Beginnings to the Babylonian
Exile* [trans. and abridged M. Greenberg; New York: Schocken Books, 1938–56
(Heb)]); I. Engnell ('Mosesböckerna', in I. Engnell and A. Fridrichsen (eds.), *Svenska Bibliskt Upplagsverk*, II [Gävle: Skolförlaget, 1948], pp. 324-42, as cited by
F.M. Cross, Jr, in *Canaanite Myth and Hebrew Epic: Essays in the History of the
Religion of Israel* [Cambridge, MA: Harvard University Press, 1973], p. 293 n. 1;
and *Gamla Testamentet: En traditionshistorisk inledning*, I [Stockholm: Svenska
Kyrkans Diakonistyrelses Bokförlag, 1945], also cited by Cross) followed recently
by Cross ('The Priestly Work', chap. 11 in *Cannanite Myth and Hebrew Epic*, pp.
293-325), argued against an independent Priestly source, but for a Priestly redaction
of the Pentateuch that took place in the exilic period. J. Van Seters has proposed a
'New Supplementary Hypothesis', which suggests that a Priestly redaction of the
Yahwist's and Deuteronomist's history (Genesis–2 Kings) was completed in the
fifth-fourth centuries. See 'The Pentateuch (Genesis, Exodus, Leviticus, Numbers,

the populace to receive tithes and that when the reconstituted community of Yehud obeyed the injunction to tithe, they brought in grain, wine, oil, and sometimes flock and herd in abundance. Never are we told how much of any commodity was collected or how many priests or Levites it would support. Nor are we told how the tithe related to the larger economy. Passages in Malachi and Haggai, as well as in Ezra and Nehemiah, suggest a troubled economy, one characterized by poverty, unfair taxation and imperial intervention. But again, no real indicators are given. This, of course, is not surprising, for the interests of the writers were different from my own: theirs were primarily theological, mine are socio-economic. If one looks to archaeology, one is helped greatly in understanding the size of the province, the number of sites, and its population. But economic indicators are problematic there as well. Most archaeologists agree, for example, that the inscribed and anepigraphic seal impressions have some economic function, but the nature of that function is unresolved. Similarly, the recently discovered text from Ketef Yeriho, while economic in nature, is of little help in understanding the larger economy of Yehud.[4] The Yehud coins that have been discovered indicate that coinage was used within the province during the latter portion of the Persian period, but little else.

If there is little help in textual or archaeological records to further one's understanding of the economy of Yehud in the Persian period, is there anywhere else we may turn? It is possible that social science theory and the 'new archaeology' may be of help at this point. If traditional archaeology was concerned primarily with ceramic typology, architectural plans and historical reconstruction of major sites, the 'new

Deuteronomy)', in Steven L. McKenzie and M. Patrick Graham (eds.), *The Hebrew Bible Today: An Introduction to Critical Issues* (Louisville, KY: Westminster/John Knox Press, 1998), pp. 3-49 (11-14); and *idem, Prologue to History: The Yahwist as Historian in Genesis* (Louisville, KY: Westminster/John Knox Press, 1992), pp. 4-7 and 19-23. For recent arguments in favor of the pre-exilic date of P, see A. Hurvitz, *A Linguistic Study of the Relationship between the Priestly Source and the Book of Ezekiel: A New Approach to an Old Problem* (Cahiers de la Révue Biblique, 20; Paris: J. Gabalda, 1982), and 'The Evidence of Language in Dating the Priestly Code: A Linguistic Study in Technical Idioms and Terminology', *RB* 81 (1984), pp. 25-46.

4. See below, Chapter 3 (pp. 164-66), for a discussion of this text and its possible significance.

archaeology' is concerned with ecological factors, subsistence strategies, scientific methodology, and, often, smaller sites. The mundane,
rather than the spectacular, is sought out for study, in the hope of learn-
ing about the life of those beyond the privileged classes. Studies by
'new archaeologists' are often rooted in cultural anthropology or the
social sciences in order to allow comparison with other cultures and the
creation and testing of hypotheses about given sites or problems. Such
an approach is needed especially when only partial data are available
for a given problem, as is the case in this study.[5]

One approach to biblical and archaeological problems that would fit
generally under the term 'new archaeology' is that of ethnoarchaeology,
in which ethnographic data are applied to archaeological problems.
While this approach has traditionally been used by anthropologists and
archaeologists concerned with reconstructing pre-historic hunting and
gathering societies, it has recently been used by biblical scholars and
archaeologists for reconstructing patterns of life in Iron Age Israel.
These scholars have used as ethnographic data taxation documents from
Syria-Palestine dating to the early Ottoman period (sixteenth century
CE) and a variety of documents from the period of the British Mandate
to study population density,[6] climate,[7] land-use patterns,[8] the ratio of

5.   For a discussion of the 'new archaeology' and its application to biblical or
Syro-Palestinian archaeology, see W.G. Dever, 'The Impact of the "New Archaeology" on Syro-Palestinian Archaeology', *BASOR* 242 (1981), pp. 15-29; 'Syro-
Palestinian and Biblical Archaeology', in D. Knight and G. Tucker (eds.), *The
Hebrew Bible and its Modern Interpreters* (Chico, CA: Scholars Press, 1985), pp.
31-74; 'The Impact of the "New Archaeology"', in J.F. Drinkard, G.L. Mattingly
and J.M. Miller (eds.), *Benchmarks in Time and Culture: An Introduction to Biblical Archaeology* (Atlanta: Scholars Press, 1988), pp. 337-57.

6.   This might be considered a least-common-denominator approach to cross-
disciplinary use of ethnographic data, although even this method has its detractors.
The bibliography on population estimates is extensive; an extended discussion of
both the method for such estimates and the problems involved in this very basic
approach to understanding and reconstructing the past is found below in Chapter 4.

7.   Typical of climatic studies are those in D. Hopkins, *The Highlands of
Canaan: Agricultural Life in the Early Iron Age* (The Social World of Biblical
Antiquity Series, 3; Decatur, GA: Almond Press, 1985), pp. 79-98, and F. Frick,
The Formation of the State in Ancient Israel: A Survey of Models and Theories
(The Social World of Biblical Antiquity Series, 4; Decatur, GA: Almond Press,
1985), pp. 101-112.

8.   Frick uses land-use maps from the Ottoman period to reconstruct land-use in
ancient Israel (*The Formation of the State*, pp. 127-28). I. Finkelstein uses statistical

bovines to caprivores,[9] diet[10] and crop yields.[11]

When I first began my research, I thought that I could use these data in order to reconstruct, perhaps quite specifically, the economy of Yehud. My dissertation,[12] upon which this work is based, included a discussion of the sources from the Ottoman period and the British Mandate of Palestine that scholars have begun to use to supplement the biblical and archaeological sources. It also presented a series of unwritten assumptions upon which these comparisons were based, and six testable hypotheses that could show the validity or question the use of such data. As I was writing that study, which was self-consciously inter-disciplinary in nature, it often felt that I was writing two separate, but related, dissertations. One was on the province of Yehud, the other on the usefulness of ethnoarchaeological data. I have decided to break the two into separate studies, the current one on Yehud, and a future study on ethnoarchaeology and biblical studies.[13]

What follows, then, is a work devoted to establishing a more complete understanding of the material culture of the province of Yehud in the Persian period.[14] To attain this, I rely on the small number of exca-

data from the period of the Mandate to do the same for the tribal area of Ephraim in *The Archaeology of the Israelite Settlement* (Jerusalem: Israel Exploration Society, 1988). See also Finkelstein's 'The Value of Demographic Data from Recent Generations for Environmental Archaeology and Historical Research', paper presented at the Society for Biblical Literature International Meeting (Sheffield, England, 1988).

9.   See B. Rosen, 'Subsistence Economy of Stratum II', in I. Finkelstein, *'Izbet Ṣarṭah: An Early Iron Age Site near Rosh Ha'ayin, Israel* (British Archaeological Reports International Series, 299; Oxford: British Archaeological Reports, 1986), pp. 156-85 (159-66).

10.   See Magen Broshi, 'The Diet of Palestine in the Roman Period: Introductory Notes', *Israel Museum Journal* 5 (1986), pp. 41-56; 'Agriculture and Economy in Roman Palestine: Seven Notes on the Babatha Archive', *IEJ* 42 (1992), pp. 230-40.

11.   Finkelstein, 'The Value of Demographic Data', 10-11; Rosen, 'Subsistence Economy of Stratum II', pp. 171-74.

12.   C.E. Carter, 'A Social and Demographic Study of Post-Exilic Judah' (PhD dissertation, Duke University, 1992).

13.   The latter is to be published by Sheffield Academic Press under the title *Filling in the Gaps: Ethnoarchaeology and the Biblical Record*.

14.   As I was completing the final revisions for this book, two studies with relevance for the study of Yehud appeared. I regret that I was unable to incorporate the insights of J. Elayi and J. Sapin's *Beyond the River: New Perspectives on Transeuphratenè* (trans. J.E. Crowley; JSOTSup, 250; Sheffield: Sheffield Academic Press,

vated sites with remains from the Persian period, and several archaeological surveys that have been conducted in the past 30 years in the territories that comprised Yehud. Based on these data, and a critical examination of some of the Persian period sources available to scholars, I
present a portrait of the site distribution, population and social setting of
Yehud from 538–332 BCE. I present this study with the conviction that
biblical scholars and archaeologists often work without an adequate understanding of one another's work. This, as William Dever has pointed
out, often leads to reconstructions that are either misinformed or misin-
forming, or more typically both. In order that the reader may better understand the scholarly context and my own methodology, I begin the
study with a presentation of both (Chapter 1). This allows the reader
quickly to determine what my own interests and even biases may be,
and is crucial for an understanding of both the need for and potential
contribution of this work. In Chapter 2, I turn to a discussion of the
boundaries of the province and the ways in which environment, geography, climate and geology combine to influence site distribution and
broader socio-economic patterns. Based upon these considerations, I
divide the province into 'environmental niches', that is, self-contained
sub-areas of Yehud that have distinct environmental traits.

Once the general boundaries of the province are determined, then it
is possible to examine the archaeological data that pertain to Persian
period sites. Chapter 3 discusses the remains from the 22 excavated
sites dating to the Neo-Babylonian and Persian periods (586–332).
Most of these were occupied sites, while some remains from tombs present additional data about the periods in question and even contribute to
the discussion of Yehud in an international context. Since the archaeological data from excavated sites are not sufficient by themselves to
allow a comprehensive reconstruction of Yehud, I then turn to the evidence from surface surveys. Chapter 4 begins with a brief history of
such surveys, the various methods used in collecting archaeological
information in surveys, their inherent strengths and weaknesses, and the
legitimate uses to which these data may be put. I am not aware of any
comparable discussion of surveys within traditional biblical studies, so I

1998) or interact with L.L. Grabbe (ed.), *Leading Captivity Captive: 'The Exile' as
History and Ideology* (JSOTSup, 278; Sheffield: Sheffield Academic Press, 1998).
Another work appeared somewhat earlier, but also too late for me to incorporate
into my study: P. Briant, *Achaemenid History. X. Histoire de l'Empire perse de
Cyrus à Alexandre* (Leiden: Nederlands Instituut voor het Nabije Oosten, 1996).

included this section in order to make this increasingly used source of data more accessible to biblical scholars. It is in this chapter that I present my preliminary reconstructions of Yehud for the Persian I (538–450 BCE) and Persian II (450–332 BCE) periods.

A discussion of the preliminary data could stop there. However, in order better to understand the implications of the data, it is necessary to continue the analysis and to understand their impact on both site distribution and population. In order to facilitate this, I then examine such issues as relative site size, changes in site distribution, site size, and population during the Persian period, and settlement history (Chapter 5). The final chapter is synthetic. In Chapter 6 I analyze the data presented and examined in Chapters 3 through 5 to see how they might inform some of the major questions that scholars have recently raised about Persian period Yehud. These include issues such as the usefulness of of J.P. Weinberg's *Bürger-Tempel-Gemeinde* (Citizen–Temple Community) model for Yehud, the social influences that led to the Persian period concerns with ritual and ethnic purity, the socio-economic setting of the province, and the rise of apocalyptic worldviews and literature. The question in all of these cases is: 'To what degree does a small, poor Yehud influence one's reading and interpretation of the community and its socio-religious, sociopolitical, and socio-economic setting?'

What This Study Is Not

The discipline of biblical scholarship is currently in a certain state of crisis. This crisis involves both methodology and the assessment—and often rejection—of previous conclusions and methods that were once considered the 'assured results' of critical scholarship. This reassessment of both methodology and former consensus opinions has led both to a reinvigoration of scholarship and a measurable backlash. Much of the discussion of late has centered around the legitimate approach to studying biblical texts and reconstructing the history of ancient Syria-Palestine, its social setting, its economic interactions and its religious/ideological commitments. And much of the discussion has become intensely political—with respect to both its use in the modern Israeli–Palestinian setting and with respect to scholarly agendas.[15] In this

15. I am keenly aware that as scholar I have no control on how others use my data, therefore I feel compelled to indicate uses of this study that I would deem

highly charged environment, the terms 'maximalist' and 'minimalist' have taken on new meanings, meanings that are often used to disparage one's opponents. It is impossible to write on the history of ancient Yehud without taking these recent developments into consideration. At the same time, these developments mean that one must be particularly clear about intent and about one's definition of terms.

In Chapter 1, I speak at greater length to the issues of the 'minimalist' and 'maximalist' debate. I want, however, to make clear that when I use the terms 'minimalist' to refer to the position of the late C.C. Torrey, and his scholarly descendants T.L. Thompson, P.R. Davies, G. Ahlström and N.P. Lemche, I am not speaking disparagingly of these scholars whom I respect and from whom I have learned a great deal. I may disagree with some of their conclusions, but I wish to engage in dialogue with them rather than diatribe against them. Therefore, when I use the term 'minimalist', I apply it in a more classical manner: those scholars whose reconstructions of the biblical worlds are written from a more skeptical perspective and who prefer a critical understanding of the biblical narratives, of extra-biblical texts and archaeological data. In this respect, my own reconstruction of Yehud is minimalistic, for it portrays a province whose boundaries and population were considerably smaller than the biblical traditions themselves—if taken uncritically—propose. Similarly, when I use the term 'maximalist', I intend it to refer to those scholars who take a more sympathetic view of the various data, and who see no reason to doubt the veracity of the biblical traditions unless serious problems require their reinterpretation. The minimalist presents the more cautious view of the data; the maximalist presents the more inclusive view of the data.

This book is also not a comprehensive analysis of the socio-economic setting of Yehud. It lays the foundation upon which such a study could be built, but it cannot do more than make programmatic observations about issues of interrelationships of settlements and environmental niches, the increase of a merchant class, the place of the temple in the provincial economy and other related matters. To go into full depth in

inappropriate. I believe that peace can only come to the modern Middle East with a meaningful resolution of the Israeli–Palestinian conflict, one that guarantees the rights of both peoples to live in peace, security and dignity. It would be a gross distortion of this study were it to be used to buttress the claims of one community over the other, or to suggest the inherent right of one or the other to the land of Israel and the West Bank/Palestine.

these socio-economic and sociopolitical areas would require a full-length study. And before *that* can be done, two additional studies must be completed: a study of the site distribution, settlement history and population of a Yehud that encompassed portions of the Shephelah and Coastal Plain, and a study of the entire area of Syria-Palestine in the Persian period.

Finally this work makes no attempt to be the final word on the social and demographic setting of Yehud. It speaks primarily to the emergence of Yehud, to the population and site distribution of the province as it is currently understood. It is by nature provisional and will therefore require periodic revisiting and changes in its projections. Already, since completing my initial study, I have had to change my site distribution and population estimates twice. And this current version is correct as of the 1996 release of *Excavations and Surveys in Israel*, which has been my primary source for updates on salvage excavations, excavations in early phases and surveys that have not yet been fully reported or released. It is my hope that despite these limitations, this study will make a substantial contribution to our understanding of what has previously been an under-analyzed and improperly understood period in ancient Israelite and Judean history.

Chapter 1

THE CHANGING FACE OF THE PERSIAN PERIOD

The study of the Neo-Babylonian and Persian periods has undergone a rather remarkable renaissance in the last two decades. Biblical scholars and archaeologists alike—though perhaps for different reasons—have devoted most of their energies to uncovering the textual and artifactual imprints of emergent Israel,[1] the 'golden ages' of the monarchy[2] and

---

1. The bibliography on each of these periods is extensive and I do not attempt here to provide a complete picture of the available work, but rather suggest the basic lines of thought. See, for example, W.F. Albright, 'Archaeology and the Date of the Hebrew Conquest of Palestine', *BASOR* 58 (1935), pp. 10-18; 'The Israelite Conquest of Canaan in the Light of Archaeology', *BASOR* 74 (1939), pp. 11-23; A. Alt, 'Die Landnahme der Israeliten in Palästina', in *idem*, *Kleine Schriften zur Geschichte des Volkes Israel*, I (Munich: Beck, 1953), pp. 89-125 (ET 'The Settlement of the Israelites in Palestine', in *idem*, *Essays on Old Testament History and Religion* [Oxford: Basil Blackwell, 1966], pp. 135-69); G.E. Mendenhall, 'The Hebrew Conquest of Palestine', *BA* 25 (1962), pp. 66-87; M. Weippert, *The Settlement of the Israelite Tribes in Palestine: A Critical Survey of the Recent Debate* (London: SCM Press, 1971); N.K. Gottwald, *The Tribes of Yahweh: A Sociology of the Religion of Liberated Israel 1250–1020 B.C.E* (Maryknoll, NY: Orbis Books, 1979); V. Fritz, 'Conquest or Settlement? The Early Iron Age in Palestine', *BA* 50 (1987), pp. 84-100; D.N. Freedman and D.F. Graf (eds.), *Palestine in Transition: The Emergence of Ancient Israel* (The Social World of Biblical Antiquity, 2; Sheffield: Almond Press, 1983); and Finkelstein, *The Archaeology of the Israelite Settlement*.
2. Frick, *The Formation of the State in Ancient Israel*; J. Flannagan, *David's Social Drama: A Hologram of Israel's Early Iron Age* (Sheffield: Almond Press, 1988); C.L. Meyers, 'David as Temple Builder', in P.D. Miller, P.D. Hanson and S.D. McBride (eds.), *Ancient Israelite Religion: Essays in Honor of Frank Moore Cross* (Philadelphia: Fortress Press, 1987), pp. 357-76; J.J.M. Roberts, 'In Defense of the Monarchy: The Contribution of Israelite Kingship to Biblical Theology', in Miller, Hanson and McBride (eds.), *Ancient Israelite Religion*, pp. 377-96; T. Ishida, *The Royal Dynasties in Ancient Israel: A Study on the Formation and Development of Royal-Dynastic Ideology* (Berlin: W. de Gruyter, 1977), and *Studies in the Period*

Israelite prophecy[3] on the one hand and setting the stage for the emergence of nascent Judaism and Christianity on the other.[4] Sandwiched in

of David and Solomon and Other Essays (Winona Lake, IN: Eisenbrauns, 1982); S. Talmon, *King, Cult and Calendar in Ancient Israel* (Jerusalem: Magnes Press, 1986); T.N.D. Mettinger, *Solomonic State Officials: A Study of the Civil Government Officials of the Israelite Monarchy* (Lund: C.W.K. Gleerup, 1971); D. Jamieson-Drake, *Scribes and Schools in Monarchic Judah: A Socio-Archaeological Approach* (The Social World of Biblical Antiquity Series, 9; Sheffield: Almond Press, 1991); D. Edelman, *King Saul in the Historiography of Judah* (JSOTSup, 121; Sheffield: Sheffield Academic Press, 1991); R. Lowery, *The Reforming Kings: Cult and Society in First Temple Juda* (JSOTSup, 120; Sheffield: JSOT Press, 1991); R. Polzin, *Samuel and the Deuteronomist* (Bloomington: Indiana University Press, 1993), and *David and the Deuteronomist: 2 Samuel* (Bloomington: Indiana University Press, 1993); B. Peckham, *History and Prophecy: The Development of the Late Judean Literary Traditions* (Garden City, NY: Doubleday, 1993); and G.N. Knoppers, *Two Nations under God: The Deuteronomistic History of Solomon and the Dual Monarchies*. I. *The Reign of Solomon and the Rise of Jeroboam* (HSM, 52; Cambridge, MA: Harvard University Press, 1993); II. *The Reign of Jeroboam, the Fall of Israel, and the Reign of Josiah* (HSM, 53; Cambridge, MA: Harvard University Press, 1994).

3.   See, e.g., the influential studies of T. Overholt, 'Prophecy: The Problem of Cross-Cultural Comparison', *Semeia* 21 (1982), pp. 55-78; and 'Seeing Is Believing: The Social Setting of Prophetic Acts of Power', *JSOT* 23 (1982), pp. 3-31; R.R. Wilson, *Prophecy and Society in Ancient Israel* (Philadelphia: Fortress Press, 1980); A.J. Heschel, *The Prophets* (New York: Harper & Row, 1962); K. Koch, *The Prophets*. I. *The Assyrian Period* (Philadelphia: Fortress Press, 1982), and *The Prophets*. II. *The Babylonaian and Persian Periods* (Philadelphia: Fortress Press, 1984); C. Westermann, *Basic Forms of Prophetic Speech* (Philadelphia: Westminster Press, 1967). J. Blenkinsopp's *A History of Prophecy in Israel from the Settlement in the Land to the Hellenistic Period* (Philadelphia: Westminster Press, 1983) marks an exception to the tendency to treat so-called 'classical prophecy' as the most significant aspect of the prophetic movement. Blenkinsopp treats the exilic and postexilic prophetic movements within the context of emergent Judaism in the Persian period. Similarly, P. Hanson's *The Dawn of Apocalyptic: The Historical and Sociological Roots of Jewish Apocalyptic Eschatology* (Philadelphia: Fortress Press, rev. edn, 1979) discusses not only the rise of this genre, but also the social setting of the postexilic community in Judah. See also R.P. Gordon (ed.), *The Place Is Too Small for Us: The Israelite Prophets in Recent Scholarship* (Sources for Biblical and Theological Study; Winona Lake, IN: Eisenbrauns, 1995), and Y. Gitay (ed.), *Prophecy and Prophets: The Diversity of Contemporary Issues in Scholarship* (Atlanta: Scholars Press, 1997).

4.   There is a marked tendency for New Testament Introductions to begin their discussion of historical backgrounds with the Hellenistic period. See, e.g., H.C. Kee,

between these two 'more interesting' periods, the 'dark age' of the pos-texilic period seemed of little consequence. When the Persian period was considered, it was common for the province of Yehud to be treated peripherally.[5] Thus, Yehud has rarely been the subject of full-length works. Instead, it has more often been examined in journal articles[6] or as part of more traditional histories of Israel,[7] of Judaism[8] or of the Persian empire or period.[9]

Understanding the New Testament (Englewood Cliffs, NJ: Prentice–Hall, 4th edn, 1983); J.B. Tyson, *The New Testament and Early Christianity*, (New York: Macmillan, 1984); S.L. Harris, *The New Testament: A Student's Introduction* (Mountain-View, CA: Mayfield, 1988); D.L. Barr, *New Testament Story: An Introduction* (Belmont, CA: Wadsworth, 2nd edn, 1995). D. Duling and N. Perrin's *The New Testament: Proclamation and Parenesis, Myth and History* (New York: Harcourt Brace Jovanovich, 1994) is the exception to this tendency and contains a brief section on Israelite history, including the Persian period. Also, the influential works on Judaism in the late Second Temple period often begin their inquiry in the Hellenistic period, e.g. E. Schürer's three-volume work *The History of the Jewish People in the Age of Jesus Christ* (ed. G. Vermes, F. Millar and M. Black; Edinburgh: T. & T. Clark, 1973); and M. Hengel's *Judaism and Hellenism* (Philadelphia: Fortress Press, 2nd edn, 1981).

5. For the purposes of this study, I use a geographic/political definition of Yehud. On the boundaries of the province, see below, Chapter 2. The stakeholders in the province included those who had remained on the land during the exile and those who returned from Babylon during the Persian period. These returnees certainly identified themselves as the 'true seed of Israel' and had at best an uneasy relationship with the 'people of the land'. But I consider both parties to be constituents of the province.

6. Among these are: P.R. Ackroyd, 'Two Old Testament Historical Problems of the Early Persian Period', *JNES* 17 (1958), pp. 13-27; 'Archaeology, Politics, and Religion: The Persian Period', *The Iliff Review* 39 (1982), pp. 5-24; and 'The History of Israel in the Exilic and Post-exilic Periods', in G.W. Anderson (ed.), *Tradition and Interpretation: Essays by Members of the Society for Old Testament Study* (Oxford: Clarendon Press, 1979), pp. 320-50; A. Alt, 'Die Rolle Samarias bei der Entstehung des Judentums', in *idem, Kleine Schriften zur Geschichte des Volkes Israel* (Munich: Beck, 1953), pp. 316-37; F.M. Cross, Jr, 'A Reconstruction of the Judean Restoration', *JBL* 94 (1975), pp. 4-18.

7. Such is the case in J. Bright's *A History of Israel* (Philadelphia: Westminster Press, 3rd edn, 1981); N.K. Gottwald, *The Hebrew Bible: A Socio-Literary Introduction* (Philadelphia: Fortress Press, 1985). See also G. Widengren, 'The Persian Period', in J.H. Hayes and J.M. Miller (eds.), *Israelite and Judean History* (Philadelphia: Westminster Press, 1977), pp. 489-538.

8. S.J.D. Cohen, *From the Maccabees to the Mishnah* (Philadelphia: Westminster Press, 1987); H.H. Ben-Sasson (ed.), *A History of the Jewish People* (Cam-

Recently, however, scholars have begun to pay more attention to the Persian period and to Yehud, spawning a number of significant studies.[10] The Society of Biblical Literature sponsored a study group devoted to the Sociology of the Second Temple;[11] the *Cambridge History of Judaism* begins with a volume on the Persian period;[12] the

bridge, MA: Harvard University Press, 1976); L.L Grabbe, *Judaism from Cyrus to Hadrian*. I. *The Persian and Greek Periods* (Minneapolis: Fortress Press, 1992).

9.   A.T. Olmstead, *History of the Persian Empire* (Chicago: University of Chicago Press, 1948); E. Bickerman, *From Ezra to the Last of the Maccabees* (New York: Schocken Books, 1962); P.R. Ackroyd, *Exile and Restoration: A History of Hebrew Thought in the Sixth Century B.C.* (Philadelphia: Westminster Press, 1968) and *idem, Israel under Babylon and Persia* (London: Oxford University Press, 1970); J.L. Berquist, *Judaism in Persia's Shadow: A Social and Historical Approach* (Minneapolis: Fortress Press, 1995).

10.   See E. Stern, *Material Culture of the Land of the Bible in the Persian Period 538–332 B.C.* (Warminster, England: Aris & Phillips Ltd, 1982); *idem*, 'The Persian Empire and the Political and Social History of Palestine in the Persian Period', in *CHJ*, I, pp. 70-87; *idem*, 'The Province of Yehud in Vision and Reality', in L. Levine (ed.), *The Jerusalem Cathedra: Studies in the History, Archaeology, Geography, and Ethnography of the Land of Israel*, I (Jerusalem: Yad Izhak Ben-Zvi Institute, 1981), pp. 9-21; T. Eskenazi, *In an Age of Prose: A Literary Approach to Ezra–Nehemiah* (Atlanta: Scholars Press, 1988); C.L. Meyers and E.M. Meyers, *Haggai, Zechariah 1–8* (AB, 25B; Garden City, NY: Doubleday, 1987); *Zechariah 9–14* (AB, 25C; Garden City, NY: Doubleday, 1993); J. O'Brien, *Priest and Levite in Malachi* (Atlanta: Scholars Press, 1990); K. Hoglund, *Achaemenid Imperial Administration in Syria-Palestine and the Missions of Ezra and Nehemiah* (Atlanta: Scholars Press, 1992). For helpful summaries of research on the exilic and postexilic periods see K. Richards, 'Reshaping Chronicles and Ezra–Nehemiah Research', in J.L. Mays, D.L. Petersen and K.H. Richards (eds.), *The Old Testament Interpretation: Past, Present, and Future. Essays in Honor of Gene M. Tucker* (Nashville: Abingdon Press, 1995), pp. 211-24; and H. Williamson, 'Exile and After: Historical Study', forthcoming in D.W. Baker and B.T. Arnold (eds.), *Faces of Old Testament Study* (Grand Rapids: Baker Book House, 1999).

11.   This in turn has given rise to two important volumes, both collections of papers presented in this section at SBL meetings: P.R. Davies (ed.), *Second Temple Studies 1: Persian Period* (JSOTSup, 117; Sheffield: Sheffield Academic Press, 1991), and T.C. Eskenazi and K.H. Richards (eds.), *Second Temple Studies 2: Temple and Community in the Persian Period* (JSOTSup, 175; Sheffield: Sheffield Academic Press, 1994). The latter volume includes some papers presented at the international meeting of the Society of Biblical Literature held in Rome in 1991 and others from the Sociology of the Second Temple group.

12.   W.D. Davies and L. Finkelstein (eds.), *The Cambridge History of Judaism*. I. *Introduction: The Persian Period* (Cambridge: Cambridge University Press, 1984).

Achaemenid History Workshop began its deliberations in the early
1980s and first published its proceedings in 1987;[13] and a new journal
dedicated to the study of the period, *Transeuphratène*, began publication in 1989. All of this activity reflects something of a shift in emphasis; indeed, it is now commonplace to see references to the Persian
period as the time in which all significant literary activity relating to
'ancient Israel'[14] occurred.[15]

13. The 1983 workshop was published as H. Sancisi-Weerdenburg (ed.), *Achae-
menid History*. I. *Sources, Structures, Synthesis* (Leiden: Nederlands Instituut voor
Nabije Oosten, 1987). Other publications include: H. Sancisi-Weerdenburg and
A. Kuhrt (eds.), *Achaemenid History*. II. *The Greek Sources* (Leiden: Nederlands
Instituut voor Nabije Oosten, 1987); A. Kuhrt and H. Sancisi-Weerdenburg (eds.),
Achaemenid History. III. *Method and Theory* (Leiden: Nederlands Instituut voor
Nabije Oosten, 1988); H. Sancisi-Weerdenburg and A. Kuhrt (eds.), *Achaemenid
History*. IV. *Centre and Periphery* (Leiden: Nederlands Instituut voor Nabije Oosten,
1990); H. Sancisi-Weerdenburg and J.W. Drijvers (eds.), *Achaemenid History*. V.
The Roots of the European Tradition (Leiden: Nederlands Instituut voor Nabije
Oosten, 1990); H. Sancisi-Weerdenburg and A. Kuhrt (eds.), *Achaemenid History*.
VI. *Asia Minor and Egypt* (Leiden: Nederlands Instituut voor Nabije Oosten, 1991);
H. Sancisi-Weerdenburg and J.W. Drijvers (eds.), *Achaemenid History*. VII. *Through
Travellers' Eyes* (Leiden: Nederlands Instituut voor Nabije Oosten, 1991); H. San-
cisi-Weerdenburg, A. Kuhrt and M. Cool Root (eds.), *Achaemenid History*. VIII.
Continuity and Change (Leiden: Nederlands Instituut voor Nabije Oosten, 1994);
M.B. Garrison and M. Cool Root (eds.), *Achaemenid History*. IX. *Persepolis seal
studies: An Introduction with Provisional Concordances of Seal Numbers and
Associated Documents on Fortification Tablets 1–2087* (Leiden: Nederlands Instituut voor het Nabije Oosten, 1996); and Briant, *Achaemenid History*, X.
    14. While I do not subscribe entirely to P. Davies's critiques of biblical schol-
arship, the quote marks around 'ancient Israel' are an explicit concession to his
point that biblical Israel is a problematic construct. See *In Search of 'Ancient Israel'*
(JSOTSup, 148; Sheffield: Sheffield Academic Press, 1992). I discuss his work
more completely in the final chapter of the present volume.
    15. The Yahwist's writing of history, the work of the Deuteronomic school, the
invention of the exodus and wilderness wandering narratives, the editing of the
Priestly school, are all placed in this period, and much of this activity is now
located in Jerusalem. See, J. Van Seters, *Prologue to History: The Yahwist as
Historian in Genesis* (Louisville, KY: Westminster/John Knox Press, 1992), and
The Life of Moses: The Yahwist as Historian in Exodus–Numbers (Louisville, KY:
Westminster/John Knox Press, 1994); G. Garbini, 'Hebrew Literature in the Persian
Period', in Eskenazi and Richards (eds.), *Second Temple Studies 2*, pp. 180-88;
R. Person, *Second Zechariah and the Deuteronomic School* (JSOTSup, 167; Shef-
field: Sheffield Academic Press, 1993).

This renewed interest in the period is heartening. But if interest in the Persian period has increased, so has an awareness of the difficulties inherent in reconstructing it. Indeed, both text and tell yield their secrets only through the interpreter's sustained effort. Numerous questions continue to be discussed, and doubtless, more should be raised. What were the boundaries of the postexilic province of Yehud? When was Yehud granted autonomy? What does 'autonomy' mean in the context of the Persian empire? What socio-economic conditions prevailed in the province? In Syria-Palestine? How important was the province to the empire and why would such a small entity as Yehud even have a significant role in imperial policy? How many sites were settled during the period, and how many people lived in Yehud? What relationship do the answers to these questions have to the biblical texts that purport to describe the period? How should these texts be approached—as history, as propaganda, as factual or as fictional? And how, if at all, can we combine the archaeological data with the textual traditions?

These questions all point toward the complicated nature of reconstructing a history of Yehud in the Persian period. The biblical texts that describe the period directly or indirectly have interests and agendas quite different from the modern historian. At the very least they must be considered tendentious. As is true of most ancient literature, political alliances, religious agendas or the self-interest of the protagonist often take precedence over 'historical fact'. So texts like Ezra–Nehemiah must be treated primarily as religious-literary texts and secondarily—if at all—as bearers of history.[16] Even if one tends to see these and other texts that date to the Persian period—and that in some way describe it—as reflecting the history and social setting that produced them, sensitivity to the nature of the texts is a necessary pre-requisite to culling them for historical information. As several scholars have aptly noted, many biblical scholars have tended to accept the general perspective of the biblical narratives—particularly those of Ezra–Nehemiah—while supplementing them with archaeological data or epigraphic sources from

16. See, e.g., Eskenazi, *In an Age of Prose*. Also following this tendency is S. Japhet, in 'The Supposed Common Authorship of Chronicles and Ezra–Nehemiah Investigated Anew', *VT* 18 (1968), pp. 330-71, and 'Sheshbazzar and Zerubbabel: Against the Background of the Historical and Religious Tendencies of Ezra–Nehemiah', *ZAW* 94 (1982), pp. 66-98.

the Neo-Babylonian or Persian periods.[17] But this approach is sorely inadequate. Typical are the comments of L.L. Grabbe:

> ...we should cease to write the history of Judah in the first part of the Persian period by lightly paraphrasing the book of Ezra, with the occasional Elephantine papyrus tossed in plus a spoonful or two of Olmstead for leavening.[18]

Archaeological studies of the period are similarly fragmentary and subject to varying interpretations. While new data are being uncovered through excavations and surveys (or are being reinterpreted on the basis of more complete understandings of the material culture of the Persian period), writing a history of the province of Yehud solely on the basis of archaeology would be difficult, if not impossible.[19] If we totally disregard the biblical literature that dates to the Persian period, in effect we fail to avail ourselves of one datum that the culture produced; it would be akin to rejecting surface survey data because they are incomplete and often inconclusive. For this reason, W.G. Dever argues for a closer relationship between archaeologists and biblical scholars, whose work is often done in isolation.[20]

17. See Davies, *In Search of 'Ancient Israel'*, pp. 22-32, and pp. 78-93; K. Hoglund, 'The Achaemenid Context', in Davies (ed.), *Second Temple Studies 1*, pp. 54-68 (55-57); L.L. Grabbe, 'Reconstructing History from the Book of Ezra', in Davies (ed.), *Second Temple Studies 1*, pp. 98-106 (105-106), and 'What Was Ezra's Mission?', in Eskenazi and Richards (eds.), *Second Temple Studies 2*, pp. 286-99 (298-99); and R.P. Carroll, 'Textual Strategies and Ideology in the Second Temple Period', in Davies (ed.), *Second Temple Studies 1*, pp. 108-24 (108-109), and 'So What Do We *Know* about the Temple? The Temple in the Prophets', in Eskenazi and Richards (eds.), *Second Temple Studies 2*, pp. 34-51 (46-51).

18. Grabbe, 'Reconstructing History', p. 105.

19. The relationship of text and archaeology and the relative place each has for reconstructing biblical history has been hotly contested of late. Few scholars would argue that there be *no* recourse to biblical traditions, but several would begin their reconstruction with archaeological rather than biblical data. See, e.g., T.L. Thompson, *Early History of the Israelite People: From the Written and Archaeological Sources* (Leiden: E.J. Brill, 1992); N.P. Lemche, *Ancient Israel: A New History of Israelite Society* (The Biblical Seminar, 5; Sheffield: Sheffield Academic Press, 1988); G. Ahlström, *The History of Ancient Palestine from the Paleolithic Period to Alexander's Conquest* (Sheffield: Sheffield Academic Press, 1993); and Davies, *In Search of 'Ancient Israel'*.

20. 'Biblical Archaeology: Death and Rebirth', in A. Biran and J. Aviram (eds.), *Biblical Archaeology Today, 1990: Proceedings of the Second International Con-*

How, then, should we proceed? Are there new methodologies or new data that will allow us to be more successful in reconstructing the socio-economic, political and religious setting of the province of Yehud than earlier scholars of the period have been? Davies has suggested that a methodology that combines the social sciences and archaeology on the one hand, and literary studies on the other hand, holds the most promise for the reconstruction of the history of biblical 'Israel'.[21] In some respects, this inclusive approach is not new. Scholars from Sir Flinders Petrie to W.F. Albright, from A. Alt to M. Noth, from B. Mazar and E. Stern to I. Finkelstein and A. Ofer have attempted to combine archaeological and textual materials.[22] However, all too frequently, textual scholars and archaeologists have neglected the advances in each others' fields. Textual scholars propose their literary solutions as if literature exists without a social or material context; archaeologists use the biblical texts and even epigraphic remains uncritically.[23] In this study, I attempt to do justice to both the literary and archaeological remains that biblical scholars and archaeologists have at their disposal. When I consult relevant biblical and extra-biblical texts,[24] I attempt to do so with appropriate sensitivity to the nature and purpose of those texts; and when I turn to archaeological data, I attempt to be as judicious and sensitive to data—both old and new—that have been unearthed. The result is a reconstruction of the size, site distribution, population and socio-economic setting of the province of Yehud from a textual, archaeologi-

gress on Biblical Archaeology (Jerusalem: Israel Exploration Society, 1993), pp. 706-22.

21. See his comments concerning the relationship between sociological and literary studies; 'The Society of Biblical Israel', in Eskenazi and Richards (eds.), *Second Temple Studies 2*, pp. 22-33; and *In Search of 'Ancient Israel'*, pp. 11-21.

22. I make no attempt here to include a bibliography for these works, since the scholars I have included are so well known that citing specific works is unnecessary. Most are cited elsewhere in this study.

23. The commentaries of Eric Meyers and Carol Meyers (*Haggai, Zechariah 1–8* and *Zechariah 9–14*), and of Philip King are notable exceptions to this trend. For the latter see *Amos, Hosea, Micah: An Archaeological Commentary* (Philadelphia: Westminster Press, 1988) and *Jeremiah: An Archaeological Companion* (Louisville, KY: Westminster/John Knox Press, 1993).

24. These would include texts such as Ezra–Nehemiah, Haggai, Zechariah, Third Isaiah and Malachi as well as relevant extra-biblical texts, ranging from the Elephantine materials, to Herodotus, to Neo-Babylonian temple texts, to the Samaritan papyri.

cal and social-science standpoint. The rest of this chapter sets the stage for this reconstruction, looking at past and present literary and archaeological constructs concerning the province, then presents the methodology for this study.

The Province of Yehud in Historical Perspective

The biblical books of Ezra and Nehemiah are the traditional starting point for discussing the reconstituted community of Yehud. While these books purport to give a history of a portion of the postexilic period, scholars appropriately question the reliability of these texts, and supplement any discussion of the period with other biblical texts that arise from a Babylonian and Palestinian provenience. Second and Third Isaiah, Haggai, Zechariah and Malachi are the most prominent of these texts, although the books of Joel, Jonah, Daniel, Ruth, Judith and 1 and 2 Maccabees are also routinely consulted as sources for the history of the Persian and Hellenistic periods. Increasingly, the studies of the period emphasize the problems involved in using any biblical texts for historical reconstruction; increasingly, therefore, a minimalist picture of Persian period Yehud prevails.[25]

The minimalist approach, however, is by no means new. Since the rise of critical scholarship, scholars have tried to solve such difficult questions as the fate of Sheshbazzar and Zerubbabel; the authenticity of the Aramaic portions of Ezra; the dating of the missions of Ezra and Nehemiah; which of the two first returned to Yehud; and the reasons for and nature of their so-called reforms. C.C. Torrey's[26] negative assessment of the validity of the Ezra traditions is cited with increasing respect by the present generation of scholars of the Persian period.

---

25. For a lively discussion on the proper methodology in reconstructing biblical history, see the exchange in the winter 1995 edition (114) of *JBL*: I.W. Provan, 'Ideologies, Literary and Critical: Reflections on Recent Writing on the History of Israel', pp. 585-606; T.L. Thompson, 'A Neo-Albrightean School in History and Biblical Scholarship?', pp. 683-98; and P.R. Davies, 'Method and Madness: Some Remarks on Doing History with the Bible', pp. 699-705. Provan's distortions of the works of Davies, Lemche, Thompson and Ahlström are unfortunate. While it will be clear that I sometimes disagree with the conclusions of the latter scholars, I trust they will find my representation of their work to be fair-minded.

26. On the context of Torrey's contribution to many of these issues, see W.F. Stinespring, 'Prolegomenon: C.C. Torrey's Contribution to Ezra Studies', in C.C. Torrey, *Ezra Studies* (New York: Ktav, 1970), pp. xi-xxviii.

According to Torrey, not only did Ezra not exist,[27] but the sources that the Chronicler used[28] and expanded into Ezra–Nehemiah tell us little or nothing reliable concerning the history of Yehud in the Persian period. No return took place under Zerubbabel or Ezra.[29] Instead, the Ezra traditions concerning the return of the Torah from Babylon were invented to validate the newly edited Torah, which was a product not of the Babylonian exile but of the resident priesthood in Yehud. In inventing the Ezra traditions and supplementing the Nehemiah Memoir, the Chronicler was thus validating and providing a history for the religious *status quo* of his day.[30]

Torrey would view the Persian period as defined not by exile and return but by the devastation of the deportation from Palestine. He believes that the exile was 'in reality a small and relatively insignificant affair' that does not deserve the central place it has been given in the history of ancient 'Israel'. The deportation to which he refers began before the destruction of the Temple in 587/586 and continued long after the so-called return from 'exile'.[31] He concludes:

> It was this catastrophe, not the exile, which constituted the dividing line between the two eras. The terms 'exilic', 'pre-exilic', and 'post-exilic' ought to be banished forever from usage, for they are merely misleading, and correspond to nothing that is real in Hebrew literature and life.[32]

According to Torrey, the gradual deportation of people from Palestine began near the end of the monarchy. It was due largely to lack of resources and changes in land tenure and availability. The ensuing eco-

27. 'The Chronicler as Editor and as Independent Narrator', in *idem*, *Ezra Studies*, pp. 208-251 (243-48).

28. Torrey identifies the Chronicler's sources as the Aramaic portions of Ezra (Ezra 4.8–6.18) and Neh. 1, 2 and 3.33–6.19. Accordingly, the rest of these works are composed by the Chronicler. See 'The Chronicler as Editor', pp. 208-251; and 'The Exile and Restoration', in *idem*, *Ezra Studies*, pp. 285-335.

29. 'The Exile and Restoration', pp. 288-301.

30. Torrey adduced as evidence for the spurious nature of the Ezra traditions the absence of Ezra in Ben Sirach 44–50, where the famous figures of Israelite history are honored, and the tradition of 2 Macc. 1.18-36 which attributes the restoration of Temple-worship to Nehemiah rather than Ezra (see Stinespring, 'Prolegomenon', p. xxi). However, Nehemiah's reforms were far-reaching and did involve the affairs of the Temple as well as so-called civil affairs. I would view neither of Torrey's objections here as conclusive.

31. Torrey, 'The Exile and Restoration', pp. 285-89.

32. 'The Exile and Restoration', p. 289.

nomic hardship over-rode the religious significance of living in Judah, near Jerusalem. Torrey has difficulty placing this in a particular historical context beyond attributing it to the monarchical period—beginning with the late eighth century BCE—and it is unlikely that the archaeological data bear out his interpretation.[33]

More important, however, is his assertion that Jerusalem was only abandoned for a short time after its destruction in 587/586. One of the effects of the destruction was the formation of at least three communities of Jews, one in Egypt, one in Babylon and one in Palestine. In Torrey's view, it was the Palestinian community that had the most authority and that created or re-worked most of the biblical literature. One of the major by-products of the forced and willful dispersion was an increased spirit of universalism. The writings dating to the Persian period show 'no condemnation of those who had left Palestine, but rather a regret that they had left and an understanding of the plight that caused them to go'.[34] Thus, the attitude of the religious authorities in Palestine became, of necessity, one that tried to make the best of the dispersion, interpreted it as a result of divine justice, accepted the good in Gentile religious traditions, and viewed Israel's destiny as bringing the nations to YHWH.[35]

While many contemporary scholars would disagree with Torrey's interpretation of these issues, several of his ideas have gained support. Lester Grabbe, for example, suggests that contemporary scholarship should revisit the consensus view that the Aramaic core of the Ezra traditions is substantially reliable and wonders how one should interpret Ezra's 'mission' if it occurred at all.[36] P.R. Davies doubts the veracity of the biblical idea of exile, the traditional scholarly view that much of the biblical material was edited during the exilic period in Babylon and that a version of the Torah was brought to Palestine by a 'historical

33. The archaeological data suggest that subsequent to the fall of Samaria in 722/721 the Southern Kingdom's population increased dramatically. It is to this period that Jerusalem's major expansion is dated. See J.M. Cahill and D. Tarler, 'Excavations Directed by Yigal Shloh at the City of David, 1978–1985', in *AJR*, pp. 35-40; See also M. Broshi and I. Finkelstein, 'The Population of Palestine in Iron Age II', *BASOR* 287 (1992), pp. 47-60.

34. Torrey, 'The Exile and Restoration', p. 308.

35. Torrey, 'The Exile and Restoration', p. 312.

36. Grabbe, 'Reconstructing History', pp. 98-99; and 'What Was Ezra's Mission?', pp. 286-99.

Ezra'.[37] Some have gone further than Torrey himself went. R.P. Carroll, for example, suggests that the fact that the dimensions of the 'Second Temple' are not given anywhere in the biblical traditions indicates that it was of little importance. He suggests that we do away entirely with the term 'Second Temple Period' and re-name the period the 'Persian-Greek Period'. In his view, the 'temple' functioned economically and socially for a minority group, one which wrote the literature about its construction in order to legitimate their perspective.[38] Carroll's call to caution is appropriate:

> What you read in the Bible are 'Biblical Facts'. Not facts in the external world but textual facts or 'history in inverted commas'. Such 'Biblical Facts' as relate to the Second Temple need to be treated in some such manner so as not to fool the modern reader into thinking that they are reading something that approximates to what *we* call history. 'Biblical Facts' require serious interpretation and evaluation as to their weight in any reconstruction of what it is we imagine we do know about the second temple—whether its origins, its structure, its nature, or its datings.[39]

A more moderate position may be found in the works of K. Hoglund, who attempts to combine literary sophistication with an archaeological perspective. Hoglund approaches the missions of Ezra and Nehemiah from the perspective of the larger Persian imperial system. For Hoglund, the social setting and historical events of the mid-fifth century BCE in Syria-Palestine must be viewed in light of the nature of empires and the social forces that sustain them.[40] He identifies four tendencies in imperial policy that affected the fortunes of Yehud in the Persian period: ruralization, commercialization, militarization, and ethnic collectivization. Each is reflected in the archaeological record, the textual traditions from the period, or both.

---

37. *In Search of 'Ancient Israel'*, pp. 40-48, 78-93, 126-30.

38. Carroll, 'So What Do We *Know* about the Temple?', pp. 34-51. He accepts the social reconstruction of Joel P. Weinberg and the *Bürger-Tempel-Gemeinde*, about which more will be said below.

39. Carroll, 'So What Do We *Know* about the Temple?', p. 46.

40. See in particular his *Achaemenid Imperial Administration*; 'The Achaemenid Context', pp. 54-68; and 'The Establishment of a Rural Economy in the Judean Hill Country during the Late Sixth Century BCE', an unpublished paper presented at the Southeastern Regional SBL/AAR/ASOR meetings, Charlotte, NC, 16–18 March 1989.

Throughout the empire, land and resources were alienable, subject to imperial needs. In most of its territories, the Persian crown pursued a policy of depopulation and/or urbanization. Within Yehud, however, a different pattern prevailed; one finds 'a deliberate decentralization of population' or what Hoglund calls a pattern of ruralization. In the traditional biblical territory of Judah, the number of settlements, most of which were unwalled villages, increased by over 25 per cent. Hoglund suggests that this difference from previous settlement patterns was not coincidental, but intentional, for two reasons: (1) the degree of discontinuity between the Iron II and Persian periods; and (2) the date the settlements in Yehud were established. He contends that a full 65 per cent of the Persian period sites in Yehud were not occupied in the Iron II period, and 24 per cent were occupied initially in the Persian period. Hoglund dates this settlement activity to the beginning of the period, a dating which seems somewhat arbitrary given the difficulty in establishing Persian period chronology.

The push toward commercialism is likewise to be found in the material culture of the Persian period. During the period, there is a marked increase in the presence of imported pottery which points toward the increase of trade. While the question of who controlled this trade must remain open to discussion, the data 'point toward extensive and protracted exchange relationships within the larger Mediterranean world'.[41] There is also an increased use of native store-jars used in transport of goods, and a number of newly established entrepots. The empire's interests were served by this increased commercialization in several ways: the commerce produced substantial revenue with little investment through increased taxation and tribute; newer patterns of regional interdependence replaced older patterns of individualization and self-sufficiency; and the increase in trade likewise stimulated production. One of the effects of this increased commercialization may have been the increase of social differentiation among the exilic community, but this occurred as a new merchant class evolved rather than from the emergence of the monied economy envisioned by Stern[42] and Kippenberg.[43]

---

41. 'The Achaemenid Context', p. 60.

42. *CHJ*, I, pp. 109-12.

43. *Religion und Klassenbildung im antiken Judäa* (SUNT, 14; Göttingen: Vandenhoeck & Ruprecht, 1978), pp. 49-53, as cited by Hoglund, 'The Achaemenid Context', p. 61.

The impetus toward militarization and ethnic collectivization bears more directly on the missions of Ezra and Nehemiah, which Hoglund dates to the mid-fifth century. In an attempt to establish the social setting of Yehud and the impact of Ezra's and Nehemiah's 'reforms', Hoglund critiques the four prevailing theories concerning the social setting of Yehud and the missions of Ezra and Nehemiah. These include Morgenstern's suggestion that a catastrophe occurred in 485 BCE, following an ill-fated revolt against Persian rule;[44] the theory that there were disturbances in the first-quarter of the fifth century throughout the Levant, which in turn are presumably visible in the archaeological record;[45] the position of Alt and his followers that Persian officials reorganized the province of Samaria and granted Yehud full political independence;[46] and the suggestion that Yehud was granted autonomy in order to engender greater loyalty to imperial rule.[47] Hoglund contends that each of the four positions is flawed and proposes a new synthesis, one that addresses issues of biblical historiography, the details of the Egyptian revolt of the mid-fifth century, the nature of the material culture and its date, and the imperial responses to the socio-political setting of the mid-fifth century.

The Egyptian revolt led by Inaros in the fifth century BCE and the ensuing Greek threat to Persian interests led to the increased militarization of Yehud. This development is reflected in the archeological record in a series of fortresses, established in the mid-fifth century BCE within the province of Yehud. These are not border fortresses, as Stern has suggested,[48] but instead had two purposes: protecting the trade routes necessary for the increased commercial activity, and providing a first line of defense for the western territories of the empire against foreign invasion.[49] This policy of militarization, in turn, provides the best context

44. For references to Morgenstern's suggestions, see Hoglund, *Achaemenid Imperial Administration*, pp. 51-61. Hoglund points out that many later scholars followed Morgenstern's theory of a revolt even though it lacks adequate evidence.

45. *Achaemenid Imperial Administration*, pp. 61-69. Here Hoglund shows that this theory is based on an unfortunate misreading of the archaeological evidence. On the archaeology of Persian period Yehud, see Chapters 3 and 4 below.

46. *Achaemenid Imperial Administration*, pp. 69-86. He rejects Alt's thesis on textual, archaeological and philological grounds.

47. *Achaemenid Imperial Administration*, pp. 86-91.

48. *Material Culture*, pp. 245-49; and 'The Persian Empire', pp. 82-86.

49. See 'The Achaemenid Context', p. 64; *Achaemenid Imperial Administration*, pp. 202-205. As a part of his discussion of the archaeological data he also

for understanding the work of Nehemiah. The fortification of Jerusalem was part of the larger imperial policy, intended not only to protect Yehud, but also to shore up the empire's defenses. As Hoglund notes, the biblical narrator associates a fortress (בירה) with the temple (Neh. 2.8), with the commander (שׂר הבירה; Neh. 7.2) controlling the entry to Jerusalem. This would explain the intensity of the protests against Nehemiah by the coalition of enemies of Yehud, who saw in these developments an increase in the status and stature of Jerusalem and therefore Yehud, and a concomitant decrease in their own authority. Thus, they threatened to appeal to the imperial throne and charge Nehemiah with sedition. This accusation would have been particularly damaging to Nehemiah, given the security concerns of the Persian empire in light of the Egyptian revolt.

Finally, Hoglund suggests that the opposition to intermarriage of both Ezra and Nehemiah is best understood in the context of a Persian policy of establishing ethnic enclaves throughout the empire. This policy included the restructuring of traditionally independent villages into collectives which were administered and taxed as a unit.[50] According to Hoglund, the concern for religious and ethnic purity, which runs throughout the Ezra and Nehemiah traditions, has as its root the economic viability of the *gôlāh* community, which perceived itself as 'slaves' living under the yoke of the empire.[51] This is further evident in the phrase, *qāhāl haggôlâh*, 'assembly of the *gôlâh*' which is 'suggestive of a corporate identity not definable by a territorial or political referrent'—that is, it is a socio-economic rather than a political term. The concern for purity of marriages, then, is not just a concern for religious purity but is rooted in the community's claim to land. A mixture of ethnicity would undermine the community's political, economic

---

establishes an architectural typology for, and dating of, these fortresses, which are found not only within the boundaries of Yehud, but also in other political contexts. His comparison of the dimensions of these buildings, the number of rooms, and percentage of the total area of the fortress devoted to the central courtyard is thorough; and his dating (arrived at in part by pottery typology) is useful in allowing for a more precise understanding of the Persian presence in Yehud. The entire discussion is found in chapter 4 of *Achaemenid Imperial Administration*, pp. 165-205.

50. 'The Achaemenid Context', pp. 65-66.

51. On this perception, see also the work of D. Smith: 'The Politics of Ezra: Sociological Indicators of Postexilic Judaean Society', in Davies (ed.), *Second Temple Studies 1*, pp. 73-97, and his larger work, *The Religion of the Landless: A Sociology of the Babylonian Exile* (Bloomington: Meyer-Stone, 1989).

and religious survival. Thus, even though the question of intermarriage was posed in theological terms, imperial concerns were always behind the actions of both reformers.[52]

The research of Joel P. Weinberg, the Latvian biblical scholar, has increasingly influenced recent analyses of the socio-economic setting of Yehud.[53] Indeed, it is rare to find contemporary works on the Persian period that do not accept some or all of Weinberg's reconstruction.[54] Weinberg proposes that Yehud be understood as an ethnically based economic enclave or collective—called a *Bürger-Tempel-Gemeinde*, or Citizen–Temple Community—centered around and controlled by the interests of the Temple. This places postexilic Judah within the context of a larger pattern of socio-economic development that Weinberg calls

52. See 'The Achaemenid Context', pp. 67-68. Hoglund's points are developed further in the final chapter of *Achaemenid Imperial Administration*.

53. Most of Weinberg's work is in Russian, Latvian and German and appeared in a series of articles in the 1970s. D. Smith-Christopher translated seven of the most important of these articles in Joel Weinberg, *The Citizen–Temple Community* (JSOTSup, 151; Sheffield: Sheffield Academic Press, 1992). These articles are: 'Bemerkungen zum Problem, "Der Vorhellenismus im Vorden Orient"', *Klio* 58 (1976), pp. 5-20; 'Demographische Notizen zur Geschichte der nachexilischen Gemeinde in Juda' *Klio* 54 (1972), pp. 45-59; 'Das Bēit 'Aḇōt im 6.–4. Jh. v.u.Z.', *VT* 23 (1973), pp. 400-14; 'Der *'ammē hā'āreṣ* des 6.–4. Jh. v.u.Z.', *Klio* 56 (1974), pp. 325-35; '*Nᵉṭînîm* und "Söhne der Sklaven Salomos" im 6.–4. Jh. v.u.Z.', *ZAW* 87 (1975), pp. 355-71; 'Die Agrarverhältnisse in der Bürger-Tempel-Gemeinde der Achämenidenzeit', *AAASH* 12 (1974), Fasc. 1-4; and 'Zentral- und Partikulargewalt im achämenidischen Reich', *Klio* 59 (1977), pp. 25-43. Weinberg wrote a concluding chapter, 'The Postexilic Citizen–Temple Community: Theory and Reality' (in *The Citizen–Temple Community*, pp. 127-38), as a retrospectus on his own work. Most references to Weinberg's work will come from Smith-Christopher's translation of these articles.

54. See J. Blenkinsopp, 'Temple and Society in Achaemenid Judah', in Davies (ed.), *Second Temple Studies 1*, pp. 22-53; P. Dion, 'The Civic-and-Temple Community of Persian Period Judaea: Neglected Insights from Eastern Europe', *JNES* 50 (1991), pp. 281-87; D. Smith-Christopher, 'Translator's Foreword', in Weinberg, *The Citizen–Temple Community*, pp. 10-16; Weinberg's influence on Smith-Christopher's analysis of the postexilic period may be seen in his studies, 'The Politics of Ezra' and *The Religion of the Landless*. See also Carroll, 'So What Do We *Know* about the Temple?', pp. 46-51, and T.C. Eskenazi and E.P. Judd, 'Marriage to a Stranger in Ezra 9–10', in Eskenazi and Richards (eds.), *Second Temple Studies 2*, pp. 266-85 (275-76).

'Pre-Hellenism'.[55] Typical of this pattern of social structure is a rapid urbanization and a concentration of power in the temples of the major deities of the emergent cities. Membership in these citizen–temple communities is restricted to the priesthood and temple-functionaries and those non-priestly citizens of the ruling class who are members of an agnatic collective called the *bêt 'abôt* in Hebrew and the *bīt abim* in Akkadian.[56]

According to Weinberg, two types of citizen–temple communities existed in antiquity: those whose temples owned large tracts of land and controlled extensive temple economies, and those in which the free, fully enfranchised members owned the land, and in which there was no true temple economy. Weinberg considers Achaemenid Judah to be representative of the latter type of *Bürger-Tempel-Gemeinde* and maintains that a clear distinction existed between it and the sociopolitical entity of the province of Judah. He suggests that the emergent community had three major population centers: one in the Central Hill country around Jerusalem, one in the Coastal Plain, and one in the Jordan Valley. In the second half of the Persian period the two separate religious and political entities combined so that by the beginning of the Hellenistic period there was no division between the political and religious spheres. All citizens of Yehud were in fact members of the citizen–temple community. Weinberg locates this sociopolitical shift within the missions of Ezra and Nehemiah. He cites as evidence for the combining of political and religious entities the increase in the number of sites—and therefore increase in population—and the increase in the number of seal impressions and coins dating to the second half of the Persian period.

The particulars of Weinberg's reconstruction and his use of textual and archaeological data are open to criticism on several levels;[57] how-

55. 'Comments on the Problem of "Pre-Hellenism" in the Near East', in Weinberg, *The Citizen–Temple Community*, pp. 17-33.

56. Weinberg discusses the form and function of the *bêt 'abôt* in several of his articles. See, e.g., 'The *Bêt Ābôt* in the Sixth to Fourth Centuries BCE'; 'Demographic Notes on the History of the Postexilic Community'; 'The Agricultural Relations of the Citizen–Temple Community'; and 'Central and Local Administration in the Achaemenid Empire', all in Weinberg, *The Citizen–Temple Community*, pp. 49-61, 34-48 (45-46), 92-104 (100-103) and 105-126 respectively.

57. I will offer a more comprehensive evaluation of Weinberg's theories below in Chapter 6.

ever, his general approach is in keeping with what may be an emerging consensus concerning the Persian period and the fortunes of the province of Yehud. He points to the need to address the sociology and socio-economic structures of the 'exile' and the 'postexilic' period. Like Hoglund and Berquist, he suggests that it is impossible to understand the period without addressing the sociology of empires in general and the needs and motivations of the Persian empire in particular.[58] He maintains that there was a substantive change in imperial policy and the fortunes of the 'postexilic' community in the mid-fifth century BCE, and that the textual and archaeological data must be consulted in tandem in order to reach a more accurate understanding of Achaemenid Judah. It is, however, in the crucial areas of his use of these two sources of data that the most serious problems in his theories become evident.

Daniel Smith has proposed one of the most thorough reconstructions of the social settings of the exilic and postexilic periods.[59] His work is characterized by a careful literary and anthropological reading of the texts in Ezra–Nehemiah and the prophetic texts that clearly date to these periods. It assumes that the starting point for understanding the Persian period and the society of both exilic and postexilic society is the historical reality of the catastrophe surrounding the destruction of Judean society in 587/586 and the subsequent deportation from Judah and forced enslavement by the Babylonians. From that vantage point he assesses the responses of minority populations 'in a conditions [*sic*] of forced removal and settlement under imperial control and power'. This, in turn, allows one to see these periods as 'a *creative response* to social realities, and not merely the desperate struggle of a culture in decline'.[60] Smith identifies four basic responses to enslavement, forced deportation or oppression, responses he calls 'mechanisms for survival'. *Structural*

58. Hoglund does interact briefly with Weinberg in his analysis of the Persian period and points out some of the limitations of Weinberg's approach. Berquist is one of the few recent scholars whose work does not refer to Weinberg's theories.

59. See in particular his *The Religion of the Landless*; 'The Politics of Ezra'; and D. Smith-Christopher, 'The Mixed Marriage Crisis in Ezra 9–10 and Nehemiah 13: A Study of the Sociology of the Post-Exilic Judaean Community', in Eskenazi and Richards (eds.), *Second Temple Studies 2*, pp. 242-65.

60. *The Religion of the Landless*, p. 10. Smith calls this perspective of minority, oppressed populations a 'Fourth World' perspective. It is important to note that his primary concern is the exilic period itself; however, I believe that his observations are pertinent to the Persian period as well.

adaptation involves changes in the ruling structure of a society, typically a 'conscious strategy of survival and resistance'. A *split in leadership* pits a new class of leaders against the traditional leaders; one group advocates physical and sometimes violent resistance to the ruling society and the other advocates what Smith calls a '*social* resistance'. *New rituals* or ritual impulses often arise that heighten the distinction and redefine the boundaries between the oppressed and any foreign influences. Such social groups also may create a new type of *hero* or *folklore* literature. For each response, Smith presents a case-study that delineates the social and anthropological aspects of a particular social group.[61] He then identifies each type of response with a development in the exilic or postexilic period. He builds upon Weinberg's suggestion that the *bêt 'abôt* represents a new social grouping among the exiles and a new strategy of leadership as an example of structural adaptation. He suggests that the conflict between Hananiah and Jeremiah is best understood as a conflict between traditional and new leadership strategies. The Priestly legislation and its concern for ritual purity is an example of ritual adaptation and boundary setting; cultic and ethnic purity function to keep the social identity of the exiles intact. Finally, Smith characterizes the Joseph, Daniel and Suffering Servant traditions as examples of 'hero literature' that provides a basis for hope for the oppressed culture. Just as Joseph, Daniel and the Servant of Deutero-Isaiah have been mistreated, but have risen to exalted positions, so the exiles will be vindicated and restored by God. Thus, these traditions function as a literature of both hope and resistance.

Although these four strategies allowed the exiles to adapt to the crises of the destruction of Judah and the deportation to Babylon, their implications were felt well into the postexilic period. The exiles developed, and to some extent maintained, a particular religious and social identity as a result of their experience. This identity, developed out of oppression and a minority status, in turn caused conflict with the Judeans who had remained in the land between 587/586 and the return of the exiles. According to Smith, this conflict underlies not only the missions of Ezra

61. The exemplars are, respectively, '(1) Japanese-American internment during World War II in the western United States; (2) South African movement of black Africans to Bantustans and the religious response of the "Zionist" churches, (3) slave societies and religious responses in pre-Civil War United States, and (4) the movement of the population of the Bikini Islands by the United States in the 1950s in order to conduct atomic tests' (*The Religion of the Landless*, p. 11).

and Nehemiah but is evident much earlier in the prophecy of Haggai. In a text that many interpreters consider a crux, Hag. 2.10-14, a portion of the community of Judeans is condemned as 'unclean'. Scholars have long interpreted this text as reflecting social and/or religious conflict, identifying the offending party along ethnic lines (Samaritans, an impure foreign element), religious distinctives (synchretists vs. 'Yahweh-alonists', or 'visionaries' vs. 'pragmatists') or class divisions (aristocracy vs. the disenfranchised). Smith argues instead that the conflict is best understood as one between the *gôlāh* community, whose minority experience purified them, and the Judeans who had remained in the land during the exilic period:

> Social boundaries erected as a mechanism for survival during the Exile led to conflicts after the return to Palestine. The exiles formed a self-consciously defined community, a *Hibakusha* community, a community of 'survivors' who returned to Palestine with a theology of acquired innocence and purity as opposed to the defilement of those who remained behind. Such a theological hubris on the part of the exile community must have created havoc and sparked the other fuel for conflicts, such as economic abuse and religious infidelity.[62]

The Status of Yehud within the Persian Empire

While the questions of the status of the province of Yehud and the date that it achieved semi-autonomous status are beyond the scope of this work, a few observations about these issues are in order. As is well known, A. Alt argued that Yehud was under control of the district of Samaria and only became a full-fledged province when Nehemiah was appointed governor.[63] His thesis focuses on the lack of mention of governors after Zerubbabel and the vigorous interference in Yehudian affairs by the governor of Samaria.[64]

---

62. *The Religion of the Landless*, p. 197.

63. A. Alt, 'Die Rolle Samarias bei der Entstehung des Judentums', in A. Alt *et al.*, *Festschrift Otto Procksch zum sechzigsten Geburtstag* (Leipzig: A. Deichert, 1934), pp. 5-28. S. McEvenue supports the Altian perspective in 'The Political Structure in Judah from Cyrus to Nehemiah', *CBQ* 43 (1981), pp. 353-64.

64. For a thorough critique of Alt's position, see M. Smith, 'Appendix: Alt's Account of the Samaritans', in *idem*, *Palestinian Parties and Politics that Shaped the Old Testament* (London: SCM Press, 2nd edn, 1987), pp. 147-53. See also the summary of Hoglund in *Achaemenid Imperial Administration*, pp. 69-75.

At the other extreme is the recent argument by M. Kochman, that the province enjoyed independence as early as the Neo-Babylonian period.[65] Kochman bases his view on the widely held theory that the Persian administrative district of *eber nāri* has its origins in the Neo-Assyrian and Neo-Babylonian periods, and identifies *eber nāri* with Syria-Palestine. In his view, the satrapy was divided into various autonomous or semi-autonomous regions; its southern region was itself divided into three parts: Samaria, Judah and Idumea, and the Transjordan. Kochman equates this block of provinces with the phrase in Ezra 4.11, 'the rest of *eber nāri*'.

Kochman argues that the province of Yehud was substantially—if not entirely—independent from the time of the edict of Cyrus, and perhaps under the Neo-Babylonian regime. He bases this conclusion upon the mention of 'Jerusalem which is in Judah' in that edict. He does not discuss the more likely possibility that Judah was merely a geographic designation.[66] However, even Kochman suggests that the purported independence of the province was in fact limited from the time of Zerubbabel until the mission of Nehemiah, when the *de jure* status of the province became *de facto* as well.

Stern[67] has argued that the province enjoyed a significant level of autonomy under Sheshbazzar and Zerubbabel, but that the latter may have been suspected of plotting rebellion against the Persian throne. This is thought to have been a result of messianic fervor associated with rebuilding the temple. In this view, Zerubbabel was deposed by Darius I as retribution for this alleged plot and rule of the province was transferred to Samaria until the mid-fifth century. With the appointment of Nehemiah as governor, and in association with his mission, Yehud was once again granted autonomy.[68]

---

65. 'Status and Extent of Judah in the Persian Period' (PhD dissertation, The Hebrew University of Jerusalem, 1980).

66. Curiously, Kochman comments that the edict of Cyrus 'was explicitly directed to the political area known by name of Judah, just as the destruction of the Temple was a political fact. It is hard to believe that the Persian kings—notwithstanding their policy of restoration—would have recognized Judah and its Temple had they ceased to exist' ('Status and Extent', p. xiii).

67. 'The Persian Empire', pp. 70-72.

68. A. Rainey suggests that from the time of Sheshbazzar to Nehemiah, Yehud functioned as a 'sub-province' of *eber nahara*. See 'The Satrapy "Beyond the River"', *AJBA* 1 (1969), pp. 51-78.

One of the major problems in reconstructing the period, as Ackroyd points out, is bridging the so-called 'governor gap'—finding adequate linkage between Zerubbabel and Nehemiah.[69] However, new sources of data have been discovered that may be of considerable use in proposing a solution to this problem and certainly call Alt's position into question. There are the cache of bullae published by Avigad[70] and the Wâdi ed-Dâliyeh papyri published by Cross.[71] With the former, C. Meyers and E. Meyers[72] have reconstructed the line of governors of Yehud from Zerubbabel to Nehemiah, and with the latter, Cross has reconstructed a list of governors and high priests for Yehud. Meyers and Meyers maintain that the line of governors after Zerubbabel included Elnathan (510–490?), whose wife was a Davidide,[73] Yeho'ezer (490–470?), Ahzai (470–?) and Nehemiah (445–433).[74] Following these more recent discoveries, then, I would suggest that during the first return allowed by Cyrus, Sheshbazzar was indeed governor of Yehud, as the Hebrew word (*pehah*) implies,[75] and that Yehud may have existed as an independent Persian province from that time.

69. Ackroyd, 'Archaeology, Politics, and Religion', pp. 11-12. Possible bridges are references to previous governors in Neh. 5.15, an obscure reference to a governor in Mal. 1.8, and the title *tirshatah*—which Ackroyd translates as 'excellency'—is also applied to Nehemiah (Neh. 10.2).

70. N. Avigad, *Bullae and Seals from a Post-Exilic Judean Archive* (Qedem, 4; Hebrew University Institute of Archaeology Monograph Series; Jerusalem: Hebrew University, 1976).

71. Cross, 'Reconstruction'.

72. Meyers and Meyers, *Haggai, Zechariah 1–8*.

73. The term used for Shelomith is *'āmāh*. See Meyers and Meyers, *Haggai, Zechariah 1–8*, p. 14. Also, E.M. Meyers, 'The Persian Period and the Judean Restoration from Zerubbabel to Nehemiah', in Miller, Hanson and McBride (eds.), *Ancient Israelite Religion*, pp. 509-521, and 'The Shelomith Seal and the Judean Restoration: Some Additional Considerations', *EI* 18 (1985), pp. 33*-38*. Stern dates this seal to the late fifth or early fourth century (*Material Culture*, p. 213).

74. Of these, Elnathan, Yeho'ezer and Ahzai have either bullae, seals or jar impressions referring to them as *phw'*, 'governor'. Sheshbazzar, Zerubbabel and Nehemiah are likewise called governors in Ezra, Haggai and Nehemiah respectively. See Meyers and Meyers, *Haggai, Zechariah 1–8*, p. 14).

75. It is important to note here, however, that the term פחה had a variety of meanings in antiquity. The comments of Ackroyd are useful: 'The title *pehah*, governor, is used very broadly, for different levels of officials. Nehemiah, we are told, was appointed governor... and this was for a fixed term. Perhaps we are making unreal distinctions if we talk of "special commissioners" and "governors" as if

The Archaeology of Yehud

The archaeological picture of Yehud is nearly as fragmentary and problematic as are the textual traditions regarding the Persian period.
Scholars often note the difficulty in distinguishing between late Iron II
pottery forms and those of the early Persian period.[76] Similar confusion
often exists between forms from the late Persian and early Hellenistic
periods, with the result that pottery from sites dating to the fourth century is often cited as Persian/Hellenistic.[77] Further, many excavations
that could have improved our understanding of the Neo-Babylonian and
Persian periods were either dug or interpreted incorrectly, or both.[78]

they were quite different. We do not know whether the Persians appointed such
officers regularly for specific periods' ('Archaeology, Politics, and Religion', p. 11).
For a similar view, see J. Kessler, 'The Second Year of Darius and the Prophet
Haggai', *Transeuphratène* 5 (1992), pp. 63-84.

76. The study of the pottery from Tell en-Naṣbeh is a case in point. Much of the
pottery for Stratum I is placed anywhere from 700–300 BCE, with two phases: 1
(seventh–early sixth centuries), and 2 ('subsequent phase or phases'; sixth–fourth
centuries). This conclusion was drawn by G.E. Wright in an analysis of remains
from the western side of the tell, and is in general agreement with those of Wampler.
More precise delineations of the period were not possible at this site (*TN*, I, p. 186).

77. A variety of excavated and surveyed sites could be cited here. An analysis
typical of excavations in the early part of this century can be found in *CBZ*. In
discussing the stratigraphy of the excavations, O.R. Sellers says '...in this volume,
because of the impossibility of making any clear-cut distinctions between so-called
EI III and H, *everything post exilic and pre-Roman is called H*, except in the very
few cases where we have material obviously from the 5th or 4th century' (p. 15
n. 7; italics added). See also A. Bergman (Biran), who said of Ras el-Kharrubeh
that it was 'a respectable village in the Perso-Hellenistic period', in 'Soundings at
the Supposed Site of Anathoth', *BASOR* 62 (1936), pp. 22-25 (24). Similarly, W.F.
Albright noted that most of the pottery from the village on the summit of Tell el-Fûl
should be dated from the seventh through the second centuries BCE and called that
pottery 'Persian-Hellenistic' (*Excavations and Results at Tell el-Fûl [Gibeah of
Saul]* [AASOR, 4; New Haven: American Schools of Oriental Research, 1924],
p. 54).

78. In particular, see the excavations at el-Jîb, conducted by J. Pritchard, who
was criticized for obscuring stratigraphic data, misinterpreting the data gathered
from the dig, and failing both to keep and to publish important pottery. See G.E.
Wright's review of 'The Water System of Gibeon' (*BA* 19 [1956], pp. 66-75), in
JNES 22 (1963), pp. 210-11; P. Lapp's review of *Winery, Defenses, and Soundings
at Gibeon* (Philadelphia: The University Museum, 1964), in *AJA* 72 (1968), pp.

Added to this is the tendency among earlier archaeologists to excavate the most important biblical sites in order to reconstruct the history of Israel and Judah. Often, even in the most recent textbooks on Syro-Palestinian archaeology, the archaeological horizon for biblical 'Israel' ends with the destruction of the Southern Kingdom in 587/586.[79]

At present there exists only one comprehensive study of the archaeology of Israel in the Persian period, Ephraim Stern's *Material Culture of the Land of the Bible in the Persian Period 538–332 B.C.* Stern has done the scholarly world a great service in bringing together in one work the wide variety of textual and archaeological data concerning the Persian period in Palestine and its material culture; it is the starting point for serious study of the archaeological data of this period. However, Stern's work is not without problems. It is sometimes misleading[80] or imprecise,[81] and it is no substitute for a careful study of the original excavation reports.[82]

Another important, but now somewhat dated, source of archaeological data is the emergency survey conducted in the West Bank and the Golan Heights after the 1967 war, published under the title *Judea,*

391-93 (which is extremely critical of virtually every aspect of Pritchard's work); and P. Paar's review of the same work in *PEQ* 98 (1966), pp. 114-18. Similarly, Wampler observed that the stratigraphy of Tell en-Naṣbeh is 'probably the most confused and uncertain of any site yet excavated in Palestine' (*TN*, I, p. 179).

79. See, for example, A. Mazar, *Archaeology of the Land of the Bible 10,000-586 B.C.E.* (New York: Doubleday, 1990); Y. Aharoni, *The Archaeology of the Land of Israel* (Philadelphia: Westminster Press, 1982).

80. For example, Stern includes a field plan for the citadel at Beth-Zur, which apparently dates not to the Persian but to the Hellenistic period (*Material Culture*, p. 37). See chapter 3 of this study for a more complete discussion of Stern's analysis of various sites, including Beth-Zur.

81. In chapter 1, in which he discusses excavation and survey data from Israel, he includes *yršlm* seals as Persian period data, and in one case considers them as partial evidence that a particular site (Azekah; a decadrachma was also discovered there) was inhabited during the Persian period. Yet in chapter 7, in which he discusses seal impressions, he correctly notes that the *yršlm* seals should be attributed to the Hellenistic period.

82. While the English translation from which his *Material Culture* was taken was published in 1982, his dissertation was completed in 1968. Evidently, however, few changes were made to update the data. Therefore the work reflects few of the advances and discoveries relating to the Persian period that were made in the intervening 14 years.

Samaria and the Golan: Archaeological Survey 1967–1968 (JSG).[83] This work contains preliminary data concerning site distribution in Palestine during the Persian period and provides a basis from which to analyze settlement patterns in all archaeological periods.

Recent advances in archaeological interpretation have allowed for a more precise nuancing of the postexilic period, advances that parallel those in biblical studies. Particularly significant in this regard is the work of Paul Lapp and Nancy Lapp, which enables scholars to assess more accurately the development from Iron II to Persian and Persian to Hellenistic periods. P. Lapp's dissertation, *Palestine Ceramic Chronology 200 B.C.–A.D. 70 (PCC)*,[84] attempts to place pottery typology for the Hellenistic period on a more firm footing. He uses pottery forms from excavations at Khirbet Qumran, Beth-Zur, and Tulul Abu el-'Alayiq to form a unified corpus of pottery, which then forms the basis for a comparative study of pottery from other sites. His stated goal is to provide '*a clear presentation of Palestinian ceramic development between 200 B.C. and A.D. 70*'.[85] It is obvious from the title and the sites considered in the study that its horizon begins well after the transition period between Persian and Hellenistic periods. Its importance for this work is that it touches on the problems involved in distinguishing between these periods and discusses a number of sites with Persian period occupations.

His groundbreaking study, 'The Pottery of Palestine in the Persian Period',[86] is based on the methodology employed in the previous study. In it, Lapp examined pottery groups from five Palestinian sites, Tell el-Fûl, Stratum V of Tell Balâṭah, Taanach (two groups) and Mughâret Abū Shinjeh, located in Wâdi ed-Dâliyeh. While Lapp himself considered the study programmatic and admitted that 'major advances' could come only from 'the careful excavation and publication of a well-stratified Persian site',[87] it remains the standard study on Persian period

---

83. Edited by M. Kokhavi (Jerusalem: The Archaeological Survey of Israel, 1972 [Heb.]).

84. Publications of the Jerusalem School, Archaeology, 3; New Haven: American Schools of Oriental Research, 1961.

85. *PCC*, p. 5. Italics in original.

86. In A. Kuschke and E. Kutsch (eds.), *Archäologie und Altes Testament: Festschrift für Kurt Galling* (Tübingen: J.C.B. Mohr, 1970), pp. 179-97.

87. 'The Pottery of Palestine', p. 187. In particular, he noted excavations at Megadim and Tel Goren. For a discussion of the latter, see Chapter 3 below.

pottery. Even so, it must be used with care, as some of the pottery that Lapp dates to the Persian period is exilic rather than the postexilic and is therefore not strictly Persian.[88]

In 1981, N. Lapp published the final report of the 1964 Tell el-Fûl excavations that had been conducted by her late husband.[89] In chapter 9, 'The Pottery from the 1964 Campaign',[90] she compares the pottery of Period III, which she dates from 640 to 538 BCE, with that of other Palestinian sites. Most important for our purposes are her discussions of the exilic and postexilic pottery of Palestine, based on the pottery forms from Tell el-Fûl IIIB.[91] She refines P. Lapp's assessment of the Stratum IIIB pottery further, concluding that the site was abandoned at the end of the Neo-Babylonian period, rather than at the end of the sixth century as P. Lapp had suggested.[92] If correct, this conclusion effectively alters the number of sites that can be dated to the Persian period.

The form, function and distribution of the *yehud* and related seal impressions from the postexilic period are the subject of the 1993 dissertation by James Christoph.[93] Christoph's study encompasses epigraphic and anepigraphic impressions from both the Persian and Hellenistic periods. He suggests that the seal impressions constitute a corpus of data that can be used effectively to help reconstruct the socio-economic setting and structure of both periods. Since previous studies of these impressions have been more narrowly focused on particular types of seals, with some emphasis on their function, this source of data has only been partially analyzed. He believes that if the distribution of the entire corpus of seals is examined and subjected to statistical testing, the results of the tests can be used to evaluate previous theories of the social setting of Yehud. Christoph follows his study of the various impres-

---

88. Most notably this is true concerning the pottery from El-Jîb, Bethel and Tell el-Fûl. For a more complete discussion of this problem, see Chapter 3.

89. N.L. Lapp (ed.), *The Third Campaign at Tell el-Fûl: The Excavations of 1964* (AASOR, 45; Cambridge, MA: American Schools of Oriental Research, 1981).

90. *The Third Campaign*, pp. 79-107.

91. Pages 84-101. For dating of stratum III, see 'Table of the Chronology of Tell el-Fûl', in *The Third Campaign*, p. xvii. There the refinement of the periodization of the site is traced. Stratum IIIA dates from 650–587 (note the discrepancy between this and the date given for the beginning of the period in chapter 9), Stratum III B spans the period from 587–538.

92. 'Tell el-Fûl', *BA* 28 (1965), pp. 2-10 (6).

93. 'The Yehud Stamped Jar Handle Corpus: Implications for the History of Postexilic Palestine' (PhD dissertation, Duke University, 1993).

sions, in which he seeks to designate internal and external consistency between and among types (such as similarities and differences in the Aramaic and Paleo-Hebrew impressions), with statistical tests designed to measure administrative, military and economic patterns in the province. In addition to his tests of the relationships among the various corpora of impressions, he seeks to identify distribution patterns in the Persian and Hellenistic periods. In this regard, he is particularly interested in the proximity of seals to either fortified sites or those designated as a *pelek* in the list of communities that aided in the refortification of Jerusalem (Neh. 3.2-22). Christoph then uses the statistical analysis to test three prominent hypotheses concerning both the function of the seals and the fiscal and political administration of Yehud in the Persian and Hellenistic periods: (1) E. Stern's suggestion that the material culture—and specifically differences in seal impressions—supports Alt's proposal that Yehud was granted autonomy in the mid-fifth century as a part of Nehemiah's mission;[94] (2) P. Schäffer's theory that there is a general continuity in administration between the Persian and Hellenistic periods;[95] and (3) theories of Y. Aharoni and P. Lapp concerning the relationship between temple and governmental control in the Persian and Hellenistic periods. Aharoni had argued that the office of High Priest controlled both temple and political affairs in Yehud by the fourth century BCE.[96] Lapp had proposed a two-pronged taxation system in the early Hellenistic period, with the *yhd-tet* impressions used by the governmental officials for taxation, and the *yršlm* pentragram seals used by the temple.[97] Christoph concludes that the data do not support Stern's

94. See Christoph, 'The Yehud Stamped Jar Handle Corpus', pp. 152-58, pp. 190-92. Stern's hypothesis is advanced in *Material Culture*, pp. 236-37, and 'The Province of Yehud', pp. 13-14 (both cited by Christoph, 'The Yehud Stamped Jar Handle Corpus', p. 190); see also Stern, 'The Persian Empire', pp. 82-86.

95. Christoph, 'The Yehud Stamped Jar Handle Corpus', pp. 158-63, 192-93. Here, Christoph is referring to P. Schäffer's study, 'The Hellenistic and Maccabeaean Periods', in J.H. Hayes and J.M. Miller (eds.), *Israelite and Judaean History* (Philadelphia: Westminster Press, 1977), pp. 539-604 (556-57).

96. Christoph, 'The Yehud Stamped Jar Handle Corpus', pp. 164-73, 193-96. The theories he analyzes are from Y. Aharoni, *Excavations of Ramat Raḥel: Seasons 1959 and 1960* (Serie Archaeologica, 2; Rome: Centro di Studi Semitici, 1962), pp. 58-59. According to Christoph, Aharoni has adapted the view proposed by Avigad in 'A New Class of Yehud Stamps', *IEJ* 7 (1951), pp. 146-53.

97. P.W. Lapp, 'Ptolemaic Stamped Handles from Judah', *BASOR* 172 (1963), pp. 22-35.

hypothesis for a radical administrative restructuring of the province of Yehud, but that Schäffer's theories of cultural and administrative continuity are substantiated through statistical testing of the seal impressions. He further concludes that the impressions and their distribution may be interpreted to support the notion of a dual office of High Priest and Governor for fourth-century Yehud. He suggests that these two offices may have been separated during the Hellenistic period; thus statistical testing may affirm both Aharoni's and Lapp's theories of political and cultic administration.[98] Finally, Christoph believes that the tests disprove the notion that the impressions were used in taxation, since they were not found throughout the province but only at certain military and administrative centers; instead, he proposes a primary function of the seals to be trade related.[99]

In addition to excavated materials, a number of important surveys have been conducted in the last decade. A. Ofer of the University of Haifa has recently completed a survey of Judea.[100] Ofer's survey divides Judea into two major sections: North, extending from the southern border of Benjamin to just north of Hebron; and South, incorporating the area from Hebron to the Negev sites.[101] Y. Magen and I. Finkelstein

98. I discuss the implications of Christoph's study, particularly regarding the political administration and socio-economic setting of Yehud in the final chapter (pp. 281-84).

99. Here, I am inclined to disagree with Christoph's analysis. The concentration of impressions in and around administrative centers seems to fit the expected pattern for a system of taxation and collection of goods-in-kind.

100. I am grateful to Dr Ofer for his willingness to share with me the preliminary results of this survey as they relate to the Persian period. Publication of the survey is expected soon.

101. In his preliminary findings, Ofer identified 28 Iron II sites in the northern section, 23 of which continuied to be occupied in the Persian period; 4 new sites were established, for a total of 27 sites. In the southern section, well south of the province of Yehud, 8 or 9 of the 23 Iron II sites were occupied in the Persian period. Ofer estimates the population of the northern section at between 10,000 and 14,000 in the Persian period ('The Judean Hill Country: From Nomadism to National Monarchy' [Heb.], in I. Finkelstein and N. Naaman (eds.), *From Nomadism to Monarchy: Archaeological and Historical Aspects of Early Israel* [Jerusalem: Yad Izhak Ben Zvi and the Israel Archaeological Society, 1990], pp. 155-214 [203-204]. A revised version of the article was translated as 'All the Hill Country of Judah? From a Settlement Fringe to a Prosperous Monarchy', in I. Finkelstein and N. Naaman [eds.], *From Nomadism to Monarchy: Archaeological and Historical Aspects of Early Israel* [Jerusalem: Yad Izhak Ben Zvi, Israel Exploration Society

recently directed a new survey of sites in Benjamin.[102] The territory is divided into seven sections, according to the 1:10,000 scale maps of the area; five of these have Persian period sites. Also important is Finkelstein's own survey of Ephraim, published in *The Archaeology of the Israelite Settlement*. While his concern in that work is primarily the Iron I period, the listing of sites includes detailed information on site histories and is useful for this study. A third survey that is important to this study was conducted by A. Kloner in the area within the municipal boundaries of Jerusalem. The results of the survey are to be published under the title *Archaeological Survey and Map of Jerusalem* but many of the sites have already been published in the series *Hadashot Archaeologiot* (*HA*) and its English counterpart, *Excavations and Surveys in Israel* (*ESI*).[103]

These surveys cover territory already studied in the 1967 survey coordinated by Kokhavi. However, they benefit from a more precise understanding of Persian period pottery and from more thorough reporting methods. They were also conducted without the time pressures under which the earlier surveys were carried out. The difference between the more recent and earlier surveys is similar to that between salvage excavations and full-scale excavations. Just as full-scale excavations provide data that are more complete and more reliable than salvage excavations, so the more comprehensive surveys in the biblical territories of Benjamin and Judah typically provide more complete data than the surveys conducted in 1967.

and Biblical Archaeological Society, 1994], pp. 92-121. However, these preliminary findings have been refined as a result of the completion of the survey. See the discussion below in Chapter 4 of this work.

102. *ASHCB: Archaeological Survey of the Hill Country of Benjamin* (Jerusalem: Israel Antiquities Authority, 1993). Most important for this study are the contributions of I. Finkelstein (Sectors 15-14, 16-14 and 17-14), U. Dinur and N. Feig (Sector 17-13), A. Feldstein and Y. Kameisky (Sectors 16-13, 16-14 and 17-14). For an analysis of the Persian period sites from *ASHCB*, see I. Milevski, 'Settlement Patterns in Northern Judah during the Achaemenid Period, According to the Hill Country of Benjamin and Jerusalem Surveys', *BAIAS* 15 (1996–97), pp. 7-29.

103. The survey represents those areas within the municipal boundaries of Jerusalem as of August 1967. Parts of four 1:20,000 maps are included: 16-13, 17-13, 16-12 and 17-12. The Old City of Jerusalem is in the northeast section of the survey, near the meeting point of the four maps.

Social Sciences and Contextual Archaeology

The social-science study of the Hebrew Bible is not new, nor are explanations about events and customs of ancient cultures by their contemporaries.[104] Scripture itself contains some 'proto-sociological' observations,[105] and classical Greek writers such as Herodotus, Plato and Aristotle comment on the social make-up and context of ancient Greek culture. To these early observations of societies one should add the comprehensive study of medieval Islamic society by Ibn Khaldûn, *The Muqaddimah: An Introduction to History*.[106] What makes Ibn Khaldûn's late fourteenth century work more than a history is his critique of the numerous historians of Islam that preceded him and his attempt to account not just for the *events* about which he wrote but also for the *reasons behind* those events. It is remarkable both in its scope and in its breadth, in its insights and its incisiveness. His work includes excurses on geography and environment, on the relationship of Bedouin culture to that of the 'civilized world' in which he lived, on kinship, on the nature of religion and its role in human societies, and on the influence of environment on human actions. He identifies the importance of group feeling, or *'aṣabiya*, for building social cohesion. While *'aṣabiya* is fundamental to the proper functioning of society in its more basic forms, Ibn Khaldûn notes that centralized government and imperial interests are often furthered at its expense. In this respect, he anticipates

104. Detailed studies on the emergence of the social sciences and their use in the study of the Hebrew Bible may be found in C.E. Carter, 'A Discipline in Transition: The Contribution of the Social Sciences to the Study of the Hebrew Bible', in C.E. Carter and C.L. Meyers (eds.), *Community, Identity, and Ideology: Social Science Approaches to the Hebrew Bible* (Winona Lake, IN: Eisenbrauns, 1996), pp. 3-36; A.D.H. Mayes, *The Old Testament in Sociological Perspective* (London: Pickering, 1989); M. Harris, *The Rise of Anthropological Theory: A History of Theories of Culture* (New York: Columbia University Press, 1968); J.W. Rogerson, *Anthropology and the Old Testament* (Atlanta: John Knox Press, 1979) and R.R. Wilson, *Sociological Approaches to the Old Testament* (Philadelphia: Fortress Press, 1984).

105. See, e.g., the writer of the Holiness Code's attempts to explain the reasons behind the purity and dietary laws (Lev. 20.22-26) and the Deuteronomic Historian's observations about prophetic developments (1 Sam. 9.8-10).

106. The definitive translation of this work was undertaken by Franz Rosenthal and published in three volumes by Princeton University Press (2nd edn, 1968). An abridged, one-volume edition, edited by N.J. Dagwood, was published in 1969 in the Bollingen Series of Princeton University Press.

Ferdinand Tönnies' assessment of the importance of community (*Gemeinschaft*) and society (*Gesellschaft*) and Emile Durkheim's distinction between the formation of simple, or 'mechanical' and more developed, or 'organic' solidarities within social groups.[107] While Ibn Khaldûn's analysis is of Islamic society, the methods he uses and the issues he raises apply to earlier as well as later societies.

Although the enlightenment provided the direct impetus for the development of the social sciences, the work of W. Robertson Smith represents one of the first detailed analyses of biblical society. Smith is considered by many to be the founder of social anthropology.[108] His *Lectures on the Religion of the Semites*[109] is still one of the classic studies of the social setting of biblical Israel, just as his earlier work, *Kinship and Marriage in Early Arabia*, laid the foundation for subsequent works on segmentary societies and kinship patterns.[110] Robertson Smith was very much a person of his times; therefore many of his theories about social evolution and Semitic culture have been superceded by more recent studies. He believed, for example, in an early, matriarchal phase of Semitic cultures that was gradually supplanted by a more traditional patriarchal society. He held that ancient widespread customs often lived on in 'survivals',[111] those relics of the past that remained in the superstitions of primitive cultures or in the underclasses of Western cultures. He maintained that cultures developed from an early, nomadic to a sedentary, agrarian phase. He also believed that sacrifice evolved from a primitive stage in which the community celebrated the presence of the deity in a spontaneous fashion, but that was gradually replaced

107. On the importance of both Tönnies and Durkheim for the social sciences, and a complete discussion of the development of social science criticism in biblical studies, see Carter, 'A Discipline in Transition', p. 6.

108. A designation suggested by M. Douglas in her influential *Purity and Danger: An Analysis of the Concepts of Pollution and Taboo* (London: Routledge & Kegan Paul, 1966), p. 13.

109. W. Robertson Smith, *Lectures on the Religion of the Semites: First Series. The Fundamental Institutions* (Edinburgh: A & C. Black, 1889).

110. This work was published by Cambridge University Press in 1885. For an analysis of the importance of *Kinship and Marriage*, see T. Beidelman, *W. Robertson Smith and the Sociological Study of Religion* (Chicago: University of Chicago Press, 1974), p. 24.

111. A term introduced by William Tylor, the originator of folklore studies. See Douglas, *Purity and Danger*, p. 14, and Rogerson, *Anthropology and the Old Testament*, particularly chapter 2, 'Survivals, Evolution and Diffusion', pp. 22-45.

by a tributary understanding, one that was more individualistic and piacular, rather than communal.

Robertson Smith wrote before the discovery of Ugaritic texts and when scholars were first discussing Akkadian texts. Thus many of the literary traditions that provide modern scholarship with the wider contexts for Israel's place in the ancient Near East were unknown to him. Yet he wrote with clarity and force, with a perception that makes his lectures worthwhile reading for scholars who are interested in the history and development of the social sciences and for those who seek better to understand Israelite culture. The second and third series of his lectures, lost for nearly 100 years, were recently discovered in the W. Robertson Smith archive of Cambridge University and subsequently edited by J. Day. These lectures deal with Smith's understanding of the priesthood, of the prophetic office and functions, and of Israelite religion in comparison with other Near Eastern traditions. Characteristic of his approach to human culture, he encourages a more sensitive, less polemical assessment of these traditions, one that foreshadowed the sentiment expressed among contemporary scholars who seek to present the Canaanite traditions in a way that presents their value rather than simply expressing their deficiencies.[112]

In the beginning of the twentieth century two European scholars wrote influential analyses of ancient Israelite culture from a social science perspective. M. Weber's *Ancient Judaism*, although seen by Weber himself as tentative and of limited value,[113] has had a lasting impact on biblical studies. The list of his preliminary observations about Israelite society that have been further developed by later scholars is impressive. It includes the significance of covenant,[114] the structure of Israelite

112. W. Robertson Smith, *Lectures on the Religion of the Semites: Second and Third Series* (ed. John Day; JSOTSup, 183; Sheffield: Sheffield Academic Press, 1995), Third Series, Lectures 1-2, pp. 59-95. A contemporary example of this concern for objectivity may be found in the paper presented in the Social and Cultural Worlds of Antiquity Group at the Society of Biblical Literature Annual Meetings in Philadelphia, November 1996, by Keith Whitelam, 'Inventing Ancient Israel: The Construction of Identity'.

113. *Ancient Judaism* (trans. H. Gerth and D. Martindale; New York: The Free Press, 1952), pp. 425-29 n. 1. Weber, who was well acquainted with the critical biblical scholarship of his day, said that he would have little, if anything, new to offer. Rather, his contribution would be in the way in which he approached the data.

114. 'Part II. The Covenant and the Confederacy', in *Ancient Judaism*, pp. 61-77. See also F.M. Cross, Jr., 'The Cultus of the Israelite League', in *idem*, *Canaanite*

society, based upon *bêt 'abôt, mishpahah* and *shevet*,[115] rejecting the idea of the bedouin or nomadic origin of Israel,[116] the Levites as carriers of cultural traditions,[117] the 'judges' as charismatic leaders,[118] Yahweh as a war god, [119] and the place of prophets in society,[120] among others. Weber's approach to sociology is generally characterized as part of the 'conflict tradition'. This tradition is concerned with the way in which competing interests in a society or culture affect one another.[121]

The French biblical scholar, Antonin Causse, wrote from a Durkeimian perspective and was particularly influenced by French sociologist Lucien Lévy-Bruhl. Causse was interested in the development of social structures and ideologies from the early, tribal period through the emergence of nascent Judaism.[122] He traced the development of Israelite

Myth and Hebrew Epic: Essays in the History of the Religion of Israel (Cambridge, MA: Harvard University Press, 1973), pp. 77-144; G. Mendenhall, 'Covenant Forms in Israelite Tradition', *BA* 17 (1954), pp. 50-76, and 'The Hebrew Conquest of Palestine', pp. 66-87; and Gottwald, *The Tribes of Yahweh*, pp. 89-114.

115. This informs Gottwald's understanding of ancient Israelite society in *The Tribes of Yahweh*, pp. 237-92, and is used by Lawrence Stager in his important study, 'The Archaeology of the Family', *BASOR* 260 (1985), pp. 1-35 (20-23).

116. In his day, Weber was rejecting this widely held belief, popularized by both W.R. Smith and by J. Wellhausen. This idealistic portrayal of the ancient Israelites was maintained by A. Alt and M. Noth and remains at the heart of the peaceful infiltration model of the origin of Israel. See, e.g., the recent work edited by Finkelstein and Naaman, *From Nomadism to Monarchy*. Weber's concerns with this model were later developed by both Mendenhall, in his essay, 'The Hebrew Conquest', pp. 68-69, and by Gottwald in *The Tribes of Yahweh*, chapter 39, 'The Pastoral Nomadic Model for Early Israel: Critique and Radical Revision', pp. 435-63.

117. Again, see Gottwald, *The Tribes of Yahweh*, pp. 695-96.

118. See Abraham Malamat, 'Charismatic Leadership in the Book of Judges', in F.M. Cross, W.E. Lemke and P.D. Miller (eds.), *Magnalia Dei: The Mighty Acts of God. Essays on the Bible and Archaeology in Memory of G. Ernest Wright* (Garden City, NY: Doubleday, 1976), pp. 126-36.

119. Cross, 'The Divine Warrior', in *idem, Canaanite Myth and Hebrew Epic*, pp. 91-111.

120. Wilson, *Prophecy and Society in Ancient Israel.*

121. For a more detailed discussion of the various social science approaches, see B. Malina, 'The Social Sciences and Biblical Interpretation', *Int* 37 (1982), pp. 229-42, and Carter, 'A Discipline in Transition,' pp. 8-13.

122. Causse's most important work is *Du groupe ethnique à la communauté religieuse: Le problème sociologique de la religion d'Israël* (Etudes d'histoire et de philosophie religieuses, 33; Paris: Alcan, 1937). See also his earlier writings: *Les*

thought from the earlier, 'group' mentality of the tribal and early monarchic periods to a more individualistic mode of thinking that, he maintained, emerged at the end of the monarchy and the exilic and postexilic periods. Causse suggested that the changes in social structure that occurred with the establishment of the monarchy led to an increased social differentiation and therefore to a widening gap between rich and poor. This, in turn, led to a protest movement, evidenced by the prophetic call for social justice and the ideology of the 'righteous poor' within the psalter. Causse's work represents the 'structural-functional' approach within sociology, an approach that traces its origin to Emile Durkheim. This tradition is concerned with the structures and institutions that a given culture constructs and their function within the wider society.[123]

After Weber and Causse, several scholars used social-science methodology in their own analyses of Israelite culture, but few did so in a comprehensive manner. Alt's contribution to the study of ancient Israel frequently used a similar methodology as that of W. Robertson Smith, and he used a Weberian perspective in his examination of the Israelite city. Noth applied Weber's notion of the centrality of the covenant in his reconstruction of tribal Israel as an amphictyony. J. Pederson and S. Mowinckel applied the perspectives of the *religiongeschictliche schule* to Israelite social and cultic settings. G. Dalman applied his extensive knowledge of nineteenth- and twentieth-century bedouin and Palestinian cultures to the study of ancient Israel in a precursor to modern ethnoarchaeology. At the same time that European scholars were applying social-science perspectives to Israelite culture, with varying degrees of success, American biblical scholarship was far more theological in orientation. W.F. Albright, whose melding of the archaeological record and biblical texts set the agenda for an entire generation

---

'pauvres' d'Israël: Prophètes, psalmistes, messianistes (Strasbourg: Librairie Istra, 1922), and *Les dispersés d'Israël: Les origines de la diaspora et son rôle dans la formation du Judaïsme* (Paris: Alcan, 1929). An article by Causse, 'Du groupe ethnique à la communauté religieuse: Le problème sociologique du judaïsme', *RHPR* 14 (1934), pp. 285-335, appears as 'From an Ethnic Group to a Religious Community: The Sociological Problem of Judaism' (trans. D.W. Baker; ed. C.E. Carter), in Carter and Meyers (eds.), *Community, Identity, and Ideology*, pp. 95-118.

123. Malina, 'The Social Sciences', pp. 233-34, and Carter, 'A Discipline in Transition', pp. 9-10.

of scholars, was suspicious of sociological models and critiqued both Weber and Causse as positivistic and reductionistic.[124]

These developments led to a hiatus in the comprehensive application of the social sciences to biblical studies that lasted until the early 1960s when G. Mendenhall first proposed the peasant revolt theory of the emergence of Israel in Canaan.[125] One of Mendenhall's major contributions to the field of biblical studies, in addition to the new model for Israelite origins and fresh analyses of biblical institutions, was methodological. He correctly criticized biblical scholars for basing their work on assumptions that not only were not clearly stated but also were often incorrect.[126] N.K. Gottwald followed Mendenhall's lead toward a renewed application of sociological and anthropological approaches to the study of the Hebrew Bible. His essay on the 'domain assumptions' that have governed biblical scholarship identifies three primary working assumptions that he considers inappropriate;[127] in their place Gottwald suggests three assumptions that place Israelite culture within a broader, more accurate social context. He followed this programmatic essay with his monumental *The Tribes of Yawheh: A Sociology of the Religion of Liberated Israel 1250–1050 B.C.E.*, which effectively altered the landscape of biblical studies. Despite the criticisms that Gottwald's work

124. On Albright's evaluation of Weber and Causse, see S.T. Kimbrough, 'A Non-Weberian Approach to Israelite Religion', *JNES* 31 (1972), pp. 197-202 (199, 202).

125. Mendenhall, 'The Hebrew Conquest'. For a more developed version of many of these ideas, see his *The Tenth Generation: The Origins of the Biblical Tradition* (Baltimore: The Johns Hopkins University Press, 1973). 'The Hebrew Conquest of Palestine' is reprinted in Carter and Meyers (eds.), *Community, Identity, and Ideology*, pp. 152-69.

126. 'The Hebrew Conquest', pp. 68-71. After reviewing the two models of the conquest popular at the time of writing and the hypotheses underlying them, he criticized the popularly held notions concerning nomadism and tribalism in the ancient world. Mendenhall was the first to suggest that the view of camel nomadism typically held by biblical scholars was naive; he argued that transhumant nomadism was more likely applicable to earliest Israel. His view of tribalism similarly altered the direction of biblical studies.

127. 'Domain Assumptions and Societal Models in the Study of Pre-Monarchic Israel', in G.W. Anderson *et al.* (eds.), *Congress Volume: Edinburgh, 1974* (VTSup, 28; Leiden: E.J. Brill, 1974), pp. 89-100. The article is reprinted in Carter and Meyers (eds.), *Community, Identity, and Ideology*, pp. 170-81.

reflects the worst of 'armchair' sociology,[128] it is an important advance
over Mendenhall, in that it exhibits a more thorough acquaintance
of sociological and anthropological theory. Some consider Gottwald's
commitment to a materialist model, rooted in Marxist social theory, to
be a weakness of the volume, one that at times leads him to positions
that the data simply do not warrant.[129]

Since Gottwald consciously builds upon Mendenhall's theories, the
strident manner in which Mendenhall has rejected Gottwald's model is
somewhat surprising.[130] On the surface, at least, these two sociologies
of Israel have much in common. However, at the heart of Gottwald's
sociology is not only a Marxist commitment, but also a cultural materialist hermeneutic.[131] This means that he sees materialist forces at the
heart of cultural change, including changes in ideology;[132] 'only as the

128. The most biting critique comes from Anson Rainey, who begins his review
of Gottwald's *The Tribes of Yahweh* by saying that is a work that has little value
and can 'safely and profitably be ignored'. See, review of *The Tribes of Yahweh:
A Sociology of the Religion of Liberated Israel 1250–1050 B.C.E.* (Maryknoll, NY:
Orbis Books, 1979), in *JAOS* 107 (1987), pp. 541-43. For more sympathetic reviews,
see those by M.J. Buss and G. Lenski, in *RSR* 6 (1980), pp. 271-75 and 271-78
respectively.

129. For example, Gottwald regards the Israelite use of an alphabetic script as an
egalitarian strategy intended to democratize writing and through which to celebrate
the victories of anti-statist Israel over stratified Canaan (See *The Tribes of Yahweh*,
p. 409). However, before Israel emerged, Ugarit—a thoroughly stratified city-state
—developed an alphabetic script using principles inherent in Akkadian syllabic
cuneiform. Further, from its inception, writing was a means of social control, usually intended to attain surplus for the ruling elite. There is little evidence that
writing functioned in a significantly different manner in Israel.

130. This is most apparent in Mendenhall's contribution 'Ancient Israel's Hyphenated History', to D.N. Freedman and D.F. Graf (eds.), *Palestine in Transition:
The Emergence of Ancient Israel* (The Social World of Biblical Antiquity, 2; Sheffield: Almond Press, 1983), pp. 91-103.

131. See in particular, 'Part X. The Religion of the New Egalitarian Society:
Idealist, Structural-Functional, and Historical-Materialist Models', in *The Tribes of
Yahweh*, pp. 591-663. For a thorough discussion of materialist approaches to cul-
tural change, see M. Harris, *The Rise of Anthropological Theory*; *idem, Cows, Pigs,
Wars, and Witches: The Riddles of Human Culture* (New York: Random House,
1979); and, *Cultural Materialism: The Struggle for a Science of Culture* (New York:
Vintage Books, 1979).

132. This is generally in keeping with Marxist readings of history. Marx himself
is often accused of being an economic determinist. For a defense of Marx on this

full *materiality* of Israel is more securely grasped will we be able to make proper sense of its *spirituality*.[133] In contrast, Mendenhall maintains that Israel's emergence in the land of Canaan was based on the radically new ideology of Yahwism. So for Mendenhall, spirituality explains materiality, while for Gottwald, materiality influences spirituality; this difference in turn explains Mendenhall's biting criticisms of Gottwald.[134]

Ironically, Gottwald may be criticized for not being consistent enough in his materialist models. He claims that the major social features of pre-monarchic Israel may be explained by its anti-statist and egalitarian ideology. It is more likely that any egalitarianism that existed in tribal Israel was due in large part to the social realities from which Israel emerged. The earliest settlements in the hill country are characterized by crude pottery and architectural traditions and a subsistence economy

charge, see M. Rader, *Marx's Interpretation of History* (New York: Oxford University Press, 1979), and L. Wacquant, 'Heuristic Models in Marxian Theory', *Social Forces* 64 (1985), pp. 17-45. Both see a complexity in Marx and contend that several models of interpretation may be found within Marx's writings. Besides the 'base-superstructure' model (changes in the superstructure—aspects of society from artistic development to political structure—are determined by changes in the mode of production), two other models are operative. The model of organic totality suggests that societies, like living organisms, are in a constant state of flux and must find a balance; the dialectical model focuses on the processes of opposition and interaction within societies.

133. *The Tribes of Yahweh*, p. xxv.

134. For a more thorough critique of cultural materialist approaches to biblical studies, see G. Herion, 'The Impact of Modern and Social Science Assumptions on the Reconstruction of Israelite History', *JSOT* 34 (1986), pp. 3-33; reprinted in Carter and Meyers (eds.), *Community, Identity, and Ideology*, pp. 230-57. Herion correctly points out that most sociologists are 'idealists' rather than 'materialists', and warns against applying models to a given society (here, biblical Israel) that may be foreign to that society. Critiquing R. Wilson's *Prophecy and Society in Ancient Israel* and Gottwald's *The Tribes of Yahweh*, he further suggests that sociological study of the biblical traditions have tended towards positivism, reductionism, relativism and determinism. By positivism he means that empirical models are espoused as the only true scientific models, leading to a false sense of objectivity. Reductionism involves explaining the complex in terms of the simple. Here he warns against a model-building in which the model and that which it is meant to explain are confused. Relativism denies the possibility of any absolute moral value in a given text or situation in the biblical world, and determinism suggests that belief systems are culturally bound if not materially caused.

with little, if any, surplus. Societies with these features tend to be egalitarian by nature, since stratification tends to result only when a substantial surplus is produced.[135] A commitment to egalitarianism, and its possible legitimation in Yahwistic religion, would probably have been secondary and socially influenced. Despite these and other criticisms, Gottwald's work is significant and in some respects has altered the face of biblical scholarship. It is fitting that in his closing remarks in *The Tribes of Yahweh* he calls for rigorous studies of particular problems in the history and religion of Israel to be written from a distinctly social-science perspective. Since the publication of *The Tribes of Yahweh* two decades ago, numerous studies of the type Gottwald envisioned have been undertaken. Among these are F. Frick's study on Israelite state-formation,[136] C. Meyer's analysis of the social setting of Israelite women,[137] J. Flannagan's study of the early monarchy,[138] and D. Smith's study of the social setting of the Babylonian exile and the early stages of the return to Yehud.[139]

Gottwald remains one of the most important methodologists for applying the social sciences to the biblical world. His most recent work is a brief but powerful proposal for a multi-disciplinary approach that blends various sources of data about ancient societies to form a view reinforced by social-science 'triangulation'. He identifies four grids that must be successively superimposed on one another to produce an accurate portrait of ancient societies: the physical grid, the cultural grid, the social organizational/political grid, and the religious grid. When one examines these grids together, one gains 'a measure of certitude that no one mode of inquiry alone can provide'.[140]

While social science criticism has become a distinct field of inquiry within biblical studies, it has received mixed reviews from traditional,

---

135. See G. Lenski, *Power and Privilege: A Theory of Social Stratification* (New York: McGraw-Hill, 1966) for a discussion of the influence of economic surplus on social stratification. In particular note chapter 3, 'The Dynamics of Distributive Systems' and chapter 4, 'The Structure of Distributive Systems', pp. 43-93.

136. *The Formation of the State in Ancient Israel*.

137. *Discovering Eve: Israelite Women in Context* (New York: Oxford University Press, 1988).

138. *David's Social Drama*.

139. *The Religion of the Landless*.

140. N.K. Gottwald, 'Reconstructing the Social History of Early Israel', *EI* 24 (1993), pp. 77*-82*.

textually oriented scholars.[141] Some of the reticence among scholars regarding social-science approaches may be influenced by the biblical writers' commitment to Israel's religious and cultural uniqueness from its neighbors. Social-science study insists on identifying elements among societies that are common as well as those that are particular to a particular culture, so that a certain leveling of human behavior is often demonstrated.[142] This approach often views Israel's theological commitments as it would any religious ideology in any other culture, either denying or at least questioning the 'truth claim' of the biblical traditions. For some, therefore, the designation of biblical theology as ideology is at once problematic and a cause for rejecting social-science interpretation of biblical cultures. In addition to this concern, scholars have expressed reservations regarding the application of modern models to antiquity,[143] the danger of social determinism[144] and the lack of

141. See, in particular, the comments of B. Halpern in *The First Historians: The Hebrew Bible and History* (New York: Harper & Row, 1988). He rejects many approaches, including the literary and sociological, as providing little of value to the serious study of the Hebrew Bible. Concerning social science approaches to biblical studies he comments: '...social scientific [methods]...call on models extrinsic not just to the text, but to the culture as a whole. They apply universal, unhistorical schematics, like those of the natural sciences, yet deal, like the human sciences, in variables (e.g., forms of society) whose components, whose atoms, are never isolated. Such tools cannot usher in a revolution in historical certainty. Their promise, like that of the positivist program of the nineteenth century, is an eschatological one' (p. 5).

142. See, for example, R. Oden, *The Bible without Theology: The Theological Tradition and Alternatives to It* (San Francisco: Harper & Row, 1987) who demonstrates that many theologically oriented explanations of biblical practices are, in fact, questionable if not incorrect (for example, the claim of the practice of cultic prostitution). More telling is the review of traditional interpretations of the uniqueness of Israelite religion by Gary Anderson in his dissertation, *Sacrifice and Offerings in Ancient Israel: Studies in their Social and Political Importance* (Atlanta: Scholars Press, 1987). Excerpts from both works are reprinted in Carter and Meyers (eds.), *Community, Identity, and Ideology*, pp. 182-229.

143. See J.M. Sasson, 'On Choosing Models for Recreating Israelite Pre-Monarchic History', *JSOT* 21 (1981), pp. 3-24, and N.P. Lemche, 'On the Use of "System Theory", "Macro Theories", and "Evolutionistic Thinking" in Modern Old Testament Research and Biblical Archaeology', *SJOT* 2 (1990), pp. 73-88. The latter is reprinted in Carter and Meyers (eds.), *Community, Identity, and Ideology*, pp. 273-86.

144. Herion, 'The Impact of Modern and Social Science Assumptions', pp. 6-9; and Lemche, 'On the Use of "System Theory"', pp. 81-82.

precision and consistency in the use of the social sciences themselves.[145] Each of these concerns raises important methodological issues
for those who would use the social sciences. Certainly, it is the case that
the more recent social-science studies of ancient Israel are more
thoroughly steeped in appropriate social-science theory than were some
of the pioneering studies mentioned here. However, one must always
guard against applying models from the social sciences to biblical
culture in overly simplified ways and must also be careful not to use
overtly deterministic methodologies. A grounding in sociological and
anthropological theory will not in and of itself guarantee a sophisticated
social-science study of biblical Israel—any more than an understanding
of Hebrew guarantees a sensitive reading of biblical texts. Such grounding is increasingly becoming necessary for the modern critical study of
biblical texts and cultures. Biblical scholars should therefore seek to
emulate the model of Max Weber, whose study and mastery of critical
biblical and ancient Near Eastern scholarship of his day was the foundation of his sociological observations in his work, *Ancient Judaism*.

A New Style of 'Biblical Archaeology'?

The debate over the name for archaeological study that is directly
related to the land of Palestine may have subsided,[146] but significant
changes in the field have occurred as a result of that debate. The
approach of the founders of the biblical archaeology movement, W.F.
Albright and G.E. Wright, which attempted to merge biblical traditions
and archaeological data,[147] has been modified and new methodologies

---

145. N.P. Lemche, *Early Israel: Anthropological and Historical Studies on the
Israelite Society before the Monarchy* (VTSup, 37; Leiden: E.J. Brill, 1985); J.W.
Rogerson, 'The Use of Sociology in Old Testament Studies', in J.A. Emerton (ed.),
Congress Volume: Salamanca, 1983 (VTSup, 36; Leiden: E.J. Brill, 1985), pp. 245-
56.

146. The chief advocate for the term Syro-Palestinian archaeology as opposed to
'Biblical Archaeology' is W.G. Dever, whose concerns for the growth of a more
professional discipline, independent of biblical concerns, are similar to those of
Binford in New World archaeology. Yet even Dever now allows for the use of the
popular term in his address to the Second International Congress of Biblical Archaeology. See 'Biblical Archaeology', pp. 706-22.

147. The problem was less that the biblical texts and archaeology were combined, but that theological concerns often set the agenda both for excavation and
interpretation. C. Meyers and E. Meyers note, concerning G.E. Wright, that 'his

have emerged from them.[148] These changes include a shift away from excavating larger, spectacular sites in favor of smaller sites; these smaller sites allow scholars to reconstruct the social setting and lifeways of the more 'ordinary' Israelite. Several scholars now use ethnographic data for population and demographic analyses. The environmental approach to Iron I, pre-monarchic Israel has allowed a greater sensitivity to issues such as crop types and yields and the interrelationship of distinct environmental areas with one another. Understanding the dynamics of state formation and making greater use of anthropological and sociological modeling have also helped to explain the archaeological record.

Long defenders of the term 'biblical archaeology', but concerned for the growth of the discipline, C. Meyers and E. Meyers have recently suggested a new form of what they call 'socio-archaeology'.[149] They welcome the impact of the 'new archaeology'[150] in biblical archaeol-

concomitant suggestion that the biblical archaeologist's "central and absorbing interest is the understanding and exposition of the Scriptures" is no longer appropriate'. In their view, biblical archaeology, once primarily located in seminaries and theological institutions, should become part of the university community, and must have a broader agenda. C. Meyers and E. Meyers, 'Expanding the Frontiers of Biblical Archaeology', *EI* 20 (1989), pp. 140*-47* (143). Similarly, Dever observes, 'The old style of relating archaeology and Biblical studies, using both as proof texts for historical and theological presuppositions is neither possible nor even desirable' ('Biblical Archaeology', p. 707).

148. Dever notes, however, that by the time the 'new archaeology' was adopted by Syro-Palestinian archaeologists, it was no longer new, but 'already obsolete' ('Biblical Archaeology', p. 708). For Dever's previous discussions of the new archaeology, see 'The Impact of the "New Archaeology" on Syro-Palestinian Archaeology', pp. 15-29; 'Syro-Palestinian and Biblical Archaeology', pp. 31-74; 'The Impact of the "New Archaeology"', pp. 337-57.

149. 'Expanding the Frontiers', pp. 142-43. For the basis of this term they seem to be following C. Renfrew, *Approaches to Social Archaeology* (Cambridge, MA: Harvard University Press, 1984), and C.L. Redman (ed.), *Social Archaeology* (New York: Academic Press, 1978) as cited in p. 147 n. 16 of their article. Another useful study is C. Redman, *Archaeological Explanation: The Scientific Method in Archaeology* (New York: Columbia University Press, 1984).

150. Meyers and Meyers point out that the 'new archaeology' and its concerns grew from a discipline with few historical or literary sources, and where, in fact, prehistory was being reconstructed. Thus, its application to biblical archaeology (or even Near Eastern archaeology) would necessarily have a different focus. This is in

ogy, but suggest that its real force is to be felt not in data collection and reportage, but in 'broadening the horizons for knowledge about an ancient culture'.[151] In their view, an 'integrative social-world approach'—one that is based on sociological theory and model-building and combines archaeological and textual data with a concern for ecology, social dynamics, gender relations, demographics, etc.—marks the ideal direction for biblical archaeology.[152]

Dever's aforementioned address also calls for a 'new style of biblical archaeology',[153] that is integrative like that of Meyers and Meyers, but which Dever calls 'contextual archaeology'. To demarcate this 'contextual' approach, Dever draws heavily on the works of Ian Hodder,[154] who has suggested a new interpretive agenda that departs significantly from certain concerns of the 'new archaeology'.[155] This newest archaeology, Dever suggests, 'now bids fair to replace the "new archaeology" as an overall paradigm'.[156]

keeping with my observations above concerning the difference in applying ethnographic data to ancient Israel in historical periods and using them for prehistoric reconstruction. See Carter, 'A Social and Demographic Study', pp. 206-317.

151. 'Expanding the Frontiers', pp. 142-43.

152. 'Expanding the Frontiers', p. 143. They note: 'the integrative goals of social and historical reconstructions, of which the use and understanding of the biblical materials is surely a part, should define the frontiers of biblical archaeology'.

153. See also 'Yigal Yadin: Prototypical Biblical Archaeologist', *EI* 20 (1989), pp. 44*-51* (51 n. 17).

154. In particular, Dever cites I. Hodder's work: *Reading the Past: Current Approaches to Interpretation* (Cambridge: Cambridge University Press, 1986). See also I. Hodder, 'The Contribution of the Long Term', in I. Hodder (ed.), *Archaeology as Long-Term History* (Cambridge: Cambridge University Press, 1987), pp. 1-8; and *idem*, 'The Identification and Interpretation of Ranking in Prehistory: A Contextual Perspective', in C. Renfrew and S. Shennan (eds.), *Ranking, Resource and Exchange: Aspects of the Archaeology of Early European Society* (Cambridge: Cambridge University Press, 1982), pp. 150-54.

155. Dever sees six aspects to this 'post-processual' or 'contextual' archaeology: (1) disenchantment with theory and its concomitant scientific orientation; (2) a more traditional 'data-based' approach, taking models from the material remains rather than importing them from external disciplines; (3) a renewed interest in history and chronology; (4) a strong 'ecological thrust' that includes society and culture; (5) 'an unabashedly "idealist" approach'; and (6) a 'reaffirmation of the place of archaeology's study of culture in modern social consciousness' that provides 'moral value in an endangered world' ('Biblical Archaeology', p. 708).

156. 'Biblical Archaeology', p. 708.

What is the significance of the contextual approach for biblical archaeology, and in turn for this study? Essentially, its focus should be two-
fold. First, the archaeologist must once again take seriously the biblical
texts themselves as potential historical sources, however ideological or
elitist they may be. Although one cannot naively accept the biblical
sources, neither can one reject them entirely; they provide the only look
at the culture of ancient Israel as viewed from within.[157] Furthermore,
Dever contends, reconstruction of histories or societies must go beyond
the material, technological or subsistence strategies and include ideology. This concern for the historical, which some practitioners of the
'new archaeology'[158] view with caution, is central to the new, 'contextual archaeology', whether it is concerned with biblical or non-biblical
cultures. According to Dever,

> we must listen patiently and respectfully to what those who lived through
> the events *thought* they meant—even if we, from our perspective, are
> convinced that they were wrong. As Hodder says, 'To study history is to
> try to get at purpose and thought'. Here lies the newest archaeology's
> imperative to look at 'the inside of events' ...and this can *only* be read
> from texts in conjunction with artifacts, both reflections of the culture
> that produced them.[159]

Such sensitivity to biblical traditions requires either training in critical
biblical scholarship, an area where American biblical archaeologists
have a decided edge over their Israeli counterparts, or serious dialogue
between biblical scholars and archaeologists of the land of Israel.

A second part of the contextual approach involves a sensitivity to
both biblical and modern historiography, a concern that Dever maintains has been lost on most Syro-Palestinian archaeologists. This means
that biblical archaeologists and historians must be concerned with writing histories that include texts and artifacts, ones that go beyond the
sort of political histories that characterized an earlier generation of biblical archaeologists. Dever envisions two parallel histories: a religious
history and a social history. Both must be integrative and contextual,

157. Dever's point here relates directly to the concerns raised in Grabbe (ed.),
Can a 'History of Israel' Be Written? The contributors of that volume discuss the
nature of historiography, the archaeological data and biblical texts.

158. See Binford, as quoted by Dever: 'The attempt to use history as the model
for archaeological investigation is ... totally inadequate... The archaeologist sees no
past events, only contemporary events' ('Biblical Archaeology', p. 710).

159. 'Biblical Archaeology', pp. 709-10 (italics added).

both must be concerned with ideological and material remains.[160] Much of Dever's discussion of 'contextual archaeology' centers on the emergence of Israel, but he suggests that the period of exile and return is particularly suited for such an approach.[161]

Thus, the biblical archaeology movement is far from being moribund as Dever had described it in earlier works. Rather, it is at an important turning point, and, strengthened by self-criticism, is emerging to a new maturity, whether it is called 'socioarchaeology' or 'contextual archaeology'. Meyers and Meyers and Dever have made important contributions to the furthering of this new style of biblical archaeology; it remains for a newer generation of biblical scholars and archaeologists to implement their methodological suggestions. Both the contextual and social approaches are fundamental to the methodology of this study. In the chapters that follow, I address the social world of the province of Yehud during the Neo-Babylonian and Persian periods, using ecofacts, material remains, textual traditions and ethnographic data. Similarly, while my orientation is somewhat more materialist than idealist, in taking the texts seriously (but applying appropriate critical tools and controls) I seek to account for both ideology and artifacts, placing each in its social, material and religious context.

---

160. Here, Dever suggests that a strictly materialist interpretative schema is inadequate, and that ideology often affects materiality. In particular he notes a reticence among scholars of Israel's earliest history to address questions of ideology as found in material remains, although he lauds the current sensitivity to ecological and technological aspects of Israelite society in this period. He notes: 'without some better understanding of the *ideology* of early Israel we shall never come to grips with the real reasons for its emergence, or appreciate the actual variety and vitality of its cultural experience. Yet the converse is true, for ideology and material culture are inextricably bound up' ('Biblical Archaeology', pp. 717-19).

161. 'Biblical Archaeology', p. 719. 'We now have rich archaeological documentation for these eras, yet even a glance at recent histories of Israel and archaeologies of ancient Palestine will show how little synthesis has been done, how isolated Biblical scholars and archaeologists still are from each other.'

Chapter 2

THE BOUNDARIES OF YEHUD

Events in Eastern Europe and the former Soviet Union in the 1980s and early 1990s remind us that national and provincial boundaries can change rapidly as imperial power ebbs and flows. So it was in Syria-Palestine in the eighth through sixth centuries BCE. Those years witnessed the waxing and waning of Assyrian hegemony, the destruction of Judah at the hands of the Babylonians, and the rapid rise of the Persian empire. What had once been a semi-autonomous kingdom, Judah, was reduced to a small piece of a world-class empire. According to the traditions of Jeremiah, 2 Kings and 2 Chronicles, many of its leading citizens were led away to Babylon while others fled to Egypt. But after the Persian conquest of Babylon, and due to the largesse of the Persian king, exiles from many national or ethnic backgrounds were allowed to return to their respective homelands. So it was that the province of Yehud was established in the late sixth century, subject to an imperial governor, but claiming to be the legitimate extension of 'pre-exilic' Judah.

These are some of the biblical claims concerning Yehud, but delineating the borders of the province is another matter. Biblical scholars and archaeologists have traditionally turned to five lists from Ezra and Nehemiah in their attempts to determine the boundaries of the province: the lists of returnees in Ezra 2 and Nehemiah 7; the list of 'districts' and 'sub-districts' of the province that sent delegations to work on the walls of Jerusalem (Neh. 3); the list of cultic officials who settled in Jerusalem (Neh. 11); and the list of singers (Neh. 12).[1] While many scholars

---

1. Some of the major reconstructions include: Z. Kallai, *The Northern Boundaries of Judah from the Settlement of the Tribes until the Beginning of the Hasmonean Period* (Jerusalem: Magnes Press, 1960 [Heb.]), pp. 82-94; M. Avi-Yonah, *The Holy Land* (Grand Rapids: Baker Book House, 1966), pp. 13-33; Stern, *Material Culture*, pp. 245-9; Y. Aharoni, *The Land of the Bible: A Historical Geography*

admit that the borders suggested by these texts are idealistic,[2] some take these lists at face value. This leads in turn to faulty and misleading reconstructions of the social history of the province.[3] The result has been maps of the province drawn from a maximalist perspective, maps that uncritically include sites listed in Ezra–Nehemiah and those discovered through excavations and surveys.

Recent literary and archaeological studies, however, suggest that more care be taken in interpreting the data available to us. The lists in Ezra–Nehemiah do not conform to the boundary lists found in the Deuteronomic history. Their authors were more interested in the socioreligious constitution of Yehud and its socio-economic and legal policies than in drawing physical boundaries of the province. This suggests that one must apply other criteria to a site discovered in an excavation or survey than its listing in a biblical text from the Persian period to determine whether or not that particular site was part of Yehud. Textual traditions and archaeological data may, in fact, be used in a discussion of the boundaries of the province, but both must be supplemented by other sources of data and other methodologies. Based on a more nuanced reading of these various data, I suggest that Yehud was a relatively small province throughout the Persian period, located in the central hills of Palestine, running along the Jerusalem corridor, from Bethel toward Hebron, and extending east to the Judean Desert. Before turning to that reconstruction, however, it will be helpful to analyze the biblical lists and past reconstructions of the province of Yehud.

(trans. A. Rainey; London: Burns & Oates, 2nd rev. edn, 1979), pp. 411-19; Kochman, 'Status and Extent of Judah', pp. xii-xiv. See also J. Blenkinsopp, *Ezra–Nehemiah* (OTL; Philadelphia: Fortress Press, 1988), pp. 86-87, 231-39 and 328-32.

2.   In this regard, see E. Stern, 'Yehud in Vision and Reality' (Heb.), *Cathedra* 4 (1977), pp. 13-25, and Blenkinsopp, *Ezra–Nehemiah*, pp. 83-84. Blenkinsopp, for example, argues that the boundary and site lists from Josh. 19 form the basis for the reconstituted province of Yehud.

3.   Most notably, J.P. Weinberg's suggestion of the two-tiered sociopolitical structure of Yehud stands (and falls!) on his naive acceptance of these lists as authentic. His province would include all the territories once comprising the kingdom of Judah. See his 'Demographic Notes', pp. 34-48. Also important for his argument are 'Comments on the Problem', pp. 17-33; 'The *Bêt Ābôt*', pp. 49-61; and 'The *'Am Hā'āreṣ* of the Sixth to Fourth Centuries BCE', in *idem, The Citizen–Temple Community*, pp. 62-74.

Past Reconstructions of Yehud

Ezra 2.1-67 and Nehemiah 7.4-69

Ezra 2 and Nehemiah 7 contain slightly different versions of a list of returnees from the exile, of the towns and villages to which they are related, of temple functionaries, slaves and animals.[4] Even though lively debate has surrounded the function, date and provenance of the lists[5]

4. H.G.M. Williamson offers a cogent discussion of the theories concerning the relationship of the lists from Ezra 2 and Neh. 7 in *Ezra, Nehemiah* (WBC, 16; Waco, TX: Word Books, 1988). After enumerating the various arguments, he concludes that the version of the list in Nehemiah is earlier and is revised by Ezra. He argues that the phrase 'in the seventh month', which follows the list, fits the context of Nehemiah better than that of Ezra, and that Ezra's list is a summary of Nehemiah's (seen particularly in the tendency to round off numbers). He draws attention to the additions and expansions in the Ezra version of the list (Ezra 2.68 adds a phrase that makes sense only in the context of Ezra; Neh. 7.72a [Hebrew, 73a] is also expanded by the redactor of Ezra) (Williamson, *Ezra, Nehemiah*, pp. 29-30). Blenkinsopp takes the opposite view and holds that theologically, linguistically and contextually the list fits Ezra better than Nehemiah (Blenkinsopp, *Ezra–Nehemiah*, pp. 43-45).

5. G. Hölscher suggested that the lists represented Persian tax rolls, dating roughly to the late fifth century ('Die Bücher Esra und Nehemia', in E. Kautzsch [ed.], *Die Heilige Schrift des Alten Testaments*, II [Tübingen: J.C.B. Mohr, 4th edn, 1923], pp. 491-562 (504a); as cited by K. Galling in 'The "Gōlā-List" According to Ezra 2//Nehemiah 7', *JBL* 70 [1951], pp. 149-58). Alt suggested that the lists were drawn up by Zerubbabel to help determine land rights ('Die Rolle Samarias bei der Entstehung des Judentums', p. 24 n. 1). Galling favored a view that the list was drawn up in response to the Samaritan challenge and intended 'to legitimate them and had to make clear the ecclesiastical and legal structure of the gōlā community' ('The "Gōlā-List"', p. 154). He dated the lists, in their original form, to 519 BCE and suggested that they were subsequently deposited in the Temple Archives. His notion that 'the orthodox "gōlā" congregation, which had so courageously begun the building of the Temple, proclaimed with all candor and conviction that they were the amphictyonical "qahal"' (p. 158), is based upon a now outdated view of pre-monarchic Israel as an amphictyony and should be rejected. More appropriate is Williamson's suggestion (*Ezra, Nehemiah*, pp. 18-20) that the author gives the name of 12 leaders of the *gôlāh* in order to call to mind the exodus of the 12 tribes of Israel from Egypt. While Williamson finds Galling's idea that the lists were intended as an answer to Tattnai's charges that the returnees were intending to revolt against Persia appealing, he notes their composite nature. He, too, dates them to early after the return from the exile, before the construction of the temple. Blenkinsopp (*Ezra–Nehemiah*, p. 83) agrees that the lists are composites but dates them

they, perhaps more than the other lists, have been the basis of scholarly discussion of the borders and 'sub-districts' of the province.

The differences between the two lists are relatively minor, generally reflecting differences in spelling, order of villages, or population. Many of these sites are located close to Jerusalem, and more are within the boundaries of the tribal territory of Benjamin than within those of Judah,[6] a pattern that is borne out in archaeological surveys and excavations. Many familiar biblical sites are listed, each with the number of returnees that populate it; these include Gibeon,[7] Bethlehem, Netophah, Anathoth, Beth-Azmaveth,[8] Kiryath Yearim,[9] Chephirah, Beeroth, Ramah, Gebah, Michmas, Bethel, Ai, Nebo, Magbish,[10] Harim, Lod, Hadid, Ono, Jericho and Sena'ah.[11] Persian period remains

---

(with Albright and Bright) to the middle of the fifth century BCE. C. Schultz also adopts the idea that the lists were used to establish legitimate inclusion in the *qāhāl*, noting that 'Only the members of the *qāhāl* can assist in the building of the temple'; see 'The Political Tensions Reflected in Ezra–Nehemiah', in W.W. Hallo, C.D. Evans and J.B. White (eds.), *Scripture in Context: Essays on the Comparative Method* (PTMS, 34; Pittsburgh: Pipwick Press, 1980), pp. 221-44 (226). J.W. Betlyon suggests that the lists of priests that accompany the site lists were subject to imperial Persian control. He sees the deletion of the names of two groups of high priests as evidence of this control and proposes that their names were expunged because of their involvement in revolts, one in the time of Zerubbabel, and one in the early fourth century. Betlyon, 'The Provincial Government of Persian Period Judea and the Yehud Coins', *JBL* 105 (1986), pp. 633-42.

6. Blenkinsopp, *Ezra–Nehemiah*, pp. 86-87. Fourteen of the 22 names of Ezra (21 of Nehemiah) or 64 per cent are from Benjamin. Blenkinsopp makes the following identifications of these place names with modern sites: Gibeon: el-Jîb; Netophah: Khirbet Bedd Faluh, near 'Ain en-Natuf; Anathoth: Ras Kharrubeh, near 'Anata; Azmaveth: Hizmah; Ramah: er-Ramm; Geba: Jiba'a; Michmas: Muchmas; Lod: Lydda; Hadid: el-Haditheh; Ono: Kefr 'Ana; and Sena'ah: Magdal-sena'a.

7. Ezra 2 reads Gibbar. This is often considered to be a corruption of Gibeon. See, e.g., Blenkinsopp, who emends the text to agree with Neh. 7.25 (*Ezra–Nehemiah*, p. 81). Williamson (*Ezra, Nehemiah*, p. 25 n. 20a) and J. Myers (*Ezra, Nehemiah: Introduction, Translation and Notes* [AB, 14; Garden City, NY: Doubleday, 1983], p. 13 n. 20) suggests reading Gibbar as a personal rather than a place name.

8. Ezra 2.24, Azmaveth.

9. Ezra 2.25, Kiryath 'Arim.

10. In the Ezra 2 list only, v. 30.

11. Note that the reference in both lists to 'the other Elam' is probably misplaced and can therefore be deleted. It may refer, instead, to one of the cities from which some of the returnees came.

have been discovered at a number of these sites through excavations or surface surveys; the total population of these villages is 7273 according to Ezra, and 7430 according to Nehemiah.

Nehemiah 3

This text from the so-called 'Nehemiah Memoir' lists the villages that supplied the workers for rebuilding the walls of Jerusalem and includes some settlements not found in the roster of Ezra 2//Nehemiah 7 (Neh. 3.1-32). It is often used to delineate the districts and/or sub-districts of Yehud, with their rulers: Mizpah,[12] Jerusalem, Beth-haccerem, Beth-Zur and Keilah. Avi-Yonah suggests that when two cities are listed in connection with a district in Nehemiah 3, the second city 'represents the administrative center of the other half'.[13] According to this reading at least three of these districts were further divided into two 'sub-districts' (Jerusalem, vv. 9 and 12; Beth-Zur, v. 16; Keilah, v. 17). Jericho and the lands surrounding it, though not mentioned in Nehemiah 3, are typically added as a separate district. There is, however, no consensus concerning the exact boundaries of these sub-districts. Avi-Yonah divides the districts as follows: Jerusalem/Ramat Rahel (which he identifies with Nethopha); Keilah/Adullam; Mizpah/Gibeon; Beth-haccerem/ Zanoah; Beth-Zur/Tekoah; and Jericho/Sana'ah.[14] Stern departs from the biblical data somewhat and suggests a very different breakdown of districts: Mizpah incorporates the 'territory of Benjamin'; the Gezer district controlled the 'north-west Shephelah'; the Jerusalem district controlled 'Jerusalem and surroundings'; Beth-Zur district included the 'hilly area south of Jerusalem'; Keilah controlled the 'south-west Shephelah'; and the Jericho district covered the entire plain of Jericho.[15] Aharoni[16] agrees with the common position that the Persian officials did not alter the administrative structure of Palestine that they took over

---

12. Listed here in Neh. 3.7, with Gibeon, as being under the 'jurisdiction' (כסא; see Blenkinsopp, *Ezra–Nehemiah*, pp. 228, 235), literally the 'throne', of the governor of *eber nahara*. Williamson translates the phrase as 'the seat of the governor of Beyond the River' (*Ezra, Nehemiah*, pp. 194, 197 n. 75). Both suggest that this reflects the fact that Mizpah (Tell en-Naṣbeh) served as the administrative center for Yehud after the destruction of Jerusalem in 587/586 BCE by Nebuchadnezzar.

13. *The Holy Land*, p. 20.

14. Blenkinsopp follows Avi-Yonah in his discussion of the province. See *Ezra–Nehemiah*, pp. 235-36.

15. See Stern, *Material Culture*, pp. 247-49.

16. *The Land of the Bible*, pp. 411-19.

from the Babylonians and Assyrians. He divides Yehud into five districts with nine sub-districts: Keilah has sub-districts of Zanoah and
Keilah; Beth-Zur is divided into the Beth-Zur and Tekoa sub-districts;
Beth-haccerem has no sub-districts; Jerusalem is comprised of the Jerusalem and Gibeon sub-districts; and the Jericho and Mizpah sub-districts are in the Mizpah district. Kallai[17] identifies the district of Mizpah
as the largest district of Yehud, extending from Sena'ah to Lod and
Ono. In his view, the Jerusalem district included Jerusalem and its
environs, Beth-haccerem encompassed sites in the Shephelah, Beth-Zur
included that site and villages surrounding it, and the Keilah district extended to Azekah and possibly included Timna.

Aaron Demsky has argued that Hebrew פֶּלֶךְ (*pelekh*) is related to
Akkadian *pilku*, which he translates 'work duty' or 'tax in the form of
conscripted labour'.[18] Nehemiah would thus be referring to work details
rather than administrative districts. Demsky points to equivalents in
the cuneiform literature to the Hebrew terms שַׂר פֶּלֶךְ, 'overseer of the
work detail' (LÚ.GAL *pilkāni*, 'chief of the work details') and שַׂר חֲצִי
פֶלֶךְ 'overseer of half of the work detail' (*mešli ṣābi*, 'half of the work
force'). While this reconstruction is not without its problems,[19] it is
somewhat more appealing in the context of Nehemiah than the traditional rendering of פֶלֶךְ as 'district'.

The Idealized Portrait of Yehud: Nehemiah 11.25-36
The list of cities in Neh. 11.25-36 includes many locales that were
almost certainly outside the jurisdiction of the province, such as Beersheba and Lachish.[20] It, more than those discussed above, represents an

17. *The Northern Boundaries of Judah*, pp. 82-94 (as cited by Stern, *Material
Culture*, p. 248).

18. '*Pelekh* in Nehemiah 3', *IEJ* 33 (1983), pp. 242-44.

19. Its primary weakness is its reliance on Neo-Assyrian administrative texts
rather than texts from the Persian period. Demsky admits that when *pilku* does
appear in cuneiform texts from the Persian period, it means 'an administratively
undefined "district, precinct, or border"' ('*Pelekh* in Nehemiah 3', p. 243). This
would seem to support the traditional translation of the Hebrew word. However, the
problems involved in sorting out the relationships between and among the rulers
over districts and sub-districts and the inclusion of sites outside Yehud make Demsky's suggestion preferable.

20. Other sites in this list may be safely excluded from Yehud: Dibon, Yek-
abzeel, Yeshua, Moladah, Beth-pelet, Hazar-shual, Ziklag, Meconah, En-Rimmon
and Zorah.

idealized portrait of Yehud, one that conforms more to Judea during the late monarchy than to the reconstituted community of the Persian period.[21] Villages or geographic areas that are first mentioned in this list are from the Judean Shephelah (Yarmuth, Zanoah, Adullam and Azekah), from Benjamin (Nob, Ananiah, Hazor, Gittaim, Zeboim, Neballat), the coastal plain (the 'Valley of the Craftsmen') and the Negev.

If these biblical lists are used to draw a composite portrait of Yehud's borders, they would indicate a rather large province, extending from Kadesh-Barnea in the south, to (Baal)-Hazor in the northeast, and to Lod, Hadid and Ono in the northwest coastal plain. Most scholars place the eastern border of the province at the Dead Sea and River Jordan. The province would have extended westward into the Shephelah, thus including sites such as Gezer and Lachish. But should these lists be taken uncritically? Were they intended boundary lists, or even as inventories of cities within the newly established province? In answering this question, it is important to note the character of each of the books in which these lists appear. The Ezra traditions are concerned largely with the protagonist's attempts to re-institute the Mosaic Torah as the law of the land—a mission purportedly underwritten by the Persian empire— and his fight against intermarriage. The Nehemiah Memoir is an often self-serving account of Nehemiah's governorship, the fortification of Jerusalem, and the redressing of social oppression. Thus, the intent of the biblical writers, in so far as it can be recovered, was not to delineate the boundaries of the province of Yehud.[22] Rather, the lists in Ezra and Nehemiah function either as indicators of the sites to which Jews had returned in the years after Cyrus's decree or sites in which returning exiles had real or fictional ancestral connections,[23] whether or not they were within the borders of the province.[24]

21. See Stern, 'The Province of Yehud', pp. 9-21; and Blenkinsopp, 'Temple and Society', p. 44. J.P. Weinberg is virtually alone in using this list as an accurate indication of the province of Yehud in the postexilic period. See, in particular, 'Demographic Notes', pp. 43-47; and, 'The *Bêt Ābot*', pp. 53-57.

22. This stands in direct contrast with the lists of tribal territories and their cities from the book of Joshua. See the discussion on this point in Blenkinsopp, 'Temple and Society', p. 44.

23. On the nature of the genealogical connections in the Persian period texts, see Weinberg, 'The *Bêt Ābot*', pp. 49-61, and Davies, *In Search of 'Ancient Israel'*, pp. 82-87.

24. A. Rainey, 'The Biblical Shephelah of Judah', *BASOR* 251 (1983), pp. 1-22 (18).

Recent Maps of Yehud

While there is general agreement that many of the villages listed in these passages were outside the actual boundaries of Yehud, there is no consensus concerning what sites were not part of the province. Reconstructions typically place the southern border of the province near En-Gedi, along the western shore of the Dead Sea. Although Hebron is listed in Nehemiah 11 (as Kiryat-Arba), its occupation in the Persian period is 'doubtful'.[25] Even if it was occupied, many contend that it was almost certainly under Edomite control.[26] According to these reconstructions, the southern border continued northwest between Hebron and Beth-Zur, extended westward to Keilah and then into the Shephelah west of Azekah and Gezer.[27] There is little agreement on the status of the northern sites of Ono, Lod and Hadid: Aharoni[28] follows Avi-Yonah[29] in placing these cities outside of the boundaries of Yehud. Avi-Yonah argues that since the Samaritans invited Nehemiah to the Vale of Ono for negotiations, this area must have been either under Samarian control or neutral, but could not have been a part of Yehud (Figure 1[30]).

Stern[31] includes these sites within the Gezer district, which encompasses sites in the northwest Shephelah (Figure 2[32]). Kallai[33] includes Lod, Ono and Hadid in the larger sub-district of Mizpah. The northern boundary of Yehud in the Persian period seems to have been roughly equivalent to its border during the late monarchy,[34] although Stern

25. Ofer, 'The Judean Hill Country', pp. 203-204.

26. Aharoni, *The Land of the Bible*, p. 416; Stern, *Material Culture*, p. 249; Rainey, 'The Biblical Shephelah', p. 18.

27. Although, as I have indicated and will discuss further below, there is serious question whether some of these sites were occupied in the Persian period (in the case of Azekah) or, if occupied, belonged in the province (in the case of Gezer).

28. *The Land of the Bible*, p. 416.

29. *The Holy Land*, pp. 28-31.

30. Adapted from Avi-Yonah, *The Holy Land*, Map 1, 'Judah under Persian Rule', p. 23.

31. *Material Culture*, pp. 248-49.

32. Adapted from Stern, *Material Culture*, Figure 379, 'Map of the Province of Judah', p. 247.

33. *The Northern Boundaries of Judah*, p. 92.

34. Aharoni, *The Land of the Bible*, p. 416; Kallai, *The Northern Boundaries of Judah*, pp. 80-93.

includes the site of (Baal)-Hazor in his map of the province, a site that is some 7.5 kilometers northeast of Bethel. Looking eastward toward the Dead Sea, Stern suggests that the province included Jericho, and to the North, Sena'ah, probably to be identified with Magdal-sena'ah.[35] Rainey's most recent reconstruction of the province places the northern boundary just north of (Baal)-Hazor, extending west toward the Coastal Plain and east to the River Jordan. He excludes the sites of Lod, Hadid and Ono in the Coastal Plain, associating them with the territory of Sidon, but includes the Shephelah and its prominent sites within Yehud, with the western border just beyond Gezer. The southern border follows a line from En-Gedi, north of Hebron, south of Beth-Zur and Keilah, then northward toward Azekah and Gezer (Figure 3[36]). L. Grabbe suggests that the boundaries of the province extended west from the Jordan River and Dead Sea, north of Sana'ah, Jericho, and Bethel, toward Upper and Lower Beth Horon (Figure 4).[37] He would include portions of the Shephelah (sites such as Azekah, Adullam and Keilah), but exclude Gezer and the Coastal Plain sites of Lod, Hadid and Ono. In his view, the southern boundary of the province passed between Beth-Zur and Hebron.

These reconstructions of the province of Yehud, while admittedly more narrowly focused than those suggested by an uncritical reading of the biblical traditions, are still problematic. Faced with the limits of textual traditions, archaeologists have turned to material remains to supplement and perhaps correct the biblical traditions. Unfortunately, there is no clear consensus concerning what types of archaeological data may be used to indicate the extent of the province's sociopolitical influence and, therefore, to determine its borders.

35. Blenkinsopp, *Ezra–Nehemiah*, p. 87; Williamson, *Ezra, Nehemiah*, p. 34. The problems with this identification center primarily on the large number of returnees who are said to have settled at Sena'ah.

36. Adapted from Y. Aharoni and M. Avi-Yonah, *The Macmillan Bible Atlas* (ed. A. Rainey and Z. Saphrai; New York: Macmillan, 3rd rev. edn, 1993), Map 170, p. 129.

37. *Judaism from Cyrus to Hadrian*, I, p. 80. Illustration adapted from Map 2, 'The Persian Province of Judah', p. 87.

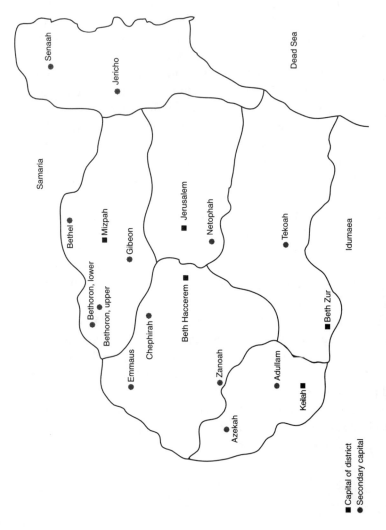

Figure 1. *The Province of Yehud as Reconstructed by M. Avi-Yonah*

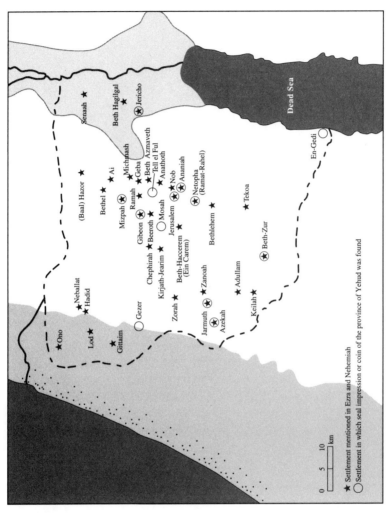

Figure 2. *The Province of Yehud as Reconstructed by E. Stern*

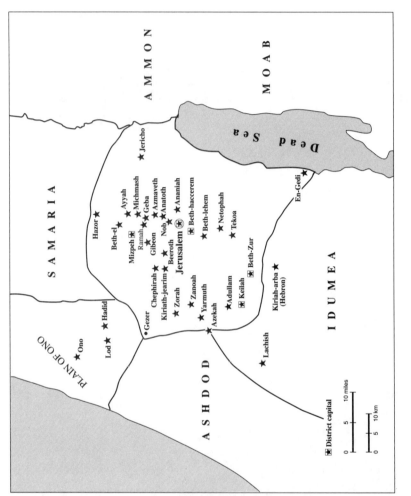

Figure 3. *The Province of Yehud According to A. Rainey*

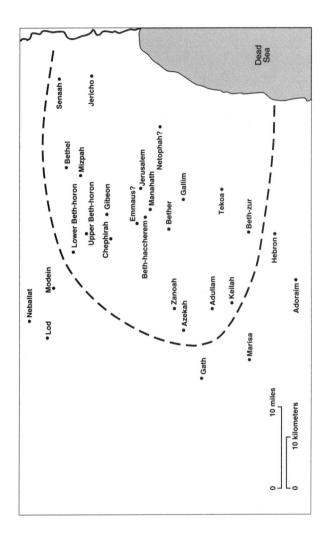

Figure 4. *The Province of Yehud as Reconstructed by L. Grabbe*

Three types of remains have traditionally been used to reconstruct the boundaries of Yehud: seal impressions, coins, and fortresses. Stern[38] and Kochman[39] assign to the province those sites at which either seal impressions or coins with the reading *yhd*, *yršlm* or *yhwd* have been discovered. Stern also interprets a series of fortresses which date to the Persian period as boundary markers. In his reconstruction, a line of fortresses extending from Beth-Zur[40] to Kh. ez-Zawiyye and Kh. el-Qaṭṭ marks the southern border of the province and a similar line of fortresses in the Shephelah (including Yarmuth, Azekah and Adullam) delimits its southwestern boundary.[41] The discovery of coins and seal impressions that Stern dates to the Persian period at two of these fortress sites would seem to support his reconstruction. A Yehud coin was excavated at Beth-Zur and a *yršlm* seal impression was discovered at Azekah.

A number of recent excavations and studies allow this theory to be tested. In 1985 R. Cohen excavated a series of fortresses in the Negev, south of Arad and Beersheva, at Horvat Mesora, Atar Haroʿa and Kadesh-Barnea. Since all of the fortresses date to the Persian period, and since a Yehud seal was discovered at Kadesh-Barnea, Cohen initially suggested that these fortresses may have marked the southern boundary of the province, following Stern's methodology.[42] But these sites are well beyond the limits of even the most maximalist recon-

---

38. See his discussions of the province and accompanying map in *Material Culture*, pp. 245-49 and in 'The Persian Empire', p. 86. C.C. McCown (*TN*, I, pp. 171-72) suggests that since no *yhd* or *yh* seals were discovered at Bethel, that city was not part of Yehud, but includes Jericho, where 10 *yh* and 3 *yhd* seals were discovered. These seals date approximately to the mid-fifth century, a period when Bethel was uninhabited, so its inclusion in the province cannot be determined by the presence or absence of seal impressions.

39. 'Status and Extent of Judah', pp. xvi-xvii, pp. 127-57.

40. Here, Stern accepts Albright's initial dating of the fortress at Beth-Zur to the Persian period, a position which is unlikely at best, since the architectural remains for the fortress most likely date to the Ptolemaic period. For a discussion of this question, see R.W. Funk, 'The History of Beth-Zur with Reference to its Defenses', in O.R. Sellers (ed.), *The 1957 Excavation at Beth-Zur* (AASOR, 38; Cambridge, MA: American Schools of Oriental Research, 1968), pp. 4-17.

41. 'The Persian Empire', p. 86.

42. 'Solomon's Negev Defense Line Contained Three Fewer Fortresses', *BARev* 12 (1986), pp. 40-45.

structions of the province,[43] and show that the existence of a fortress in a strategic area does not necessarily imply that it was intended to defend provincial boundaries. Since the discovery of one seal impression is not an appropriate indicator of a site's inclusion within Yehud, Cohen ultimately concluded that Kadesh-Barnea was outside the province and that the seal may instead indicate that 'large numbers of Jews lived south of Judah'.[44] K. Hoglund has questioned Stern's assignment of fortresses to boundaries from a strategic point of view. In his discussion of the fortresses in the south-central hill country, Hoglund observes:

> The fortress [Kh. ez-Zawiyye] is located on the northern side of the ridge it sits on, and faces to the north toward Yehud. Any Edomite force that might come upon the fortress would command the higher elevation to the south and could easily overwhelm what forces may have been deployed in the fortress.[45]

He maintains that rather than indicating borders, the fortresses represent an imperial concern to protect trade routes and communication lines necessary to maintain control of the empire.

Is the interpretation that coins and seal impressions may be used as markers of the boundaries of Yehud more defensible? Two issues must be addressed to answer this question: (1) the appropriate date of the seal or coin; and (2) the location in which the artifact was discovered. Stern's analysis is inconsistent on both counts. Stern assigns a Persian period date to any site at which a Yehud coin or seals impressed with *yhd*, *yhwd*, *yhd*-plus-symbol, or *yršlm* was discovered. But of these, only the *yhd* and *yhwd*[46] impressions date to the Persian period. The latter two are more accurately dated to the early Hellenistic period, as Paul Lapp had suggested in 1963 and as the excavations at the City of David have confirmed.[47] This casts doubt upon Stern's inclusion of

43. Cohen also suggests that they were under Arabian rather than Jewish control, citing a tradition in Herodotus that the Arabs controlled trade routes from South Arabia to Gaza via Transjordan and through the central Negev ('Solomon's Negev Defense Line', p. 45).

44. 'Solomon's Negev Defense Line', p. 45. In this way he harmonizes the archaeological data with the mention of Negev sites in Neh. 11.30.

45. *Achaemenid Imperial Administration*, pp. 202-203.

46. This would include the composite *yhwd* impressions, i.e. *yhwd* plus personal name, or *yhwd phw'* seals.

47. See Lapp, 'Ptolemaic Stamped Handles', pp. 22-35. On the impressions from the City of David excavations, see the discussion of Jerusalem below in Chapter 3, pp. 134-48.

Azekah in the province, since the impression from that site is a *yršlm* seal, and therefore not Persian period.[48] As for location, not only has a *yhd* seal been discovered at Kadesh-Barnea, but another impression interpreted as a *yhd* seal was excavated at Tel Michal.[49] While these impressions may indicate something of their economic function, and perhaps show intra-provincial relations, they cannot demonstrate inclusion within the province.[50]

A Geographic Approach to the Boundaries of Yehud

The complex issue of the boundaries of Yehud, which has evoked so many different hypotheses but no consensus, is perhaps best approached by considering the historical and geographic parameters.[51] In 1894, G.A. Smith observed that Palestine may be divided into six vertical strips, from the coastal plain to the Arabian desert.[52] These natural divisions often formed the basis of geopolitical entities and were the occasion of many conflicts in the history of Israel.[53] Further, the limits on political

48. This would leave just one artifact, an Attic decadrachma, that could date to the Persian period. One find, and particularly one rare coin, is insufficient evidence for the occupation of Azekah in the Persian period. Further, Gezer—which Stern includes in his reconstruction of the province—while possessing minimal remains from late in the period, may not have been controlled by Yehud until the Ptolemaic period. On the latter assertion, see Lapp, 'Ptolemaic Stamped Handles', p. 31 n. 45.

49. The impression is unpublished, and in poor, barely readable condition. I examined this impression in Jerusalem in 1994 at the Israel Antiquities Authority facility in Romeima. I would qualify the identification as only possibly a *yhd* seal, due to the deteriorated nature of the inscription.

50. J. Christoph offers a more complete assessment of the function of the seal impressions in his study, 'The Yehud Stamped Jar Handle Corpus', pp. 174-201. Christoph does not analyze Stern's use of the impressions as boundary indicators, but rather accepts the boundaries presented below.

51. This general approach was suggested to me by K. Hoglund; the reconstruction that follows is my own.

52. *The Historical Geography of the Holy Land* (London: Hodder & Stoughton, 25th edn, 1931; repr.; Gloucester, MA: Peter Smith, 1972), p. 54 (page reference is to reprint edition).

53. C.L. Meyers, 'Of Seasons and Soldiers: A Topological Appraisal of the Pre-Monarchic Tribes of Galilee', *BASOR* 252 (1983), pp. 47-59. Although Meyers's study deals with the Galilee rather than the tribal areas of Benjamin or Judah, her methodology and conclusions are useful for our study. While she does note that ecological concerns alone cannot determine boundaries and that sometimes 'historical-

influence are often determined in part by the power of a central government to overcome these natural boundaries.[54] That this control is often fragile is seen in the ease with which the 'Israelite monarchy' divided after the death of Solomon. What the Deuteronomic Historian presents as a pre-existing geopolitical entity (the ten northern tribes) that had been subject to a larger central government was able to break away from the monarchy as a unit. This was due in part to the natural geographic divisions that placed many important cities beyond the effective sociopolitical control of the Jerusalem bureaucracy.

With respect to the question of the boundaries and size of Yehud, it is unlikely that a governing body with limited resources and limited autonomy, one that itself may have been undergoing internal conflict, would be able to extend its influence beyond certain natural topographical boundaries. More specifically, from a geographic standpoint alone, I would seriously question any reconstruction of the province of Yehud that includes sites in the Shephelah (Gezer, Azekah, Ain Shems), or the Coastal Plain (Lod, Hadid, Ono). The Shephelah is 'a homogeneous zone of Eocene limestone separated on the east from the Cenomanian limestone hills of Judah by a long, narrow trough created by the exposure of Senonian chalk' that forms a natural buffer between the Coastal Plain and the central hill country of Judah.[55] It has two levels: the first consists of rolling hills with an approximate elevation of 300 to 400

---

cultural factors can result in the drawing of boundaries that may not, and often do not, coincide with natural borders' (p. 53), Meyers does see geographic, ecological and subsistence strategies as significant factors in contributing to tribal distinctions and delineation (p. 56).

54. If the biblical traditions regarding the 'united monarchy' are accurate, Solomon both used and subverted these geopolitical divisions. He set up districts of the kingdom according to ancient tribal land holdings, but used these districts in service (both in terms of human and economic terms) of the larger government, thus 'fulfilling' the warning of the Deuteronomic Historian as delivered through Samuel (1 Sam. 8). See G.E. Wright, 'The Provinces of Solomon (I Kings 4:7-9)', *EI* 8 (1967): pp. 58*-68*; and Mettinger, *Solomonic State Officials*, pp. 112-21. It is also possible that the bureaucracy of the 'united monarchy' established these 12 districts, but sought to legitimate them by attributing them to an earlier, tribal period. The point of the historian is the same whether the events recorded in 1 Kgs 4 are accurate and 'historical' or fictive: an entity that coheres geographically and is distinct from a central government can easily establish its independence if it has the will or the reason to do so.

55. Rainey, 'The Biblical Shephelah', pp. 1-2.

meters above sea level; and the second, closer to the plain, is up to 150 meters in elevation.[56] According to the Deuteronomic Historian, this relatively fertile land[57] was the source of conflict between the Philistines and the Israelite tribes in the early history of Israel;[58] only under David's rule was this territory brought under the control of the emerging monarchy. Though controlled by the united monarchy, and subsequently by Judah, it remained a self-contained geographic entity, one which was divided into as many as three administrative districts.[59]

One result of the Babylonian conquest in 587/586 BCE may have been a return to more natural geographic borders, borders that had been expanded as the monarchy's geopolitical influence grew. Such contraction of borders in times of military crisis is well attested,[60] as is the difficulty of controlling territories located a significant distance from the ruling entity's heartland.[61] Given this difficulty, empires have tended to divide their provinces into geographically self-contained units,[62] and there is no reason to believe that either the Neo-Babylonian or the Persian empire would have acted differently.[63] The Shephelah, contiguous to but geographically distinct from the central hill country, would more likely have formed a separate district from Yehud.[64]

56. D. Baly, *The Geography of the Bible* (New York: Harper & Row, rev. edn, 1974), pp. 140 43.

57. C.C. McCown observes that the Shephelah 'was a valuable asset both economically and strategically, and the rival powers of the mountains and plains both coveted it' ('Palestine, Geography of', in *IDB*, III, p. 631).

58. F. Frick discusses the various theories of the 'Philistine problem' and its relationship to the emergence of the monarchy in *The Formation of the State in Ancient Israel*, pp. 25-30, 191-204.

59. Rainey, 'The Biblical Shephelah', p. 6; see also Figure 1, p. 8.

60. R. Collins, 'Some Principles of Long-Term Social Change: The Territorial Power of States', in L. Kriesberg (ed.), *Research in Social Movements, Conflicts, and Change*, I (Greenwich, CT: JAI Press, 1978), pp. 1-34 (2), and 'Does Modern Technology Change the Rules of Geopolitics?', *JPMS* 9 (1981), pp. 163-77.

61. Collins, 'Some Principles', pp. 24-25; 'Rules of Geopolitics', pp. 164-67.

62. Hoglund, 'The Establishment of a Rural Economy'.

63. See also Kochman, 'Status and Extent of Judah', pp. xix-xxiii, who argues along similar lines, but with different results.

64. The existence of a north-south road that extended from Beersheva, to Keilah, and north to Aijalon may support such a hypothesis. D. Dorsey points out that the road 'followed a natural route created by the narrow Senonian chalk valley that runs north-south along the western edge of the Judean hills, *creating a distinct line of demarcation between the rugged highlands of Cenomanian limestone to the east,*

The conclusion that the Shephelah was outside the province of Yehud was also reached by Kenneth Hoglund, who used Christaller's Central Place Theory in his analysis.[65] Christaller had suggested that the socio-economic relationship between larger, central sites and smaller satellite sites was best represented graphically through a series of interconnected hexagons, with the large site in the center surrounded by smaller towns, villages, and hamlets (Figure 5[66]). This ideal model would have been modified by topographic or ecological features, and, perhaps, by the subsistence strategies of the villages and urban centers.[67] Drawing circles with a radius of approximately 20 kilometers from the central places of Jerusalem, Lachish and Gezer, the latter two of which have architectural remains that can be interpreted as administrative complexes, Hoglund finds that the spheres of influence of these cities intersect at about the border of Shephelah and hill country (Figure 7, A[68]). This finding may be even more clearly demonstrated by applying the observations of G.A. Johnson, who tested and refined Christaller's theory.[69] Johnson, studying site distribution in the Diyala region of Iraq, found that spheres of economic influence of the three major urban centers (Tutub, Eshnunna, and the Northern Cell) exhibited a rhomboid rather than hexagonal pattern (Figure 6).[70] Given the differing topographic features of Palestine, an ellipse would perhaps be more appropriate in examining the relationships among settlements. Plotting such a

and the lower rolling hills of Eocene limestone to the west' (*The Roads and Highways of Israel* [Baltimore: The Johns Hopkins University Press, 1991], p. 153 [emphasis added]).

65. W. Christaller, *Die zentralen Orte in Süddeutschland: Eine ökonomisch-geographische Untersuchung über die Gesetzmässigkeit der Verbreitung und Entwicklung der Siedlungen mit städtischen Funktionen* (Jena: Gustav Fischer, 1933).

66. Adapted from C.L. Redman, *The Rise of Civilization: From Early Farmers to Urban Society in the Ancient Near East* (San Francisco: W.H. Freeman and Company, 1978), Figures 7-8, 'Central Place Model of Hexagonal Settlement Distribution', p. 240.

67. Redman, *The Rise of Civilization*, p. 241.

68. Adapted from Hoglund, 'The Establishment of a Rural Economy', pp. 6-7.

69. 'A Test of the Utility of Central Place Theory in Archaeology', in P.J. Ucko, R. Tringham and G.W. Dimbleby (eds.), *Man, Settlement and Urbanism* (Cambridge, MA: Schenkman Publishing Co., 1972), pp. 769-85.

70. Johnson suggested that the rhomboid pattern was probably determined by the 'roughly parallel paths of major watercourses in the Diyala' ('A Test of the Utility of Central Place Theory', p. 771, as cited by Redman, *The Rise of Civilization*, pp. 241-42). Figure 4 was adapted from Johnson, 'A Test of the Utility of

pattern (Figure 7, B),[71] the spheres of influence would follow the natural boundaries between the coastal plain and central hills almost exactly. The western border of the province should thus be located at the edge of the central hill country.

In a recent study of votive figurines dating to the Persian period from Tell Halif, E. Beach also concludes that the Shephelah was culturally distinct from the central hills.[72] Over 500 figurines were discovered in fill on the western edge of Tell Halif in the 1992 and 1993 excavations. Beach compares the figurines with those discovered at three other core Shephelah sites: Tell 'Erani, Lachish, and Maresha, and analyzes them typologically as follows: (1) woman with child: this type has two variations in the Shephelah—the child seated on the woman's left shoulder, and the child on the woman's left hip; (2) standing robed men; most are bearded, with the left hand on the waist; some clean-shaven, with right hand raised and palm extended.

Also discovered were several nude male 'heroic figures' and a geographically distinct rendering of the popular horse and rider figurine. In this form, the riders' cape is divided, their arms and legs 'abbreviated' and unarticulated, their faces 'abstract', and the horses are skirted. All of the figurines have general parallels in the Coastal Plain, such as Machmish and perhaps Dor, but a clearly distinct typology is evident in the Shephelah and absent from the Central Hills.[73] Beach suggests that the sites of Safi and Sippor, situated near the edge of the Shephelah and Coastal Plain, may have been provided for both cultural and economic links between the two regions.[74]

Central Place Theory', Fig. 2 (E), 'Derivation of the Proposed Settlement Lattice'.

71. As suggested by Hoglund, 'The Establishment of a Rural Economy', pp. 6-7.

72. Eleanor Beach, 'Cultural Relations in the Shephelah in the Persian Period: Preliminary Observations from the Tell Halif Figurines', paper presented in the Literature and History of the Persian Period Group of the Society of Biblical Literature, Philadelphia, 20 November 1995.

73. This may be a function of typologically similar figurines either not being excavated or not being reported as yet. Some figurines that match this typological corpus have been associated with Hebron and Beersheba, but are from a questionable archaeological context.

74. Based on the culturally and geographically distinct collections, Beach concludes: 'I believe the field of common symbols defines an area of cultural cohesion on the foothill shelf that matches Carter's outline of the Shephelah's geographic and political cohesion. This line of inquiry can be extended to questions of social realities in both the Shephelah and neighboring Judea' (Cultural Relations', pp. 7-8).

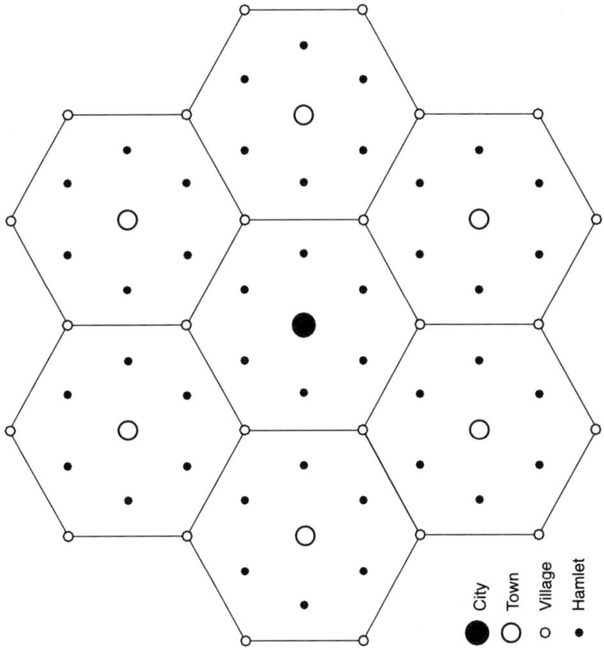

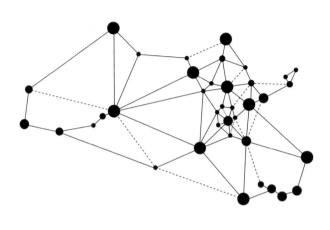

Figure 6. *Economic Interrelationships in the Diyala Region: G.A. Johnson's Revised Central Place Model*

Figure 5. *Ideal Model of Christaller's Central Place Theory*

City
Town
Village
Hamlet

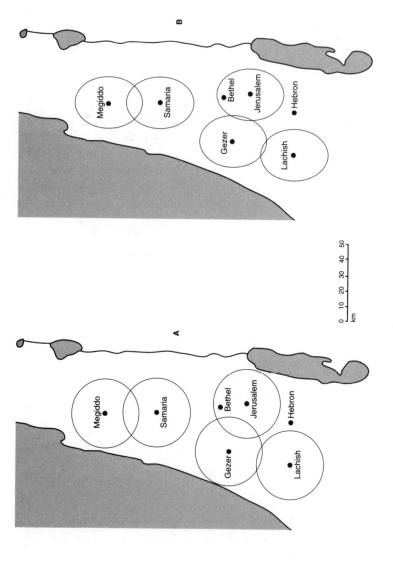

Figure 7. *The Central Place Theory Applied to Palestine*

There are other reasons for excluding the Shephelah and Coastal Plain sites from the core of the province of Yehud. As noted above, the biblical data are subject to a number of interpretations. More importantly, the biblical texts in Ezra and Nehemiah do not claim to be border lists or even suggest that their concern lies with the extent of the province of Yehud. Virtually all of the lists contain some sites that either were not occupied or were well outside of the borders of the province (i.e. Azekah, included in the list of the wall-builders in Neh. 3; Kadesh-Barnea listed in Neh. 11). Rather than impose on the lists a modern scholarly concern for the borders of the province, it seems more appropriate to recognize that the lists simply suggest either sites in which returning exiles had ancestral connections, or sites to which exiles returned, whether or not they were within the borders of the province.[75] Thus, at issue in these texts is the extent of Jewish settlement in Palestine rather than the extent of the province itself. This interpretation is borne out in the account of the invitation extended to Nehemiah to meet the delegation from Samaria in the Vale of Ono. This, according to M. Avi-Yonah, suggests that Ono was outside the jurisdiction of the province.[76] Further, the plots of Sanballat, Tobiah and their co-conspirators, to interrupt the work of fortifying the walls of Jerusalem, were made known by 'some of the Jews who lived near them', indicating that Jews whose loyalties lay with the province of Yehud and its leaders lived outside the province itself.[77]

Another textual support of this conclusion may lie in the funerary inscription of the Sidonian king, Eshmun'ezer II.[78] Eshmun'ezer, who reigned in the mid-fifth century BCE, claims to have received from the Persian overlords

> Dor and Joppa, the mighty lands of Dagon, which are in the Plain of Sharon, in accordance with the important deeds which I did. And we added them to the borders of the country, so that they would belong to Sidon forever.[79]

75. See Rainey, 'The Biblical Shephelah', p. 18.
76. *The Holy Land*, pp. 13-18.
77. See Neh. 4.7-15.
78. *CIS*, Pars Prima: Inscriptiones Phoenicias Continens, Tomus I, Inscription 3, pp. 9-20. I am grateful to Professor Anson Rainey for referring me to this inscription.
79. Translation of F. Rozenthal in *ANET*, p. 662.

According to Anson Rainey[80] the mention of these lands shows that the entire northern Coastal Plain (the Plain of Sharon) was under Sidonian control and was therefore outside of the control of the province of Yehud. This, too, would exclude sites like Lod, Hadid and Ono from the province, and it would suggest that the Persians saw coastal plain and hill country as separate entities.[81]

The eastern border of the province was most likely in the rift valley, although exactly where is difficult to determine. A number of sites are attested in the desert fringe during the Persian period and are close enough to the major cities and villages of that period to have been controlled by a provincial governor. Whether or not the two occupied sites in the Judean desert (Jericho and En-Gedi) would have been attached to the province of Yehud is open to debate. However, I have included them within the province inasmuch as it is equally unclear what other province would have been able to control these sites which are isolated from any other known geopolitical entity.

The northern and southern borders of Yehud are more difficult to establish. In the early Persian period, the southern border may have reached from En-Gedi, on the shore of the Dead Sea, northwest toward Tekoa, and then continued westward to Beth-Zur and from there towards Keilah, until it reached the western border just east of this Shephelah site. A series of fortresses were constructed in the mid-fifth century along a route north of Beth-Zur, although, as noted above, *they are not to be considered border fortresses*.[82] In the later portion of the Persian period, the border would have extended to just south of Hebron and then continued westward until it reached the western border at the edge of the hill country. Here I am consciously departing from the conventional view that the area south of Beth-Zur and north of Hebron

---

80. Personal communication. See also his discussion in 'Tel Gerisah and the Inheritance of the Danite Tribe' (Heb.), *Annual of the Eretz Israel Museum* 23–24 (1987–89), pp. 59-72.

81. One may suggest that a funerary inscription is not a legitimate historical source, given the tendencies of ancient Near Eastern rulers for exaggeration and political propaganda. As I have noted above, the traditions of Ezra and Nehemiah are no less tendentious. See, e.g., the frequent petition from Nehemiah that YHWH 'look upon me for good' on account of his deeds (Neh. 5.19; 13.14, 31). Neither the biblical nor the extra-biblical texts may be used uncritically as disinterested historical sources, but they may reflect a genuine social and/or geographic reality.

82. See the discussion above, pp. 88-90.

was under Edomite control in the Persian period.[83] As Hoglund notes, the notion of Edomite control of Hebon is based on the textual witness that this area was under Edomite hegemony in the Maccabean period (1 Macc. 4–5) and thus must have been controlled by them in the earlier period. However, no archaeological or textual evidence places the Edomites here in the Persian period. Rather, the closest attested Edomite presence to Hebron in the Persian period is from Horvat Qitmit, which is located in the eastern Negev. This site, which may have been cultic in nature is dated to the late seventh or early sixth centuries BCE, continuing into the Neo-Babylonian and Persian periods.[84] The archaeological data, therefore, do not demand an Edomite presence in the hill country in the early Persian period.[85]

The northern border seems to have extended toward the hill country of Ephraim. As noted above, the province of Yehud was comprised primarily of the tribal territories of Judah and Benjamin. During the period of the Judges, the northern border of Judah which formed the southern border of Benjamin followed the Sorek Valley. Benjamin's northern boundary ran just north of Jericho, Michmas, et-Tell and Bethel, then along the Beth-Horon pass toward Gezer.[86] When the monarchy split, the northern border of the kingdom of Judah fell just south of the ancient tribal boundaries between Ephraim and Benjamin. During the reign of Josiah, however, the territory of Judah probably extended well beyond Bethel and both Beth-Horons. Then, after the Assyrian and Babylonian conquests, the old tribal boundaries would, according to

83. Stern, *Material Culture*, pp. 249-50.

84. I. Beit-Arieh, 'New Light on the Edomites', *BARev* 14 (1988), pp. 28-41. Beit-Arieh's final report suggests that the site's final phase may have dated to the seventh century BCE (I. Beit-Arieh [ed.], *Horvat Qitmit: An Edomite Shrine in the Biblical Negev* [Tel Aviv: Institute of Archaeology of Tel Aviv University, 1995]).

85. Environmental analysis also supports the contention that the area around Hebron should be included in the province. The geographical division between the central hill country and the Negev falls approximately 8-10 kilometers south of Hebron, at which point the average rainfall drops below 300 millimeters annually, the amount necessary to support traditional agrarian subsistence strategies. See Hoglund, 'The Establishment of a Rural Economy', pp. 7-8.

86. See Aharoni, *The Land of the Bible*, pp. 251-56. Dorsey also considers this the northern border of Benjamin and notes the existence of a road from Jericho to Bethel, which merged with the Bethel to Beth-horon roads. See *The Roads and Highways of Israel*, pp. 134, 183-85, 201-204.

my reconstruction, provide a logical northern limit of the reconstituted community of Yehud.

According to this analysis, the boundaries of Yehud in the late fifth–early fourth centuries BCE extended approximately from Jericho (coordinates 1920/1422) in the northeast, northwest to Bethel (1483/1733), and continued to Beit Ur et-Tahta (1580/1450). The southern border extended from Tel Goren (1872/0963), northwest toward Hebron (although the site was not occupied during the Persian period) and continued westward to the border between the hill country and the Shephelah.[87]

Environmental Niches and the Province of Yehud

The location of the province of Yehud in the central hill country of Palestine itself reveals something about the ecological setting of the province and its essential subsistence strategies. However, a better and more nuanced understanding of Yehud can be obtained by dividing the province into sub-areas, designated here as *environmental niches*. An environmental niche is a self-contained area separated from other niches by features of topography, climate, soil type, rainfall patterns and geomorphology. The relationship of factors that influence these environmental niches may be stated as follows:

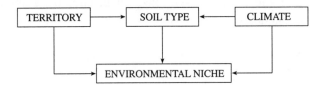

Figure 8. *Interrelationship of Constants and Variables that Create Environmental Niches*

Environmental niche is a function of territory, climate and soil type (Figure 8).[88] In this model, environmental niche functions as a dependent

87. See Chapter 4, Table 3, 'Excavated and Surveyed Sites in Persian Period Yehud' (pp. 190-95), for a list of the excavated sites that fit within these borders.

88. This descriptive model, and those that follow, diagrams the basic *endogenous* forces that influence the dependent variable, all things being equal. These 'path diagrams' or flow charts are used to attempt to delineate the different variables and constants that influence particular social forces or developments. The diagrams are intended to aid both the author and the reader, adding clarity to the research, thus

variable and is affected by territory (a constant), soil type (which functions as an independent variable) and climate. *Territory* specifies a geographic area that is separated from other areas by features of geography or topography. *Climate* may be considered both a constant and an independent variable, depending on the timeframe one considers. The climate of the hill country of Judah has not changed significantly in its basic make-up since the last ice age,[89] but may vary considerably from year to year.[90] *Soil type* is determined by both climate and territory, in

furthering scholarly debate. Path diagrams are frequently, though not exclusively, used as an aid in causal modeling. In the social sciences, model building has tended to follow two lines, axiomatic and causal. Causal models develop a series of statements that specify the hypothesized effects of particular constants and/or variables on other variables. Axiomatic models also attempt to define the relationships between and among variables, but express those relationships hierarchically. See Chapter 1, 'The Nature of Sociological Theorizing', in J. Turner, *The Structure of Sociological Theory* (Chicago: Dorsey Press, 4th edn, 1986), pp. 1-33 (16-21).

89. See the discussion on climate in Hopkins, *The Highlands of Canaan*, pp. 77-108. N.P. Lemche places the last climatic shift at about 3000 BCE, in *Ancient Israel*, p. 17. Figures on annual rainfall patterns in the discussion below are taken from N. Roseman, 'Climate, IV/2: Rainfall', in *Atlas of Israel: Cartography, Physical Geography, Human and Economic Geography, History* (Jerusalem: Survey of Israel, Ministry of Labor; Amsterdam: Elsevier Publishing Co., 2nd edn, 1970).

90. Biblical traditions from all periods attest to extended periods of drought resulting in famine. Drought is portrayed as a divine curse in Deut. 28.22; the conflict between Elijah and Ahab (1 Kgs 17–18); and, in the Persian period, drought is brought upon Yehud by YHWH as punishment (Hag. 1.11). Also indicative of the instability of climate are rainfall data from Jerusalem from 1920–21 through 1961–62 as analyzed by Frick in *The Formation of the State in Ancient Israel*, pp. 103-106. He charts a dry cycle of years (1920–21 to 1937–38) and a rainy cycle (1947–48 to 1961–62) and finds a negative deviation (rainfall below the annual average) in 27 of the 36 years (75 per cent) that comprise the two cycles. In the dry cycle there were 4 positive deviations, but none of 30 per cent or more, whereas there were 7 negative deviations of 30 per cent or more, 2 of which were more than 50 per cent below the norm. During the rainy cycle, 5 positive deviations were recorded, 2 of which were 30 per cent or higher, and 5 negative deviations of 30 or higher. In the dry cycle, 14 straight years were below average. Even in the rainy cycle, 10 of the last 12 years reflected a negative deviation, 2 exceeding 50 per cent. His conclusion that this represents a 'considerable degree of agricultural risk' is certainly well founded. The figures above are taken from the histogram on p. 105 of Frick's book. Note that the accompanying table on p. 104 incorrectly lists the number of years with positive deviations in the rainy cycle as four, whereas the his-

that the geomorphology of the particular territory is constant. Soil is produced by the erosion of the basic rock structures of the territory through exposure to the natural elements, a part of which is determined by climate, and by micro-organisms that grow on, and subsequently break down, these rock formations.[91] So, for example, while the terra rossa soils, the most common soil type in the central hills of Palestine, are derived from turonian and cenomanian limestones, the rendzina soils of the mountains come from chalk, marl, or a combination of these base rocks.[92]

In the previous section I have argued that the province of Yehud excluded the Shephelah and that it extended from just north of Bethel to just south of Hebron at the end of the Persian period. The area of the entire province is roughly 1900 square kilometers (680 square miles), slightly smaller than one-half of the area of the state of Rhode Island. The province of Yehud can be divided into four major environmental niches (Figure 9; they are abbreviated to EN in the discussion below), three of which may in turn be subdivided. At the western edge of Yehud are the slopes that mark the transition from the central spur of Palestine towards the Shephelah and Coastal Plain. Next is the central spur or Judean hills, followed by the desert fringe, which then leads toward the Judean desert. Based upon the recent surveys of Benjamin and the Judean hills mentioned in Chapter 1, I have subdivided these major

togram lists five years; three of those five years had a positive deviation of 30 per cent or more rather than two as listed in the chart.

91. For a detailed study of the process of soil formation and types in Palestine see Hopkins, *The Highlands of Canaan*, pp. 123-33, and Ephraim Orni and Elisha Ephrat, *Geography of Israel* (Jerusalem: Israel Program for Scientific Translations, 1964), pp. 49-56; M. Rim, 'Interpretation of Polymorphic Profiles in Soils of the Eastern Mediterranean: An Analysis of the Geophysical Factor in Soil Genesis', *IEJ* 4 (1954), pp. 266-77; and D.H. Yaalon, 'Calcareous Soils of Israel: The Amount and Particle-size Distribution of the Calcareous Material', *IEJ* 4 (1954), pp. 278-85. In the pages that follow, the careful reader will see my indebtedness to the studies of the relationship of the environment to settlement patterns and the socio-economic context of ancient Israel by D. Hopkins (*The Highlands of Canaan*), F. Frick (*The Formation of the State in Ancient Israel*), I. Finkelstein (*The Archaeology of the Israelite Settlement*), and A. Ofer ('The Highlands of Judah during the Biblical Period, I' [PhD dissertation, Tel Aviv University, 1993]). I have attempted to apply their methodology in my analysis of the environmental niches of the province of Yehud.

92. S. Ravikovitch, 'Geomorphology II/3, Soil Map', in *Atlas of Israel*.

niches as follows (Figure 10):[93] EN 1, Northwestern Hills; EN 2, North Central Hills; EN 3, Northern Desert Fringe; EN 4, Southwestern Hills; EN 5, Central Hills; EN 6, Southern Desert Fringe; EN 7, South Central Hills; and EN 8, Judean Desert.

1. *Northwestern Hills.* This area is approximately 200 square kilometers, 61 per cent of which was in the biblical tribal territory of Benjamin and 39 per cent in the area of Judah. The elevation ranges from 600 to 800 meters above sea level. These hills are separated from the North Central Hills by a complex series of routes. The border follows the modern road from Ramallah to the Beth Horon pass, turns south towards Biddu, then follows the winding Nahal Samwil. It heads southwest and then joins and follows the Nahal Sorek system until it bisects the Nahal Rephai'im system, which also separates this niche from the adjoining Southwestern Hills. Annual rainfall in this environmental niche ranges from 500 to 600 millimeters (see Figure 11 for rainfall patterns in the province), with most of the area averaging 500 millimeters. The geological substructure of this zone is characterized by limestone from the Lower Cenomanian period (see Figure 12 for soil types in the province),[94] which produces terra rossa soil,[95] the type most predominant in the central hills.[96] It is most suited for cultivation of grains

93. In the survey of Benjamin five distinct topographical areas were identified: foothills (outside the borders of Yehud), slopes, central hills, desert fringe, and desert. The survey of Judah was divided into ten areas: the southern Shephelah, the Negev hills, the southwestern Judean desert, the 'southern springs', the mountain heights, the southern desert fringe, the Arkub triangle, the northern central hills, the northern desert fringe, and the Jerusalem hills. Borders for my EN 1 through EN 3 are based on the Benjamin survey; borders for my EN 4 through EN 7 are composites from the Judah survey (EN 4 is part of the Arkub triangle, EN 5 is equivalent to Ofer's northern central hills [his zone 8], EN 6 includes all of his northern desert fringe and part of his southern desert fringe [his zones 6 and 9], EN 7 is equivalent to Ofer's zone 5). EN 8, the Judean desert, is represented in both surveys. See *ASHCB* for a complete discussion of the nature of their zones.

94. The sources of geological data for the following discussion are D.H.K. Amiran and D. Nir, 'Geomorphology II/1, Geomorphology', in *Atlas of Israel*, and L.Y. Picard and U. Golani, *Geological Map of Israel* (Jerusalem: Survey of Israel, 1987 [1965]).

95. These soils are red or brownish red, tend to be 'clayey' in texture, and have a depth of up to 50 cm. They are generally quite fertile, with the deeper soils used for agriculture and the shallower, more rocky soils suited for afforestation (see *Atlas of Israel*, 'Soil Map').

96. For a discussion of geomorphology of the highlands of Canaan and the soil

although traditionally a mixed oil and grain economy has characterized its subsistence strategy. While the rich terra rossa soil predominates in this environmental niche, there are also pockets of the Mediterranean brown forest soils[97] as well as mixtures of these two soil types in which terra rossa is dominant. Along the Beth Horon Pass is a small area of colluvial-alluvial soils.[98]

2. *North Central Hills*. These hills are comprised of the southern extremity of the Bethel Hills and all of the lower Jerusalem saddle. Its southern boundary is marked by the Nahal Repha'im system, while its eastern boundary extends along the so-called watershed road, the main road that extends from Nablus to Hebron. Its area is approximately 155 square kilometers, 69 per cent of which was in the tribal area of Benjamin and 31 per cent in that of Judah. It comprises 8 per cent of the total province of Yehud. Its elevation is between 800 and 875 meters above sea level, with the area around Jerusalem being lower than the Bethel or Hebron hills by about 100-200 meters. The subsoil of this region is comprised of three types of limestones: lower cenomanian is predominant in the area of Ramallah and el-Bireh, and a mixture of upper cenomanian and turonian is most common in the Jerusalem area.

types created by the various types of rock formations see Orni and Ephrat, *Geography of Israel*, pp. 5-15, 49-66; and Hopkins, *The Highlands of Canaan*, pp. 58-63. The information on soil types comes from Hopkins, *The Highlands of Canaan*, pp. 123-33; Frick, *The Formation of the State in Ancient Israel*, pp. 112-29; A. Reifenberg, *The Soils of Palestine: Studies in Soil Formation and Land Utilization in the Mediterranean* (London: Thomas Murby & Co., 2nd rev. edn, 1947), 73-85; and *Atlas of Israel*, 'Geomorphology II/3, Soil Map'. The *Atlas of Israel* identifies 24 types of soil that are from two basic categories based upon the climate of the region in which they are found: '(a) soils of the Mediterranean zone, and (b) soils of the desert zone'.

97. These soils come from harder limestones of the highlands, called 'nari' limestone, and are either brown, dark brown or greyish-brown in color. They tend to maintain a depth of between 40 and 60 cm, and are considered 'productive' but the shallower, more rocky soils are used either for pasturage or forests (*Atlas of Israel*, 'Geomorphology II/3, Soil Map').

98. These soils are found either at the foot of the hills or in the wadi beds that cut across the hill country. They are very fertile and productive, tend to be 'comparatively deep', and have a texture of either clay or loam. They are formed from the parent soils of the mountains that are washed down from the hills and hillsides by the rains. In the Judean hills, colluvial-alluvial soils would be a mixture of the terra rossa, Mediterranean brown forest soils, and rendzina soils of the mountains (*Atlas of Israel*, 'Geomorphology II/3, Soil Map').

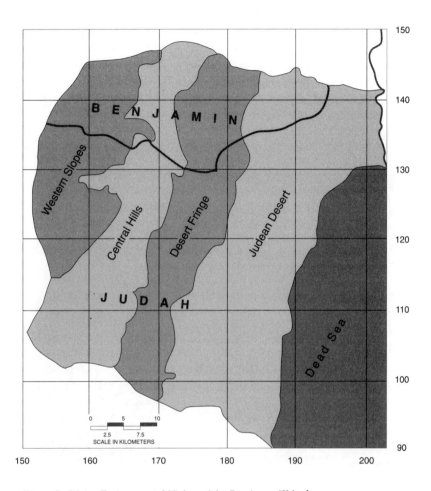

Figure 9. *Major Environmental Niches of the Province of Yehud*

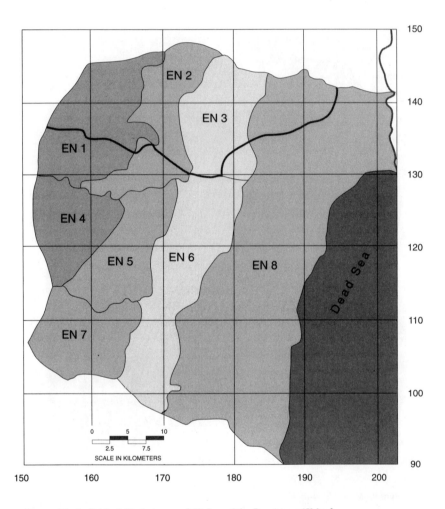

Figure 10. *Individual Environmental Niches of the Province of Yehud*

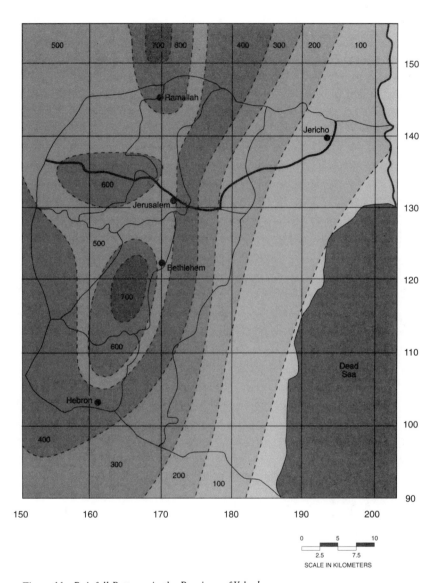

Figure 11. *Rainfall Patterns in the Province of Yehud*

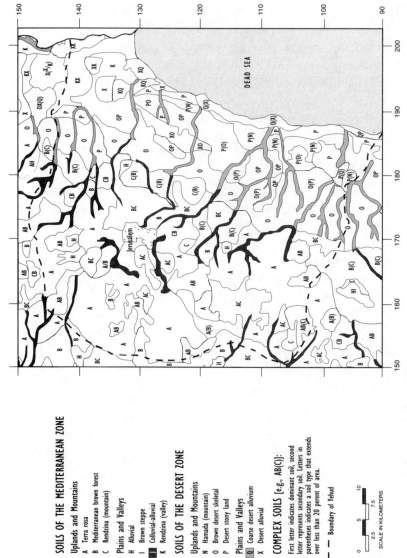

Figure 12. *Soil Types in the Province of Yehud*

Approximately 50 per cent of the soil in this niche is terra rossa. In the northern sector of the niche, southeast of the modern city of Ramallah, is a pocket of mixed terra rossa and Mediterranean brown forest soil. In this sector are also two areas of alluvial soils[99]—one just north of el-Jîb and the other west of the watershed road, near er-Ram. In the area around el-Jîb is a mixture of Mediterranean brown forest soil and the mountainous rendzina soil.[100] A large area of mixed terra rossa and rendzina soil is located along the border between EN 2 and EN 5, west of Jerusalem. Colluvial-alluvial soils are located along the border between EN 1 and EN 2 in the Wadi Shaul and Nahal Sorek systems. Rainfall in this niche also averages between 500 and 600 millimeters annually. The area between Bethel and Ramallah averages 600 millimeters annually as does an area of about 65 square kilometers, that begins approximately two to three kilometers west of Jerusalem.

3. *Northern Desert Fringe.* This niche is comprised of hills that range in elevation between 500 and 800 meters above sea level. Of the 150 square kilometers (comprising 7 per cent of the total area of the province), 20 per cent of the area is located in the tribal allotment of Judah, and 80 per cent in that of the tribe of Benjamin. At its eastern edge, the elevation falls rapidly to approximately 300 and 400 meters. Rainfall in this area is between 300 and 500 millimeters annually with most of the area averaging 400 millimeters. The geomorphology of this region is also varied, with turonian limestone being most common, but with upper cenomanian, a mixture of cenomanian and turonian, and, in the area of Hizma, an area of coniacian-santonian. This niche has a complex soil map. In the northwestern quadrant of the niche, along the watershed road, terra rossa soil is predominant. The next largest soil group is a mixture of Mediterranean brown forest and rendzina soils,

99. The alluvial soils are found in the highlands of Canaan in the intermontane basins as well as the Huleh Basin, the Plain of Jezreel and the Haifa Plain. They are generally brown in color and tend to be quite deep. These are some of the most productive agricultural soils in the highlands. See *Atlas of Israel*, 'Geomorphology II/3, Soil Map'.

100. Two types of rendzina soils are found in Palestine: the rendzina of the mountains and the rendzina of the valleys. In Yehud, with the exception of small areas in the Jordan Valley, most of the rendzinas are, naturally, of the mountainous type. They are light brown, or occasionally greyish-brown in color, and their texture is 'loam to clay', and have a depth of between 40 and 70 cm. This type of soil tends to quite high in lime content (between 30 and 80 per cent); only the soils with lower percentages of lime are suitable for cultivation.

with smaller areas of each individual soil; Mediterranean brown forest soil tends to be represented in the northeastern area and rendzina in the southeastern sector. The colluvial-alluvial soils are commonly found along the major wadi systems of this niche, such as the Wadi Makkuk, Nahal Michmas, and the Wadi Qilt. While the soil is relatively fertile, the Desert Fringe is the area most adaptable to a mixed agrarian and pastoral economy due to its lower average annual rainfall.

4. *Southwestern Hills*. This small niche, called the Arkub Triangle,[101] ranges in elevation between 550 and 750 meters above sea level. Its annual rainfall is approximately 500 millimeters. The soil tends to be terra rossa, coming from a substructure of upper cenomanian limestone, although there are two pockets of a mixed terra rossa and Mediterranean brown forest soil in this niche. It comprises 6 per cent of the area of the province and is itself 125 square kilometers. It is separated from EN 1 by the Wadi es Surar and from EN 7 by the Wadi Musrir.[102]

5. *Central Hills*. This area extends from just south of Jerusalem to south of Bethlehem and is approximately 140 square kilometers, 80 (66 per cent) of which have been completely surveyed. It comprises 7 per cent of the province of Yehud. The elevation ranges between 700 and 970 meters above sea level, with the northern section of the niche at approximately 800 meters, the western border with the southwestern hills averaging 700 meters. Between Jerusalem and Bethlehem the hills rise to between 900 and 970 meters, and fall to approximately 700-800 meters south of Bethlehem. Limestones of the upper cenomanian, lower cenomanian, upper cenomanian and turonian, and turonian are represented, with the most prevalent being upper cenomanian and turonian types, either appearing alone or mixed. The three major soil types of the central hills are all represented here, with terra rossa accounting for approximately 40 per cent of the area. Small pockets of both Mediterranean brown forest soil and rendzina soil exist in the niche. Mixtures of terra rossa with rendzina and terra rossa with Mediterranean brown forest soils are also represented. Along the border between EN 2 and EN 5 is an area of colluvial-alluvial soil. Rainfall in this area varies between 500 and 700 millimeters annually. Bethlehem is situated on the border between the 500 and 600 millimeter area. Most of the niche

---

101. According to Ofer, 'The Highlands of Judah' (Volume 1, Part 2, p. 9), this area was first identified as the Arkub by C.R. Conder and H.H. Kitchener in *SWP*, III. See the latter work, pp. 4-5, for a description of the area.

102. *SWP*, III, p. 4.

receives 600 millimeters of rain annually while an area of about 40 square kilometers has an annual rainfall of 700 millimeters.

6. *Southern Desert Fringe*. This niche extends from approximately El-Ezariyah in the north to southeast of Hebron in the south and has an area of approximately 245 square kilometers, making up 13 per cent of the province of Yehud. It is characterized by hills approximately 400 to 650 meters in elevation in the northern sector of the zone and between 400 and 800 meters above sea level in its southern sector. As with the northern desert fringe, the elevation drops off quite rapidly at its border with the Judean desert. Base rock formations for this niche include coniacian-santonian and campanian in the northern part of this niche and in the southern part, from west to east, upper cenomanian-turonian and turonian limestones, and coniacian-santonian.

Soils of the three major types are represented in EN 6, with Mediterranean brown forest soils and rendzina soils being predominant. In the northwest sector of the niche is an area of Mediterranean brown forest soil followed by an area of mixed Mediterranean brown forest and rendzina, followed by a pocket of rendzina. Similar patterns continue as one travels southward in the niche, with forest soils giving way to a mixed forest soil and rendzina, and pure rendzina soils along the eastern edge of the niche. An area of terra rossa soil is present in the south central sector of the niche, which in turn gives way to a mixed terra rossa and Mediterranean brown forest soil and a pocket of pure Mediterranean brown forest soil in the southern end of the niche. The southeastern corner is marked by a small area of mixed Mediterranean brown forest and rendzina soils. The wadi systems that transverse EN 6 are flanked by rich colluvial-alluvial soils. Annual rainfall in EN 6 is approximately 400 millimeters.

7. *South Central Hills*. These hills extend to just south of the modern city of Hebron (which was not inhabited during the Persian period); the niche is approximately 140 square kilometers, making up 7 per cent of the province. Along the western border with the Shephelah the elevation of the niche is roughly 700 kilometers above sea level. The area between Halhul and the border with the desert fringe is characterized by high ridges and valleys, with the hills approximately 1020 meters and the valleys between them averaging 900 meters above sea level. Rainfall in these hills averages between 400 and 600 millimeters annually. The geomorphology of this area is dominated by upper and lower cenomanian limestones, with a small pocket of upper cenomanian-turonian

limestone in the southwestern corner of the niche. The primary soil type generated by these limestones is, not surprisingly, terra rossa, accounting for approximately 80 per cent of the soil of this niche. Smaller pockets of rendzina, terra rossa and rendzina mixed soils, and mixed terra rossa and Mediterranean forest brown soils are also represented. In addition, there are pockets of colluvial-alluvial soils in the intermontane valleys that characterize this niche.[103]

8. *Judean Desert.* This strip of rugged wasteland has been inhabited only sparsely in the periods with which this study is concerned. Its area is approximately 790 square kilometers, 41 per cent of the province's total size. Elevation is approximately 300 to 400 kilometers above sea level in its western border but goes to below sea level at its lowest point along the shores of the Dead Sea. Aside from oases at Jericho and En-Gedi it was not suited for habitation or agriculture unless irrigation was used to overcome the area's small amount of rainfall (between 100 and 200 millimeters annually). The geomorphology of this niche is varied but is dominated by two rock types: the coniacian-santonian and campanian formations, both found in the desert fringe. Also represented are alluvium, where the Jordan flows into the Dead Sea (notably in the area of Jericho), upper campanian-eocene, and upper campanian-paleocene (in small pockets). Near the western shore of the Dead Sea narrow latitudinal strips of limestones (turonian, lower cenomanian-turonian, and upper cenomanian, respectively, west to east) are present.

The soil types from this niche are as varied as its geomorphology. Along the many wadi systems that cut across the niche are areas of coarse desert alluvium.[104] The western section of the niche is characterized by brown desert skeletal soils.[105] As one travels eastward, these soils give way to either stony desert land[106] or a mixture of these two

103. Avi Ofer, personal communication.

104. The soil in these wadi beds is formed from the parent desert soils, and tends to be made up of stones, gravel and sand. It is generally quite deep, but has very little, if any, agricultural value. See 'Geomorphology II/3, Soil Map', in *Atlas of Israel*.

105. This soil type comes 'from hard and semi-hard limestone, chalk and chalky marls', is usually light brown in color, and tends to be fairly shallow (between 20 and 50 cm). Soil texture usually ranges between sandy and clay loam, and can be used for agriculture if it is deep enough and has small amounts of gravel (see 'Geomorphology II/3, Soil Map', in *Atlas of Israel*).

106. This land is characterized by large areas of stone and rock, with some shallow patches of soil. The soil, brownish-yellow in hue, is between 10 and 20 cm in

types of soils. In the Jordan Valley, near Jericho, is an area of desert alluvial soil[107] and a smaller pocket, southeast of the city, of the rendzina soil of the valleys.[108] All of the soils of the region are represented along the shore of the Dead Sea, with an area of desert alluvial soils where the Jordan River empties into the Dead Sea, followed by a mixture of the latter soil and the coarse desert alluvial soils. In the area surrounding En Gedi are the brown desert skeletal soils, a mixture of the latter soil with desert stony land, and, along the wadi beds, coarse desert alluvium.

This chapter has presented a new reconstruction of the borders of the province of Yehud, one based on sensitivity to the wide variety of topographic, environmental and geological features that exist in Syria-Palestine in general and the central hill country in particular. This sets the stage for the analysis of the numerous excavated and surveyed sites that date to the Neo-Babylonian and Persian periods.

depth, and has no agricultural value (see 'Geomorphology II/3, Soil Map', in *Atlas of Israel*).

107. This soil, found here and in the 'Arava, is of 'mixed origin'. It tends to be deep, and either sandy or clay in texture, and brown in color. It has a relatively high lime content (5 to 50 per cent) and is quite saline—as are most desert soils. It can be used for agriculture when irrigated and when the excess salts are removed (see 'Geomorphology II/3, Soil Map', in *Atlas of Israel*).

108. This soil type, formed from the Lisan Marls, is also common in the Beth Shean Valley and the Huleh Basin. It is grey in color and either 'clay loam or silty clay loam'. It is generally quite deep, quite high in lime content (between 30 and 75 per cent) and often quite saline. Soils of this type are generally fairly fertile when low in salt (see 'Geomorphology II/3, Soil Map', in *Atlas of Israel*).

Chapter 3

YEHUD IN THE PERSIAN PERIOD: EXCAVATED SITES

This chapter is the first of two concerned with reconstructing the province of Yehud during the Persian period—the number and size of sites, the distribution of those sites, and the population of the province. The focus of this chapter is the excavated sites of the Persian period, while Chapter 4 will discuss survey methodology, sites discovered through archaeological surveys of the last 30 years, and the population of the province of Yehud. Just as it was necessary to set the boundaries of the province before discussing its demography, so it is necessary to suggest a relative chronology for the Persian period before analyzing either excavated or surveyed sites that belong in the province. The discussion that follows first considers periodization, then turns to an analysis of the excavated sites from the period of 587/586–332 BCE.

Excavations, Yehud and Archaeological Periods

The biblical lists of returnees in Ezra 2//Nehemiah 7, though composites and almost certainly telescoped, provide us with a rather high number of returnees, approximately 50,000. Archaeological data from excavations and surface surveys suggest a very different reconstruction. Twenty-two sites excavated in Palestine this century have been attributed by various scholars to the province of Yehud and up to 103 sites have been identified on the basis of surface surveys.[1] But before discussing population and site distribution, we must address a more

1. This excludes excavated sites such as Gezer and 'Ain Shems and surveyed sites such as Adullam and Azekah that are outside the borders of Yehud as I have drawn them.

basic question: How should the period from 587/586–332 BCE be designated, and how, if at all, should it be divided? A brief survey of recent treatments of the periods shows that scholars have been divided in their identification of archaeological ages for the exilic and postexilic periods. For example, Albright refers to the period between the Babylonian destruction and the beginning of the Hellenistic period as Iron III,[2] as does O.R. Sellers.[3] C.C. McCown, discussing the pottery of Tell en-Naṣbeh, refers to this period as Late Iron.[4] As pottery typology became more exact, scholars began to distinguish between Iron II, 'Sixth Century'[5] and Persian period pottery.[6] Recent archaeological chronologies have referred to the periods from 587/586 to 332 as 'Babylonian and Persian Periods',[7] or less correctly referred to the entire period as Persian.[8] P. King, in his recent history of the American Schools of Oriental Research, sees the Iron IIC period extending from 605 to 539, but identifies the years 539–332 as Persian.[9]

2.   See, e.g., the chronological chart 'Table of Archaeological Periods Employed', in *Excavations and Results*. Similarly, 'Table of Archaeological Periods', in *The Archaeology of Palestine and the Bible* (New York: Fleming H. Revell, 1932), p. 10. See also W.F. Albright and O.R. Sellers, 'The First Campaign of Excavation at Beth-Zur', *BASOR* 43 (1931), pp. 2-13 (5).

3.   *CBZ*, pp. 15, 41.

4.   'The Cultural History of the Site', in *TN*, I, p. 62.

5.   L.A. Sinclair, 'Bethel Pottery of the Sixth Century B.C.', in W.F. Albright and J.L. Kelso (eds.), *The Excavations of Bethel (1934–1960)* (AASOR, 39; Cambridge, MA: American Schools of Oriental Research, 1968), pp. 70-76.

6.   Lapp, 'The Pottery of Palestine', and *PCC*, pp. 2-4.

7.   'The Historical-Archaeological Periods in Palestine', in *NEAEHL*, IV, p. 1529; and 'The Archaeological Periods in Palestine', in A. Negev (ed.), *The Archaeological Encyclopedia of the Holy Land* (New York: Prentice–Hall, 1990), p. 416.

8.   Z. Gal ('Khirbet Roš Zayit—Biblical Cabul: A Historical-Geographical Case', *BA* 53 [1990], pp. 88-97) refers to this time period (587/586–332) as the Persian period. This is particularly surprising since he has argued for more precision in describing the Iron Age, dividing it into Iron I (1200–1000), Iron II (1000–733) and Iron III (733–586).

9.   Appendix VI, 'The Archaeological Periods of Syria-Palestine', in *American Archaeology in the Mideast: A History of the American Schools of Oriental Research* (Philadelphia: American Schools of Oriental Research, 1983), pp. 282-83. He divides the Iron Age as follows: Iron I (1200–930), Iron IIA (930–721), Iron IIB (721–605), Iron IIC (605–539).

In this respect, it is apparent that the same difficulty in differentiating material culture from late Iron II to early Persian has affected the question of periodization. However, on the basis of historical, material cultural and textual evidence I divide the years 586–332 into three periods: the sites inhabited between 587/586 and 538 represent Neo-Babylonian or Iron IIC sites; those inhabited during the years 538 to c. 450 are Persian I, those inhabited from 450 to 332 are Persian II sites.

From a historical standpoint, it is clear that Babylonian control of Judah had ceased by 539 with the rise of the Persian empire; Persian control ended in 332 with the conquest of Alexander the Great. Thus the beginning and ending points of the Persian period are easily established. The material-cultural evidence points to a period of transition in the sixth century, when many typical Iron II forms continued in use but showed a clear decline in quality. Thus, although the destruction in Judah at the hands of the Babylonians from 598–587/586 was extensive, it did not lead to an immediate change in material culture, a fact which may suggest that this period should be identified as Iron Age rather than Neo-Babylonian.[10]

The transitional forms that began in the mid-sixth century gradually gave way to more distinct Persian period pottery. This pottery has typically been identified as 'early' or 'late', with no real indications of the criteria for these designations. But there is ample evidence for significant changes in the nature and status of Yehud during the fifth and fourth centuries—evidence that supports a break in the period. As Hoglund has pointed out, the fortresses constructed in Syria-Palestine (and in Yehud in particular) during the mid-fifth century BCE represent a new phase in imperial policy.[11] The number of seals increased during

10. The controversy regarding the best way of identifying the period between the Babylonian destruction of 586 and the beginning of the Persian period will no doubt continue. I recognize that the division here is historical rather than being based on material culture. For an argument in favor of treating the period of 586–538 as Iron Age, see Gabriel Barkay, 'The Redefining of Archaeological Periods: Does the Date 588/586 B.C.E. Indeed Mark the End of the Iron Age Culture?', in *BAT 1990*, pp. 106-109. Barkay concludes: 'The end of Iron Age civilization should be dated to around 520 B.C.E.' (p. 109).

11. See Hoglund's *Achaeminid Imperial Administration*, pp. 202-205, and the discussion of his work above in Chapter 1, pp. 42-46.

the late fifth century; coinage became more prominent in the late fifth and early fourth centuries, and Attic ware became more common during this period. In addition, more than a few sites were settled later than even the fortresses (many seem to have been founded in the late fifth or early fourth centuries); some of these present scholars with a mix of Persian and Hellenistic pottery that is as problematic as the mix of Iron IIC and Persian period pottery is for the early period sites. Added to the archaeological data is the literary witness to a strategy of fortification, at least for Jerusalem, as indicated in the book of Nehemiah.[12] This in turn led to the re-population of the city and resulted in a significant change in the status of Yehud within Syria-Palestine, if not the empire. No one of these shifts alone provides sufficient reason to divide the Persian period in the mid-fifth century, but taken together, they support such a position.

With this division of the period from 587/6–332 in mind, the study now may turn to a discussion of excavated sites dating to the Neo-Babylonian, Persian I and Persian II periods (Table 1). A cursory reading of the table shows that I have omitted Moṣah, Azekah, and Gezer, sites that Stern includes in his discussion of sites from Yehud.[13] The site of Moṣah was not excavated, and, strictly speaking, is a surveyed site, as Stern himself notes.[14] I have already discussed, above in Chapter 2, the reasons for deleting Gezer and Azekah. The number of Persian period sites excavated would shrink further if, as is possible, Tell el-Fûl and el-Jîb were inhabited only until the end of the Neo-Babylonian period.

12. Ephraim Stern has suggested the end of the fifth century BCE, when Attic ware becomes more prevalent, as another possible date for the break between Persian I and II (personal communication).
13. *Material Culture*, pp. 31-40.
14. *Material Culture*, pp. 34-35.

Table 1. *Excavated Sites from the Neo-Babylonian*
and Persian Periods

Neo-Babylonian (587/586–538)	*Persian I (538–450)*
Bethel I[15]	Jerusalem[16]
El-Jîb	Ketef Hinnom
Tell el-Fûl	Mamilla
Tell en-Naṣbeh[17]	Kh. er-Ras (W)
Ḥorvat Zimri (Pizgat Ze'ev 'D')	Wadi Salim
Kh. er-Ras (S)	Ramat Rahel
	Jericho
	Tel Goren

Persian II (450–332)
Bethel II
Ras el-Kharrubeh
El-'Ezariyeh (Bethany)
Ketef Yeriḥo
Khirbet et-Tubeiqah (Beth-Zur)
Khirbet Abu et-Twein
'Ain 'Arrub
Khirbet 'Almith
Khirbet Nijam (Har Adar)

15. A chronology is given in the final report of the Bethel excavations (p. xiv), but note that it lacks a detailed stratigraphic analysis. What I call Bethel I is called a 'sixth century phase' and given the dates 587/586 to the late sixth century. Bethel II refers to the period the excavators identified as 'Late Persian and Early Hellenistic'.

16. Even though many excavations have been conducted in Jerusalem in the last 100 years (for a full discussion, see below, pp. 134-48), it is still unclear how soon after its fall in 587/586 Jerusalem began to be inhabited again. In the period directly after the Babylonian conquest, Mizpah (Tell en-Naṣbeh) was the regional capital. It has frequently been suggested that sacrifices began to be offered in Jerusalem soon after its fall. Among these, see Kochman, 'Status and Extent of Judah', pp. xii-xiii. J. Berquist proposes this cultic activity in Neo-Babylonian Jerusalem (*Judaism in Persia's Shadow*, pp. 142-62). If this is the case, one would expect some small level of settlement to have begun before the first return to Yehud in 538. However, the most we can say on the basis of the archaeological evidence is that Jerusalem was resettled sometime during the sixth century.

17. This site, as we shall see below, was not completely destroyed during the Babylonian conquest and continued to be inhabited through the Neo-Babylonian and Persian periods.

Excavated Sites from Yehud Dating to the Neo-Babylonian Period

El-Jîb (Gibeon)

From 1956 through 1960 excavations were undertaken at the site of el-Jîb, 12 kilometers northwest of Jerusalem. These excavations, directed by James Pritchard, uncovered significant occupation of the Early Bronze, Middle Bronze, Iron I and II, and Roman periods, including some 60 inscriptions and seal impressions that proved conclusively that el-Jîb was in fact biblical Gibeon.[18] In Pritchard's view, the evidence for a Persian period occupation of Gibeon is tenuous at best. Characteristic of his interpretation of the assembled data is his view that

> The evidence for occupation during the Persian period consists principally of a gold ring which had been dropped into a crevice of the demolished Iron Age city wall, a silver ring inscribed with the letters *mr(?)tsmm* and 5 *mṣh* stamps on handles.[19]

The preliminary reports and final publications of the Gibeon excavations are imprecise and inconsistent. For example, Pritchard speaks both of a seventh-century end to the occupation of the site, positing a break

18. The principle publication of these epigraphic finds is in J.B. Pritchard's *Hebrew Inscriptions and Stamps from Gibeon* (Philadelphia: University of Pennsylvania Press, 1959). For reviews of this work and differing interpretations of the dating of these finds see: W.F. Albright, 'Reports on Excavations in the Near and Middle East (Continued)', *BASOR* 159 (1960), pp. 37-39 (37); N. Avigad, 'Some Notes on the Hebrew Inscriptions from Gibeon', *IEJ* 9 (1959), pp. 130-33; F.M. Cross, Jr, 'Epigraphical Notes on the Hebrew Documents of the Eighth Centuries B.C. III. The Inscribed Jar Handles from Gibeon', *BASOR* 168 (1962), pp. 18-23; A. Demsky, 'The Genealogy of Gibeon (I Chronicles 9:35-44): Biblical and Epigraphic Considerations', *BASOR* 202 (1971), pp. 16-23. The most significant indicator of the correspondence between el-Jîb and Gibeon was the large number of jar handles having the reading of גבען. This laid to rest the controversy in which Albright, following Robinson, held el-Jîb to be Gibeon, and Alt and Noth located Gibeon at nearby Nebi Samwil.

19. 'Gibeon's History in Light of Excavation', in G.W. Anderson *et al.* (eds.), *Congress Volume: Oxford, 1959* (VTSup, 7; Leiden: E.J. Brill, 1960), pp. 1-12. See also 'The Wine Industry at Gibeon: 1959 Discoveries', *Expedition* 2 (1959), pp. 17-25 (25). Similarly, he writes regarding the ceramics that 'although there are pottery forms which may be dated as late as the end of the sixth century, these are limited in number, *and do not represent a major occupation of the site*' (*Winery, Defenses, and Soundings at Gibeon* [Philadelphia: The University Museum, 1964], p. 39; emphasis added).

between Iron II and Persian settlements, and of continuity of settlement at least into the early sixth century.[20] Further, it is never clear exactly what period he is referring to as Persian. Does 'Persian' designate any material-cultural remains that post-date 587/586, as is the case for many scholars, or would he begin this period with the correct date of 539/538?

Perhaps more problematic is his analysis of the pottery. In *Winery*, he often dates to the Iron II period pottery which he admits has parallels from other sites in clear Persian period contexts.[21] It is true that one of the major difficulties of designating early Persian period pottery from Syria-Palestine is its similarity to Iron II forms. However, it would seem that had Pritchard taken more care in his comparison of the pottery from other sites he would have been more aware of what is almost certainly a significant occupation of Gibeon during the Neo-Babylonian period. In his review of 'The Water System of Gibeon', G.E. Wright suggests that 'the wine jugs from which the inscribed jar handles derive' be dated 'not much before the middle and preferably in the second half of the sixth century'.[22] This is consistent with the adjusted dating of the paleographic evidence from the handles themselves to the middle of the sixth century.[23] Together, the pottery and paleographic evidence would suggest that what Pritchard identifies as the primary industry of

20. Note his oft-mentioned destruction of the city wall in the seventh century ('Gibeon's History', p. 11) while speaking of a 'thriving wine industry' in the late seventh and early sixth century. He similarly notes the mention of Gibeon in the account of the assassination of Gedeliah by Ishmael in Jer. 40–41; see 'The Bible Reports on Gibeon', *Expedition* 3 (1960), pp. 2-9. Yet the mention by Jeremiah in these chapters of the presence of 'soldiers, women, children, and court officials from Gibeon' is curious if the city met its end in the late seventh century.

21. See, e.g., *Winery*, pp. 19-21, where it is not uncommon for him to date pottery to eighth-sixth centuries while noting parallels into the fifth and fourth centuries.

22. Wright, review of 'The Water System of Gibeon', pp. 210-11 (211 n. 1). Wright cites a parallel with Tomb 14 at Beth Shemesh and Stratum V of Shechem.

23. Here, see Cross, 'Inscribed Jar Handles', p. 23: 'In the case of some (formal) letters, *dalet* and *he*, traits appear which have parallels only in post-Exilic seals and the archaeizing paleo-Hebrew script of the Greek period. In view of this evidence, it does not appear feasible to date the group before *ca.* 600 B.C. ...Perhaps we can do no better than to date the Gibeon handles broadly to the sixth century B.C.' Note also the view of Albright, who feels 'certain that most—probably all—of these graffiti belong to the Babylonian Exile or immediately after it in the sixth century B.C.' ('Reports on Excavations', p. 37). Avigad dates these same inscribed handles to the late eighth century in 'Some Notes on the Hebrew Inscriptions', p. 132.

Gibeon, the 'winery', was at its high point in the Neo-Babylonian or perhaps the early Persian period, not the late Iron II period. Pritchard's analysis of the water system, notably the so-called pool of Gibeon, and of the defense systems have also come under considerable scrutiny.[24]

Most critical of Pritchard's excavations and publications is Paul Lapp.[25] He maintains that not only were Pritchard's choices of what pottery to publish poor, but his analysis of the published forms was inaccurate. According to Lapp, much, if not most, of the pottery that Pritchard dates as Iron II was clearly Persian;[26] further, many of the parallels he cites to support his Iron II dating were inappropriate and/or incorrect. Lapp also notes that much of the pottery that would have clarified the stratigraphy of the site ended up in the dig's dump, 'from which several Palestinian archaeologists have gathered their teaching collections for the Persian period'.[27] He also questions Pritchard's analysis of the 'wine cellars', which he suggests are better interpreted as grain silos. Lapp concludes that it is not possible 'to adduce any clear evidence for wine cellars. In fact, there is no incontestable evidence for a wine industry at el-Jîb.' Rather, the storage facilities 'are ordinary silos, everywhere associated with Iron age and subsequent occupation in Palestine'.[28] If he is correct, even this part of Pritchard's interpretation of the excavation is flawed. Instead of a flourishing wine industry, Gibeon had storage facilities for grain dating to the exilic or possibly the early Persian period settlement. This interpretation is supported by numerous parallels with evidence of grain storage facilities, particularly

24. Wright, review of 'The Water System of Gibeon', interprets the evidence from the water systems in the exact opposite manner from Pritchard, suggesting that the 'pool' was dug after the tunnel was engineered and was never used. For a critical review of Pritchard's interpretation of the defense system, see Paar, review of *Winery, Defenses, and Soundings at Gibeon*, pp. 114-18.

25. See Lapp, review of *Winery, Defenses, and Soundings at Gibeon*, pp. 391-93; and 'The Pottery of Palestine', p. 181 n. 14.

26. Here, however, one should note that Lapp seems to include as Persian remains what this study identifies as exilic. Such is the case in his discussion of the material from Tell el-Fûl, Bethel sub-104 and el-Jîb. Nancy Lapp makes a similar corrective; see 'The Pottery from the 1964 Campaign', in her *The Third Campaign*, p. 84.

27. Lapp, review of *Winery, Defenses, and Soundings at Gibeon*, p. 392.

28. Lapp, review of *Winery, Defenses, and Soundings at Gibeon*, p. 392.

Tell el-Hesi,[29] Tell el-Fûl and Tell en-Naṣbeh. Commenting on the silos from Tell el-Fûl, Nancy Lapp suggests:

> Silos with similar contents and a similar geological makeup are recorded from Tell en-Naṣbeh, and the 'wine cellars' found at Gibeon are comparable to the Tell el-Fûl silos. It is probable that at all three sites (which have similar occupational histories and are in the same geographical area), the silos housed storage jars filled with grain or liquids.[30]

Stern does not discuss pottery typology in his summary of the Gibeon excavation though he does observe that 'it is strange that the excavator disregarded the significance of a stratum of settlement of the Persian period at Gibeon'.[31] Apparently Pritchard misunderstood much of the material discovered in the six years of excavation at Gibeon. Although the published material does not allow for an accurate reconstruction of its stratigraphy, Gibeon was evidently occupied during the Neo-Babylonian and perhaps even the early Persian period. What is perhaps most surprising is that even after several reviews critical of his publications appeared Pritchard still maintained that there was only 'scant evidence' of any occupation from the late sixth century until the beginning of the Roman Period.[32]

Tell el-Fûl (Gibeah of Saul)[33]

Excavations at Tell el-Fûl were conducted in three seasons, two directed by W.F. Albright in 1922–23 and 1933, and one in 1964 by Paul Lapp. While there is much Iron I and II material that is of general interest to

29. See L.E. Stager, 'Climatic Conditions and Grain Storage in the Persian Period', *BA* 34 (1971), pp. 86-88; J. Betlyon, 'Archaeological Evidence of Military Operations in Southern Judah during the Early Hellenistic Period', *BA* 54 (1991), pp. 36-43; and W.J. Bennett, Jr, and J.A. Blakely (eds.), *Tell el-Hesi: The Persian Period (Stratum V)* (Winona Lake, IN: Eisenbrauns, 1989), pp. 341-55.

30. 'Fûl, tell el-', in *NEAEHL*, II, p. 448. For a complete discussion of Tell el-Fûl, see below.

31. *Material Culture*, p. 33.

32. See his entry on Gibeon in *EAEHL*, II, pp. 446-50. The encyclopedia was published in 1975–78, clearly allowing Pritchard enough time to have made appropriate adjustments to his theories about Gibeon. His assessment of the site remains unchanged in the newly revised *NEAEHL*, II, pp. 511-14.

33. For a discussion of the identification of Tell el-Fûl with Gibeah of Saul, see J.A. Graham, 'Previous Excavations at Tell el-Fûl: A Survey of Research and Exploration', in Lapp (ed.), *The Third Campaign*, pp. 2-5. According to Graham, Albright conducted the excavations at the suggestion of G. Dalman, who thought

archaeologists,[34] this discussion will be confined to the village associated with this relatively small site. Albright dated the remains to a period spanning from the eighth to the seventh centuries to the first century BCE and identified the majority of the pottery dated from the sixth through second centuries as 'Persian-Hellenistic'.[35] Using these same data, but refined by additional finds from his later excavations, Paul Lapp suggested adjusting the beginning dates down one century and posited a break from the end of the sixth century to the beginning of the Hellenistic period.

Lapp had published only a preliminary report of his 1964 salvage excavation before he died.[36] He held that the site was strongly fortified in the late seventh and early sixth centuries, a conclusion justified by the discovery of one of the latest casemate walls known in Palestine.[37] There is slight evidence of destruction, probably dating to 597 BCE; but then the site increased in size during the sixth century. As is true of many Neo-Babylonian and Persian period sites, there is evidence for building outside the fortification line of the settlement.[38] Significant amounts of pottery were dated to the second half of the sixth century, and Lapp therefore concluded that the occupation of the site ended in about 500 BCE, the same time that Gibeon and Bethel were abandoned.

Nancy Lapp further refined the archaeological history of Tell el-Fûl with publication of the full report of the final campaign of the site's excavation in 1981.[39] She suggests that the destruction that P. Lapp and

that such excavations might shed light on the controversy concerning the location of Gibeah.

34. Particularly the so-called 'Fortress of Saul' which Albright used to substantiate his identification of the site with Gibeah. See Albright, *Excavations and Results*.

35. *Excavations and Results*, p. 23.

36. 'Tell el-Fûl', pp. 2-10.

37. 'Tell el-Fûl', pp. 4-5. See also Nancy Lapp, 'Casemate Walls in Palestine and the Late Iron II Casemate at Tell el-Fûl (Gibeah)', *BASOR* 223 (1976), pp. 25-42.

38. On this point, see L.A. Sinclair in 'An Archaeological Study of Gibeah (Tell el-Fûl)', *BA* 27 (1964), pp. 52-64 (60); Lapp, 'Tell el-Fûl', p. 6; and Lapp, *The Third Campaign*, p. 44). A similar pattern is evident at Tell en-Naṣbeh and Bethel, and according to K. Hoglund (*Achaemenid Imperial Administration*, p. 221) is characteristic of the Persian period as a whole, during which fortified sites were the exception rather than the rule. This seems to have been a result of Persian Imperial policy.

39. *The Third Campaign*.

Sinclair had dated to 597 should date instead to 587 and divides Stratum III into two periods. Stratum IIIA dates from 650 to 587 and Stratum IIIB dates from 587 to 538. This interpretation is based primarily on a homogeneous grouping of pottery from Cistern 1. While P. Lapp considered the site to have been abandoned from about 500 BCE until 200 BCE, N. Lapp notes that the 'common Persian pottery forms do not appear, and it is probable that Tell el-Fûl was abandoned before the period of Balâṭah Stratum V'.[40] She thus concludes that the site's sixth century occupation ends before the Persian period begins, namely, in 538. She also suggests that the pottery from el-Jîb likewise is pre-Balâṭah V (contra G.E. Wright[41]). The logical conclusion, then, is that el-Jîb and Bethel should also be identified as 'Neo-Babylonian' sites, abandoned during the Persian period. Some would contend that Paul Lapp and Nancy Lapp are too narrow in their dating of the pottery from Tell el-Fûl. However, Paul Lapp demonstrated parallels between the pottery of this site and that from Neo-Babylonian contexts from other sites, including locus sub-104 from Bethel, Tomb 14 from Beth She-mesh, several tombs from Lachish, el-Jîb, Samaria, and cisterns from Tell en-Naṣbeh.[42] If Nancy Lapp is correct in her assessment that Tell el-Fûl IIIB ends in 538, then it follows that Bethel and el-Jîb were also abandoned at that time. Her discussion of the pottery of Tell el-Fûl[43] is thorough and well documented, and clarifies the ceramic transition from the Iron IIC to Persian periods.

Bethel

This important cult site of the northern kingdom was excavated by Albright and Kelso in four seasons: 1934, 1954, 1957 and 1960. Kelso suggests that it was destroyed by the Assyrians in the late eighth century BCE, probably some time after 724.[44] After the fall of the Assyrian

40. N. Lapp, 'The 7th–6th Century Occupation: Period III', in her *The Third Campaign*, p. 40.

41. See above, n. 22.

42. See Lapp, 'The Pottery of Palestine', p. 181 n. 14; and Lapp, 'Fûl, Tell el-', p. 448.

43. Lapp, 'Fûl, Tell el-', p. 448; and 'The Pottery from the 1964 Campaign', pp. 79-107.

44. W.F. Albright and J.L. Kelso, *The Excavation of Bethel (1934–1960)* (AASOR, 39; Cambridge, MA: American Schools of Oriental Research, 1968), p. 51. Kelso suggests the date of 721 BCE in 'Bethel', in *NEAEHL*, I, p. 192.

empire, it was evidently taken into the southern kingdom by Josiah and seems to have been one of the many sites not destroyed by the Babylonians in 587/586. However, the site was subsequently destroyed, possibly during the transition from Babylonian to Persian control.[45] A gap in occupation followed its destruction, but according to Kelso it was a small village by the time of Ezra.[46]

Associated with the Neo-Babylonian period at Bethel, but purchased from villagers from the modern city of Beitin was a conical seal, dating to the sixth or possibly the fifth century. This seal depicts a person worshiping standing before an incense altar, worshiping a Babylonian deity, perhaps Marduk. Albright and Kelso interpreted it as an indication of the Babylonian influence in the sixth century BCE.[47] Similar seals have been discovered at En-Gedi[48] and Kh. Nijam.[49] A stone scarab that Albright and Kelso judged as 'Neo-Babylonian work'[50] was discovered in the 1960 campaign in a mixed context.

45. Albright and Kelso posit a date 'sometime between 533 and 521' (*The Excavation of Bethel*, p. 37) but also suggest that Bethel was destroyed 'either by Nabonidus, or by the Persians in the period just preceding the reign of Darius' (*The Excavation of Bethel*, p. 51). Kelso reiterates this in the *NEAEHL*, I, entry on Bethel (p. 194). P. Lapp dates the pottery midway between 587 and 550, with a probable date of 570; he suggests an abandonment of the site in about 500 BCE ('The Pottery of Palestine', p. 181 n. 14). N. Lapp concurs with Albright's suggestion of destruction by Nabonidus, 'in conjunction with the Syrian revolts of 553 B.C.' (*The Third Campaign*, p. 84).

46. 'Bethel', p. 192. Albright and Kelso's earlier assessment of the site suggested that there were only scant remains from the postexilic period. In suggesting a mid-fifth century occupation they seem to be influenced by the Ezra–Nehemiah traditions, which attribute a population of between 123 and 223 for Bethel and Ai. The archaeological evidence suggests that there may have been a settlement gap of nearly two centuries. See *The Excavation of Bethel*, p. xiv ('Chronology of Bethel'), and pp. 37-40.

47. Exact dating is impossible since it was unstratified; even if it had come from a fifth-century context its origin was probably earlier. See *The Excavation of Bethel*, pp. 51 and 91.

48. Two such seals were discovered, one in Building 234 and one along Wall 25. These are interpreted as fifth-century finds by the excavators. See B. Mazar and I. Dunayevsky, 'En-Gedi: Fourth and Fifth Seasons of Excavations', *IEJ* 17 (1967), pp. 133-43 (140).

49. M. Dadon, 'Har Adar', *ESI* 14 (1994), pp. 87-88. I discuss the seal below on p. 169.

50. *The Excavation of Bethel*, p. 91.

The most important pottery group, according to Paul Lapp and Nancy Lapp, is that from sub-104 group, discovered in Area II of the 1934 excavations. This, as noted above, dates to about 570 BCE and is 'the latest sixth century horizon'[51] from Bethel. The major question remaining, given the evidence presented here, is the length of the gap in occupation at Bethel. The destruction layer is clear and its date to the first third of the sixth century seems certain.

Tell en-Naṣbeh
This site with an area of 32 dunams[52] is located 12 kilometers north of Jerusalem, overlooking the modern road from Jerusalem to Nablus. It is one of the most completely excavated sites in Palestine, having been dug in five seasons by W.F. Badè during the years from 1926 to 1935. Although one of the most advanced excavations of its time with respect to methodology of recording finds, its stratigraphy is notoriously problematic.[53] This remains true despite the significant work of T.L. McClellan[54] and Jeffrey Zorn,[55] both of whom have clarified the nature of the stratigraphic remains for the Iron II and perhaps the Neo-Babylonian periods (see Table 2 for a comparison of the three major analyses of the site).[56]

51. Lapp, 'The Pottery of Palestine', p. 181 n. 14.

52. One metric dunam is equivalent to 0.25 acres and 0.1 hectares.

53. See the comments of Wampler above in Chapter 1, p. 25 n. 77; similarly, Jeffrey Zorn notes: 'It is dificult to speak of a site-wide, unified stratigraphy in the 1947 report', largely because Wampler and McCown, who published the report after Badè's death, did not work from a comprehensive understanding of the site in their respective contributions on stratigraphy (Wampler) and architecture and defenses (McCown). See Zorn, 'Tell en Naṣbeh: A Re-evaluation of the Architecture and Stratigraphy of the Early Bronze Age, Iron Age and Later Periods' (PhD dissertation, University of California, Berkeley, 1993), pp. 16-17.

54. 'Town Planning at Tell en-Naṣbeh', *ZDPV* 100 (1984), pp. 53-69. His main concern is with the Iron II period though he discusses the Persian period briefly.

55. See Zorn, 'Tell en Naṣbeh: A Re-evaluation'; *idem*, 'Naṣbeh, Tell en-', in *NEAEHL*, III, pp. 1098-1102; *idem*, 'Estimating the Population Size of Ancient Settlements: Methods, Problems, Solutions, and a Case Study', *BASOR* 295 (1995), pp. 31-48; and *idem*, 'Mizpah: Newly Discovered Stratum Reveals Judah's Other Capital', *BARev* 23.5 (1997), pp. 28-37, 66.

56. This table is patterned after, but differs from, Zorn's Table A. 3.1, 'Stratigraphic Divisions of Tell en-Naṣbeh', in his 'Tell en-Naṣbeh: A Re-evaluation', p. 33. Zorn interprets McCown's and Wampler's Stratum II as only corresponding to his Stratum 4, and their Stratum I as equivalent to his Strata 3-1, dividing their

Table 2. *Analyses of Tell en-Naṣbeh's Stratigraphy*

	McCown/Wampler	McClellan	Zorn
Stratum:	LC/EB I	Not discussed	5
	II (Early: 1100–1000)	A	4 (1200–1000)
	II (Late: 1000–700)	B	3C (1000–900)
	II (Late: 1000–700)	B+C	3B (900–850)
	II (Late) and I (Early: 700–586)	B+C	3A (850–586)
	I (Late: 586–400)	C	2 (586–400?)
	I (Late 400–?)	D	1 (332–37?)[57]

Occupied first at the beginning of the Early Bronze Age (Zorn's Stratum 5), Tell en-Naṣbeh was abandoned from the end of EB I or EB II until the beginning of the Iron Age; it was then inhabited almost continually from the Iron I through the Hellenistic/Roman periods.[58] It has

Stratum I into two phases. While he characterizes his chart as a 'general comparison' of the three studies concerned, closer analysis of the McCown/Wampler studies shows that they divided Stratum II into two phases and Stratum I into two or three, as indicated in the table below. See the discussions and datings in *TN*, I: Wampler dates Stratum II from the eleventh/twelfth centuries until the seventh century BCE (p. 180), and Stratum I from 700 to 400 BCE, noting finds from the Hellenistic period and later, but not assigning a specific phase in that stratum to these period due to lack of architectural evidence (pp. 185-86). See also McCown's discussion of the architectural features of the site, especially pp. 224-47. Although McCown and Wampler seem to have worked fairly independently of one another, Wampler does refer to McCown's stratigraphic analysis (see *TN*, I, p. 221). Both cited G. Ernest Wright's pottery analysis of ceramic remains from areas AE, AF and AG) which roughly agreed with their phasing of the site.

57. Zorn has identified Stratum 1 with various dates in his writing. His original study dates the stratum from about 300 BCE but gives it no terminal point. The dates above are from 'Mizpah: Newly Discovered Stratum', pp. 32-34.

58. This settlement history follows Zorn's interpretation from 'Naṣbeh, Tell en-', p. 1098, his dissertation, 'Tell en-Naṣbeh: A Re-evaluation', pp. 15-16, pp. 88-93, and 'Mizpah: Newly Discovered Stratum', pp. 32-34. Wampler and McCown had suggested that the site was occupied at the end of the Chalcolithic or beginning of the Early Bronze Age, had remains from the Middle Bronze Age, a gap in occupation during the Late Bronze Age, and continuous subsequent occupation from Iron I through the middle of the Persian period. Zorn suggests that there was a short break in occupation until perhaps the beginning of the Hellenistic period when the final phase of settlement began. This phase lasted through the beginning of the Roman period.

been identified by various scholars as Gibeon, Beeroth and Ataroth.[59] Badè, followed by most scholars, identified Tell en-Naṣbeh as biblical Mizpah,[60] which played a significant role in the newly formed Babylonian province and was the site of the murder of the pro-Babylonian Gedeliah (2 Kgs 25.22-26; Jer. 40.7–41.18).[61] Although their stratigraphic context is uncertain, significant pottery, architectural and epigraphic remains from both Neo-Babylonian and Persian periods exist at Tell en-Naṣbeh. It is evident that the site sustained partial damage at the end of its Iron II occupation, perhaps during the Babylonian conquest, but was not totally destroyed.[62] McClellan divides Tell en-Naṣbeh's history into four phases. During Phase A the earliest city wall was built; this wall underlies later casemate walls, and McClellan suggests that buildings may have existed within the walls of this phase. In Phase B a casemate defense wall was constructed, with a number of three- or four-room houses built 'against or into the casemate system'.[63] The major defensive wall was built in Phase C and made the Phase B wall obsolete. All building that post-dates the destruction of the Phase C wall is included in McClellan's Phase D. Wampler had already noted significant building over the city walls and attributed it to the postexilic period in general.[64] He further notes that the main area of occupation in the city is found in the southwest sector of the tell, as is true of the Iron II period at Tell en-Naṣbeh. According to both Wampler and McClellan,

59. For a concise discussion of these identifications, see J. Muilenberg, 'Survey of the Literature of Tell en-Naṣbeh', and 'The Literary Sources Bearing on the Question of Identification', in *TN*, I, pp. 13-22 and 23-45 respectively; and Zorn, 'Naṣbeh, Tell en-', p. 1098.

60. Note that Albright maintained that Nebi Samwîl was the most likely site of Mizpah; see Muilenberg, 'Survey of the Literature', p. 16.

61. C.C. McCown notes that the site 'serves to provide extremely valuable data regarding the cultural history of the southern kingdom and the Persian province...' (*TN*, I, p. 172).

62. Zorn suggests that the site was 'deliberately, but not violently leveled' at the end of Stratum 3A, and that the construction of Stratum 2 began almost immediately. See 'Tell en Nasbeh: A Re-evaluation', p. 163.

63. McClellan, 'Town Planning', p. 54.

64. 'The Stratifications of Tell en-Naṣbeh', in *TN*, I, pp. 179-86, 221. He notes, e.g., that rooms 299, 302 and 303 were built over the city wall and suggests that many walls are from the latter part of the sixth century. In particular, he considers the date of the remains from the area of the city gate to be the exilic or postexilic period.

an additional factor that makes establishing a clear stratigraphy of the site more difficult is the reuse of Iron II buildings in the Persian period.

J. Zorn identifies five strata at Tell en-Naṣbeh, four dating from the Iron I through Hellenistic (and perhaps later) periods. Stratum 4 dates from 1200 through 1000 BCE and represents the first phase of its resettlement. Zorn cites the presence of Philistine pottery and collared-rim store jars to establish this dating, although the architectural and agricultural installations (winepresses, storage silos, etc.) are more difficult to date with certainty. Stratum 3 represents the Iron II occupation (equivalent to McClellan's Phases A-C): 3C dates to 1000–900 BCE; 3B represents the period from 900 to 850 BCE, and 3A was occupied from 850 to 586 BCE. Stratum 3 included construction inside the fortified city as well as its 'suburbs'—buildings constructed outside the city walls.[65]

From the standpoint of this study, Zorn's greatest contribution is his ability to untangle the stratigraphic puzzle of Tell en-Naṣbeh, clearly delineating remains from the Neo-Babylonian and Persian periods (Zorn's Stratum 2). Zorn assigns six four-room houses to Stratum 2 (Buildings 93.03, 110.01, 125.01, 127.03, 145.02 and 194.01).[66] Some are built over Iron II buildings, and their orientation marks a departure from the city's original plan. The size and construction techniques mark them as post-Iron II, and according to Zorn they are 'of finer construction than any other dwellings on the site'.[67] In particular, whereas the Iron II buildings (Strata 3C-3A) tend to be constructed with one-stone thickness, the Neo-Babylonian/Persian (Stratum 2) walls fall under two major construction types (Zorn identifies four types of walls in the various strata). They typically combine one-stone thick walls with walls built with two-stone thickness (Zorn's Type 1), are entirely constructed with the latter technique, or have walls constructed with large, roughly cut, often square stones (Zorn's Type 3).[68] These buildings often have

65. Zorn, 'Naṣbeh, Tell en-', p. 1101. The term 'suburb' is perhaps not ideal, but Zorn is quite correct when he observes that these extra-mural settlements are typically not considered when the population of ancient cities is estimated.

66. For a full discussion of these buildings, see his 'Tell en-Naṣbeh: A Reevaluation', pp. 503 (93.03; Plan, p. 979); 537-45 (110.01; Plan, p. 1032); 567-70 (125.01; Plan, p. 1034); 591-605 (127.03; Plan, p. 1040); pp. 706-710 (145.02; Plan, p. 985); and pp. 897-910, (194.01; Plan, p. 993).

67. 'Naṣbeh, Tell en-', p. 1101.

68. 'Tell en-Naṣbeh: A Re-evaluation', pp. 167-69. While these two building styles are predominant in Stratum 2, Zorn identifies two other styles of wall con-

stone-paved floors and stone monoliths supporting a roof or in some cases a second storey. The three- and four-room buildings are between 1.3 and 2.2 times larger than their Stratum 3 counterparts, with an average size of 133.3 m². Zorn notes that the three-room buildings from Stratum 2 are as large as the largest of the Stratum 3 buildings.[69] In addition to the several four-room domestic buildings a large public building with two areas of stone pavement was discovered in the northeast portion of Tell en-Naṣbeh (Building 74.01); adjacent to the pavement were walls more substantial than those of the four-room, private dwellings. Although the entire area was not excavated, Zorn suggests that the building contained several connected chambers and that 'the remains are indicative of a structure far larger than any other found'.[70] He identifies two long chambers discovered in the south-central portion of the site as store-rooms (Building 160.10), as he does other wall fragments east of these chambers and on the southwest sector of the site. Located west of the city gate was a 26-meter long 'enclosure wall', though its function remains unclear.[71] Zorn concludes that the size of structures as well as their construction techniques, their different orientation within the city plan and their construction over Iron II structures best fit the Neo-Babylonian period and conform to what one would expect for Tell en-Naṣbeh as the provincial capital. Ceramic remains from Stratum 2 are similar to the Iron II assemblage, as one would expect for the Neo-Babylonian period. A portion of a bronze circlet inscribed with a dedicatory formula inscribed in Neo-Babylonian cuneiform was also discovered. Zorn suggests that Stratum 2 ended sometime in the late fifth century and that the site was subsequently intentionally dismantled before the founding of Stratum 1.

Stratum 1 of Tell en-Naṣbeh dates either from the late Persian through the Byzantine,[72] or the early Hellenistic through the Roman or Byzan-

---

struction. Zorn's Type 2 wall is composed of two rows of typically undressed stones; his Type 4 wall is comprised of small (usually 20 cm or less) stones and is of 'flimsy' construction.

69. 'Tell en-Naṣbeh: A Re-evaluation', pp. 172-73.
70. 'Naṣbeh, Tell en-', p. 1102.
71. On the storehouses and enclosure wall, see Zorn, 'Tell en-Naṣbeh: A Re-evaluation', pp. 164-65, 172-75, 695.
72. These dates are suggested in Zorn, 'Naṣbeh, Tell en-', p. 1102.

tine periods,[73] and is equivalent to McClellan's Phase D and McCown's and Wampler's Late I. It is marked by wall fragments that often cut across 'stratum 2 walls, and over the town wall and outer gate'.[74] In addition, Zorn dates two kilns to the Persian period, and notes the presence of a wine-press in the northern portion of the site which dates to the Neo-Babylonian or Persian period.

An abundance of pottery forms from both Neo-Babylonian and Persian periods was also discovered at Tell en-Naṣbeh. This includes both native Palestinian forms and a large amount of Attic red and black ware. In Cistern 304 some East Greek 'Clazomenian' ware was discovered in the form of an amphora with parallels to the sixth century, probably dating to the 'latest phase' of this type, c. 540 or 530 BCE.[75] Room 502 yielded a 'wall and handle' of a skyphos, decorated with a sphinx-like figure and palmette, dating to about 500 BCE. Cistern 361 contained a fragment of an oinochoe, with black glaze and ivy-branch decoration.[76] From Silo 157 part of an Attic black cup or plate was recovered, decorated with an impressed design; this dates to the second half of the fifth century. A piece of a red Attic cup was discovered in a test trench; the inside of this cup was decorated, but it was 'characterized by poor workmanship'.[77] Parallels to this vessel are from Rhodes and date to the last quarter of the sixth century.

Equally important are the epigraphic remains. Over 60 stamped jar handles dating generally to the exilic or postexilic period were discovered. Most enigmatic are the *m(w)ṣh/mṣp* seals, 30 of which were found at Tell en-Naṣbeh. This seal impression is also known from Jericho, Ramat Raḥel, Beth Hanina, el-Jîb and Jerusalem.[78] In addition, one

---

73. See Zorn, 'Tell en-Naṣbeh: A Re-evaluation', p. 199. There are scant remains from the Byzantine period in the area of Tell en-Naṣbeh, including a church, but Zorn believes that the mound of Tell en-Naṣbeh itself ceased to be occupied sometime in the Roman period. In 'Mizpah: Newly Discovered Stratum' (p. 34), he assigns the dates 332–37 BCE, as noted above.

74. Zorn, 'Tell en-Naṣbeh: A Re-evaluation', pp. 186-99.

75. D. von Bothmer, 'Greek Pottery', in *TN*, I, pp. 175-78 (175). Von Bothmer notes, however, that such amphorae are found as late as the fourth century.

76. Von Bothmer, 'Greek Pottery', p. 176.

77. Von Bothmer, 'Greek Pottery', p. 177.

78. Ramat Raḥel and Beth Hanina each yielded one *mṣh* impression; two were discovered at Jericho, four were found in Jerusalem and five at Gibeon. See 'Table 3.2: Moṣah Stamped Jar Impressions of Yehud', in Christoph, 'The Yehud Stamped Jar Handle Corpus', p. 232. However, note that Christoph lists only four at Gibeon

yršlm seal,[79] two 'four letter seals', probably *yhwd* impressions, eighteen 'two letter stamps', most of which were *yh* but some read initially *yhw* (and read correctly by Sukenik as *yhd*), and six *yhd* impressions were discovered.[80] McCown suggests a Neo-Babylonian or early Persian period date for the *mṣh/mṣp* seals and assumes that they ceased being used either between 538 and 516, when he believes Jerusalem was first resettled, or in the mid-fifth century BCE, during the mission of Nehemiah.[81] Zorn associates the *mṣh/mṣp* impressions to the Neo-Babylonian period and the *yhd* seals to the Persian period. He bases the date of the former in part to their geographic distribution, which he contends 'conforms very closely to the area of the tribe of Benjamin, which was most likely the heart of the Babylonian province'.[82]

Horvat Zimri (Pisgat Ze'ev 'D')

Located in the northern section of Jerusalem, between Jerusalem's Pisgat Ze'ev section and the village of 'Anata, Horvat Zimri/Pisgat Ze'ev D was located in a survey by Shimon Gibson in 1981. Subsequently, Yonatan Nadelman conducted excavations from July to November 1990. Although the site is poorly preserved, due to erosion, removal of stones and construction of terraces in the Byzantine period, six distinct strata from the Iron IIC through the early Islamic periods were discovered; Strata 6-4 are most significant for this study.[83] Stratum 6 represents the earliest occupation of the site, with evidence of architectural and ceramic remains dating to the late seventh and early sixth centuries BCE. Stratum 5 dates to the Neo-Babylonian period and is

---

and one at Jericho. See also Table 28 below in Chapter 6 (pp. 261-62). One additional *m(w)ṣh* impression was discovered at the crusader site of Belmont Castle in some mixed fill in a wall. No other Neo-Babylonian or Persian remains were discovered at the site, so it does not represent an occupation. See J. Zorn, J. Yellin and J. Hayes, 'The *m(w)ṣh* Stamp Impressions and the Neo-Babylonian Period', *IEJ* 44 (1994), pp. 161-83 (168).

79. As noted above in Chapter 2, the *yršlm* seal impressions correctly date not to the Persian period but to the Ptolemaic period.

80. McCown, 'Inscribed Material Including Coins', in *TN*, I, pp. 156-74.

81. 'Inscribed Material Including Coins', p. 172.

82. Zorn, 'Naṣbeh, Tell en-', p. 1102. See also Zorn, Yellin and Hayes, 'The *m(w)ṣh* Stamp Impressions', pp. 182-83.

83. Y. Nadelman, 'Jerusalem—Pisgat Ze'ev "D"', *HA* 99 (1993), pp. 49-51, and *idem*, 'Jerusalem, Pisgat Ze'ev D (H. Zimri)', *ESI* 12 (1993), pp. 54-56.

represented primarily by numerous potsherds that carry on Iron II traditions yet are clearly distinguished both from Iron II and the later Persian
period forms. These shards were discovered in the fill in the casemate
walls of the Stratum 4 fortress. Two types of cooking pots were discovered: one type is globular in shape with a high neck, the other type
is a low pot with an out-turned neck. For this type of pot, the shapes as
well as the ware itself is markedly similar to Iron II cooking pots. Also
dating to this period were elongated 'carrot'-shaped bottles and storage
jars that resemble the *lmlk* and rosette-stamped tradition of the Iron II
period. Nadelman contends, however, that all of the Stratum 5 ceramic
remains are different enough from the late Iron II and subsequent Persian period types to represent the transitional forms that one would
expect in the Neo-Babylonian period.

Stratum 4 contains significant Persian period remains, including a
60 × 70 meter fortress with casemate walls. Large amounts of pottery
were discovered in the northwestern corner near the entrance of the
fortress. Inside the fortress were some remnants of a floor, a tabun, and
a cistern from which seven characteristic Persian period vessels were
restored. Storage jars, large flasks, cooking pots, lamps, krater fragments with triangular wedge/reed impressions, and elongated bottles
were all discovered, as were a stamped seal impression of a lion's leg
and several loom weights. The excavation also yielded considerable
numismatic remains, with 74 coins dating from the Persian through
Byzantine periods discovered. Two Yehud coins, probably dating to the
fourth century but both from unstratified contexts, were discovered. On
one coin, an owl is visible along with the letters *yhd*; the other is decorated with a winged lynx but the inscription is not readable. Nadelman
suggests that it is a type of *yhzqyh* coin, similar to that found at Beth-
Zur.[84]

Kh. er-Ras (S)
In the course of salvage excavations on a spur located to the south of
the Manahat section of Jerusalem in December 1990 through March

---

84. Of the other coins discovered, 39 are Jewish coins minted during the Hasmonean period, 10 are Hellenistic with foreign origins, and 4 are Herodian, with
dates from Herod the Great through the destruction of Jerusalem. One of those four
was minted in the fourth year of the first revolt against Rome. Nineteen date from
Roman through Byzantine periods (Y. Nadelman, personal communication).

1991, A. Zehavi discovered a large storehouse with 'late Iron Age-Persian period' remains. The building included two broad rooms measuring 2 × 5 meters and a long room 2.5 × 5.0 meters. Sixteen winepresses were discovered in the courtyard of the storehouse. All have a similar plan with a treading area and collecting vat. Zehavi dates one of them to the 'Late-Iron-Persian Period' and suggests that the similarity in plan of the 16 installations points to their construction and use in that period.[85] He also notes the existence of an ancient agricultural terrace in the vicinity of the site.

Conclusions
Of the six sites classified here as Neo-Babylonian, only three, Tel en-Naṣbeh, Horvat Zimri (Pisgat Ze'ev 'D'), and Kh. er-Ras (S) definitely continued into the Persian period. It is unlikely that Bethel I was occupied much later than the mid-sixth century, according to the assessment of both Paul and Nancy Lapp that the gap in occupation at that site began about 550 BCE. Tel el-Fûl and el-Jîb are somewhat more difficult to determine. On the basis of parallels with Tel el-Fûl IIIB and Bethel I (primarily taken from the sub-104 group), Nancy Lapp suggests an end of occupation at both of the former sites (el-Jîb and Tel el-Fûl) at about 538; neither, she concludes, dates to the Persian period.[86]

*Excavated Sites from Yehud Dating to the
Persian I Period (538–450 BCE)*

Jerusalem, the Provincial Capital
The destruction of Jerusalem at the hands of the Babylonians in 587/586 was evidently widespread if not complete; and it is unclear to what extent, if any, settlement continued at the site after the defeat and exile. According to 2 Kings 25, the seat of Babylonian control of vanquished Judah transferred to Mizpah, where Gedeliah—installed by the new ruling empire as governor—was eventually assassinated. From the standpoint of the biblical traditions, Jerusalem itself then faded into darkness throughout the exilic period, only to rise from oblivion with the missions of Haggai and Proto-Zechariah, Third Isaiah, and then, in the mid-to-late fifth century, with the missions of Ezra–Nehemiah.

85. A. Zehavi, 'Jerusalem, Manahat', *ESI* 12 (1993), pp. 66-67.
86. Lapp, 'The Pottery from the 1964 Campaign', p. 85.

While it is probable that some settlement in Jerusalem continued into the exilic age, both text and artifact agree that it is only with the return from exile that it gradually regained its prominence. The debate concerning when Jerusalem was again designated the capital of an autonomous province must be left for others to answer.[87] But the archaeological remains of the city allow us to draw some general conclusions about its size and patterns of growth in the Persian period.[88]

The results of excavations in six areas—the City of David, the Ophel, the Tyropean Valley, Mount Zion, Ketef Hinnom and Mamilla—are most relevant for a discussion of Persian period remains. The campaigns of Crowfoot in the Tyropean Valley and MacAlister and Duncan on the Ophel provided significant epigraphic finds, while those of Kenyon and Shiloh in the City of David contributed data on the extent of the Persian period settlement of this site (Figure 13).

87. As noted above, Chapter 1, p. 51, Kochman suggests that Jerusalem was the capital of an autonomous Yehud in the Neo-Babylonian period, a position that he alone holds. Gustav Hölscher, while not claiming Jerusalem as provincial capital in the Neo-Babylonian period, suggested that sacrifices were offered at the temple site before its rebuilding. See his *Geschichte der israelitischen und jüdischen Religion* (Giessen: Alfred Töpelmann, 1922), pp. 117-18, as cited in Causse, 'From an Ethnic Group' , p. 96 n. 2. See also G. Hölscher, 'Les origines de la communauté juive à l'époque perse', *RHPR* 6 (1926), pp. 105-26 (110-11).

88. The bibliography for Jerusalem's excavations is extensive; see the reports listed in E.K. Vogel, 'Bibliography of Holy Land Sites', *HUCA* 42 (1971), pp. 1-96; *idem*, 'Bibliography of Holy Land Sites, Part II', *HUCA* 52 (1981), pp. 1-92; and *idem*, 'Bibliography of Holy Land Sites, Part III', *HUCA* 58 (1987), pp. 1-67. Also helpful are the articles collected in *AJR*. The most up-to-date summary of Jerusalem's archaeological remains can be found in Shiloh, 'Jerusalem: The Early Periods and the First Temple Period. Excavation Results', in *NEAEHL*, II, pp. 701-12. For a graphic representation of excavation activity through 1976 see Yigal Shiloh, 'Tables of Major Archaeological Activities in Jerusalem since 1863', in Yigal Yadin (ed.), *Jerusalem Revealed: Archaeology in the Holy City 1968–1974* (Jerusalem: Israel Exploration Society, 1976), pp. 131-35.

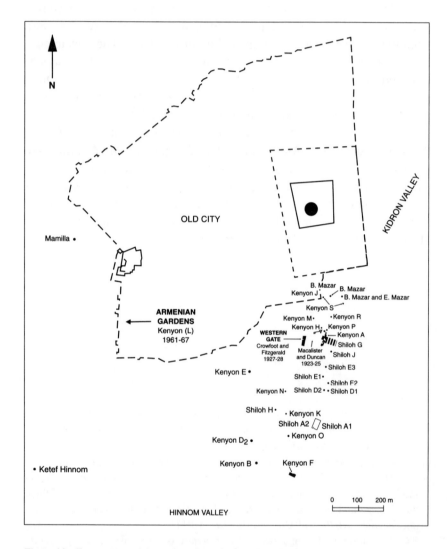

Figure 13. *Excavations of Jerusalem Consulted for This Study*

During Crowfoot's 1927 excavations, which were concerned with the period from 70 CE to the Arab conquest, several seal impressions were discovered in what the excavators called a 'disturbed' context in a house in the middle of the valley. These include: one circular seal reading *yh*, dated by Crowfoot to the fourth century; three circular, two-line stamps, read *y-t-r* (or *-d*), and *-h*, which almost certainly should be read *yhwd*; and two *yršlm* seals.[89] In the course of the MacAlister and Duncan excavations, five types of inscribed seals were discovered: *yh*; *yhd* (read initially as *yhw*); two-line seals (probably *yhwd* impressions); *yršlm* pentagrams; *yhd* plus symbol; and the so-called Latin-F stamp, which MacAlister relates to the letter *yodh*.[90]

In both of these early excavations, then, seals were found that date to a period extending from the mid-fifth century to the late fourth or early third centuries BCE, that is, to the Persian and Ptolemaic periods.

Kenyon's excavations of 1961–67 established the line of the post-exilic walls of Jerusalem.[91] The discovery during the 1962 campaign of the eastern line of the wall within the line of the city wall that was used from the Middle Bronze Age to the Iron II period led her to conclude that 'there is now clear evidence that on the eastern side, post-exilic Jerusalem shrank very greatly in size'.[92] This wall was built on a rock scarp that had been constructed in an earlier period; remains next to the wall were dated generally to the fifth to third centuries BCE.[93] In 1965

89. J.W. Crowfoot and G.M. Fitzgerald, *Excavations in the Tyropean Valley, Jerusalem 1927* (*PEFA* 5 [1929]), pp. 67-68. On the context for the finds, see pp. 25-26.

90. R.A.S. MacAlister and J.G. Duncan, *Excavations on the Hill of Ophel, Jerusalem, 1923–1925* (*PEFA* 4 [1926]), pp. 189ff. Note also the existence of rosette and cross (Hebrew *taw*) stamps, with parallels at Ramat Raḥel. The number of the stamps is not given. The best solution for the Latin F stamp is offered by D.T. Ariel and Y. Shoham (see below, pp. 144-45), who consider it a ligature of a *yodh* and a *he*.

91. It is remarkable that Kenyon's finds had been anticipated by Avi-Yonah in 1954. See 'The Walls of Nehemiah: A Minimalist View', *IEJ* 4 (1954), pp. 239-48. He notes that 'it is obvious that in the absence of excavations all reconstruction of the ancient walls of Jerusalem must be hypothetical'. Kenyon's excavations brought Avi-Yonah's reconstruction out of the realm of the hypothetical.

92. K. Kenyon, 'Excavations in Jerusalem, 1962', *PEQ* 95 (1963), pp. 7-21 (15).

93. J. Cahill suggests that the wall was constructed much earlier than Kenyon had thought, with a probable Late Bronze Age date. See her forthcoming article, 'Stratum 9: Stratigraphy and Pottery'.

and 1966, excavations in three areas (R, M and K) successfully demarcated the southwest and western sides of the wall; these three sections
of the wall were dated to the postexilic period, but closer to the Hellenistic than the Persian period.[94]

In the final year of Kenyon's excavations, walls that connected to the
platform of the Haram esh-Sharif were discovered in area SII. Because
the fill along these walls contained Persian period remains Kenyon concluded that although the wall was much earlier than this period, it had
been incorporated into Nehemiah's wall. Near the southeast corner of
the Haram esh-Sharif is a joint between Herodian period remains and
earlier remains, which Kenyon suggested also dated to the Persian period. The temple platform of that period was shorter than that of the
Herodian period and Kenyon proposed that it should be identified with
Zerubbabel's temple,[95] an identification now generally rejected.[96]

In connection with the excavations of Kenyon were a series of excavations in the Armenian Garden, conducted from 1962 through 1967
and recently published by A.D. Tushingham.[97] Of great interest to the
excavators was the Herodian palace and wall, the fill of which contained abundant pottery from the Iron II, Persian and Hellenistic periods. While the volume makes an important contribution concerning the
history and archaeology of Jerusalem, its significance for the Persian

94. 'Excavations in Jerusalem, 1965', *PEQ* 98 (1966), pp. 73-88 (83-84); and
'Excavations in Jerusalem, 1966', *PEQ* 99 (1967), pp. 65-71 (69). One can infer
that the Persian period wall also followed this line. Avi-Yonah suggests that inasmuch as Nehemiah reduced the size of Jerusalem on the eastern side, 'it would have
been most unreasonable not to use the old line of wall on the western side of this
hill' ('The Newly Found Wall of Jerusalem and its Topographical Significance',
IEJ 21 [1971], pp. 168-69).

95. 'Excavations in Jerusalem, 1967', *PEQ* 100 (1968), pp. 97-109 (104-105).
Kenyon says that the style of the masonry is not Solomonic and notes the comments
of M. Dunand who 'saw in it a strong resemblance to the masonry of the Persian
period found in Lebanon. This is a possibility well worth pursuing, for such an
identification would suggest that we have here the platform of the Temple of
Zerubbabel, completed c. 516 B.C.' For a useful treatment of the size of postexilic
Jerusalem, see H.G.M. Williamson, 'Nehemiah's Walls Revisited', *PEQ* 116 (1984),
pp. 81-88.

96. See Y. Tsafrir, 'The Walls of Jerusalem in the Period of Nehemiah' (Heb.),
Cathedra 4 (1977), pp. 31-42; and Cahill, 'Stratum 9: Stratigraphy and Pottery'. I
am grateful to Ms Cahill for allowing me to use an early draft of her study.

97. *Excavations in Jerusalem 1961–1967*, I (Toronto: Royal Ontario Museum,
1985).

period is somewhat limited. Tushingham concludes that there is no evidence of Persian period architectural remains in the compound and that the Persian period pottery was brought to the area as fill for the base of the Herodian buildings.[98] The pottery itself is said to represent two phases in the Persian period, one in the late sixth and early fifth centuries, the other extending from the late fifth through the end of the fourth centuries. Tushingham relates these phases to similar findings from En-Gedi,[99] but Barkay[100] contends that much of the pottery that Tushingham dates to the Persian period (perhaps phase I of the period) is instead exilic or Neo-Babylonian.

Subsequent to the work of Tushingham, M. Broshi and E. Netzer conducted excavations in two fields on Mount Zion in 1971–72, in the courtyard of the Armenian church. While there were no architectural finds dating to the Persian period, several unstratified artifacts that Broshi dates to the fourth century were discovered. Two Yehud stamped handles were found, as was a silver Yehud coin with an owl and lily on the reverse.[101] However, Broshi maintains that these finds are not sufficient to indicate settlement on the western ridge of Jerusalem.

Yigal Shiloh, who directed the City of David excavations from 1978 to 1985, opened 11 areas on the southeastern hill of Jerusalem, south of the Temple Mount. Persian period remains were found in areas D1, D2, E1 and G, although pottery from this period was found in most other areas.[102] Shiloh, who was able to provide a more accurate stratigraphy

98. Tushingham, *Excavations in Jerusalem*, p. 38.

99. Tushingham, *Excavations in Jerusalem*, p. 38. For a detailed discussion of the excavations from En-Gedi, see below, pp. 157-60.

100. Personal communication.

101. M. Broshi, 'Excavations on Mount Zion, 1971–1972', *IEJ* 26 (1976), pp. 81-88 (82-83). Broshi notes that the coin was only the second *Yehud* coin (at that time) to have been discovered in a controlled excavation. The other was discovered at a citadel in Giv'at Sarfatit (French Hill) and published in *HA* 31–32 (1969), p. 18 (Hebrew) by Ora Negbi (as cited by Broshi, 'Excavations on Mount Zion', p. 83 n. 6).

102. Yigal Shiloh, *Excavations at the City of David*. I. *1978–1982, Interim Report of the First Five Seasons* (Qedem, 19; Jerusalem: Institute of Archaeology, The Hebrew University of Jerusalem, 1984), p. 29. For useful summaries, see Shiloh, 'Jerusalem', pp. 701-712; and Cahill and Tarler, 'Excavations', pp. 31-45. See also the subsequent reports as follows: D.T. Ariel (ed.), *Excavations at the City of David*. II. *1978–1985, Directed by Yigal Shiloh. Imported Stamped Amphora,*

for the southeastern hill of the city than any of his predecessors, identified 21 strata from the Chalcolithic through the 'Medieval and later'
periods (fourteenth to the twentieth centuries). The Persian period level,
dating from the sixth to the fourth centuries BCE, is Stratum 9. According to Shiloh, it was partially represented in area E1 and fully represented in areas D1, D2 and G. Area E1 was occupied continuously from
the Middle Bronze Age through the Early Roman period. Area D2 was
occupied from the eighth century through the Early Roman period. In
Area D1, Persian period remains were found directly on top of eighth
century remains, and occupation continued through the Early Roman
period. Area G, which is the best attested, contained remains from Stratum 10 (seventh-sixth centuries BCE) followed by Stratum 9. It was
abandoned in the Early Hellenistic period and resettled from the second
century BCE until the Early Roman period.[103]

Areas D1 and D2 contained evidence of the quarrying associated
with rebuilding efforts for Jerusalem, and very likely served as dumping
grounds for the quarrying. While most of the remains were in the form
of gravel, some Persian period pottery was found among this debris.[104]
In Area D2 architectural remains were discovered in the form of Wall
804 and a structure interpreted by Shiloh as a columbarium. The wall,
1.5 meters high, continued for a distance of 10 meters; it was built
above remains from Stratum 10 and beneath walls and fill from Strata 8
and 7. Pottery associated with this wall was also dated to the Persian
period.[105] Area D2 also yielded a silver Lycian coin with a lion walking

---

Handles, Coins, Worked Bone and Ivory, and Glass (Qedem, 30; Monographs of
the Institute of Archaeology; Jerusalem: The Hebrew University, 1990); D.T. Ariel
and A. DeGroot (eds.), *Excavations at the City of David*. III. *1978–1985, Directed
by Yigal Shiloh. Stratigraphical, Environmental, and Other Reports* (Qedem, 33;
Jerusalem: Institute of Archaeology, The Hebrew University of Jerusalem, 1992),
and *Excavations at the City of David*. IV. *1978–1985, Directed by Yigal Shiloh*
(Qedem, 35; Jerusalem: Institute of Archaeology, The Hebrew University of Jerusalem, 1996).

103. Shiloh, *Excavations at the City of David*, I, Table 1, 'Preliminary Scheme
of Strata–City of David (1978–1982)', and Table 2, 'Strata and Distribution of
Remains in the City of David (1978–1982)', pp. 3-4.

104. Shiloh notes that his dating of the quarrying to the Persian period is
contrary to the conclusions of Weill and Kenyon, both of whom dated it to the Late
Roman and Byzantine periods (*Excavations at the City of David*, I, p. 8).

105. Shiloh, *Excavations at the City of David*, I, p. 9.

and devouring its prey depicted on the obverse and 'Triskeles in incuse square' on the reverse; the coin dates to between 500 and 440 BCE.[106]

In the 1984 season, outside the line of the Iron Age city wall (also in Area D2), a large Iron II public building was discovered, evidently abandoned about 701. The northwest corner of this building was disturbed by a 'round, columbarium-like structure', 4.8 meters in diameter, containing 8 niches.[107] In the final season, Shiloh again excavated the 'columbarium' and concluded that it should be dated to the Persian period, since the structure damaged the Iron II building and its east side was damaged by later terraces of the Hellenistic period.[108]

Area E1 contained rich Iron II remains, including the so-called 'Ashlar House' and a clearly delineated destruction layer for the buildings and city wall. As in Areas D1 and D2, dumps containing white gravel associated with quarrying activity were found and one wall (Wall 237) was discovered. Within the Ashlar House, a deep pit yielding Persian period remains on top of hard-packed limestone floors was discovered.[109]

Area G, located close to the acropolis of the ancient city, was excavated previously by MacAlister, Crowfoot and Kenyon. While its earliest remains date to Stratum 16, perhaps the most significant remains of this area are from Stratum 10. The three major Iron II structures from the stratum are the so-called 'House of Ahiel', 'Burnt Room' and 'House of the Bullae'.[110] What is perhaps most important about the Persian period material from this area is that Area G is located *outside* the line of the postexilic city walls. Most of the finds from Stratum 9

106. 'Coins, Flans, and Flan Moulds', pp. 99-100, 111-13 in Ariel (ed.), *Excavations at the City of David*, II.

107. Y. Shiloh, 'News and Notes: Jerusalem, City of David, 1984', *IEJ* 35 (1985), pp. 65-67 (66).

108. Y. Shiloh, 'News and Notes: Jerusalem, City of David, 1985', *IEJ* 35 (1985), pp. 301-303 (303).

109. Shiloh, 'City of David, 1984', p. 6.

110. These bullae date from Stratum 10B (seventh–sixth century BCE); one of the most interesting of these reads: 'Gemaryahu son of Shaphan', which Shiloh identifies with the scribe of the same name active in the court during the reign of Jehoiakim (608–597). 51 bullae, of which 41 are legible, were discovered; 4 are pictorial and bear no inscription. The bullae contain 51 different names, a high percentage of which contain the theophoric element -*yahu* (19). See Shiloh, *Excavations at the City of David*, I, pp. 19-20, and Y. Shiloh, 'A Group of Hebrew Bullae from the City of David', *IEJ* 36 (1986), pp. 16-38.

were discovered in squares D-E 3-5 and included a number of walls and layers of stone that 'formed a stratigraphically well-defined layer',[111] although Shiloh considered the nature of the occupation there 'unclear'. The pottery discovered in this area comprises a 'rich repertory' of typical Persian period forms. In addition to the pottery remains, a large number of *yhd, phw'* and animal seal impressions were discovered. These discoveries 'fix the stratigraphical and the chronological ascription of Stratum 9 in the Persian period'.[112]

J. Cahill now suggests that two strata can be designated in Area G.[113] Stratum 9b is characterized by soil, pebbles, cobblestone and boulder fills and stone support walls that were apparently used to buttress the construction in that area. It is also possible that walls constructed of boulders that currently stand at three courses high functioned as either the foundation for a fortification or some type of rectangular podium. The remains that comprise Stratum 9b are laid directly on top of the destruction layer at the end of the Iron II period. Stratum 9a is located primarily in squares E3 and E4 and consists of 'a thick layer of gray clay' that contained Persian period remains but may have been laid during the construction of the later Stratum 8. While this phasing is tentative, it is consistent with that suggested in the study of the epigraphic remains.[114] Cahill's study also identifies numerous pottery types that Shiloh alludes to in the first volume dedicated to the City of David excavations. In the course of the excavations of the Persian Period strata of Area G, 22 bowls, 12 kraters, 5 cooking pots, 3 decanters, 4 jars, 1 flask, 1 lekythos, 2 juglets, 1 alabaster vessel, 1 bottle, 1 'twin vessel', 1 stand and 1 lamp were discovered. This comprises the most complete pottery assemblage dating to the Persian period excavated in Jerusalem.[115]

---

111. Shiloh, *Excavations at the City of David*, I, p. 20. Some walls (746, 754) supported debris of buildings from Stratum 10. Walls 303 and 307 supported fill from Stratum 9. This 'well-defined layer' also included walls 311 and 314, and stone layers 763 and 806.

112. Shiloh, *Excavations at the City of David*, I, p. 20.

113. 'Stratum 9: Stratigraphy and Pottery'.

114. See the discussion of the suggestions of D.T. Ariel and Y. Shoham immediately below.

115. J. Cahill, personal communication.

Throughout the areas excavated in the City of David project, 11 'spatulas', 5 glass objects and several chalk vessels were discovered. The 11 spatulas dating to Stratum 9 were manufactured from worked animal bone.[116] Eight were discovered in area E1 and three recovered from area G; two were discovered on Persian period floors, two on 'earth layers' and the rest in either fill or pits. While the function of these implements remains an issue of debate, the 84 spatulae recovered during the City of David excavations are all held to have been manufactured in Jerusalem. The excavations also produced five glass objects from Stratum 9: one 'core-formed' glass fragment[117] with possible parallels to Rhodian glass vessels[118] and four glass beads. As with the spatulae, these were recovered from areas E1 and G.[119] Twenty-five chalk vessels from the late Persian/early Hellenistic period were discovered in D1-2, E1-3 and G.[120] The variety of types of vessels included numerous ledge-rimmed bowls, a fragment of a lamp, four trumpet bases and a vessel tentatively identified as an inkwell. Of these vessels, three date to the Persian period: a lid[121] and a goblet (discovered in Area D2), and a bowl (retrieved in area E1).[122] All of these artifacts were manufactured from locally available chalk, either white or multi-colored, and seem to be imitations of imported alabaster ware. Their presence in Jerusalem points to a vibrant local artisan community and an industry that 'appear[s] to have flourished in the Persian/early Hellenistic periods',[123]

116. 'Part III. Worked Bone and Ivory', in Ariel (ed.), *Excavations at the City of David*, II, pp. 127-34.

117. Of the four core-formed fragments discovered, one was in an Iron II context, one in a Persian context, and two from a Roman period context. The Iron II and Persian discoveries may actually date to earlier periods. See 'Part IV. Glass', in Ariel (ed.), *Excavations at the City of David*, II, pp. 149-52.

118. 'Part IV. Glass', pp. 152-53.

119. The core-formed fragment was discovered in Area G, as were two of the jewelry beads; the other two beads were discovered in Area E1 ('Part IV. Glass', pp. 153 and 159).

120. J. Cahill, 'Chalk Vessel Assemblages of the Persian/Hellenistic and Early Roman Periods', in Ariel and DeGroot (eds.), *Excavations at the City of David*, III, pp. 190-278.

121. This was discovered in a disturbed tenth-century BCE locus that contained Iron II and Persian period remains (Cahill, 'Chalk Vessel Assemblages', p. 196).

122. Two vessel fragments were found in contiguous loci, one dating to the Persian period and the other to the Hellenistic period (Cahill, 'Chalk Vessel Assemblages', pp. 190-98).

123. Cahill, 'Chalk Vessel Assemblages', p. 196.

although Cahill contends that the uniqueness of some of the vessels compared with their imported alabaster counterparts indicates 'that the local chalk vessel industry possessed an individual vitality not wholly dependent on external influences'.[124]

The seal impressions from Stratum 9 are to be published by D.T. Ariel and Y. Shoham in a future volume of the Qedem series to be dedicated to the City of David excavations.[125] A total of 171 stamped pottery handles and body fragments were found in Strata 9 through 5 during the eight seasons of excavations, all of which were considered to be local in origin. All but two impressions were from storage jars. According to Ariel and Shoham, 109 (62 per cent) are datable according to previous schema; of these 50 (46 per cent) came from the strata to which they actually date.[126] Seventy-four seal impressions that date generally to the Persian period were found in the course of the excavations; of these 33 (45 per cent) were discovered in Stratum 9, 32 (43 per cent) in Strata 8-5, and 9 (12 per cent) were unstratified. Of the impressions discovered in Stratum 9, ten were anepigraphic (eight of these were depictions of a lion), two were *mṣh* seals, two read *yhwd ḥnnh*, one *yhwd/yhʿzr/pḥwʾ*, six had the reading *lʾhzy/pḥwʾ*, one read *yhwd*, two were *yhd* seals, and nine were *yh* impressions. All were inscribed in Aramaic script. Five other objects were discovered in Stratum 9: four unclassified seal impressions and a handle with a gem impression. The latter has parallels in gems with similar styles from a Persian period phase from Shiqmona[127] and En-Gedi. Thus, a total of 38 impressions

124. Cahill, 'Chalk Vessel Assemblages', p. 197.

125. The volume number is as yet undecided. However, the title of the study will be 'Locally Stamped Handles and Associated Body Fragments of the Persian and Hellenistic Periods'. I am grateful to the authors, and to the general editor of the City of David publication team, Mr Alon DeGroot, for allowing me to use the manuscript for the present study and to see photographs and line drawings of all of the seal impressions found in the City of David excavations.

126. Others, then, were from strata subsequent to the period from which the impressions date. For example, a total of four *mṣh* impressions were discovered; two were found in the Persian period stratum (Stratum 9), one was found in Stratum 5, and one was unstratified. This distribution of seal impressions in subsequent strata is typical of the impressions that are generally dated to the Persian period in the excavations and surveys of Yehud.

127. See J. Elgavish, *Archaeological Excavations at Shikmona, Field Report No. 1: The Levels of the Persian Period. Seasons 1963–1965* (Haifa: Museum of Ancient Art, 1968), p. 56.

were discovered in Stratum 9, comprising 22 per cent of the whole.

The seal impressions serve to confirm the dating of seals from other excavations, as well as to make possible the phasing of Stratum 9 from the City of David excavations. For example, the *yhwd/yh'zr/phw'* are the first of its type that was discovered in a 'homogeneous Persian stratum'.[128] Several impression types that are often attributed to the Persian or Hellenistic period, such as the *yhd-ṭeṭ* impression and the so-called Latin-F impression,[129] were not found in Stratum 9. Their absence from the Persian period stratum from Jerusalem in turn lends support to their Hellenistic date. As to the phasing of the Persian period stratum, Ariel and Shoham suggest that the earliest phase is represented by the *mṣh* and *yh* impressions found in loci 2114 and 2115. An intermediate phase is to be identified with locus 2113 where two *l'hzy/phw'* impressions were discovered, followed by the latest phase, represented by loci 2092 and 2104 in which two *l'hzy/phw'* seals were found along with one *yhd* impression. If this proposed stratigraphic interpretation is correct, then it would tend to support the general dating schema of J. Naveh for the *mṣh* seals, and may suggest that the *yh* seals are somewhat earlier than is generally thought. This phasing, however, remains very tentative.

Ketef Hinnom and Mamilla Tombs

Two other recent excavations outside of the walls of postexilic Jerusalem also deserve mention. One excavation, directed by Gabriel Barkay, was conducted in five seasons at Ketef Hinnom on the grounds of the Scottish Presbyterian Church.[130] Persian period remains were found in Chamber 25 of Cave 24 and under a Byzantine church. Cave 24 is a monumental, multi-chamber burial cave. In one chamber a repository was discovered containing over 1000 objects (120 of which were silver). The cave reflects the burial traditions of the late Iron Age. It was apparently first used in the seventh century but continued in use through the sixth and possibly into the fifth century. Of the 1000 objects discovered in this chamber, over 300 were intact ceramic finds, some of which date

128. Ariel and Shoham, *Locally Stamped Handles*, p. 13.

129. These are identified by the authors as a ligature of the letters *yodh-he*, a solution to the type of impression that is attractive. If they are correct, the impression probably evolved from the *yh* type that is common in the Persian period.

130. The report of the finds given here is based upon a conversation held with Professor G. Barkay in Jerusalem, 1990 and on his recent publication, 'Excavations at Ketef Hinnom in Jerusalem', in *AJR*, pp. 85-106.

to the Persian period. In Chamber 25 of Cave 24 a silver archaic Greek coin was discovered, dating to the latter part of the sixth century BCE.[131]

Barkay also took several soundings underneath a Byzantine church located on the northern side of Ketef Hinnom. These soundings yielded rich Iron Age assemblages, including several royal seal impressions and a wide variety of domestic vessels. These remains had an earlier point of beginning (probably eighth century) than the tombs and they included vessels with parallels to Lachish Stratum III. Barkay suggested that these vessels represent some kind of settlement—perhaps related to either a hamlet or a fortress that stood opposite the Iron Age walls of Jerusalem. The fill from the soundings also included Persian period vessels. He uses the nature of the vessels—domestic rather than tomb related[132]—to support his hypothesis that the area was settled rather than a burial ground. He further concludes that the continued use of the Ketef Hinnom tombs for burial into the sixth and fifth centuries demonstrates that Jerusalem, while destroyed in the Neo-Babylonian conquest of 586 BCE, was inhabited by a 'small remnant' and that 'ritual activities were still carried on in the ruined Temple'. In his view, 'the evidence from the burial caves of Ketef Hinnom points to continuous settlement in Jerusalem throughout the 6th century BCE and until the return to Zion and the days of Persian overlordship'.[133]

The second excavation of interest here is the salvage excavation conducted as a result of the Mamilla Street construction project across from Jaffa Gate.[134] Three tombs were found near Ha'emeq Street, located 100

131. See R. Barkay, 'An Archaic Greek Coin from the "Shoulder of Hinnom" Excavations in Jerusalem', *INJ* 8 (1984–85), pp. 1-5. Barkay notes that the coin was well worn and probably in use for a considerable time before being deposited in the tomb. It bears the image of a crab on the obverse and is thus probably from the mint of Cos. She posits that 'it is not improbable that [coins of this type] reached this area as a result of trade along the coasts of the Aegean and neighboring areas' (p. 2). It is the first such coin discovered in a controlled excavation, and one of four archaic Greek coins found in Jerusalem (one was found in Givat Ram, another on the slope of Mount Zion, and the third in the City of David excavations).

132. Most were cooking pots, kraters and deep bowls rather than the more traditional grave goods of juglets, lamps, etc.

133. Barkay, 'Excavations at Ketef Hinnom', p. 106.

134. See R. Reich, 'Tombs in the Mamilla Street Area, Jerusalem', in A. Drori (ed.), *Highlights of Recent Excavations* (Jerusalem: The Israel Antiquities Authority, 1990), pp. 16-17; 'The Ancient Burial Ground in the Mamilla Neighborhood,

meters southwest of the Old City walls. Of these tombs, one (Tomb 1) contained primarily Hellenistic material, one (Tomb 7) late Iron Age finds (seventh to early sixth centuries BCE) and one (Tomb 5) was in use from the late Iron Age through the Hasmonean period. Several objects were recovered from the Neo-Babylonian and Persian periods, including a terracotta figurine of a mounted horseman, a pottery bottle and a bronze carrot-shaped bottle. The latter two objects were discovered in a crevice cut into the rock tomb and are considered by the excavator, R. Reich, to have been placed there intentionally. Reich correctly draws a parallel between Tomb 5 and its contents and the tombs in use during the Neo-Babylonian and Persian periods in the Ketef Hinnom burial chambers.[135] Subsequent excavations in the Mamilla area were carried out from 1991 to 1993 and resulted in the discovery of two distinct tomb types: burial caves with rock shelves carved into the rock around a central pit, containing a repository for bones; and square shaft tombs. Artifacts contained in the tombs dated from the late Iron II (seventh–sixth centuries BCE), Persian, Hellenistic and Byzantine periods.[136] The floor of Tomb 19, one of the square shaft tombs, contained two levels of remains. The lower level held pottery from the end of the Iron Age; the upper level had what Reich and Shukron call 'an unusual [pottery] assemblage of the Persian period'.[137] Among the contents were:

a bronze mirror, kohlstick and fibula; a small hematite swan-shaped weight; a cylinder seal; several silver rings set with bits of blue glass; a tiny Egyptian vessel of some blue glass-like material and a black Attic amphoriskos dating from the mid-5th century BCE.

The excavators conclude that this and the other tombs from the Mamilla area show that tombs cut in the late Iron Age were used throughout subsequent periods, including the Persian period.

Conclusions. On the basis of these excavations it is possible to discuss the size of Jerusalem in the Persian period. It is unlikely that the city extended onto the western hill during this period; rather, most settlement was confined to the southeastern spur and the Temple Mount. The western wall of the Persian period settlement was evidently identical

Jerusalem', in *AJR*, pp. 111-18; and R. Reich, E. Shukrun and Y. Bilig, 'Jerusalem, Mamilla Area', *ESI* 10 (1991), pp. 24-25.

135. 'The Ancient Burial Ground in the Mamilla Neighborhood', p. 116.
136. R. Reich and E. Shukron, 'Jerusalem, Mamilla', *ESI* 14 (1994), pp. 92-96.
137. Reich and Shukron, 'Jerusalem, Mamilla', p. 93.

with that of the Iron II city, and the eastern wall was located within the lines of the Iron II eastern wall but it joined that wall near the Temple Mount (Figure 14).[138] In addition, settlement outside the Persian period city walls is attested in areas D2 and G, with some form of settlement possibly existing on Ketef Hinnom as well. Shiloh estimates that during the tenth through eighth centuries BCE the size of Jerusalem was approximately 160 dunams, with 100 dunams associated with the Temple Mount, 49 dunams with the southeastern spur, and 11 dunams on the eastern slope, evidently beyond the line of the Iron II city walls.[139] Because the data from excavations in the City of David seem to indicate that the eastern wall of the city was above the Iron I and II wall, I would estimate that the maximal size of Jerusalem in the Persian period was between 130 and 140 dunams, with 80 dunams dedicated to the Temple Mount and between 50 and 60 dunams settled, including intra- and extra-mural occupation. This would represent the size of the city after the mission of Nehemiah and the effort, imperially sanctioned if not imposed, to repopulate and fortify Jerusalem. Before that time (i.e., between the first return under Sheshbazzar and the mission of Nehemiah) it is impossible to arrive at a conclusive estimate of Jerusalem's size. Given the textual traditions of Haggai and Nehemiah, both of which suggest an impoverished Jerusalem, I would doubt that Jerusalem was more than half of its Persian II size.[140]

Kh. er-Ras (W)
Located on the Shufat ridge in the area of the Jerusalem forest, a large number of sites, architectural remains and agricultural installations were discovered that date from the Iron II through the Byzantine period. Excavations at Kh. er-Ras (W), directed by A. Onn, uncovered architectural and ceramic remains from the end of the Iron Age and the Persian period.[141]

138. This map of Jerusalem is based on the reconstructions of A. Rainey (in Aharoni and Avi-Yonah, *The Macmillan Bible Atlas*, Map 169, p. 129), D. Bahat, *The Illustrated Atlas of Jerusalem* (trans. S. Ketko; New York: Simon & Schuster, 1990), p. 36, and G.J. Wightman, *The Walls of Jerusalem from the Canaanites to the Mamluks* (Mediterranean Archaeology Supplement, 4; Sydney: Meditarch, 1993), Figure 15, p. 73.
139. Shiloh, *Excavations at the City of David*, I, p. 3.
140. For a discussion of the population of the city see Chapter 4, pp. 201-202.
141. A. Onn and Y. Rapuano, 'Jerusalem, Kh. er-Ras', *ESI* 13 (1993), p. 71.

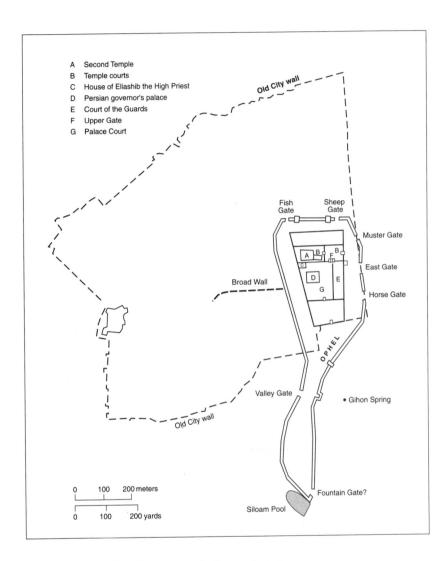

Figure 14. *The Walls of Jerusalem in the Persian Period*

The site was comprised of several rectangular stone towers measuring 4.0 × 8.0 meters, each two storeys high. Each of the buildings had a stone fence that enclosed a courtyard (20 to 30 m²), and a long room and an adjacent small room that led to a staircase allowing access to the second floor. The structures were erected in the eighth to seventh centuries BCE, based evidently on the pottery forms. Onn and Rapuano note the presence of Persian period potsherds throughout the site, attesting to the village's continued occupation.[142]

Wadi Salim
In the course of construction of the road from Jerusalem to Ma'ale Adumim, G. Edelstein and Y. Fleitman conducted salvage excavations near 'Isawiye, north of Jerusalem. Associated with Wadi Salim were two 'agricultural units' consisting of remains of stone buildings with terraces nearby. Each unit was approximately 2 dunams. On the floors of these units, shards from the Iron II, Persian and Hellenistic periods were discovered. A cistern and several similar farmsteads were discovered near the settlement.[143]

Ramat Raḥel
Located four kilometers southwest of Jerusalem, this ten-dunam site was excavated in five seasons, first in 1954, and then from 1959 to 1962. Its strategic location along the road from Jerusalem to Bethlehem provided Jerusalem protection from attack from the south. It seems to have been a significant site in the late Iron II period, perhaps a royal citadel. After the initial three seasons of excavation, Aharoni divided the site into five strata, identifying Stratum IV as 'The Period of the Second Temple', extending from the fifth century BCE to the first century CE.[144] In the course of the fourth season, Aharoni was able to subdivide the stratum into two levels. Stratum IVB covered the period from

142. The preliminary nature of the report makes it difficult to date the site more specifically within the Persian period. I have placed Kh. er-Ras (W) in the Persian I period somewhat arbitrarily, although it is apparent that the site was not occupied during the Neo-Babylonian period based on the absence of pottery dating to that period. Further, it is possible that the site was abandoned before the end of the Iron II period, given the eighth-seventh century date of the structure assigned by Onn and Rapuano.

143. I. Pommerantz (ed.), 'Isawiye—Survey of New Road', *ESI* 1 (1982), pp. 54-55.

144. *Excavations at Ramat Raḥel: Seasons 1959 and 1960*, pp. xiii, 4-5.

the fifth to the third centuries (Persian to early Hellenistic) and Stratum
IVA extended from the third century BCE to the first century CE (Hellenistic to Roman periods). Through the five seasons of the excavations
Aharoni maintained that a citadel existed in the Persian and Hellenistic
periods but no remains of such a structure were found. In the report of
the final season Aharoni admitted that the 'latter [i.e. Persian period]
citadel and its date are still extremely problematical'[145] and concluded
that

> Since we did not strike floors from the Persian or Hellenistic period
> anywhere in the whole area excavated, this citadel evidently cannot have
> been particularly large; and if there was a civilian settlement on the site,
> it apparently did not occupy the highest part of the hill, but was perhaps
> dispersed over the surrounding area.[146]

According to Aharoni, this citadel was built some time in the fifth century and remained in use until the early Hellenistic period. A short gap
in occupation separated Strata IVB and IVA; the civilian settlement of
Stratum IVA was established in about 100 BCE.

Ramat Raḥel was rich in epigraphic finds. Here it will suffice to catalogue the various seal impressions discovered and the contexts in which
they were found: 69 *yh* seals, many from pit 380 in the central courtyard of the Iron II citadel and many from fill near an Iron II defense
wall; 49 *yhd* impressions, many coming from the same loci; 28 one-line
yhwd seals and 11 *yhwd* seals inscribed in 2 lines. These tended to be
impressed on the body of the jar, rather than on the handles. In addition,
14 *phw'* impressions were found, many with personal names or preceded by *yhwd*.[147] There were also 45 anepigraphic animal stamps,
4 *taw* stamps, 1 rosette stamp, 1 *mṣh* stamp, and 1 stamp resembling a
Latin F. Also, one oval stamp reading *yhwd/ḥnnh* was found during the
third season,[148] as was an impression that reads *'zbq ṣdqyh*. Aharoni

---

145. *Excavations at Ramat Raḥel: Seasons 1961 and 1962* (Serie Archaeologica, 6; Rome: Centro di Studi Semitici, 1964), p. 120.

146. *Excavations at Ramat Raḥel: Seasons 1961 and 1962*, p. 120.

147. According to Aharoni, four read *yhwd/yhw'zr/phw'*, five read *l'ḥyw/phw'*
and four read *yhwd/phw'*. More likely, the impressions he interpreted as *l'ḥyw/phw'*
should be read *l'ḥzy/phw'*. See Avigad, *Bullae and Seals*, p. 22. Six such seals were
discovered in Stratum 9 of the City of David excavations.

148. On the basis of this seal impression, Aharoni suggests that a similar seal,
found at Jericho, should be restored [*yh*]*wd* [*ḥn*]*nh* rather than [*yh*]*wd b'nh* (*Excavations at Ramat Raḥel: Seasons 1961 and 1962*, p. 47).

cautiously related the impression to the family of a certain Nehemiah ben Azbuk, who was ruler of the half district of Beth-Zur, according to traditional translations of Neh. 3.16.[149] In addition to these seals, which date generally to the Persian period, are the 21 *'ha'ir'*[150] and the 23 *yršlm* impressions. Although the *yršlm* seals were discovered in similar contexts to the rest of the seal impressions catalogued above, Aharoni correctly identified them as Ptolemaic rather than Persian.

The seals, then, represent the most significant evidence of Persian period occupation at Ramat Raḥel. The few walls that date to this period that were uncovered do not allow for any substantial building phase. Most of the pottery found in the same fills with the seal impressions dates generally to the fifth or fourth centuries BCE, though some dates to the sixth century. Aharoni calls all of the pottery 'transitional'.

Aharoni identifies the site as Beth-haccerem and suggests, almost solely on the epigraphic evidence, that it was an administrative center throughout the Persian period. In the original reports, he similarly asserts that there was a citadel at the site during this period; the most recent publication suggests the inner citadel of Stratum VA was not rebuilt in Stratum IVB, and that while there are some 'strong walls' dating to the Persian period, it is difficult to date the architectural remains definitively.[151] In light of the evidence, the suggestion that Ramat Raḥel was a fortified administrative center in the Persian period appears to be based upon circular reasoning: a citadel existed in the Iron II period, the abundance of epigraphic evidence confirms that it was an administrative center; on the basis of these two assertions, a citadel must date to the Persian period. In contrast, I suggest that the scant evidence that

149. Noting that 'there are, of course, no grounds for identifying the owner of the stamp in question with one of these officials', he suggests that as the practice of papponymy was widespread in the early second temple period that 'it is quite possible that this is the seal impression of a Judean official from the same family a generation or two later' (*Excavations at Ramat Raḥel: Seasons 1961 and 1962*, p. 47). Alternatively, using the translation of פלך suggested above, this Nehemiah was overseer of the work detail from Beth-Zur. On papponymy, see Cross, 'Reconstruction', pp. 6-7.

150. In both volumes Aharoni referred to these seals in this manner, but noted that they should instead be read *yhd* plus a symbol (*Excavations at Ramat Raḥel: Seasons 1959 and 1960*, p. 30).

151. Y. Aharoni, 'Ramat Raḥel', in *NEAEHL*, IV, pp. 1261-67.

exists does not warrant either assertion. The citadel has been, and will remain, a hypothetical construct without sufficient evidence to support its existence.[152]

Khirbet et-Tubeiqah (Beth-Zur)
This 1.5 hectare site, located within the city limits of Halhul, 30 kilometers south of Jerusalem, was first excavated in 1931 by W.F. Albright and O.R. Sellers.[153] In 1957 a final season of excavations was conducted by a team led by Sellers and including P. Lapp and N. Lapp.[154] As is the case in many of the excavations of the early part of the century, the lack of refinements in pottery typology made the stratigraphy of the site difficult to establish,[155] particularly regarding the transition from the Persian to Hellenistic periods.[156]

A variety of problems make the analysis of this site difficult even today. In 1931 Albright and Sellers noted an abrupt break in pottery from the late seventh to mid-fifth centuries.[157] This gap was confirmed by the 1957 excavations.[158] While a small amount of mid-fifth century pottery has been found at the site, the extent of settlement it represents remains in question. In the 1957 excavations of Field II, Paul Lapp noted that there was no evidence of occupation between 587 and 200 BCE.[159] In Fields I and III some 'chalky' orange ware that predates 450 BCE was discovered, but is limited to eight large storage jars with

---

152. G. Barkay has recently conducted soundings at Ramat Raḥel and is in general agreement with Aharoni concerning both the size and importance of the site during the Persian Period (personal communication).

153. 'The First Campaign', pp. 2-13. The preliminary report of the excavations, *The Citadel at Beth-Zur* (*CBZ*) (Philadelphia: Westminster Press) was published by Sellers in 1933.

154. See O.R. Sellers (ed.), *The 1957 Excavation at Beth-Zur* (AASOR, 38; Cambridge, MA: The American Schools of Oriental Research, 1968). Also important is Sellers's preliminary article, 'The 1957 Campaign at Beth-Zur', *BA* 21 (1958), pp. 71-76.

155. Albright and Sellers note finding 'hundreds of baskets of characteristic pottery from the Hellenistic and EI III' ('The First Campaign', p. 5).

156. In particular, see the quote of Sellers in Chapter 1, p. 53 n. 77.

157. 'The First Campaign', p. 9.

158. See, in particular, Paul Lapp and Nancy Lapp, 'Iron II-Hellenistic Pottery Groups', in Sellers (ed.), *The 1957 Excavation at Beth-Zur*, pp. 54-79 (70-71).

159. Paul Lapp, 'The Excavation of Field II', in Sellers (ed.), *The 1957 Excavation at Beth-Zur*, pp. 26-34.

parallels to pottery from Lachish[160] and lacks a distinct stratigraphic context. A large corpus of Persian period pottery was discovered in the 1931 excavations. However, arguing for the existence of a settlement on the basis of this cache is ill-advised in that it was found in a cistern (Reservoir 44) southeast of the citadel; this may mean only that the cistern continued to be used into the fifth century.

The citadel excavated in 1931 seems to date to the Ptolemaic and Hellenistic periods rather than the Persian period.[161] In areas of the citadel with remains prior to the Persian period there was typically a break in ceramics between the Iron II and Hellenistic periods.[162] In only two areas was there found any pottery associated with the Persian period (called Iron III by Sellers). Sellers notes the discovery of nine jars set in a rock trench in the Hellenistic street. While Sellers concluded that they were older than the street and were thus 'Iron III', the question remains how they survived the construction of that street. In locus 59, seven more 'Iron III' jars were discovered, one of which contained an Attic tetradrachm.[163]

More recently, R. Reich has proposed that the citadel was a residence for the regional governor during the Persian period.[164] Reich cites parallels for a similar 'Assyrian style' residence at Lachish Level I. The residence from Lachish is comprised of a large central courtyard (18×18 m) surrounded by a combination of broadrooms and smaller rectangular rooms. Most important is a room that Reich interprets as a 'throne room' or 'reception suite' for the local governor. A wide entrance linked the courtyard and the suite, which has two broadroom-style chambers (a northern and southern hall). Each of the chambers has adjacent smaller rooms.

When Reich compares his reconstruction of the Beth-Zur citadel with the Lachish residency, he observes that some of the elements found in

160. Lapp and Lapp, 'Iron II-Hellenistic Pottery Groups', p. 70.
161. Contra Albright, who dated Phase I to the Persian period; see Sellers, 'Echoes of the 1931 Campaign', in *idem* (ed.), *The 1957 Excavation at Beth-Zur*, pp. 1-3, and Stern, *Material Culture*, pp. 36-38, who follows Albright.
162. See *CBZ*, pp. 20-24, noting particularly the area south and west of the 'Wine Shop', the area near the eastern gate of the city, and the cistern near the middle of the citadel.
163. *CBZ*, pp. 15, 20. Note, however, that in his catalog of the coins (p. 71) he identifies the context as Hellenistic.
164. 'The Beth-Zur Citadel II: A Persian Residency?', *TA* 19 (1992), pp. 113-23.

the latter are either missing or 'hard to locate' in the Beth-Zur building. These elements include the pairs of columns that divided the broad-rooms and their adjacent chambers and components of the doorways (thresholds and door sockets). Further, he notes that the 'corresponding location' of the wide staircase so clearly outlined in the Lachish residence is 'unclear' in his Beth-Zur proposal. There are other aspects of the building plan of the Beth-Zur citadel that do not correspond to the Lachish building. At Lachish, the central courtyard is surrounded by rooms of various shapes and sizes. In the Beth-Zur citadel, there are no rooms on the eastern side of the building and a combination of broad-rooms (two each on the western and southern sides) and rectangular rooms of a fairly consistent size. Thus, merely from a typological standpoint, Reich's proposed parallel between the Lachish residency and the plan of the Beth-Zur citadel is weak. However, not only has Reich based his conclusions about Beth-Zur solely on architectural parallels, but he has also failed to incorporate the pottery finds from Fields II and III into his discussion. The pottery from these fields, as discussed above, suggest that only a minimal settlement existed at the site. This makes his conclusion even more surprising:

> It seems, therefore, that Beth-zur [*sic*] was a prominent site in the Persian period (5th-4th centuries BCE), with a residency, perhaps even two, located on its summit. They probably served as the official residence of Nehemiah son of Azbuq, Governor of the half-district of Beth-zur.[165]

Given the difficulties involved in establishing a meaningful chronology for Beth-Zur, the numismatic evidence takes on somewhat greater importance. A Yehud coin decorated with an Athenian owl and bearing the name *yḥzqyh hpḥh* was discovered in Reservoir 44. While Albright and Sellers[166] suggest that the coin is Ptolemaic, Mildenberg[167]

---

165. 'The Beth-Zur Citadel II', p. 122.

166. The coin was first read *yḥzqyh yhḥn[n]* by Albright, but was correctly identified as a Yehud coin by Sukenik ('Paralipomena Palestinensia', *JPOS* 14 [1935], pp. 178-84 and Pl. III). On the dating see Sellers, 'Echoes of the 1931 Campaign', p. 2.

167. 'Yehud: A Preliminary Study of the Provincial Coinage of Judea', in O. Markholm and N.M. Waggoner (eds.), *Greek Numismatics and Archaeology: Essays in Honor of Margaret Thompson* (Belgium: Wettern, 1979), pp. 183-96. Mildenberg dates the *yḥzqyh* coins to the period of 340–332 BCE, just prior to the Alexandrian conquest.

and Meshorer[168] date it to late in the Persian period.[169] Six other coins
dated by Sellers to the fifth and fourth centuries were found during the
1931 excavations, but the stratigraphic context for them was not recorded. These include:[170] one imitation Attic drachm bearing the Greek letters AΘE; one Palestinian obol, probably minted at Gaza; two Philisto-
Arabian obols; one Tyrian hemiobol; and one Sidonian trihemiobol.[171]

With these data in mind, some tentative conclusions are in order. The
nature of the finds from the site make proposing a definitive dating extremely difficult. Neither the ceramic remains from the cistern in the
center of the citadel and from Reservoir 44 nor the various numismatic
discoveries can by themselves be used to indicate actual occupation of
the site during the Persian period. Other explanations, such as the use of
the reservoir by squatters or travelers, may account for the pottery discovered there. The mere existence of coins, particularly when they are
unstratified, does not necessarily indicate a settlement: coins tend to
remain in use for a considerable period of time and could conceivably
have been deposited at Beth-Zur long after they were minted. If a hoard
of coins had been found, or if those recovered came from a clear Persian period stratum, one could use them more confidently. To com-
plicate matters further, the architectural remains in field II point toward
a gap between 587 and roughly 200 BCE.[172] This leaves us with rela-

---

168. *Ancient Jewish Coinage*. I. *Persian Period through Hasmonaeans* (Dix
Hills, NY: Amphora Books), pp. 13-34.

169. Note, however, the theories of J.W. Betlyon. See 'The Provincial Government', pp. 633-42; and his dissertation, *The Coinage and Mints of Phoenicia* (HSM,
26; Chico, CA: Scholars Press, 1982). In the former, Betlyon ties the minting of
particular coins to the revolts in the mid-fourth century in which, he asserts (but
without adequate evidence), Yehud participated. Thus he would date the *yḥzqyh*
coins, including the Beth Zur exemplar, to 358–346 BCE.

170. This list is adapted from Sellers's 'Catalog of the Coins', in *CBZ*, pp. 71-
73.

171. Of these coins, all but the Attic drachm would date to the fourth century
BCE. Numismatists agree that the Philisto-Arabian coinage was struck from roughly
400 to 333 BCE and that the Tyrian and Sidonian coins would be contemporaries of
these coins. See Betlyon, The Provincial Government', pp. 636-38, 642; L. Mildenberg, 'On the Money Circulation in Palestine from Artaxerxes II till Ptolemy I:
Preliminary Studies of Local Coinage in the Fifth Persian Satrapy. Part 5', *Transeuphratène* 7 (1994), pp. 63-71 (67-70); Meshorer, *Ancient Jewish Coinage*, I, p. 17.

172. In this respect, Stern's comment that 'The latest excavations at the site (in
1957) shed little new light on the settlement of the Persian period' (*Material*

tively isolated pottery and coin finds. With respect to the pottery discovered in the 1931 and 1957 excavations, Paul Lapp and Nancy Lapp suggest that a small occupation of Beth-Zur is indicated in the early fifth century, or perhaps as early as the late sixth century.[173] Based on these considerations, I suggest that a small settlement existed at Beth-Zur in the early fifth century, and agree with Funk's assessment that 'occupation during the Persian period was sparse';[174] only a meager village existed.

Tel Goren (En-Gedi)

This site, located 800 meters west of the Dead Sea, is 41 kilometers southeast of Jerusalem, between Nahal 'Arugot and Nahal David. In the biblical period it was evidently an important point along a trade route that extended from the Transjordan, crossed the el-Lisan peninsula, passed through En-Gedi, and then headed northwest to Tekoa and Jerusalem.[175] A survey of agricultural remains in the vicinity of the site was conducted in 1905 by G. Sandel and a cache of pottery from En-Gedi was obtained in 1908 by H.A. Clark.[176] The modern exploration of the site began in 1949 with a general survey conducted by B. Mazar, T. Dothan and A. Reifenberg. In 1956 a second survey was conducted by Y. Aharoni, and a third was completed in 1957 by J. Naveh.[177] The

Culture, p. 38) is misleading. In fact the 1957 excavations suggest that there may have been no Persian period settlement at this site.

173. See their contribution to Sellers (ed.), *The 1957 Excavation at Beth-Zur*, pp. 70-71; Lapp, 'The Pottery of Palestine'; and Lapp, 'The Pottery from the 1964 Campaign', pp. 86-87. While most of her discussion concerns Reservoir 44, she notes that the orange ware 'must represent a slight occupation into the 5th century'.

174. R.W. Funk, 'Beth Zur', in *NEAEHL*, I, p. 261.

175. B. Mazar, T. Dothan and I. Dunayevsky, *En-Gedi: The First and Second Seasons of Excavations, 1961–1962* ('Atiqot, 5; Jerusalem: Department of Antiquities and Museums,1966), pp. 2-3. However, D. Dorsey notes that there is no archaeological evidence on either side of the Dead Sea for the route from the Transjordan, along the el-Lisan peninsula, to En-Gedi; see *The Roads and Highways of Israel*, p. 148.

176. Mazar, Dothan and Dunayevsky, *En-Gedi*, p. 10. The pottery dates primarily to the Iron II period, with some vessels from the Persian and Hellenistic periods. The results of Sandel's survey, 'Am Toten Meer', may be found in *ZDPV* 30 (1907), pp. 79-106.

177. B. Mazar, 'En-Gedi', in *NEAEHL*, II, pp. 399-405.

five seasons of excavations that ran from 1961 to 1965 were considered an extension of this survey.

Tel Goren has an area of 0.35 hectares on its top and approximately 0.9 hectares when the slopes, which were terraced in antiquity, are included. The terracing, which facilitated both settlement and agricultural development, has impaired the preservation of remains from the oldest strata of the site, Stratum V (Iron II) and Stratum IV (Persian). Stratum V is dated to the period of the late seventh and early sixth centuries BCE, with close parallels in pottery to Ain Shems Tomb 14 and Ramat Raḥel Stratum V. Stratum IV dates to the fifth/fourth centuries BCE and represents a rare increase in size in the Persian period over that of the Iron II settlement.

In the first two seasons of excavations, Stratum IV pottery was discovered on the north, west and south slopes of the tell. Most significant of the finds were two jar handles inscribed with *yhd*. Building remains included traces of walls, found primarily on the south slope. Wall 25, which extended for approximately 20 meters, was intersected by Walls 201, 202 and 204. This installation was built on the destruction debris of Stratum V. Locus 104, located between Walls 201 and 202, yielded a 'small amount' of Persian period pottery. Building 32, from area C10 (also on the south slope), was found to contain some Persian period pottery and one Attic potsherd.[178] On the north and west slopes Stratum IV finds 'consisted of remains of buildings and plastered installations of unclear character'.[179]

During the third season, the excavators concentrated their efforts on two major fronts: a trial trench dug on the north slope of the tell, and the plateau between Nahal 'Arugot and Nahal David. On the basis of the latter area, the excavators concluded that in Stratum IV, the settlement 'covered the entire slope, down to the base of the hill and onto the plain to the north'.[180] They were unable to find the outer limits of the Stratum IV, suggesting that the site was much larger than the top of the tell and its terraced slopes. Excavation of the trench produced similarly significant results. Among the pottery types discovered were store jars, cooking pots, bowls, flasks, jugs, juglets and lamps. Also unearthed was a jar fragment with an Aramaic inscription dating to the mid-fifth century and pottery with inscribed seals including those reading *yhd*, *yhwd*,

178. Mazar, Dothan and Dunayevsky, *En-Gedi*, p. 39.
179. Mazar, Dothan and Dunayevsky, *En-Gedi*, p. 39.
180. Mazar and Dunayevsky, 'Third Season', p. 124.

yh and *b'*, along with an anepigraphic seal depicting a roaring lion. Many jars decorated with characterisic Persian period wedge-shaped and circular reed impressions were also discovered. Finally, the trench yielded a 'significant amount' of Attic pottery, some of which dated to the first half of the fifth century, but most to the third quarter of that century.[181]

In the final two seasons most of the work relating to Stratum IV was concentrated in Building 234, discovered when the trench was dug. The building was fully excavated and had an area of at least 550 square meters. At least part of the building, during its initial phase, had two storeys.[182] Three distinct divisions were evident to the excavators: the western wing, comprised of six rooms (234, 235, 236, 229a and 229b and 231); the eastern sections, in which a large central room (248), rectangular in shape, was surrounded by eight rooms (249, 251-253, 258 and 260-262); and the northern segment, which included five rooms (236, 263, 266, 268 and 271). Room 231 seems to have been used as a workshop, possibly for the perfume industry long associated with this site,[183] based on the finds of basalt grinding tools, storage jars and cooking pots. Also supporting the theory that the room was a workshop— but unrelated to the perfume industry—was the discovery of what the excavators identified as clay loom weights.[184] The initial phase of the building is thought to date to about the beginning of the fifth century and to have been in use until about 400, when it was destroyed. In the second phase of the building, which extended from the end of the fifth century until the middle of the fourth century BCE, only the western section of the building was occupied. After the mid-fourth century, the building seems to have been abandoned.[185]

Other important finds from this building include some Stratum V seal impressions reading *lmlk*, *ziph* and *lmr'*. Among the Persian period remains were a fragment of a rhyton with a relief of a lionness decorating

---

181. 'Third Season', p. 126. The writers note the 'special chronological significance' of this pottery, which they see as important for determining the limits of Stratum IV.

182. The northern rooms of the east and west wings. Mazar and Dunayevsky, 'Fourth and Fifth Seasons', pp. 135-36.

183. See Mazar, Dothan and Dunayevsky, *En-Gedi,* pp. 4-9; also Mazar and Dunayevsky, 'Fourth and Fifth Seasons', p. 136.

184. Mazar and Dunayevsky, 'Fourth and Fifth Seasons', p. 136.

185. Mazar and Dunayevsky, 'Fourth and Fifth Seasons', p. 138.

it[186] discovered in locus 246,[187] an Aramaic ostracon discovered in locus 234, and a conical chalcedony seal, similar to the one discovered at
Bethel, recovered in locus 248. A similar seal was discovered on the
southern slope of the tell.[188]

The excavators concluded that this building was not an isolated find
but rather represents 'a densely populated quarter, with houses separated by narrow alleys clustering both west and east of building 234'.[189]
Another large structure, above Building 234, may have been a public
building, and remains from the south, eastern, and western slopes also
indicate a 'prosperous settlement in the time of Nehemiah and Bagoas,
governors of the province of Judah'.[190]

Jericho
The first excavations of this important biblical site were conducted by
E. Sellin and C. Watzinger in 1908 and 1909; these were followed by
K. Kenyon's monumental excavations in the years 1952 to 1958. Sellin
and Watzinger discovered some architectural remains that may be dated
generally to the Persian period and a variety of pottery types of the sixth
through the fourth centuries, with some ceramic remains they dated
to the early Hellenistic period;[191] Kenyon likewise identified Persian

---

186. Mazar, 'En-Gedi', p. 403.
187. See E. Stern, 'Achaemenid Clay Rhyta from Palestine', *IEJ* 32 (1982), pp.
36-43 (41-42).
188. Mazar, 'En-Gedi', p. 403.
189. Mazar and Dunayevsky, 'Fourth and Fifth Seasons', p. 140; See also Mazar,
'En-Gedi', pp. 402-403.
190. Mazar and Dunayevsky, 'Fourth and Fifth Seasons', p. 140; See also
Mazar, 'En-Gedi', pp. 402-403. This is in general agreement with their conclusion
based on the first three seasons of excavations: 'The Judean settlement at En-Gedi
was renewed at some time early in the period of the Return from Exile, i.e., in the
days of Darius I (and perhaps even in the time of Zerubbabel, governor of Judah); it
reached a fairly flourishing state in the days of Artaxerxes I... and in the days of
Darius II (424-405), and declined about 400 B.C.' (Mazar and Dunayevsky, 'Third
Season', p. 126). As the pottery seems to be consistently from the fifth and fourth
centuries BCE, it is doubtful that the settlement was established as early as Mazar
and Dunayevsky suggest.
191. E. Sellin and C. Watzinger, *Jericho: Die Ergebnisse der Ausgrabungen*
(Wissenschaftliche Veröffentlichung der deutschen Orient-gesellschaft, 22; Leipzig: J.C. Hinrichs, 1913), pp. 79-82.

period remains at Tell es-Sultan.[192] Stern notes the presence of the wedge- and reed-decorated pottery and of Attic vessels, which he dates to the fifth-fourth centuries.[193]

As at Ramat Raḥel, some of the most important finds were epigraphic. During the Sellin and Watzinger excavations ten *yh* and three *yhd* seals[194] were discovered and dated by the excavators to the fourth century.[195] The Kenyon excavations uncovered a seal inscribed in two lines, which was read first as אוריה/צגנד ('*uryw/sgnd*),[196] and correctly read by Avigad as אוריה/יהוד ('*uryw/yhwd*), as well as one *mṣh* impression.[197] Hammond's assertion that the former seal was discovered in a context that 'is clearly Iron Age II'[198] is contested by J.R. Bartlett (of the Kenyon excavations), who considers the statement unjustified.[199]

192. See Kenyon's brief discussion of the Iron II and Persian period strata in 'Jericho, Tell es-Sultan', in *NEAEHL*, II, pp. 680-81.

193. *Material Culture*, p. 38.

194. As with the seals from Jerusalem, the *yhd* impressions were initially read as *yhw*. See above, p. 135.

195. *Jericho*, p. 159.

196. P.C. Hammond, 'A Note on Two Seal Impressions from Tell es-Sultan', *PEQ* 89 (1957), pp. 68-69. Hammond changed his reading to אורית/להגר in 'A Note on a Seal Impression from Tell es-Sultan', *BASOR* 147 (1957), pp. 37-39.

197. 'A New Class of Yehud Stamps', pp. 146-53. Avigad identified the owner of the seal with a certain Uriah, the father of Meremoth referred to in Neh. 3.4, 21. He suggested a dating early in the Persian period and related the seal directly to temple taxation, stating that the seal 'bears the name of the priest in charge of the temple treasury whom we have been able to trace in biblical records' (p. 151). Albright accepted Avigad's reading of *yhwd*, but rejected the connection between the seal and the figure mentioned in the book of Nehemiah. He would date the seal to the second half of the fourth century and says that the owner of the seal lived about 100 to 150 years after the Uriah of Nehemiah. See 'The Seal Impression from Jericho and the Treasurers of the Second Temple', *BASOR* 148 (1957), pp. 28-30.

198. 'A Note on Two Seal Impressions from Tell es-Sultan', pp. 68-69. However, in 'A Note on a Seal Impression from Tell es-Sultan', Hammond referred to the archaeological context in which the seal impression was found 'disturbed', and dates it to the fourth or third centuries BCE, with the possibility of a fifth/fourth century horizon.

199. J.R. Bartlett, 'Appendix A: Iron Age and Hellenistic Stamped Jar Handles from Tell es-Sultan', in K.M. Kenyon and T.A. Holland (ed.), *Excavations at Jericho. IV. The Pottery Type Series and Other Finds* (Jerusalem and Oxford: British School of Archaeology and Oxford University Press, 1982), pp. 537-45.

Thus Stern is correct in noting that the find was essentially unstrati-fied.[200] Also discovered by the Sellin/Watzinger expedition were one seal impression reading *lyhw'zr*, 'belonging to Yehoezer' with a parallel to a *phw'* seal from Ramat Raḥel, and one *mṣh* seal. Exact dating of any of the seals is difficult. Avigad placed the *Yehud/Urio* seal before the missions of Ezra and Nehemiah,[201] a dating that is almost certainly too early. Albright's dating for this impression was approximately mid- to late-fourth century.[202] J.R. Bartlett, who provides the best discussion of the date of the seals, suggests a late fourth century date for the *mṣh* impressions (probably too late for these seals), dates the *yhwd/'uryw* seal broadly to the fourth century, and places the *yh* seals in either the fifth or fourth century BCE.[203] Troubled by the paucity of architectural finds during this period, Bartlett concludes:

> The fact that occupation and building levels from these centuries have not been evidenced at Tell es-Sultan requires explanation, as does the absence of certain types of seal impressions, but the explanation is not that Jericho did not exist in this period.[204]

The conclusions of Albright and Bartlett fit well with the general dat-ing of the site of Jericho during the Persian period suggested here. The site was abandoned sometime in the Persian period, and the Hellenistic period site of Jericho was settled at nearby Tulul Abu el-'Alayiq.[205]

Excavated Sites from Yehud Dating
to the Persian II Period (450–332 BCE)

Bethel II
Albright and Kelso note that the buildings that post-date the confla-gration are meager and poorly built.[206] As at Tell el-Fûl and Tell en-

200. *Material Culture*, p. 38.
201. 'A New Class of Yehud Stamps', p. 151.
202. Albright, 'The Seal Impression from Jericho', p. 30.
203. 'Iron Age and Hellenistic Stamped Jar Handles', pp. 543-44. According to Bartlett, 'the *yh* impressions in Aramaic script are equally difficult to date with precision'.
204. 'Iron Age and Hellenistic Stamped Jar Handles', p. 544.
205. Kenyon, 'Jericho: Tell es-Sultan', p. 681; E. Netzer, 'Jericho: Hellenistic to Early Arab Periods', in *NEAEHL*, II, p. 681; T.A. Holland suggests that the settlement at Tulul Abu el-'Alayiq began sometime in the Persian period and reports that a bronze barbed arrowhead was discovered at that site. This artifact, he

Naṣbeh, building in this period tended to be outside of or on top of previous fortifications, 'in valleys and on low exposed spurs',[207] concentrated near the springs to the south of the tell.[208] While Albright identified the pottery associated with these remains as Persian, he noted that the Persian period materials were probably late and suggested that 'only in the Hellenistic period did the town prosper again'.[209] Albright and Kelso suggested a rather short gap in settlement, but Albright noted that Area II contained 'continuous phases of building during the late Persian and the Hellenistic periods'.[210] Kelso concludes that the site was occupied again during the middle of the fifth century and became a major settlement again during the Hellenistic period.[211]

Ras el-Kharrubeh

In conjunction with preliminary excavations at 'Anata, A. Biran (Bergman) conducted a survey and soundings at this site in 1936.[212] Located 4.5 kilometers north of Jerusalem and 800 meters south-southwest of 'Anata, Ras el-Kharrubeh yielded architectural remains including a watchtower and a building near the summit of the hill. Next to the walls of the building were found a rim and two handles of a vessel from the Persian-Hellenistic period and the top of a flask dated by Biran to the Persian period. Two cisterns were discovered on the northwest side of the hill; the first contained pottery from the Iron II to Byzantine periods and the second had sherds from what was then identified as the Iron III to the Roman period.

Biran suggests that Ras el-Kharrubeh was occupied from the Iron II to Byzantine periods. He maintains that it reached its peak in the eighth to sixth centuries and 'was a respectable village in the Perso-Hellenistic period'.[213] He concludes that the site could not have been biblical

concludes, 'attests to at least the presence of Persian warriors or their subjugates' ('Jericho', in *OEANE*, III, pp. 221-24 [224]).

206. In *The Excavation of Bethel*, p. 38, they note that 'little remained of the first reoccupation except fragments of rude walls, probably sheepfolds'. Cf. also Albright, 'The Kyle Memorial Excavation at Bethel', *BASOR* 56 (1934), pp. 1-14.

207. *The Excavation of Bethel*, p. 38.

208. *The Excavation of Bethel*, p. 38.

209. *The Excavation of Bethel*, p. 40.

210. 'The Kyle Memorial Excavation', p. 14.

211. Kelso, 'Bethel', p. 194.

212. 'Soundings', pp. 22-25.

213. 'Soundings', p. 24.

Anathoth, a site that should have had more pottery remains from the Iron I period, when it was a large walled city.[214] This view differs from that of Albright and Alt, both of whom had identified Ras el-Kharrubeh with Anathoth.[215] The former site was surveyed by Uri Dinur and Nurith Feig in 1988, who identify the site as Anathoth,[216] as does Stern.[217]

Ras el-Kharrubeh was excavated again in 1983 under the auspices of the Nelson Gleuck School of Biblical Archaeology of Hebrew Union College. Architectural remains were found from both Persian and Hellenistic periods, as was a wide variety of pottery types.[218] No architectural remains from the Iron II period were discovered, and only 40 potsherds from the seventh and early sixth centuries were unearthed. For this reason, Biran again rejects the possibility of Anathoth being located at this site. He also rejects his earlier identification of Anathoth with el-'Isawiyah.[219] Instead, he locates Jeremiah's home town with nearby Kh. Deir es-Sidd, located 1400 meters east of the modern village of Anata. There, significant architectural remains dating to the seventh century BCE were excavated along with some seventh-sixth century pottery.

Ketef Yeriḥo

This site, located one kilometer west of ancient Jericho, was excavated in 1986. The decision to excavate this cave followed a fortuitous discovery of a wooden comb that had parallels in the Judean Desert caves. In the cave were found sherds from a variety of periods, including the Persian and Hellenistic periods, with most pottery dating to the Roman period. The most important finds were again epigraphic, notably pieces of six documents and several dozen small fragments. Of these, only one was fairly complete. It is written in an Aramaic script identified as

214. 'Anathoth?', *BASOR* 63 (1936), pp. 22-23. Biran suggests that Anathoth should be located at the modern village of el-'Isawiyeh and identified Ras el-Kharrubeh with biblical Laish.

215. Albright, 'Additional Note', *BASOR* 62 (1936), pp. 25-26.

216. Site 450 (17-13/45/1) in *ASHCB*, p. 358 (*60). Note that the survey does not identify a Persian period level, though the excavations uncovered Persian period architectural and ceramic remains.

217. *Material Culture*, p. 34.

218. A. Biran, 'On the Problem of the Identification of Anathoth', *EI* 18 (1985), pp. 209-14 (209-10). See also his 'Ras el-Kharubbe (Anathoth)', *ESI* 2 (1983), p. 89.

219. 'On the Problem of the Identification of Anathoth', pp. 210-11.

'formal cursive'[220] and measures 16 centimeters in length and 7 centimeters in width. Writing is preserved on both sides of the document, with Side A containing 13 lines and Side B containing 2 columns each with 6 lines of text. The text is a list of names, often with either a patronymic or an epithet, followed by a symbol and a number, which together represent an amount of money.[221] Line 13 of side A and line 7 of column 2 on side B gives a monetary total for each respective side of the document.

Eshel and Misgav suggest that the document is a list of loans and repayments; side A lists the loans given, side B the repayments. Since the total on side B is less than that of side A, they theorize that some debtors defaulted and the difference between the two sides represents the amount still outstanding. However, it seems to bear more resemblance to Cowley 22, a list of donations to the temple of Yaho in Elephantine which Eshel and Misgav cite as a parallel. In Cowley 22, 120 donors are listed, each giving a donation of two sheqels.[222] Although the Ketef Yeriho document probably does not indicate temple taxation, it could be a local or imperial tax roster. Eshel and Misgav offer the following explanation for the document's deposit in the cave. During the Persian military response to the rebellion of Coele Syria that took place during the reign of Artaxerxes III (358–338), at which time they maintain Jericho was destroyed, some Jews fled to the cave to avoid exile. Accordingly, Eshel and Misgav date the document, primarily on epigraphic grounds, to the last third of the fourth century,[223] noting that it

220. H. Eshel and H. Misgav, 'A Fourth Century B.C.E. Document from Ketef Yeriho', *IEJ* 38 (1988), pp. 158-76 (172). See also H. Eshel, 'Ketef Yeriho', *ESI* 5 (1986), pp. 58-59.

221. Three symbols are used: ש stands for *sheqel* or *sheqlin*, ר for *rib'in*, and מ for *ma'at*. Eshel and Misgav give the following values: there are six *m'h* in one *rb'*, and four *rb'n* in one *sheqel* ('A Fourth Century B.C.E. Document from Ketef Yeriho', p. 165 n. 8).

222. See B. Porten, Appendix IV, 'The Collection List', in *idem, Archives from Elephantine* (Berkeley: University of California Press, 1968), pp. 319-27.

223. 'A Fourth Century B.C.E. Document from Ketef Yeriho', p. 175. Despite their claims, there is no direct evidence that Yehud participated in the Tennes rebellion nor that Jericho was destroyed (Hoglund, personal communication). There is no destruction layer dating to the fourth century from Jericho, and it is as likely that it was simply abandoned at the end of the Persian period. See Kenyon, 'Jericho, Tell es-Sultan', p. 681.

may have originated during the first half of the century.[224]

El-'Ezariyeh (Bethany)

Excavations were conducted at this site, which is located about three kilometers west of Jerusalem, from 1949 to 1953. The excavators discovered pits, cisterns, caves and tombs dating from the sixth or fifth centuries BCE to the fourteenth century CE. However, the nature of the area excavated is such that none of the finds was from a clear stratigraphic context. In the final excavation report, it is not uncommon to read statements such as 'the context makes any date possible from the Persian period onwards' or 'the context suggests the Persian or early Hellenistic periods'.[225] Most of the finds dating broadly to the Persian period were found in locus 65, the columbarium, and were probably dumped there when a medieval cistern was dug.[226] Saller's dating of initial settlement as early as the sixth century BCE was also somewhat skewed by an incorrect dating of the four seal impressions discovered at the site. One *yršlm* and three *yhd* plus symbol (read by Saller as *ha'ir*) were dated to the sixth or fifth centuries;[227] they are, however, almost certainly Ptolemaic rather than Persian. Therefore, whatever settlement dating generally to the Persian period was apparently quite small and should be placed later rather than earlier in the period. The site was recently surveyed by Dinur and Feig, who identified a small amount of Persian period pottery.[228]

Khirbet Abu et-Twein

During a survey in 1968, Z. Kallai discovered ruins at this site, located 19 kilometers southwest of Jerusalem.[229] A. Mazar subsequently exca-

---

224. Eshel and Misgav also allow for the possibility that it was written later than the papyri from Wâdi ed-Dâliyêh, i.e. after 335 BCE, in which case it would be a Hellenistic rather than Persian period document ('A Fourth Century B.C.E. Document from Ketef Yeriho', pp. 175-76).

225. S.J. Saller, *The Excavations at Bethany (1949–1953)* (Publications of the Studium Biblicum Franciscanum, 12; Jerusalem: Franciscan Press, 1957), pp. 222, 237.

226. Approximately 78 vessels or fragments are considered either Persian or Persian-Hellenistic.

227. *Excavations at Bethany*, pp. 192-96.

228. *ASHCB*, site 436, pp. *58 and 351.

229. A. Mazar, 'Abu Tuwein, Khirbet', in *NEAEHL*, I, pp. 15-16.

vated Kh. Abu et-Twein in two short seasons in 1974 and 1975.[230] Architectural remains were found at the top of the hill on which the *khirbeh* is located and on the southeast side of the foot of the hill. The remains from the *khirbeh* are in the form of a building that measures 29.5 × 31 meters, with a central courtyard 12 × 13.5 meters in size. Around the courtyard were a series of double rooms, divided by standing monolithic pillars. The main gate to the building, on the eastern side, was flanked by a small room that may have functioned as a guard room. Mazar considered many of the excavated rooms to be either store-rooms, industrial rooms (room 2 contained loom weights) or stables.[231] While he did not give a percentage of space that would have been used for human occupation, he noted that one 'could not rule out' the possibility that the building may have had two storeys, the second intended to house the troops.[232] He interprets the building as a fortress,[233] on analogy with buildings with similar plans from the Negev and the central hill country. However, the Negev sites, though initially dated to the early Iron II period, have recently been re-dated to the Persian period by Cohen.[234] Further indicating that the fortress should be dated to the Persian period is the similarity of the building's plan with the typology of Persian period fortresses developed by Hoglund.

Mazar dates the building to the Iron II period and suggests that it was abandoned for a time after the Babylonian conquest, then occupied later in the sixth–fifth centuries.[235] His dating is based almost primarily on pottery evidence from the building; but Hoglund contends that Mazar failed to take adequate methodological cautions in his interpretation.[236]

---

230. A. Mazar, 'Iron Age Fortresses in the Judean Hills', *PEQ* 114 (1982), pp. 86-109.

231. 'Iron Age Fortresses', p. 95.

232. 'Iron Age Fortresses', p. 96.

233. Mazar addresses other possible interpretations, noting that it could be an administrative center, or simply the major building of a large estate, but based on the similarity of the building's plan with other fortresses, rejects these interpretations ('Iron Age Fortresses', p. 97).

234. See Chapter 2, pp. 88-89.

235. 'Abu Tuwein, Khirbet', p. 15.

236. *Achaemenid Imperial Administration*, pp. 191-96. While Hoglund is quite correct in this observation, it is curious that Mazar interpreted the evidence in the manner that he did, for he himself urged caution based upon the disturbed nature of the finds: 'there was a gradual collapse and fall of the upper parts of the walls. The pottery sherds collected from the fallen debris should, therefore, be treated with

He points to the fact that some pottery from Kh. Abu et-Twein is clearly Persian (i.e. sixth–fourth centuries BCE); even Mazar notes the difficulty in differentiating between Iron II and Persian forms for some sherds.[237] Hoglund also argues that the Iron II pottery discovered in the building was from the walls that had collapsed onto the floors[238] of the fortress and suggests, on the basis of both ceramic and architectural typologies, that the fortress should be dated not to the Iron II period but to the mid-fifth century BCE.[239] Hoglund further points out that the main parallels Mazar uses for his reconstruction of the history of the site are in fact mid-fifth-century fortresses. This would make the excavations at Kh. Abu et-Twein particularly important as the only excavated mid-fifth-century fortress in the Judean hill country.

The buildings found at the foot of the hill, though discussed only in passing by Mazar, may also be related to the fortress. Ten such buildings were discovered, but evidently not excavated. The pottery found in the survey of the buildings was from the Iron II period,[240] not the Persian period. Perhaps, however, excavations would reveal ceramic remains similar to those found in the fortress, making the settlement and fortress contemporaneous. If such a relationship existed, it is possible that the buildings found there served as barracks for the imperial troops. Mazar notes a similar arrangement at Kh. el-Qaṭṭ, where a village was discovered near a fortress.[241] The fortress at Kh. Umm el-Qal'a is located 200 meters away from Kh. Jrish, a 3-dunam settlement containing 12 buildings, and may be interpreted as a third example of this

caution: it is not a homogeneous pottery assemblage found at one spot, and the sherds could originate from various sources: fill of ceilings and walls, broken vessels which fell from upper parts of the building, etc.' See Mazar, 'Iron Age Fortresses', pp. 99-101.

237. 'Other forms, including many of the jars and jugs, are characteristic of the end of the Iron Age (seventh century B.C.) yet some of them continue during the sixth century and probably also the fifth century B.C. A few of the sherds are not earlier than the Persian period' ('Iron Age Fortresses', p. 104).

238. Mazar himself admits this, noting that 'sherds were found among the fallen stones in the various rooms. In most cases the rooms contained only one floor level, laid close to bedrock, and thus it was impossible to isolate pottery from the building deposits.' See 'Iron Age Fortresses', p. 104.

239. *Achaemenid Imperial Administration*, pp. 191-98.

240. Mazar, 'Iron Age Fortresses', p, 105; 'Abu Tuwein, Khirbet', p. 15.

241. 'Iron Age Fortresses', p. 107.

type of arrangement.[242] A fourth example may be the fortress of Kh. ez-Zawiyye, which is evidently related to an 8-dunam site discovered in a survey by Avi Ofer.[243]

Khirbet Nijam (Har Adar)

In a salvage excavation conducted in May 1991, remains of a Persian period fortress were discovered.[244] It measured 21.8 × 25.8 meters, with a central courtyard measuring 10.0 × 11.9 meters in which a cistern was discovered. Several rooms were constructed around the courtyard. The ceramic remains were not discussed, but the most interesting find was a bronze ring containing a seal depicting a religious motif: 'a fire-cult scene—an altar and next to it a seated figure (deity?) and a standing figure in a praying attitude'.[245] The excavator interprets the building as a fort along the northern border of the province and dates it to the fifth century. In the Hellenistic period the building was evidently converted into a farmhouse.

'Ain Arrub

In 1971, a salvage excavation of two tomb-caves, one of which was from the Persian period, was conducted near this site. The tomb, located two kilometers west of Beit Fajjar and 11 kilometers north of Hebron (coordinates 1637/1139), yielded what Stern called 'the first homogeneous group originating in the Judean Hills to be published'.[246] Of particular significance, according to Stern, were the five cups that represent a new form, one that is perhaps an 'imitation of some Achaemenian

242. Kokhavi observes that the fortress, though 35 × 55 meters in its present state, had two phases. In the first, the building was 20 × 20 meters, and in the second phase, a 30 × 40-meter addition was added to the eastern side of the initial fortress (but evidently incorporating some of the earlier structure within the whole). While Iron Age pottery was present at the site, the primary pottery type was Persian. The plan of the early phase is smaller than most of the mid-fifth century fortresses in the Judean hill country, but does have a parallels in the Negev, Ḥorvat Mesora and Meṣad Naḥal Haroʻa, which are also 20 × 20 meters. See Hoglund, *Achaemenid Imperial Administration*, pp. 188-91.

243. See site list for Yehud below, Chapter 4, pp. 190-95.

244. Dadon, 'Har Adar', pp. 87-88.

245. 'Dadon, Har Adar', p. 87.

246. E. Stern, 'A Burial of the Persian Period near Hebron', *IEJ* 21 (1971), pp. 25-30.

type'.[247] In addition to these cups, three flasks, three juglets dating to the fifth or fourth centuries BCE, one jug, an alabastron vessel, an earring, rings and eye-beads were found near the skeleton. The flasks are dated to the sixth or early fifth centuries on the basis of parallels to vessels from En-Gedi, Lachish, Tell Jemmeh and Khirbet esh-Sheikh Ibrahim. Stern concludes that the tomb dates to the fifth century BCE.[248] Nancy Lapp dates the flasks and burial more specifically to late in the fifth century, noting several problems with Stern's parallels.[249]

Khirbet 'Almit

A tomb dated to the Persian period was excavated in 1981 by G. Lipowitz, Z. Ehrlich, A. Mazar and U. Dinur. Dinur reports that most of the ceramic remains date to the fifth century; other periods represented include Iron II, Roman and Byzantine. The burial cave had a 3.3 × 3.5 meter entrance chamber, a burial chamber carved in the shape of a trapezoid (3.3 × 1.5 meters) and two circular burial pits. Finds included cosmetic vessels, including 'a small bottle, a small alabaster bowl, a bronze kohl stick, and a grinding palate'. The pottery assemblage included decanters, jugs, flasks, cooking pots, lamps and store-jars.[250]

Dinur also reports that five caves, used for burial and habitation, were discovered in 1973. Pottery that Dinur dates to the Persian period was discovered in one of the caves, used for storage or living space, including three seal impressions. However, two of the seal impressions Dinur dated to the Persian period are actually Hellenistic (*yehud* plus symbol and *yršlm* seals); the third, identified as a 'cruciform', is also typically called a 'taw' impression and is known from Persian and/or Hellenistic strata at Ramat Rahel and Jerusalem.[251] Dinur equates Kh. 'Almit with biblical Elam.

247. 'A Burial of the Persian Period', p. 28.

248. 'A Burial of the Persian Period', p. 30.

249. 'The Pottery from the 1964 Campaign', pp. 88, 91. Lapp notes that many of Stern's parallels are either incorrect (i.e. the Gezer parallels) or otherwise problematic. For example, the En-Gedi flasks are dated to the end of the fifth century, those from Tell Jemmeh are from the fifth rather than sixth century, which Stern 'overlooks', and those from Lachish are likewise from late in the fifth century.

250. U. Dinur, 'Khirbet 'Almit', *ESI* 5 (1986), p. 1.

251. Four such impressions were discovered at Ramat Rahel, Stratum IVA, and dated to the Persian Period by Aharoni; see *Excavations of Ramat Rahel: Seasons 1961 and 1962*, pp. 20ff. The 'taw' impression is know from the City of David

In order to complete the picture of the settlement history and site distribution for the province of Yehud it is necessary to supplement the excavation data. The next chapter will discuss survey methodology and the results of recent surveys of Benjamin and Judah as they relate to the Persian period. Based on the more comprehensive data, it will be possible to estimate the population of the province for the Persian I and Persian II periods.

excavations, with the first stratified impressions coming from the Hellenistic period, in Stratum 8.

Chapter 4

YEHUD IN THE PERSIAN PERIOD:
SURVEYS, SITE DISTRIBUTION AND POPULATION

Data from archaeological excavations are foundational for reconstructing the various material cultural traditions of antiquity. Yet comparatively few sites in any area can be excavated due to limited resources of time, finances, and the pressures of contemporary urban development projects. When full excavations are impractical or when building projects uncover archaeological remains, archaeologists often conduct salvage excavations.[1] These excavations provide a provisional rather than a comprehensive understanding of the site's occupational history, typically focusing on a more limited section of a site than an extensive excavation would.

An equally important source for data concerning the ancient past comes from regional reconnaissance and survey projects.[2] Since even salvage excavations of every archaeological site is not feasible, archaeologists and historians have increasingly turned to such projects in order to examine settlement patterns and the interrelationship of villages, cities, provinces and even states. In the earliest stages of archaeological research, surveys were used to reconnoiter an area and identify

1. See G. Schwartz, 'Salvage Excavations: An Overview', in *OEANE*, IV, pp. 159-61, and R. Cohen, 'Salvage Excavations: Salvage Excavation in Israel', in *OEANE*, IV, pp. 461-63.

2. For an introduction to the methodology and use of reconnaissance and surveys in archaeology, see M.B. Schiffer, A.P. Sullivan and T.C. Klinger, 'The Design of Archaeological Surveys', *WA* 10 (1978), pp. 1-28; and A.J. Ammerman, 'Surveys and Archaeological Research', *ARA* 10 (1981), pp. 63-88; J.A. Blakely, 'Site Survey', in *OEANE*, V, pp. 49-51; T.E. Levy, 'Survey, Archaeological', in *OEANE*, V, pp. 101-104; R.J. Sharer and W. Ashmore, *Archaeology: Discovering our Past* (Mountain View, CA: Mayfield, 2nd edn, 1993), pp. 186-237.

sites worthy of full excavation. It is only in the last 30 years that surveys have become an accepted method for identifying the larger settlement patterns of particular areas.[3] Given the relatively few excavated sites dating to the Persian period, one must turn to the archaeological surveys that have been carried out in the last 30 years in order to develop an accurate understanding of the number of sites and their distribution within the province.[4] An understanding of the place of surveys in archaeological research as well as their strengths and weaknesses will aid readers in their interpretation of the survey data that relate to Yehud.

Historical and Methodological Perspectives on Archaeological Surveys

Historical Context
The first survey in Syria-Palestine was conducted in 1802 by Ulrich Seetzen, who discovered the ancient sites of Jerash and Philadelphia (modern Amman).[5] The explorations of Edward Robinson and Eli Smith in 1838[6] are often considered to have been the first *scientific* survey[7] conducted in the Middle East. Those that followed, by Félician de Saulcy,[8] Fredrick Bliss,[9] and Charles Wilson and Charles Warren,

---

3.   Schiffer, Sullivan and Klinger ('The Design of Archaeological Surveys', p. 1) and Ammerman ('Surveys and Archaeological Research', p. 63). Both point to the defense of surveys as an appropriate method for recovering regional archaeological data by R.J. Ruppé, 'The Archaeological Survey: A Defence', *AA* 31 (1966), pp. 313-33.

4.   These include surveys conducted or edited by M. Kokhavi (*JSG*), I. Magen and I. Finkelstein (*ASHCB*), A. Ofer ('The Highlands of Judah, I') and A. Kloner (ed.), *Archaeolgical Survey of Jerusalem* (Jerusalem: Israel Antiquities Authority, forthcoming) as discussed above in Chapter 1, pp. 54-59.

5.   Levy, 'Survey', p. 101. Seetzen's work was published in English as *A Brief Account of Countries Adjoining the Lake Tiberias, the Jordan and the Dead Sea* (London: Palestine Association of London, 1810).

6.   E. Robinson, *Biblical Researches in Palestine, Mount Sinai and Arabia Petraea* (London: J. Murray, 1856).

7.   Blakely, 'Site Survey', pp. 49-50; Levy, 'Survey', p. 101.

8.   *Voyage autour de la Mer Morte et dans les terres bibliques: Exécuté de décembre 1850 à avril 1851* (2 vols.; Paris: Gide & J. Baudry, 1853).

9.   'Narrative of an Expedition of Moab and Gilead in March 1895', *PEFQS* (1895), pp. 203-204. See also F. Bliss, *Excavations at Jerusalem 1894–1897* (London: Palestine Exploration Fund, 1898), and F.J. Bliss and R.A.S. MacAlister, *Exca-*

provided valuable information about Palestine that subsequently led to excavations.[10] Similarly, Conder and Kitchener's *Survey of Western Palestine* (*SWP*), Conder's survey of the Transjordan[11] and Charles Wilson's survey of Jerusalem[12] are precursors of modern regional projects. Although the explorations of Syria-Palestine were often conducted for religious, military or political purposes rather than as modern, scientifically controlled surveys,[13] they nonetheless continue to provide scholars with important information concerning the topography, environment, archaeology and pre-modern culture of western Palestine. Many settlements previously lost to western culture were rediscovered as a result of these early surveys and their association of Arabic toponyms with biblical sites, a methodology first applied by Robinson and Smith and used since that time in the field of historical geography.[14] Like many modern surveys, they painstakingly mapped sites, environmental and topographic features, and various archaeological remains. Thus, even though their intent was not strictly archaeological, they had an enormous influence on the general understanding of Palestine and subsequent archaeological fieldwork and interpretation.

vations in Palestine during the Years 1898–1900 (London: Committee of the Palestine Exploration Fund, 1902).

10. For a listing of important explorations of the Transjordan in the nineteenth and early twentieth centuries, see Figure 7, '19th and Early 20th Century Travelers Cited in Site Descriptions', in J. Maxwell Miller (ed.), *Archaeolgoical Survey of the Kerak Plateau* (Atlanta: Scholars Press, 1991), p. 28.

11. C.R. Conder, *Survey of Eastern Palestine* (London: The Committee of the Palestine Exploration Fund, 1889); see also Conder's *Heth and Moab* (London: A.P. Watt, 1889).

12. *The Ordnance Survey of Jerusalem* (London: HMSO, 1865); reprinted in 1980 under the same title by Ariel House Publishers in Jerusalem.

13. Niel Silberman's *Digging for God and Country: Exploration in the Holy Land, 1799–1917* (New York: Doubleday, 1991) chronicles the struggle for power and influence in Palestine among the British, French, German and, to a lesser extent, American governments. Beginning with the campaign of Napoleon in Egypt at the end of the eighteenth century, this European presence laid the groundwork for the spheres of influence that were cemented with the fall of the Ottoman empire and the division of the region into the modern Middle East.

14. See A. Rainey, 'Historical Geography: The Link between Historical and Archaeological Interpretation', *BA* 45 (1982), pp. 217-23. Classic works on historical geography include Smith, *The Historical Geography of the Holy Land* and Aharoni, *The Land of the Bible*.

Nelson Glueck's survey of the regions of Moab, Edom and Ammon in the Transjordan is one of the earliest comprehensive archaeological surveys of the biblical world. Between 1932 and 1947, Glueck surveyed, identified and collected artifacts from over 1000 sites in Jordan[15] and was one of the first archaeologists to propose a settlement history of the survey area through applying a sophisticated ceramic typology to the survey data.[16] He then applied this same methodology to identify some 500 sites in the Negev, in a survey that lasted from 1952 until 1964.[17] Glueck's and many of the early surveys conducted in Syria-Palestine may be considered 'source-driven', seeking as they do to shed light on the biblical record. However, since the 1960s surveys have been more 'problem-oriented',[18] seeking to address specific research questions. Robert McC. Adams conducted three major surveys in Mesopotamia and through them was able to reconstruct the settlement history of the Diyala plains region,[19] the Euphrates floodplain[20] and the Uruk countryside.[21] Adams' work employed up-to-date survey methods, and collected geographic, environmental, climatological, geological, floral/botanical and archaeological data. He combined these with textual, historical and previously known archaeological information to provide a comprehensive analysis of the regions under study from their earliest human habitation to late Islamic periods. What differentiates Adams

15. Reports of his survey were published in a series of four *AASOR* volumes under the title *Exploration in Eastern Palestine* (14, 15, 18/19 and 25–28; New Haven: American Schools of Oriental Research, 1934–51). For a synthesis of his findings, see *The Other Side of the Jordan* (Cambridge, MA: American Schools of Oriental Research, rev. edn, 1970). See also J. Maxwell Miller, 'Archaeological Survey South of Wadi Mujib: Glueck's Sites Revisited', *ADAJ* 23 (1979), pp. 79-81, and 'Introduction', in *idem, Archaeological Survey of the Kerak Plateau*, pp. 16-17; S. Gitin, 'Glueck, Nelson', in *OEANE*, II, pp. 415-16; and Levy, 'Survey', p. 102.

16. Gitin, 'Glueck', p. 416; Levy, 'Survey', p. 102.

17. N. Glueck, *Rivers in the Desert: A History of the Negev* (New York: W.W. Norton, 1968).

18. This terminology comes from Levy, 'Survey', p. 101. Levy locates the beginning of the problem-oriented approach somewhat earlier, in the 1940s and 1950s.

19. *Land behind Baghdad: A History of Settlement on the Diyala Plains* (Chicago: University of Chicago Press, 1965).

20. *Heartland of Cities: Surveys of Ancient Settlement and Land Use on the Central Floodplain of the Euphrates* (Chicago: University of Chicago Press, 1981).

21. R.McC. Adams and H.J. Nissen, *The Uruk Countryside: The Natural Setting of Urban Societies* (Chicago: University of Chicago Press, 1972).

work from the earlier surveys is its multi-disciplinary approach and its ability not only to interpret site distribution and population patterns but also to address broader agricultural, socio-economic and sociopolitical developments. Its macro- rather than micro-focus (i.e. concern with an entire region's history than of a particular site or site-cluster) contributes to the current understanding of the region, and makes it foundational to any future excavations or explorations of each specific area.

The number of such regional projects for the Levant has increased dramatically in the last two decades. The study of Israelite origins has been the concern of two major projects: the survey of the Galilee by Yohanan Aharoni in the 1960s[22] and that of Ephraim by Israel Finkelstein have lent support to Alt's peaceful infiltration hypothesis for the settlement period.[23] Since early 1964 most areas under Israeli control have been surveyed in a series of systematic regional projects while other regional projects have been undertaken in concert with major site excavations.[24] In the Transjordan, some surveys have concentrated on the broader settlement history and interrelationships of particular regions, such as those surrounding the Kerak plateau,[25] Hesban,[26] Wâdi el-Hasa[27] or the Ghors region.[28] Others have combined regional concerns with specific archaeological periods, such as the Baq'ah valley

22. See the discussion of Levy, 'Survey', p. 102.

23. Y. Aharoni, *The Settlement of the Israelite Tribes in the Upper Galilee* (Jerusalem: Hebrew University, 1957 [Heb.]); and Finkelstein, *The Archaeology of the Israelite Settlement*.

24. R. Cohen, 'Survey of Israel', in *OEANE*, V, pp. 104-106; see also Z. Gal, 'Regional Survey Projects: Revealing the Settlement Map of Ancient Israel', in *BAT 1990*, pp. 453-58.

25. Miller, *Archaeological Survey of the Kerak Plateau*.

26. R.D. Ibach, Jr, *Archaeological Survey of the Hesban Region: Catalogue of Sites and Characterizations of Periods* (Hesban, 5; Berrien Springs, MI: Andrews University, 1987).

27. See B. MacDonald, G. Rollefson and D.W. Roller, 'The Wadi el-Hasa Survey 1981: A Preliminary Report', *ADAJ* 26 (1982), pp. 117-31; and B. MacDonald, *The Wadi el Hasa Archaeological Survey 1979–1983* (Waterloo, Ontario: Wilfrid Laurier University, 1988).

28. B. MacDonald, *The Southern Ghors and Northeast Arabah Archaeological Survey* (Sheffield Archaeological Monographs, 5; Sheffield: University of Sheffield, 1992).

project—which concentrates on the Late Bronze and Early Iron Ages[29] —and the *Liumus Arabicus* project—which examines the central plateau of Jordan during the Roman and Byzantine periods.[30]

Survey Methodology

Schiffer, Sullivan and Klinger define archaeological surveys as 'the application of a set of techniques for varying the discovery probabilities of archaeological materials in order to estimate parameters of the *regional archaeological record*'. They define regional archaeological record as 'a more or less continuous distribution of artifacts over the land surface with highly variable density characteristics'.[31] The methodology and the appropriate interpretation of the results of surveys continues to be an issue of debate. It is generally agreed that an area to be surveyed should be divided into a series of *quadrants* (square sample units), *transects* (linear sample units of uniform width) or *points* (samples taken at the point where geographical coordinates intersect).[32] Surveys ideally record more than archaeological remains—artifacts, ecofacts and architecture—but also document major environmental, geographical and geological features that might have influenced settlement patterns and subsistence strategies. Remains are collected in various ways. Archaeologists generally agree that the pedestrian recovery method is most accurate; this involves trained field-workers who walk the quadrant or transect in overlapping fields in order to identify the major features and/or remains of the sample area. Surveyors sometimes use shovels or corers to probe beneath the surface of a site in order to provide a more complete sample and thereby to fill out its settlement history.

Numerous technological developments enhance site identification, location and data collection and analysis on surveys. These include: satellite imagery (such as the Landsat images); SLAR (side-looking

29. P.E. McGovern, *The Late Bronze/Early Iron Age of Central Transjordan: The Baq'ah Valley Project, 1977–1981* (Philadelphia: University of Pennsylvania Museum, 1986).

30. S.T. Parker (ed.), *The Roman Frontier in Central Jordan: Interim Report on the Limes Arabicus Project, 1980–1985* (British Archaeological Report International Series, 340; Oxford: British Archaeological Reports, 1987).

31. 'The Design of Archaeological Surveys', p. 2.

32. Sharer and Ashmore, *Archaeology*, pp. 139-46, 187-209; Schiffer, Sullivan and Klinger, 'The Design of Archaeological Surveys', pp. 11-14.

airborne radar) images; the Global Positioning System units (which calibrate site location through using satellite signals); ground penetrating radar; geophysical diffraction tomography (a technology that identifies underground features through sound-waves); resistivity detectors (which measure the varying degrees to which electrical impulses pass through soil between two probes); metal detection; and the use of Geographic Information Systems (GIS), a sophisticated computer database system that aids in the analysis and mapping of the entire data set. Through the use of the GIS, site size and site distribution, environmental, geographic, climatological and geological data can be examined separately or in tandem to produce a much more detailed understanding of the region under consideration.[33]

Other methodological considerations in surveys involve the sampling strategy: Will the survey be probabilistic or non-probabilistic (often referred to as 'purposive')? How much of a given area will be surveyed? And (how) will the results be stratified and then interpreted? Most archaeologists prefer probabilistic sampling when 'total data acquisition'[34]—a complete survey of an entire quadrant or transect—is impossible. Probabilistic sampling involves surveying random areas within the total study area, and projecting from those findings by statistical analysis the probable number of sites and, in some cases, the relationship among sites. The sampling technique(s), the sample size or population (total number of units in the sample area to be surveyed), and the methods for data analysis should be determined by the survey team and statistician *before* fieldwork begins. This allows a higher level of accuracy in the final projections of site distribution, site relationships and the settlement history of the area surveyed.[35] There are three major types of probabilistic sampling techniques. Simple random sampling is the least accurate; in this type of sampling, the statistician establishes

33. For more detailed information on these various technologies, see Sharer and Ashmore, *Archaeology*, pp. 209-220; Blakely, 'Site Survey', p. 50, and Levy, 'Survey', pp. 103-104. For a more detailed treatment of various computer applications within archaeology, see the new *BAR* international series, *Computer Applications and Quantitative Methods in Archaeology* (British Archaeological Reports International Series, 548–; Oxford: British Archaeological Reports, 1989–) (cited by Blakely, 'Site Survey', p. 51); five volumes have appeared in the series to date.

34. This term is taken from Sharer and Ashmore, *Archaeology*, pp. 140-41.

35. For a helpful discussion of the use of statistics in archaeology, see Christoph, 'The Yehud Stamped Jar Handle Corpus', pp. 109-118. See also my 'A Social and Demographic Study', pp. 216-31.

the specific units to be examined, not in a 'hit-or-miss' manner, but in a way that assures that 'each unit in the sampling frame has a statistically equal chance for selection'.[36] Since random sampling treats all data relatively equally, it is considered least reliable for the type of sophisticated analysis typical of the more recent surveys.[37] Systematic sampling begins by choosing a beginning point within the survey area randomly, but then examines points in predetermined number and distance from the point of origin. It is considered more accurate than simple random sampling and is more likely to be useful for reconstructing site relationships and/or hierarchies. Stratified sampling is most useful when a prior knowledge of the area to be surveyed alerts archaeologists to factors that could potentially influence site distribution and/or settlement patterns. Based on this prior knowledge, the survey team divides the data set into particular levels or strata that reflect the known patterns. These strata are examined and analyzed in isolation and then together, thus providing a more comprehensive understanding of the survey area.[38]

Non-probablistic or purposive, sampling techniques are often considered less objective, for they may introduce human biases to the collection of data. Bias may be introduced through interviewing local inhabitants of a survey area and using them to discover important sites that might go undetected through random survey techniques. Purposive techniques add to the data universe through methods such as aerial photographs, satellite images, and through predictive techniques such as sensitivity to natural and/or environmental features that may have influenced settlement patterns and artifact production.[39] While it is true that a strictly probabilistic survey is more 'objective', collection of data is the true priority of surveys, and thus a combination of purposive and probabilistic methods holds the most promise for a reconstruction of the

---

36. Sharer and Ashmore, *Archaeology*, pp. 142-43.

37. Sharer and Ashmore, *Archaeology*, pp. 142-43.

38. Sharer and Ashmore, *Archaeology*, pp. 143-44; Schiffer, Sullivan, and Klinger, 'The Design of Archaelogical Surveys', pp. 4-6; Ammerman, 'Surveys and Archaeological Research', pp. 78-79.

39. Schiffer, Sullivan and Klinger, 'The Design of Archaelogical Surveys', p. 5. See also the discussion of Sharer and Ashmore, *Archaeology*, pp. 141-46 and 224-26.

settlement and artifactual history of a given area.[40] In fact, as Ammerman points out, the debate surrounding random sampling versus the more sophisticated methods, such as cluster analysis, systematic sampling and stratified random sampling, has deflected attention from other, more compelling issues in survey methodology.[41]

Another pressing question in survey methodology is site definition. Biblical scholars are well acquainted with the difficulties of connecting a particular archaeological site with its biblical counterpart.[42] Such identification has often been somewhat haphazard, falling between the interests and expertise of biblical scholars and Syro-Palestinian archaeologists. Very often, a tentative identification becomes what J.M. Miller refers to as 'commonly accepted scholarly opinion' through sheer frequency of citation. In some cases, these identifications, while widespread, are based on erroneous assumptions and upon closer examination are found to be incorrect. Miller notes that often, even when a once-accepted identification is challenged and corrected in the scholarly literature, it is not corrected in the field as a whole. Frequently these erroneous site identifications remain on maps of a particular biblical period for decades; some are never corrected.

The problem of site identification is of a different nature for surveys and may be posed as a question of what constitutes an archaeological site. What differentiates a sherd splatter—which might indicate casual occupation—from a homestead, small settlement, village or city?[43] Surveyors often distinguish between 'sites' and 'non-sites'. Sites are defined as areas that have significant artifactual remains (large amounts of

---

40. Schiffer, Sullivan and Klinger, 'The Design of Archaelogical Surveys', pp. 2, 5, 15-19.

41. Ammerman, 'Surveys and Archaeological Research', p. 79.

42. On this problem, see H.J. Franken, 'The Problem of Identification in Biblical Archaeology', *PEQ* 108 (1976), pp. 3-11; J. Maxwell Miller, 'Site Identification: A Problem Area in Contemporary Biblical Scholarship', *ZDPV* 99 (1983), pp. 119-29; and Rainey, 'Historical Geography'.

43. This question was first posed to me by J. Maxwell Miller after my presentation of a paper, 'Reconstructing the Past with Analogies from the Present: Establishing the Appropriate Limits for Ethnoarchaeological Approaches to Biblical Archaeology', at the Southeast regional SBL/AAR/ASOR meetings, March 1991. It remains an important issue, one that is not often discussed by those who use surveys in their research, and one for which I have not found a satisfactory answer.

pottery; evidence of architecture or installations); Levy's definition is perhaps most satisfying:

> Surface concentrations of flint tools and debitage; pottery sherds; fragments of architectural remains such as foundation stones and mud bricks; inscriptions; and ash and other human-deposited sediments identify an ancient site.[44]

In contrast, non-sites, or 'low density artefact scatters',[45] are typically defined as areas with sparse remains. For the purposes of this study the question is this: once a site is identified as having Persian period potsherds, how does one determine whether or not it represents a true settlement? Typically Persian period sherds represent only a small percentage of the total found at a particular site, sometimes as minimal as 1 or 2 per cent. But percentages themselves may be misleading; for example, Kh. esh-Sheik Suleiman, a site outside the borders of Yehud, but surveyed by Finkelstein in the new Benjamin survey, had only 34 potsherds, 1 of which (3 per cent) dated to the Persian period. Persian period pottery also accounted for three per cent of the pottery discovered at Beit Ur et-Tahta, but there that percentage represented five potsherds. One feels rather ill at ease when attributing a major settlement for a surveyed site on the basis of three or five sherds, even given the recent progress in survey methodology. Faced with these same problems in his survey of Ephraim, Finkelstein estimated that although 92 sites had Persian period remains, far fewer actually represented occupied sites.[46] But it is appropriate to ask, which ones? On what basis does one consider surveyed sites to be settlements versus areas that were used only casually?

Other methodological issues include the degree to which specific areas are surveyed, the relative expertise of the surveyor and the mapping of sites discovered within a survey. Few quadrants in any survey are canvassed entirely due to limitations of time and resources and different quadrants may be canvassed unevenly in the same survey. Thus,

---

44. Levy, 'Survey', p. 101.

45. See Schiffer, Sullivan, and Klinger, 'The Design of Archaeological Surveys', pp. 2, 14.

46. I. Finkelstein, 'The Land of Ephraim Survey 1980–1987: Preliminary Report', *TA* 15–16 (1988–89), pp. 117-83 (154-55). He concluded that in the Persian period the number of sites was less than half of that of the Iron II period, and that the Persian period population was probably no more than 25 per cent of the preceding period.

quadrants in which more time is spent will probably yield higher percentages of pottery and numbers of sites than those in which less survey time is spent.[47] Even the character of the same site may be interpreted quite differently if the surveyors canvass different areas of that site. The site of Beit Ur-el Fauqa was surveyed in connection with the survey of Benjamin by two teams: one led by Feldstein and Kameisky, the other by Finkelstein. According to Feldstein and Kameisky, the major occupation was in the Iron II period (this period was also the first settlement of the site, according to their data), followed by a break in settlement during the Persian period, with renewed occupation during the Hellenistic period. Finkelstein's survey found some sherds dating as early as the Middle Bronze Age, major occupation in the Iron II period, and a Persian period settlement (four per cent of the pottery discovered in the survey dated to this period). Both found the same percentage of pottery in the Hellenistic period, but Feldstein and Kameisky found significant occupation in the Roman and Byzantine periods, whereas Finkelstein found no Roman period pottery and only a few sherds dating to the Byzantine period. Critics might allege that this discrepancy shows that survey data are unreliable. However, it is significant that both surveys are in agreement regarding the major periods of settlement (Iron II and Hellenistic); information from other periods serves to fill out the occupational history of the site.[48]

Ammerman has critiqued surveys for their tendency to treat periods in a homogeneous fashion, without regard for the changes in settlement patterns and site distribution that invariably occur over an extended period of time, a problem that results in what he calls 'overestimated maps' of a region or period.[49] This problem has, in fact, characterized the use of survey data to understand the Persian period. It is seen most often in maps that include all sites from a given period, even though some, or even many, of those sites may date to only a portion of that

47. In Ofer's survey of the Judean hill country, only two quadrants were surveyed entirely; one cut through three of Ofer's ten zones, the other bisected two zones. Of the other areas included within the borders of Yehud, the Jerusalem highlands were not surveyed, 12 of the 88 square kilometers of the mountain highlands were completely surveyed, 80 of the 120 square kilometers of the northern central hills were surveyed, and 26 of the 64 square kilometers of the northern desert fringe were completely surveyed.

48. *ASHCB*.

49. Ammerman, 'Surveys and Archaeological Research', pp. 77-78.

period. I have attempted to avoid this by separating the period into Persian I and II with the dividing line being the middle of the fifth century BCE. However, it is much more difficult to distinguish between Persian I and II sites based on survey data and any such distinction must be considered extremely tentative. Despite this difficulty I have identified 22 sites as Persian II (see Table 3 below). Among these sites are nine fortresses dated clearly to the mid-fifth century (at the beginning of Persian II) and twelve other sites with pottery identified by the surveyors as 'Persian-Hellenistic'.[50] The fortresses were perhaps inhabited by imperial conscripts who may or may not have been native Yehudites.

Summary
Archaeological surveys have developed from their early form as explorations of the Levant with the intent of recovering biblical history, into the sophisticated, problem-oriented reconnaisance and recovery tools that characterize modern regional projects. With the application of appropriate methodology and diverse and increasingly accurate technologies, surveys have the capacity to analyze many different types of data together in order to present a comprehensive understanding not only of settlement patterns, but also of the interrelationships among sites and regions, of the influence of geology, geography and environment on subsistence strategies, settlement history, and social, economic and political structures. It is important for the reader to consider, however, that the survey data used for the following reconstruction of the province of Yehud do not come from a single regional survey project, but from four surveys, each of which was conducted by different teams, at different times and with distinct methodologies (Figure 15). While this does not make the sites identified any less important, it does introduce a level of unevenness that would not be present were we taking data from one, 'Yehud regional project'.

---

50. Aside from the fortresses, it was impossible to differentiate between Persian I and Persian II sites for the survey data from Judah. Ofer identifies the Persian period as 586-332 BCE; his data came to me in the form of a site list that does not include percentages of pottery in specific archaeological periods. Note that I did not include Ḥorvat Zimri in this list of Persian II sites even though it is a fortress and was in use in the Persian II period. As the excavation report indicates, this fortress had a Neo-Babylonian phase and was occupied throughout the Persian period.

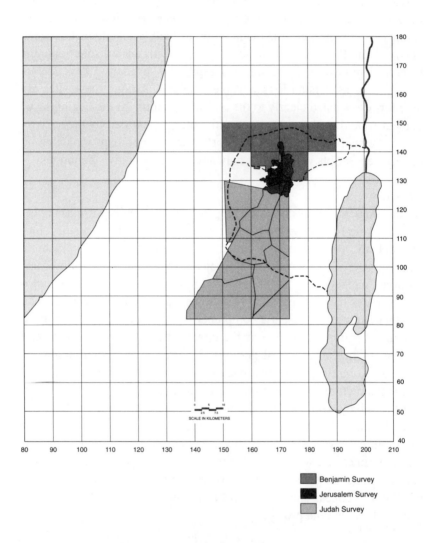

Figure 15. *Recent Surveys of Jerusalem, Benjamin, and Judah*

Site Distribution in the Province of Yehud

Site distribution refers to the relative placement of sites within a particular geopolitical area, and is a function of territory, soil type, climate and environmental niche (Figure 16). In the discussion that follows, site distribution applies specifically to the number of sites in the major and individual environmental niches identified in Chapter 2 and the number of sites in each biblical tribal territory that made up the province of Yehud.[51] This model asserts that site distribution is influenced by the interrelationships that cause environmental niches, as well as the environmental niches themselves. It predicts that settlement will be more dense in environmental niches with adequate rainfall and more arable land than in those with either deficient rainfall or those with poor quality soils, although socio-economic or geopolitical factors may at times override these factors of the natural environment. There may also be some feedback (i.e. counter-influence) from site distribution that may affect environmental niches, although this effect is somewhat indirect.

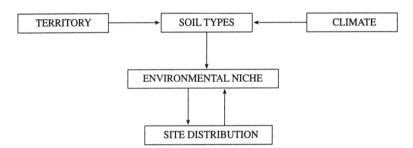

Figure 16. *Interrelationships of Constants and Variables that Affect Site Distribution*

Excavations and surveys show a total of 132 sites in the province of Yehud that may date to the Persian period, of which 125 were occupied (Figure 17).[52] Of these sites, 59 (47 per cent) were located in the biblical

---

51. The term 'site distribution' may also refer to the distances between and among sites.

52. The cave at Ketef Yeriḥo may not have been occupied, and if it was it would represent a minimal occupation; the site of 'Ain Arrub is a tomb-cave. It is also important to note that some of these sites may have been Neo-Babylonian rather than Persian, as discussed above (see, e.g., el-Jîb and Tell el-Fûl). Also note the difficulty in determining which period to place the sites from Ofer's survey.

tribal territory of Benjamin (Chart 1), and 66 (53 per cent) in the biblical territory of Judah. The number of sites in the four major and eight individual environmental niches is also of interest. The western slopes (WS) contained 32 sites (26 per cent); 68 sites (54 per cent) were located in the central hills (CH); the desert fringe (DF) contained 23 sites (18 per cent); and 2 sites (2 per cent) were located in the Judean desert (JD; see Chart 2). The breakdown by individual environmental niche is as follows (Chart 3): EN 1, the northwestern slopes—24 (19 per cent of all sites); EN 2, the north central hills—18 sites (14.4 per cent); EN 3, the northern desert fringe—17 sites (13.6 per cent); EN 4, the southwestern slopes—8 sites (6 per cent); EN 5, central hills—37 sites, of which 36 were occupied (29 per cent of all sites); EN 6, southern desert fringe—6 sites (5 per cent); EN 7, south central hills—14 sites (11 per cent); and EN 8, the Judean Desert, contained 3 sites, of which 2 represent settlements (2 per cent). Table 3 (below) shows excavated and surveyed sites, coordinates, estimated size and excavator or surveyor of each site. The survey data from Avi Ofer's survey of Judah includes his own estimate of each site's size in metric dunams. This estimate is based on two formulae that take into account the maximal size of the site, the pottery density of each archaeological period for a particular site,[53] and the proportion of pottery from each period. The first formula yields the site's 'calculated size':

$$\frac{P_x}{P_m} \times S_{max} = S_m$$

where P_m equals the maximum amount of the pottery, P_x equals the pottery dating to a particular archaeological period, S_{max} equals the maximum size of the site, and S_m is the minimum size of the site in the period in question. Ofer then calculates the average size of the site[54] using a constant (from 1-10, usually 2) and the site's minimum and maximum sizes (as determined through the first formula):

$$\frac{S_m \times K + S_{max}}{(K + 1)} = S_n$$

53. Pottery density is defined as the number of rims collected in one hour of survey, divided by the number of centuries in each period, and multiplied by the average calculated size of that site.

54. Evidently the average size of the site within a particular archaeological period.

● Very small

▲ Small

◆ Medium

■ Large

★ Very large

+ Unoccupied site

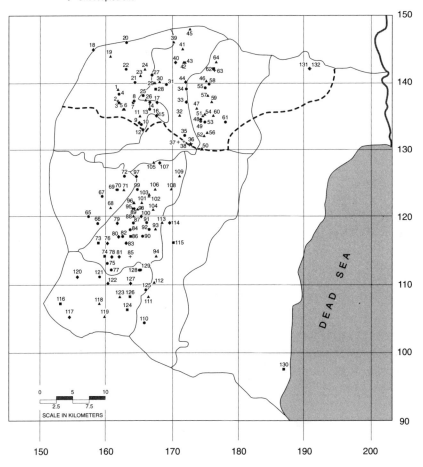

Figure 17. *Site Distribution in the Province of Yehud, Persian Period II*

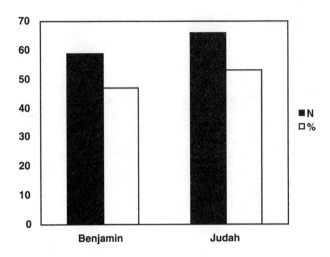

Chart 1. *Site Distribution by Biblical Territories,*
Persian Period II Yehud

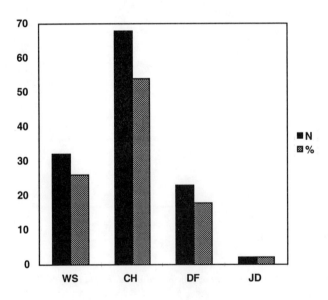

Chart 2. *Site Distribution by Major Environmental Niches,*
Persian Period II Yehud

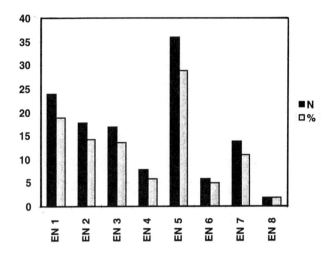

Chart 3. *Site Distribution by Individual Environmental Niches,*
Persian Period II Yehud

where S_m refers to '(minimum) calculated size', K refers to the constant, S_{max} is the maximum size of the site and S_n is the site's average size. This procedure, while perhaps imperfect,[55] represents an improvement over the more subjective estimates to which one often must resort. For this reason, I have applied where possible a slightly revised formula to the data from the survey of Benjamin.[56] To arrive at the minimum calculated size, I use the simple percentage of pottery dated by the various surveyors to the Persian period:

$$P_x \times S_{max} = S_m$$

where P_x refers to the uncalibrated percentage of the Persian period discovered at the site in question. I then enter the minimum calculated

55. Its point of departure is still pottery percentages, generally apart from architectural remains.

56. This change, reflecting a difficulty in arriving at a calibrated percentage for the Persian period versus the other periods represented in the sites of the Benjamin survey, was suggested to me by Avi Ofer in the summer of 1990 as we discussed survey methodology.

size arrived at through this formula in Ofer's second formula (unchanged)[57] to arrive at the average size of the site.

When using these formulae has not been possible (often due to a lack of either pottery percentage or of maximum size of the site in the survey report), I have estimated the size of the sites, and placed them into the following five categories:[58] Very Small (VS), 1–2.0 dunams (median 1.5); Small (S), 2.1–5.0 dunams (median 3.5); Medium (M), 5.1–12.0 dunams (median 8.5); Large (L), 12.1–25.0 dunams (median 18.5); Very Large (VL), more than 25 dunams.[59]

Table 3. *Excavated and Surveyed Sites in Persian Period Yehud*

Excavated Sites[60]

Site Name	Coordinates	Size	Excavator/Surveyor
Bethel I	1728.1481	10	Albright and Kelso
El-Jîb	1676.1394	L	Pritchard
Tell el-Fûl	1719.1367	M	Albright; P. Lapp
Tell en-Naṣbeh	1706.1436	17	Badè; McCown
Kh. er-Ras (W)	1709.1354	S	Onn and Rapuano
Jerusalem	1728.1313	60	Kenyon; Shiloh
Ketef Hinnom	1714.1307	T	Barkay
Mamilla	1714.1513	T	Reich

57. I have used a constant of 2 throughout these calculations.

58. Milevski proposes a site hierachy with three tiers: small sites are those 0.5–9.9 dunams, medium sites range from 10–19.9 dunams, and large sites are those over 20 dunams ('Settlement Patterns', p. 18). This division is based not on the possible size of the site during the Persian period, but its overall or maximal size. It is therefore of little value in attempting to reconstruct settlement sizes during the Persian period, and obscures, rather than clarifies, the issue.

59. The site list included here is patterned after those of M. Broshi and R. Gophna in their studies of the population of the Early and Middle Bronze Ages, and the Roman-Byzantine period. See M. Broshi, 'The Population of Western Palestine in the Roman-Byzantine Period', *BASOR* 236 (1980), pp. 1-10; M. Broshi and R. Gophna, 'The Settlements and Population of Palestine during the Early Bronze Age II-III', *BASOR* 253 (1984), pp. 41-53; M. Broshi and R. Gophna, 'Middle Bronze Age II Palestine: Its Settlements and Population', *BASOR* 261 (1986), pp. 73-90. The five categories of site sizes that I use here seem more appropriate than the schematization that Broshi and Gophna use for the Early or Middle Bronze Age in that the Persian period sites are markedly smaller than those of the periods that they analyzed.

60. The size of many of these sites is obscured due to the existence of modern villages or forests above the ancient site. However, in order to estimate the popula-

Site Name	Coordinates	Size	Excavator/Surveyor
Wadi Salim	1743.1344	4	Kloner
Kh. er-Ras (S)	1672.1281	3	Zehavi
Ramat Raḥel	1706.1274	S	Aharoni; Kloner
Tel Goren	1863.0960	L	Mazar
Jericho	1908.1424	M	Sellin and Watzinger; Kenyon
Ketef Yeriḥo	1908.1424	C	Eshel and Misgav
'Ain 'Arrub	1637.1139	T	Stern
Ras el-Kharrubeh	1746.1350	S	Dinur and Feig; Biran
El-'Ezariyeh	1744.1309	S	Saller; Dinur and Feig
Kh. et-Tubeiqah (Beth Zur)	1590.1108	2	Seller; P. Lapp and N. Lapp; Ofer
Bethel II	1728.1481	S	Albright and Kelso
Kh. 'Almith	1758.1369	S	Dinur and Feig

Surveyed Sites: Persian I

Benjamin

Kh. Ras el-Mughar	1619.1387	8	Feldstein and Kameisky; Kallai
Kh. el-Kafira	1620.1375	5	Feldstein and Kameisky; Eshel and Amit
Kh. el-Murran	1627.1359	8	Feldstein and Kameisky
Kh. el-Bawaya	1629.1364	3	Feldstein and Kameisky
Kh. Ein el-Keniseh	1646.1369	2	Feldstein and Kameisky
Mevasseret Zion	1652.1339	S	Stern
Kh. Beit Mizza	1652.1349	4	Feldstein and Kameisky
Unnamed 2	1667.1361	2	Feldstein and Kameisky
Unnamed 3	1667.1368	3	Feldstein and Kameisky
Kh. el-'Alawina	1675.1354	3	Milevski; Feldstein and Kameisky
Unnamed 4	1677.1351	11	Feldstein and Kameisky
Beit 'Ur el-Tahta	1582.1446	10	Finkelstein

tion of the province, I have included them in the above list and have, for consistency's sake, considered them either as Very Small or Small villages. While designating these sites in this manner may appear arbitrary, it will allow a more accurate picture of the population of the province than would deleting them from consideration. The villages so affected are Kh. Ras el-Mughar, Beit Surik, Hizma, El-'Eizariya, Husan and el-Jaba'. Note also these additional abbreviations: C = Cave; T = Tomb. All sizes are in metric dunams. A more detailed listing of sites may be found in the Appendix, 'Excavated and Surveyed Sites in the Province of Yehud', pp. 324-48. That list includes population figures, biblical territory and environmental niche of each site. It is numbered to correspond with the map of site distribution (Figure 17, p. 185). Note that three fortresses that have been excavated are included in the final category of this table ('Imperial Fortresses'); these are Ḥorvat Zimri, Kh. Nijam, and Kh. Abu et-Twein.

Site Name	Coordinates	Size	Excavator/Surveyor
Beit 'Ur el-Fauqa	1608.1436	5	Finkelstein; Feldstein and Kameisky
Kh. Badd Abu Mu'ammar	1645.1403	1	Feldstein and Kameisky
Kh. el-Jufeir	1653.1411	S	Feldstein and Kameisky; Kallai
Kh. el-Latatin	1660.1418	S	Finkelstein; Kallai
Unnamed 5	1657.1378	2	Feldstein and Kameisky
Kh. Abu Leimun	1661.1370	6	Feldstein and Kameisky
Unnamed 6	1666.1416	6	Feldstein and Kameisky
Kh. 'Id	1675.1402	6	Feldstein and Kameisky
Judeira	1688.1406	S	Feldstein and Kameisky
Ras et-Tahuneh (S)	1702.1462	S	Kallai
Kh. Nisieh	1717.1449	5	Feldstein and Kameisky
Unnamed 8	1720.1429	1	Feldstein and Kameisky
er-Ram	1721.1402	10	Feldstein and Kameisky
Unnamed 9	1743.1343	VS	Gibson
Ras Abu Subeitan	1748.1321	4	Dinur and Feig
Kh. Herabat 'Audeh	1749.1340	3	Dinur and Feig
'Anata	1749.1356	S	Gibson
Unnamed 10	1750.1389	VS	Dinur and Feig
Ras Tumeim	1754.1382	S	Dinur
Jurrat es-Saqqawi	1756.1398	VS	Dinur and Feig
Kh. Deir es-Sidd	1762.1353	S	Dinur and Feig; Biran
Unnamed 11	1780.1344	VS	Dinur and Feig
Kh. el-Hara el-Fauqa and Mukhmas	1763.1424	16	Feldstein and Kameisky
Unnamed 12	1767.1422	T	Feldstein and Kameisky
Tell el-'Askar	1767.1430	4	Feldstein and Kameisky

Judah

Kh. el-Kabarah	1607.1215	S	Kokhavi
Husan	1627.1244	S	Kokhavi
Kh. el-Yahudi	1628.1264	VS	Kokhavi
Kh. Judur	1588.1156	14	Kokhavi; Ofer
Beit Ummar	1598.1143	13	Ofer
Kh. Huveilah	1602.1157	9	Ofer
Kh. 'Umm ed-Durj	1608.1124	2	Ofer
Kh. Kufin	1609.1143	6	Ofer
Kh. Beit Zakariyeh	1617.1189	10.4	Ofer
Deir Sha'ar	1619.1170	11	Ofer
Kh. el-Keren	1620.1140	6	Ofer
Suweir	1625.1172	1	Ofer
Kh. Umm et-Tal'ah	1630.1160	5.8	Ofer
Rujm es-Sebit	1636.1178	2	Ofer
Kh. Bericuth	1637.1168	15	Ofer

Site Name	Coordinates	Size	Excavator/Surveyor
Kh. Pe'or/Kh. Zakandah	1640.1193	22	Ofer; Kochavi
Kh. Humeidiyah	1641.1197	5	Ofer
Kh. Shanah	1642.1144	2	Ofer
Salmuneh	1655.1172	1	Ofer
Marsiya'	1661.1187	1	Ofer
Shem'ah	1665.1181	1	Ofer
Halil Isma'el	1674.1175	3	Ofer
Wadi 'Arrub	1675.1135	2.4	Ofer
Kh. Jumeia'	1641.1214	6	Ofer
Kh. Merah ej- Jumeia'	1642.1217	3	Ofer
Kh. Abu Shaven	1646.1263	9	Ofer
Kh. Gharab	1647.1212	4	Ofer
Rujm el-Khadar	1647.1235	1	Kokhavi; Ofer
Kh. Umm el-Qita'	1653.1202	6	Kokhavi; Ofer
Kh. 'Aliye'	1654.1224	4	Ofer
Neimar	1665.1229	3	Ofer
Kh. el-Khwakh	1671.1214	5	Kokhavi; Ofer
Ras el-Kebir	1674.1237	5	Kokhavi; Ofer
Sharafat	1681.1278	11	Ofer
Bethlehem	1698.1235	4	Ofer[61]
Kh. 'Arabieh	1658.1042	2	Ofer
Kh. el-Seimar	1664.1080	3	Ofer
Kh. Za'aphran	1672.1102	4	Ofer
Beidah	1683.1194	3	Ofer
Kh. Sib'ah	1695.1185	6	Ofer
Kh. et-Tuqu'	1700.1157	15	Kokhavi; Ofer
Kh. et-Tayyibeh	1531.1072	18	Kokhavi; Ofer
Taffuh	1545.1052	12	Kokhavi; Ofer
Kh. Dahdah	1590.1074	4	Ofer
Gebel Namra	1598.1048	3	Ofer
Kh. 'Arnav	1557.1108	6	Ofer
Halhul	1603.1095	11.4	Ofer
Kh. Beit 'Anun	1621.1078	4	Ofer
Kh. el-'Udiseh	1632.1064	3	Kokhavi; Ofer
Rujm el-Qesar	1664.1092	1	Ofer
Kh. Ras et-Tawil	1636.1083	23	Ofer
Si'ir	1637.1102	6	Kokhavi; Ofer
Kh. Zawiyye	1652.1122	8	Ofer

61. Only the area surrounding Manger Square was surveyed; the actual area of Bethlehem occupied in the Persian period may have been larger.

Site Name	Coordinates	Size	Excavator/Surveyor
	Surveyed Sites: Persian II		
Benjamin			
Kh. Judeida	1623.1381	3	Feldstein and Kameisky
Beit Surik	1642.1367	9	Feldstein and Kameisky
Unnamed 1	1650.1341	11	Feldstein and Kameisky
Qaluniya (Moṣah?)	1656.1333	13	Feldstein and Kameisky
Kh. el-Burj	1678.1367	12	Feldstein and Kameisky
Kh. el-Ballut	1692.1395	2	Kallai
el-Khalis			
Kh. el-Hafi	1633.1455	2	Finkelstein
Unnamed 7	1718.1434	1	Feldstein and Kameisky
Kh. Irha	1724.1394	4	Dinur and Feig
Hizma	1754.1382	S	Dinur and Feig
Jaba'	1749.1405	S	Kallai; Feldstein and Kameisky
Judah			
Kh. Jrish	1616.1241	3	Kokhavi
el-Jab'a	1573.1203	VS	Kokhavi
Imperial Fortresses			
Kh. Abu et-Twein	1587.1192	M[62]	Mazar
Deir Baghl	1594.1228	1	Kokhavi;[63] Ofer

62. This size reflects both the fortress and the associated settlement. For a comparison, see the fortress of Kh. ez-Zawiyye and the 8 dunam site adjacent to it, Kh. Zawiyye. The problem of estimating the population of the fortresses is complex and requires more study. Some seem to have had settlements associated with them. But were the settlements for the conscripts or were the fortresses built next to already existing settlements to provide a tax or commodity base for them? Is it appropriate to apply the normal population coefficient to the size of the site, given that so much of the fortress was public in nature? Or should another type of areal analysis be used, such as Narrol's ratio of 1 person per 10 square meters (R. Narrol, 'Floor Area and Settlement Population', *AA* 27 [1962], pp. 587-89), or Casselberry's formula of P = 1/6 F (population is equal to one-sixth the floor area; S.E. Casselberry, 'Further Refinement of Formulae for Determining Population from Floor Area', *WA* 6 [1974], pp. 117-22).

The fortress at Kh. Abu et-Twein is a case in point. The total floor area is 914.5 square meters, but at least 34 per cent of that area is public (courtyard, entrances, storerooms, workshops). This would leave at the most 606.7 square meters for human occupation (although it is likely that closer to 50 per cent of the floor area was used for purposes other than lodging the troops), or enough space to house up to 61 people. The matter is complicated, however, by another factor; Mazar does not rule out the possibility of an upper storey, which would leave up to 690 square meters for occupation, or enough space for 69 people. If the upper storey were used

Site Name	Coordinates	Size	Excavator/Surveyor
Kh. el-Qaṭṭ	1602.1127	1	Kokhavi; Ofer
Kh. Umm el-Qalʻa	1617.1243	1	Kokhavi; Ofer
Rujm Abu Hashabe	1632.1419	VS	Kallai
Kh. ez-Zawiyye	1651.1121	1	Kokhavi; Ofer
Kh. Kabar	1665.1231	1	Kokhavi; Ofer
French Hill	1725.1343	VS	Kloner
Ḥorvat Zimri	1738.1363	VS	Gibson; Nadelman
Har Adar (Kh. Nijam)	1623.1372	VS	Dadon

The Population of the Province of Yehud

Population may be estimated in a variety of ways, including spatial analysis,[64] paleodemography, food remains analysis,[65] carrying capacity,[66] water supply[67] and areal analysis. The latter approach is best suited to the data available for Yehud. In using this procedure, I build largely on the work of Y. Shiloh,[68] Broshi and Gophna,[69] and I. Finkelstein.[70] All

as living space, it is reasonable to assume that the first storey was almost entirely public in nature. Using Casselberry's suggestion, the maximal population would have been approximately 100, a figure that is almost certainly too high.

63. According to Kokhavi, Iron II pottery was found here, with a subsequent gap until the Roman period. Hoglund includes this site as a mid-fifth century fortress since it conforms to his architectural typology (*Achaemenid Imperial Administration*, pp. 195-97).

64. Narrol, 'Floor Area and Settlement Population'; and Casselberry, 'Further Refinement of Formulae for Determining Population'. The formulae suggested by each author seem to be somewhat inflated. However, since most of the sites included in the province of Yehud in the Persian period have been surveyed rather than excavated, neither formula can be applied consistently.

65. For a discussion of these two methods of population estimates, and a general discussion of the problems of such estimates, see R.M. Schacht, 'Estimating Past Population Trends', *ARA* 10 (1981), pp. 119-40. Also helpful is F.A. Hassan, 'Demography and Archaeology', *ARA* 8 (1979), pp. 137-60.

66. M. Broshi, 'Methodology of Population Estimates: The Roman-Byzantine Period as a Case Study', in *BAT 1990*, pp. 420-25.

67. J. Wilkinson, 'Ancient Jerusalem: Its Water Supply and Population', *PEQ* 106 (1974), pp. 33-51.

68. 'The Population of Iron Age Palestine in the Light of a Sample Analysis of Urban Plans, Areas and Population Density', *BASOR* 239 (1980), pp. 25-35.

69. Broshi, 'The Population of Western Palestine'; Broshi and Gophna, 'The Settlements and Population of Palestine', and Broshi and Gophna, 'Middle Bronze Age II Palestine'.

have used ethnographic data to reconstruct certain aspects of Israelite
society, although each with differing emphases and levels of success.
Their studies estimate population through combining the total area of
the settled sites during a particular period with population-to-land area
coefficients. Shiloh used a coefficient of 40 to 50 persons per dunam (a
figure that has been shown to be far too high) in his estimate of the population of Palestine in the Iron Age. This coefficient was based, in part,
upon a figure of eight persons per household, which also is inflated.[71]
The primary value of Shiloh's work, then, is methodological. He suggests four controls to ensure the validity of one's estimates:

(1)   In towns that are to serve as statistical samples, a considerable area must
        have been excavated.

(2)   The outlines of the town plan must be clearly defined.

(3)   It must be possible to define with certainty the limits of the residential
        area of the individual dwelling units.

(4)   The dwelling units must be clearly defined architecturally, so as to make
        it possible to arrive at a reasonable classification of all dwellings making
        up the residential area.[72]

These controls are useful for Iron Age and Bronze Age estimates but
are less useful for the Persian period (at least in Yehud) since most
excavations do not provide these types of data. Another of Shiloh's
suggestions is more to the point for this study: that a variety of site
types existed, and that these should be differentiated in any reconstruction. These include: (1) royal centers; (2) provincial towns; and (3) rural
settlements, estates and central fortresses.[73] In the Persian period, perhaps more than in the Iron Age, the majority of the sites would fit in the
third category.

Broshi and Gophna use a methodology similar to Shiloh's. In his early
work, Broshi suggested that the population of Palestine in the Roman
period was approximately 1,000,000 persons. He based this study on an
analysis of 26 urban sites, which have a total area of 1240 hectares, and
reasoned that about one-third of the total population of Palestine was

70. *The Archaeology of the Israelite Settlement*; 'The Value of Demographic
Data'; and Broshi and Finkelstein, 'The Population of Palestine', pp. 47-60.

71. See the discussions in Stager, 'The Archaeology', pp. 18-24, and Finkelstein,
'The Value of Demographic Data', p. 13.

72. Shiloh, 'The Population of Iron Age Palestine', p. 28.

73. 'The Population of Iron Age Palestine', p. 28.

located in these cities. Using a coefficient of 400 persons per hectare and a correction factor of 0.25 (for public space), he arrived at a figure of 372,000 persons in these urban centers. He then multiplied this by three, and arrived at his population estimate of 1,116,000 persons. Broshi has since confirmed this figure by analyzing the carrying capacity of the land.[74]

In their later studies on the Early and Middle Bronze ages, Broshi and Gophna use a population coefficient of 250 persons per hectare, a figure that is confirmed in several ethnographic studies.[75] For the Iron Age, Broshi and Gophna suggest a figure of 270 persons per hectare, based on 54 dwellings per hectare at Tel Masos and 5 persons per family per dwelling.[76] I prefer a coefficient of between 4.0 and 4.5 persons per family per dwelling, which would yield between 220 and 240 persons per hectare,[77] a figure that accords well with Broshi and Gophna's estimates.

Finkelstein likewise integrates land area and population coefficients, measuring the size of villages in the Iron I period in dunams rather than in hectares. Finkelstein also bases his population to area ratio on ethnographic data from a wide variety of sources, including the 'Village Statistics' recorded during the period of the Mandatorial Government of Palestine[78] and the studies of both Watson and Kramer. While he uses a figure of 25 persons per dunam, the figure I use here, Finkelstein notes that during the period of the British Mandate, figures varied from 9.9 to 21.2 persons per dunam, based upon the ecological niche in which particular villages were located.[79] My own research confirms this con-

74. 'Methodology of Population Estimates', pp. 421-23.

75. It is unclear whether Broshi would revise his figures in the Roman-Byzantine period from 400 persons to 250 persons per hectare. If so, this would yield a total population of 700,000. Among the ethnographic studies Broshi and Gophna cite are: C. Kramer, *Ethnoarchaeology: Implications of Ethnography to Archaeology* (New York: Columbia University Press, 1979), and P.J. Watson, 'Ethnoarchaeology in the Near East, Lettre d'Information', *AO* 5 (1982), pp. 72-79.

76. 'The Settlements and Population of Palestine', p. 42.

77. For a discussion of family size in antiquity based on a wide variety of data, see my 'A Social and Demographic Study', chapter 4, pp. 183-85.

78. I describe the Village Notebooks and other sources of data from the period of the British Mandate and evaluate their usefulness for demographic studies in 'A Social and Demographic Study', pp. 193-210.

79. 'The Value of Demographic Data', pp. 13-15. Finkelstein draws exclusively upon information from the Mandatorial period for these figures. The average figure

clusion. The ratio of persons per dunam in villages from the Mandatorial period that were located within the borders of biblical Yehud
varied from a low of 6.9 to a high of 22.9 (average 12.4) in one district
and from 6.6 to 36.5 (average 15.1) in another. This suggests that the
generally accepted figure of 25 persons per dunam should be considered
maximal, despite being approximately one-half of the coefficient that
Shiloh used.[80]

A recent study by J. Zorn[81] applies a multi-layered approach to
population estimates. As Zorn points out, understanding the relative
population of a site is important both for micro-level (understanding the
history of the site itself) and macro-level (understanding the site in relationship to others and its role within a region) reconstructions of antiquity. He suggests further that regional estimates of population and site
distribution can be sharpened by providing a hierarchy of site functions,
proposing a division of sites into 'major administrative centers, unwalled
villages, border fortresses, cult sites',[82] for example. Zorn approaches
the population of Tell en-Naṣbeh from the combined perspective of
areal analysis, carrying capacity, water resources, family size and spatial
analysis. Tell en-Naṣbeh lends itself to this type of overlapping analysis
since so much of the site was excavated (approximately 66 per cent),
and since numerous contiguous dwellings were uncovered, allowing a
convergence of estimates from the perspectives identified above. Combining these various approaches to the problem of population estimates,
Zorn is able to project a reasonable population range between 800 and
1000 for Tell en-Naṣbeh during the Iron IIC period and between 400
and 500 in the Neo-Babylonian and Persian periods.[83] Zorn's methodology is similar to that suggested by Shiloh[84] in that it recognizes the

for 113 modern villages located within the boundaries of a recent survey conducted
by Finkelstein was 20 persons per dunam; that of villages from the center of the hill
country of Ephraim was 17 persons per dunam.

80. 'The Population of Iron Age Palestine', pp. 25-35.

81. 'Estimating the Population Size', pp. 31-48. A useful chart on the variety of
methods and range of population estimates is provided on p. 34 ('Table 1: Population Estimates').

82. 'Estimating the Population Size', p. 34.

83. 'Estimating the Population Size', p. 44. Zorn suggests that the population
density would be between 400 and 450 persons per hectare in the Iron IIC period,
but would have dropped to about 200 to 250 during the subsequent Neo-Babylonian
and Persian periods.

84. 'The Population of Iron Age Palestine'.

various site types and functions and uses an excavated site to 'test' the various approaches to population estimates. However, since so few sites in the province of Yehud have been excavated to the degree of either Jerusalem or Tell en-Naṣbeh, the population estimate that follows is by necessity based primarily on areal analysis.

Nuancing and Interpreting the Data

Taking the Neo-Babylonian and Persian periods together, the settled area of the province of Yehud was approximately 723 dunams, with an estimated population of 18,100.[85] Broshi and Gophna suggest adding a factor of 20 per cent of the area to account for sites that were not discovered by surveys.[86] With this corrective added, the total settled area of Yehud would be 868 dunams with a maximal population of 21,700.

However, by dividing the Persian period into periods I and II, it is possible to revise these figures and arrive at a more accurate estimate of the population for each portion of the period (Table 4). A total of 9 sites dating roughly to the Persian I period have been excavated, with a maximum area of approximately 121 dunams. The 87 surveyed sites would add approximately 492 dunams for a total of 613 dunams. With the 10 per cent factor for sites missed in surveys the adjusted total is 662 dunams, allowing for a total population of 16,550. This figure itself is misleading, however, for it does not account for the considerable flux that existed within the Persian period. It is impossible to determine on the basis of the published surveys when the sites that I have dated to Persian I and Persian II were established. Further, judging from the excavated sites, many villages that may have existed in the beginning of

85. Using a population coefficient of 25 persons per dunam.

86. 'Middle Bronze Age II Palestine', p. 73. While Broshi and Gophna add the 20 per cent in area based upon the total area computed, derived both from surveys and from excavated sites, I add a corrective factor only for the surveyed sites. Further, Hoglund notes that during visits to fortress sites in 1986, he and Christoph discovered sites with Persian period remains that had not been reported in *JSG*, a fact that would confirm the necessity to adjust the total area of settlements upwards. Even though new surveys of Benjamin and Judah are more thorough than those in *JSG*, the selective nature of surveying still makes a corrective factor necessary; I have used a corrective of 10 per cent for Benjamin and 20 per cent for Judah. This is based on the relative completeness of the Benjamin survey and Ofer's suggestion of using 20 per cent for Judah, given its less comprehensive nature.

the period were abandoned by the end of the sixth century (e.g. el-Jîb, Tell el-Fûl and Bethel I). Others seem to have been settled near the beginning of the fifth century, such as Tel Goren and Ramat Raḥel. In addition, the estimated size of Jerusalem of 50 to 60 dunams, based on Shiloh's studies, is clearly not accurate until after the mission of Nehemiah, and would therefore represent Jerusalem's size only in the late fifth and early fourth centuries BCE.

With these issues in mind I propose making the following adjustments in order to approximate more accurately the total settled area of Yehud and its population. Since Bethel I, Tell el-Fûl and el-Jîb were abandoned by the end of the sixth century (and may actually have been Neo-Babylonian rather than Persian period sites), I have excluded them from the final calculations for Persian I. I estimate that the maximum size of Jerusalem for the Persian I period was 30 dunams, based in part upon the textual evidence from Nehemiah, Haggai and Zechariah 1–8, all of which point to decidedly rustic conditions for that city. Finally, I have used the correction factor of 10 per cent rather than the usual 20 per cent to reflect sites not discovered in surveys in order to account for the likelihood that some sites existing in the early years of the Persian period were abandoned by the first third of the fifth century BCE. With these adjustments, the estimated total settled area of the province would be 651 dunams, with an approximate population of 16,300 persons.

Yet even this figure may be too high. As indicated above, in his survey of the hill country of Judah, Ofer has not indicated where chronologically within the Persian period any of the sites should be placed. Nor are his data reported in a fashion that would allow a division into Persian I and II. Thus, with the Judah sites, which are themselves more numerous than those located in Benjamin, the possibility of an inflated 'settlement map' for the Persian I period is distinct. In order to compensate for this problem I suggest applying the percentage of sites from Benjamin that are clearly datable to Persian II to the sites from Judah, with the assumption that the same general conditions that led to a gradual increase in sites in Benjamin existed in Judah as well, and that a similar increase in the number of sites (and therefore population) occurred there.[87] In the territory of Benjamin 48 surveyed sites have been dis-

87. Of course it is possible that this assumption is not accurate and that the two geographic areas had different settlement trajectories. If the settlement patterns for the two tribal areas were distinctly different, it might indicate that the destruction of 587/586 BCE by the Babylonians was more severe in Benjamin and in the areas

covered dating to the Persian period. Of these, 12 (25 per cent) date to
the Persian II period, accounting for approximately 28 per cent of the
settled area from that territory. Applying these percentages to the 55
sites from Judah (excluding the fortresses), one may estimate that approximately 41 sites would have dated to the Persian I period. To
attempt a more objective estimate I have taken a stratified random sample of the Judah sites, which yields a settled area of about 239 dunams.
Added to the excavated sites (which account for 93.5 dunams in the
Persian I period) and those from Benjamin (161.5 dunams) the total
area of settled Yehud in this period would have been approximately 534
dunams; this would, in turn, allow for a population of 13,350.

Dating to the Persian II period there are 5 additional excavated[88] and
23 additional surveyed sites. This would add approximately 188 dunams
from surveyed sites and 52 dunams from excavated sites. By the end of
the fifth century, it is likely that Jerusalem would have grown to its full
size of approximately 60 occupied dunams (approximately 70 to 80
dunams would have been dedicated to the temple and administrative
complex; this, however, is considered public space rather than settled
area).

Table 4. *Settled Area in the Province of Yehud, Persian I and II*

	Persian I	Persian II
Excavated Area (in dunams)	93.5	141
Surveyed Area	400.5	591
Correction Factor	40	94
Total	534	826
Population Coefficient	×25	×25
Approximate Population	13,350	20650

This would mean, then, that Jerusalem during this period was inhabited
by a maximum of 1500 people at any given time.[89] The following totals

around Jerusalem than in the southern sector of the province.

88. This does not include, of course, the sites of Ketef Yeriho or Ain 'Arrub,
neither of which represent settlements.

89. Contrast this with Broshi's estimate of approximately 4500 persons in the
postexilic period ('Estimating the Population of Ancient Jerusalem', *BARev* [1978],
pp. 10-15 [12]). Broshi and I have arrived at a similar area for the city. The discrepancy between our population estimates comes from two factors. Broshi used

are probable, then, for the Persian II period: 685 dunams discovered in surveys (including a correction factor of 10 per cent in Benjamin and 20 per cent in Judah for sites not yet discovered), and 141[90] from excavated sites for a total of 826 dunams settled. The approximate population would be 20,650. These figures should all be considered provisional, at best. I have presented them with the conviction that some attempt to estimate the population of Yehud, however tentative, is preferable to leaving the issue unexamined.[91]

Table 5. *Area, Site Distribution, Population and Density*
in the Province of Yehud, Persian Period II (450–332 BCE)

	EN 1	EN 2	EN 3	EN 4
Size	197	155	150	125
Area %	10	8	8	6
Population	3500	3725	1700	700
Pop. %	17	18	8	3
Density	18	24	11	6
Settlements	24	18	17	8
Site %	19	14.4	13.6	6

	EN 5	EN 6	EN 7	EN 8	Totals
Size	141	246	139	790	1943
Area %	7	13	7	41	100
Population	6150	1000	3350	525	20650
Pop. %	30	5	16	3	100
Density	44	4	24	0.7	11
Settlements	36	6	14	2	125
Site%	29	5	11	2	100

the entire area (30 acres = 120 dunams) for his estimate, not accounting for public space—a factor that he has addressed in his later writing on population estimates ('The Population of Western Palestine', pp. 1-10). He also used a higher population to land ratio than I do—his being 150 people per acre (= 37.5 per dunam), as compared to my 25 people per dunam.

90. Note the following differences in size from Persian I to Persian II: Jerusalem 50-60 dunams, up from 30 dunams; Tell en-Naṣbeh (decreased from 24 dunams to 17 dunams); Tel Goren, remained Large, but reduced from 18.5 to approximately 12.5 dunams; Ramat Raḥel, increased from Small to Medium; Jericho increased from Small to Medium.

91. Milevski, e.g., considers my division of sites into Persian I and II to be 'dangerous' and concludes, 'While the population estimates provided by Blenkinsopp and Carter seem to be *prima facie* more accurate than those of Weinberg, it

Also of interest, given the figures provided in Table 4, is the distribution of the population among the major and individual environmental niches (see Table 5 and Chart 4). A look at the major environmental niches of the province shows that, not surprisingly, most of the population resided in the central hills. This area, accounting for only 22 per cent of the area of Yehud, contained 64 per cent of its population. The western slopes comprised 16 per cent of the province and held 20 per cent of the total population. Approximately 13 per cent of the population lived in the desert fringe, which accounted for 21 per cent of the area of Yehud. And the Judean desert, which represented 41 per cent of the province's area, accounted for only 3 per cent of the population of Yehud.

A look at the eight individual environmental niches reveals the following distribution. During the Persian II period, an estimated 3500 people (17 per cent of the total population) lived in EN 1, which comprises approximately 10 per cent of the total area of the province; the population density was 18 people per square kilometer (18 P/km^2). EN 2, which accounts for 8 per cent of the area of Yehud, had a population of about 3700 (18 per cent of the province's population), and a population density of 24 P/km^2. 1700 people (8 per cent of the total population) lived in EN 3, which accounts for 8 per cent of the area of Yehud; its population density was 11 P/km^2. EN 4, comprising 6 per cent of the province's area, contained only 700 people (3 per cent of the total), and had a population density of about 6 P/km^2. EN 5 was the most densely populated environmental niche of the province; approximately 6150 people (30 per cent of the total) lived in only 7 per cent of the total area of the province. Its population density was 44 P/km^2. EN 6, which accounted for approximately 13 per cent of the area of Yehud, had about 1000 inhabitants (5 per cent of the total pop-

is suggested to leave the question untouched until new information becomes available and an accurate chronology is acheived for the period' ('Settlement Patterns', p. 18). While I agree with Milevski that such periodization and population estimates are provisional, I still maintain that the proposals here further our understanding of the Persian period as a whole, and clarify its context within other archaeological periods. The certainty that Milevski waits for will not, I believe, be forthcoming without an extensive and systematic program of Persian period excavations.

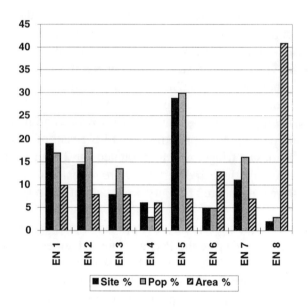

Chart 4. *Population, Site Distribution and Area in the Province*
of Yehud, Persian Period II (450–332 BCE)

ulation), and a population density of only 4 P/km^2. EN 7 was the second
most densely populated niche, with a population of 3350 (16 per cent of
the total) in 7 per cent of the area of the province, and a population density of 24 P/km^2. Finally, EN 8, the largest niche (accounting for 41 per
cent of the province's total area), had a population of approximately
550 in two sites (3 per cent of the total population); its population density was 0.7 P/km^2.

Excursus: Yehud in the Persian I Period

Given the nature of the survey data and the difficulty in attributing
surveyed sites from Judah to either Persian I or II, it was not possible in
my original study to present a detailed analysis of site distribution and
population during the Persian I period. With the stratified random
sample discussed above, it is now possible to present a provisional (but
hypothetical) analysis of site and population distribution in the first half
of the Persian period (Figure 18; Table 6). Based on these projections,
41 sites (48 per cent) were located in the biblical territory of Benjamin

and 45 sites (52 per cent) in Judah (Chart 5). Site distribution among the major environmental niches is as follows (Chart 6): 19 sites (22 per cent) were located in the western slopes, 48 (56 per cent) in the central hills, 17 (20 per cent) in the desert fringe, and 2 sites (2 per cent) were located in the Judean desert. Approximately 65 per cent of the population (8675 people) resided in the central hills, 17 per cent lived in the western slopes (2325 people), 14 per cent settled in the desert fringe (1800 inhabitants), and 4 per cent (550 people) lived in the Judean desert.

The distribution within the eight environmental niches is as follows (Table 7; Charts 7 and 8). Approximately 2075 people inhabited EN 1 (16 per cent of the total population); its density was 11 P/km^2. EN 2 was the second most densely populated area of the province, with 2600 people (20 per cent of the total), and a population density of 17 P/km^2. EN 3, the northern desert fringe, contained 1350 people (10 per cent of Yehud's population) and a population density of 9 P/km^2. EN 4, the southwestern hills, was the least populated area of the province, with a total of 250 inhabitants (2 per cent of the total population) and a density of 2 P/km^2. 4025 people settled in EN 5, the central hills, accounting for 30 per cent of the population; it had a population density of 29 P/km^2. EN 6, the southern desert fringe, had a population of 450 (3 per cent of Yehud's population) and a density of 2 P/km^2. EN 7, the southern central hills, was the third most populated area with 2050 people (15 per cent of the total) and a density of 15 P/km^2. The Judean desert, EN 8, had a population of approximately 550 people (4 per cent of the total), but a population density of only 0.7 P/km^2.

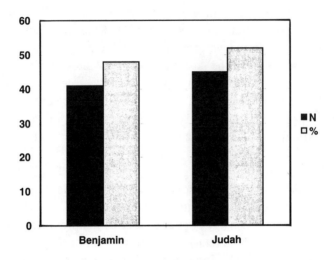

Chart 5. *Site Distribution by Biblical Territory,*
Persian Period I Yehud

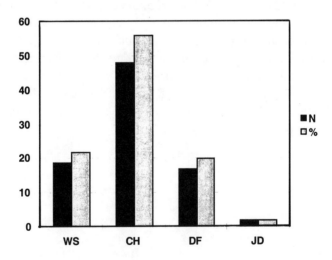

Chart 6. *Site Distribution by Major Environmental Niches,*
Persian Period I Yehud

Table 6. *Excavated and Surveyed Sites in the Province*
of Yehud, Persian Period I (Hypothetical Reconstruction)

Site Name	Coordinates	Size	Excavator/Surveyor
Benjamin			
Environmental Niche 1			
Kh. Ras el-Mughar	1619.1387	8	Feldstein and Kameisky; Kallai
Kh. el-Kafira	1620.1375	5	Feldstein and Kameisky; Eshel and Amit
Kh. el-Murran	1627.1359	8	Feldstein and Kameisky
Kh. el-Bawaya	1629.1364	3	Feldstein and Kameisky
Kh. Ein el-Keniseh	1646.1369	2	Feldstein and Kameisky
Mevasseret Zion	1652.1339	S	Stern
Kh. Beit Mizza	1652.1349	4	Feldstein and Kameisky
Unnamed 2	1667.1361	2	Feldstein and Kameisky
Unnamed 3	1667.1368	3	Feldstein and Kameisky
Kh. el-'Alawina	1675.1354	3	Milevski; Feldstein and Kameisky
Unnamed 4	1677.1351	11	Feldstein and Kameisky
Beit 'Ur el-Tahta	1582.1446	10	Finkelstein
Beit 'Ur el-Fauqa	1608.1436	5	Finkelstein; Feldstein and Kameisky
Kh. Badd Abu Mu'ammar	1645.1403	1	Feldstein and Kameisky
Kh. el-Jufeir	1653.1411	S	Feldstein and Kameisky; Kallai
Kh. el-Latatin	1660.1418	S	Finkelstein; Kallai
Environmental Niche 2			
Unnamed 5	1657.1378	2	Feldstein and Kameisky
Kh. Abu Leimun	1661.1370	6	Feldstein and Kameisky
Unnamed 6	1666.1416	6	Feldstein and Kameisky
Kh. 'Id	1675.1402	6	Feldstein and Kameisky
Judeira	1688.1406	S	Feldstein and Kameisky
Ras et-Tahuneh (S)	1702.1462	S	Kallai
Tell en-Nasṣbeh	1706.1436	17	Badè; McCown; Zorn
Kh. er-Ras (W)	1709.1354	S	Onn and Rapuano
Kh. Nisieh	1717.1449	5	Feldstein and Kameisky
Unnamed 8	1720.1429	1	Feldstein and Kameisky
er-Ram	1721.1402	10	Feldstein and Kameisky
Jerusalem	1728.1313	30	Kenyon; Shiloh
Ketef Hinnom	1714.1307	T	Barkay
Mamilla	1714.1313	T	Reich

Site Name	Coordinates	Size	Excavator/Surveyor
Environmental Niche 3			
Ḥorvat Zimri	1738.1363	VS	Gibson; Nadelman
Unnamed 9	1743.1343	VS	Gibson
Wadi Salim	1743.1344	4	
Ras Abu Subeitan	1748.1321	4	Dinur and Feig
Kh. Herabat ʿAudeh	1749.1340	3	Dinur and Feig
ʿAnata	1749.1356	S	Gibson
Unnamed 10	1750.1389	VS	Dinur and Feig
Ras Tumeim	1754.1382	S	Dinur
Jurrat es-Saqqawi	1756.1398	VS	Dinur and Feig
Kh. Deir es-Sidd	1762.1353	S	Dinur and Feig; Biran
Unnamed 11	1780.1344	VS	Dinur and Feig
Kh. el-Hara el-Fauqa and Mukhmas	1763.1424	16	Feldstein and Kameisky
Unnamed 12	1767.1422	T	Feldstein and Kameisky
Tell el-ʿAskar	1767.1430	4	Feldstein and Kameisky
Judah			
Environmental Niche 4			
Kh. el-Kabarah	1607.1215	S	Kokhavi
Husan	1627.1244	S	Kokhavi
Kh. el-Yahudi	1628.1264	VS	Kokhavi
Environmental Niche 5			
Kh. Judur	1588.1156	14	Kokhavi; Ofer
Beit Ummar	1598.1143	13	Ofer
Kh. Kufin	1609.1143	6	Ofer
Deir Shaʿar	1619.1170	11	Ofer
Kh. el-Keren	1620.1140	6	Ofer
Suweir	1625.1172	1	Ofer
Kh. Umm et-Talʿah	1630.1160	5.8	Ofer
Rujm es-Sebit	1636.1178	2	Ofer
Kh. Bericuth	1637.1168	15	Ofer
Kh. Peʿor/Kh. Zakandah	1640.1193	22	Ofer; Kochavi
Kh. Shanah	1642.1144	2	Ofer
Salmuneh	1655.1172	1	Ofer
Marsiyaʿ	1661.1187	1	Ofer
Shemʿah	1665.1181	1	Ofer
Halil Ismaʿel	1674.1175	3	Ofer
Ras el-Kebir	1674.1237	5	Ofer
Wadi ʿArrub	1675.1135	2.4	Ofer

Site Name	Coordinates	Size	Excavator/Surveyor
Kh. Merah ej-Jumeia'	1642.1217	3	Ofer
Kh. Abu Shaven	1646.1263	9	Ofer
Kh. Gharab	1647.1212	4	Ofer
Rujm el-Khadar	1647.1235	1	Kokhavi; Ofer
Neimar	1665.1229	3	Ofer
Kh. el-Khwakh	1671.1214	5	Kokhavi; Ofer
Kh. er-Ras (S)	1671.1282	3	Kloner
Bethlehem	1698.1235	4	Ofer
Ramat Raḥel	1706.1274	S	Aharoni; Kloner

Environmental Niche 6

Kh. 'Arabieh	1658.1042	2	Ofer
Kh. Za'aphran	1672.1102	4	Ofer
Beidah	1683.1194	3	Ofer
Kh. Sib'ah	1695.1185	6	Ofer

Environmental Niche 7

Kh. et-Tayyibeh	1531.1072	18	Kokhavi; Ofer
Taffuh	1545.1052	12	Kokhavi; Ofer
Kh. Dahdah	1590.1074	4	Ofer
Kh. et-Tubeiqah (Beth Zur)	1590.1108	2	Sellers; P. Lapp and N. Lapp; Ofer
Gebel Namra	1598.1048	3	Ofer
Halhul	1603.1095	11.4	Ofer
Kh. Beit 'Anun	1621.1078	4	Ofer
Kh. el-'Udiseh	1632.1064	3	Kokhavi; Ofer
Rujm el-Qesar	1664.1092	1	Ofer
Kh. Zawiyye	1652.1122	8	Ofer

Environmental Niche 8

Tel Goren	1863.0960	L	Mazar
Jericho	1908.1424	S	Sellin and Watzinger; Kenyon

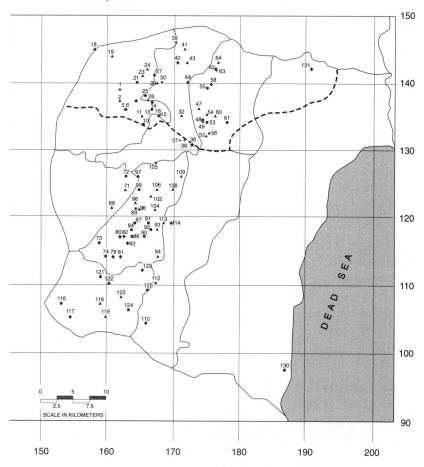

Figure 18. *Site Distribution in the Province of Yehud, Persian Period I
(Hypothetical Reconstruction)*

Table 7. *Area, Site Distribution, Population and Density
in the Province of Yehud, Persian Period I (538–450 BCE)*[92]

	EN 1	EN 2	EN 3	EN 4
Size	197	155	150	125
Area %	10	8	8	6
Population	2075	2600	1350	250
Pop. %	16	20	10	2
Density	11	17	9	2
Settlements	16	12	13	3
Site %	19	14	15	3

	EN 5	EN 6	EN 7	EN 8	Totals
Size	141	246	139	790	1943
Area %	7	13	7	41	100
Population	4025	450	2050	550	13,350
Pop. %	30	3	15	4	100
Density	29	2	15	0.7	7[93]
Settlements	26	4	10	2	86
Site %	30	5	12	2	100

92. The figures for the Persian I period are based on projections from a stratified random sample of surveyed sites in the tribal territory of Judah (EN 4-7) and the excavated sites that date to this period. The percentage of sites used for this sample was based upon the percentage of surveyed sites in the tribal area of Benjamin that date to the Persian I period.

93. This figure represents the average population density for the entire province of Yehud.

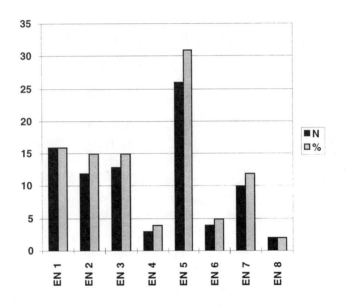

Chart 7. *Site Distribution by Individual Environmental Niches,*
Persian Period I Yehud

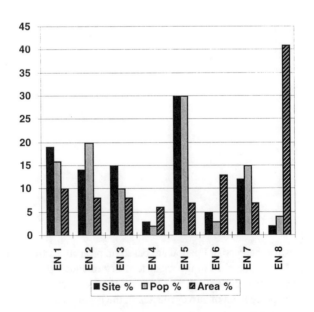

Chart 8. *Population, Site Distribution, and Area*
by Environmental Niches, Persian Period I Yehud (538–450 BCE)

Conclusion

These figures provide the basis for a new analysis of the social setting of the province of Yehud during the Persian period. Numerous questions, however, remain. How well do these projections of site distribution and population fit with previous estimates—from Albright's to Weinberg's—of the nature and status of Yehud? What do the data suggest about relative continuity from the Iron II through the Hellenistic periods? How do the site distribution, site size and population figures vary from one environmental niche to another?

Do these variations suggest anything about the social structure of the province? These questions are the subject of the next chapter and are foundational to one's larger understanding of the social, literary and religious history of Yehud, to which the final chapter of this work is dedicated.

Chapter 5

YEHUD IN THE PERSIAN PERIOD:
CONTINUITY AND CONTEXT

In his study based upon the *JSG* survey of 1967 and the scant information on excavations, Kenneth Hoglund suggests that the province of
Yehud was comprised primarily of small, unwalled villages. It formed a
village-based, agrarian economy subject to imperial needs, and showed
a marked distinction from the settlement pattern of the Iron II period.[1]
He observes that in the territory of Judah there was a 25 per cent increase in the number of sites and that this increase reflects an imperial
policy of ruralization that stands in stark contrast with the settlement
patterns in other areas of the empire and even in Palestine. In the
Judean desert and the hill country of Benjamin, one finds a 'dramatic
and pervasive drop in the number of settlements'; this demonstrates a
policy of depopulation and/or urbanization.[2] In the Judean desert, for
example, the number of sites dropped from 27 to 2 (a 93 per cent decline). The territory of Benjamin had a less precipitous drop, but significant nonetheless, from 51 to 15 sites (a drop of 71 per cent). Hoglund
notes that only 65 per cent of the Persian period sites in Judah had a
prior Iron II occupation and that 24 per cent were established in the Persian period. Taken together, Hoglund maintains, these figures demonstrate that many of the returnees formed new settlements instead of
returning to 'ancestral lands', and thus undermine the widely held
notion of a protracted conflict between those returning from Babylon
and those who had remained in Judah. Both, he contends, were 'reorganized' according to Imperial concerns. He concludes: *The presump-
tion of a class struggle between exiles and "remainees" over land rights*

1. Hoglund, 'The Achaemenid Context', pp. 54-72.
2. 'The Achaemenid Context', pp. 57-58. Note that the computations that follow are based upon his Figure 1, 'Comparative Numbers of Settlements in Traditional Regions of Eretz-Israel'.

does not fit the evidence of the pattern of these Persian period villages.[3]

The new excavation and survey data call for an analysis of this general portrait. Certainly nothing in the new data calls into question the notion that the province was comprised primarily of small, unwalled villages. With the exception of Jerusalem from the mid-fifth century and perhaps Tell en-Naṣbeh and Ramat Raḥel, there appear to be no other walled settlements in Yehud during the Persian period.[4] The number of sites that can be dated to the Persian period has increased markedly since Hoglund's study with the advent of the new excavations and surveys, and in fact has increased significantly since I completed my initial study on Yehud in 1991. One can, in fact, expect a *continued increase* in projections of the site distribution and population of the province as new archaeological research is conducted. What this means is that the presentation below, while accurate in terms of general site distribution and population estimates, will be dated within as little as three to five years. Despite that volatility, it is still possible to discuss several important features of both population and site distribution; many of these features will, I believe, remain accurate as a pattern even as the specifics fluctuate.

In the analysis in Chapters 3 and 4, I proposed a site hierarchy that was divided into five categories from Very Small to Very Large as follows: Very Small sites are those between 0.1 and 2.0 dunams, with a population of up to 50 persons; Small sites ranged between 2.1 and 5.0 dunams, with a population between 51 and 125; Medium sites are those with a size of 5.1 to 12 dunams and a population that ranged between 126 to 300 persons; Large sites ranged between 12.1 and 25 dunams, with a corresponding population of 301 to 625. Very Large sites are those larger than 25.1 dunams and a population of more than 625.[5]

3.   'The Achaemenid Context', pp. 59-60.

4.   The only site that has clear evidence of being walled is Jerusalem. It is likely that during the Neo-Babylonian period Tell en-Naṣbeh re-used the Iron II walls when it served as a Babylonian capital for the province and similarly likely that during the later Persian period those walls fell out of use. During this time some buildings appear to be constructed over the Iron II wall. Ramat Raḥel similarly lacks evidence of external walls, but I identify it as possibly being walled since both Y. Aharoni and G. Barkay deem it to be an important site, perhaps a fortified settlement. However, as I pointed out in Chapter 3, this view is based on an *a priori* belief in the importance of the site rather than on the archaeological evidence itself.

5.   The median size and corresponding populations for each category (which I

Among the settlements in the province of Yehud, only Jerusalem reached a size of Very Large; it is quite possible that it reached that size only in the latter half of the Persian I period or the beginning of the Persian II period. These data alone suggest that the population range for villages and towns in the province of Yehud was quite small during the Persian period, a conclusion that is not at all surprising given the socio-political context within Syria-Palestine in the sixth through fourth centuries BCE. This conclusion is even more striking when one analyzes the province as a whole and its environmental niches according to the relative size of the villages.

Site Distribution by Size Hierarchy in the Persian I Period

In the early Persian period, as reconstructed through the stratified random sample outlined in Chapter 4, 21 of the 86 sites were Very Small, 37 were Small, 18 were Medium, and 9 were Large. Only Jerusalem could be identified as Very Large (Table 8[6]).

Table 8. *Relative Site Size during the Persian Period I*

Size	VS	S	M	L	VL	N
Number	21	37	18	9	1	86
Percent	24	43	21	10.5	1	99.5

This means that only 11.5 per cent of the villages had a population of over 465 persons. Twenty-four per cent of the settlements had a population of 50 or less, 67 per cent had a population of 125 or less, and 88 per cent had a population of up to 300 persons. Thus, during the initial part of the Persian period, it would appear that Hoglund is quite correct

used in computing the population for those sites that could not be identified to an approximate size in metric dunams are as follows: VS, 1.5 dunams, population: 37.5; S, 3.5, population: 87.5; M, 8.5, population: 212.5; and L, 18.5, population: 462.5. These raw numbers were then rounded up to the nearest whole number in the population estimates.

6.   The following abbreviations are used in the tables in the rest of the chapter: N refers to the number of sites (or total percentage) in a particular environmental niche or biblical 'tribal' territory. Percent (Y) refers to the percentage of sites in Yehud, Percent (B) to the percentage of sites in the 'tribal' territory of Benjamin, and Percent (J) to the percentage of sites in the 'tribal' territory of Judah. When the four major environmental niches are compared, they are abbreviated as WS (Western Slopes), CH (Central Hills), DF (Desert Fringe), and JD (Judean Desert).

in identifying the economy as village-based, comprised of numerous farmsteads that are associated with small villages. The picture within the two former 'tribal' territories of Benjamin and Judah is very similar (Table 9), with each having a majority of sites that are Very Small, Small or Medium (Benjamin, 95 per cent; Judah, 82 per cent). The major difference between them is in the number of Large sites: Benjamin contained only two sites larger than 12.1 dunams (5 per cent of its 41 sites) whereas Judah contained nearly four times that number of sites, accounting for 16 per cent of its 45 sites.

Table 9. *Relative Site Size by Biblical Territory, Persian Period I*

	Benjamin					
Size	VS	S	M	L	VL	N
Number	10	20	9	2	0	41
Percent (Y)	12	23	10	2	0	47
Percent (B)	26	49	22	5	0	100

	Judah					
Size	VS	S	M	L	VL	N
Number	11	17	9	7	1	45
Percent (Y)	13	20	10	8	1	52
Percent (J)	24	38	20	16	2	100

Within the major environmental niches (Table 10), the western slopes contained four Very Small sites, ten Small sites and five Medium sites. Seven of the nine Large sites of the Persian I period were located in the central hills. That environmental niche also contained 10 Very Small sites, 18 Small sites, 12 Medium sites, and the province's only Very Large site. In desert fringe, the majority of the sites were Very Small (seven) or Small (eight) added to one Medium and one Large site. The two sites in the Judean desert, En-Gedi and Jericho, were Large and Small respectively. Also significant is the relative percentage of sites within each niche (Table 10): 21 per cent of the sites in the western slopes were Very Small, 53 per cent of the sites were Small, and 26 per cent of the sites were Medium. In the central hills, 21 per cent of the sites were Very Small, 37.5 per cent were Small, 25 per cent were Medium, 14.5 per cent were Large, and 2 per cent were Very Large. 41 per cent of the sites in the desert fringe were Very Small, 47 per cent were Small, and 12 per cent Medium (six per cent) or Large (six per cent).

Table 10. *Relative Site Size by Major Environmental Niches,*
Persian Period I

	VS	S	M	L	VL	N
			Number			
Size	VS	S	M	L	VL	N
WS	4	10	5	0	0	19
CH	10	18	12	7	1	48
DF	7	8	1	1	0	17
JD	0	1	0	1	0	2
N	21	37	18	9	1	86
			% in EN			
WS	21	53	26	0	0	100
CH	21	37.5	25	14.5	2	100
DF	41	47	6	6	0	100
JD	0	50	0	50	0	100
			% in Yehud			
WS	19	27	28	0	0	
CH	48	48.5	66.6	78	100	
DF	33	21.5	5.5	11	0	
JD	0	3	0	11	0	
N	100	100	100.1	100	100	

The breakdown of the sites by size within Yehud is also important. Of the 21 Very Small sites, 4 (19 per cent) were located in the western slopes, 10 (48 per cent) were located in the central hills, and 7 (33 per cent) were located in the desert fringe. Ten of the 37 Small sites (27 per cent) were located in the western slopes, 18 (48.5 per cent) were located in the central hills, 8 (21.5 per cent) were located in the desert fringe, and 1 (3 per cent) was located in the Judean desert. There were 18 Medium sized sites in the province of Yehud during the Persian I period. Of these, 5 (28 per cent) were located in the western slopes, 12 (66.6 per cent) in the central hills, and 1 (5.5 per cent) in the desert fringe. There were no Large sites in the western slopes during the Persian I period. The desert fringe and the Judean desert each contained one of the nine Large sites (11 per cent each). The remaining eight Large sites (78 per cent) were located in the central hills.

Table 11. *Relative Site Size by Individual Environmental Niches,*
Persian Period I

Number	VS	S	M	L	VL	N
EN 1	3	8	5	0	0	16
EN 2	1	5	4	1	1	12
EN 3	6	6	0	1	0	13
EN 4	1	2	0	0	0	3
EN 5	7	10	5	4	0	26
EN 6	1	2	1	0	0	4
EN 7	2	3	3	2	0	10
EN 8	0	1	0	1	0	2
N	21	37	18	9	1	86

% in EN

Number	VS	S	M	L	VL	N
EN 1	19	50	31	0	0	100
EN 2	8	42	33	8	8	100
EN 3	46	46	0	8	0	100
EN 4	33	67	0	0	0	100
EN 5	27	38	19	15	0	99
EN 6	25	50	25	0	0	100
EN 7	20	30	30	20	0	100
EN 8	0	50	0	50	0	100

% in Yehud

Number	VS	S	M	L	VL
EN 1	14	22	28	0	0
EN 2	5	14	22	11	100
EN 3	29	16	0	11	0
EN 4	5	5	0	0	0
EN 5	33	27	28	44	0
EN 6	5	5	5.5	0	0
EN 7	9.5	8	16.6	22	0
EN 8	0	3	0	11	0
N	100.5	100	100.1	99	100

Table 11 analyzes site size by the eight individual environmental niches. A few observations are in order. The largest percentages of Very Small sites within the province were located in the northern desert fringe (EN 3, 29 per cent) and the heart of the central hills (EN 5, 33 per cent). The other niches contained between one and three Very Small sites, with the exception of the Judean desert. The Small sites were spread fairly evenly throughout the northern sector of the province, with the north central hills containing 5 sites (14 per cent), the northern desert fringe containing 6 sites (16 per cent) and the northwestern slopes containing eight sites (22 per cent). Together, these three niches contained just over half of the Small sites of the province (52 per cent). Ten small sites (27 per cent) were located in the central hills between Jerusalem and just north of the Hebron Hills. A similar pattern existed for the Medium sites. Nine of the 18 sites (50 per cent) were located in the northern section of the western hills (EN 1; 5 sites, 28 per cent) and the northern central hills (EN 2; 4 sites, 22 per cent). Five were located in the central hills (EN 5, 28 per cent). The southern desert fringe contained only one Medium site (EN 6, 5.5 per cent) and the southern central hills contained three sites of the Medium range (EN 7, 16.6 per cent). The highest percentage of the Large sites were located in the central hills (EN 5, 4 sites accounting for 44 per cent of the total), with the southern central hills (EN 7) containing two sites (22 per cent of the total number of Large sites). The northern central hills (EN 2), the northern desert fringe (EN 3) and the Judean desert (EN 8) account for the three remaining Large sites (11 per cent each). Thus, just as the highest percentage of sites is concentrated in the central hills (ENs 2, 5 and 7), the northern sector of the province (EN 1-3) accounts for nearly half of the sites (48 per cent). But of those 41 sites, fully 29 (70 per cent) were Very Small (10 sites, 24 per cent) or small (19 sites, or 46 per cent) and had a maximum population of 125 persons.

Site Distribution by Size Hierarchy in the Persian II Period

As one would expect, the size and number of sites in the province of Yehud increased substantially from the middle of the fifth century through the end of the Persian period. Of the 125 inhabited settlements (Table 12), 33 (26 per cent) were Very Small, 48 (38 per cent) were Small, 31 (25 per cent) were Medium, 12 were Large (10 per cent) and only 1, Jerusalem, was Very Large.

Table 12. *Relative Site Size in Yehud*
during the Persian Period II

Size	VS	S	M	L	VL	N
Number	33	48	31	12	1	125
Percent	26	38	25	10	1	100

This means that the majority of the sites (112, or nearly 90 per cent) were less than 12.0 dunams in size and had a population of less than 300 persons. Nearly two-thirds (64 per cent) of the villages in Yehud were less than 5.0 dunams, with populations up to 125, and just over one-fourth (26 per cent) ranged between 0.1 and 2.0 dunams, with populations less than 50 persons.

The breakdown of the site size according to the biblical territories that comprised the province reflects similar patterns (Table 13).

Table 13. *Relative Site Size by Biblical Territory, Persian Period II*

Benjamin

Size	VS	S	M	L	VL	N
Number	15	28	13	3	0	59
Percent (Y)	12	22	10	2	0	47
Percent (B)	25	47	22	5	0	99

Judah

Size	VS	S	M	L	VL	N
Number	18	20	18	9	1	66
Percent (Y)	14	16	14	7	1	53
Percent (J)	27	30	27	14	2	100

As in the Persian I period, each has a majority of sites that are Very Small, Small or Medium (95 per cent in Benjamin, 84 per cent in Judah). The differences in the relative percentage of the site sizes within the biblical territories are equally important. The number of Very Small and Small sites in each territory is very similar, with Judah containing a total of 38 Very Small or Small sites, and Benjamin containing 43 (three fewer Very Small sites, but eight more Small sites). Those numbers account for 25 per cent (Very Small) and 47 per cent (Small) of the sites within the territory of Benjamin and 27 per cent and 30 per cent of the sites in the territory of Judah. So, while the raw numbers of Very Small and Small sites differ by merely five sites, the percentages differ by 15 percentage points. Further, while both Benjamin and Judah have more small sites than any other category (28 and 20 respectively, Judah has a much higher number of Medium sized sites than does Benjamin (18 and 13 respectively, accounting for 27 per cent and 22 per cent of the sites in each territory). Finally, Judah has three times the number of large sites as Benjamin (nine in Judah, three in Benjamin) accounting for 14 per cent and 5 per cent of each territory's settlements. *Seventy-*

five per cent of the towns with populations over 300 were located in the biblical territory of Judah.

The major environmental niches reflect changes similar to those reflected in the biblical territories (Table 14).

Table 14. *Relative Site Size by Major Environmental Niches, Persian Period II*

Size	VS	S	M	L	VL	N
WS	10	12	9	1	0	32
CH	17	22	20	8	1	68
DF	6	14	1	2	0	23
JD	0	0	1	1	0	2
N	33	48	31	12	1	125
			% in EN			
WS	31	38	28	3	0	100
CH	25	32	29	12	1	99
DF	26	61	4	9	0	100
JD	0	0	50	50	0	100
			% in Yehud			
WS	30	25	29	8	0	
CH	52	46	65	67	100	
DF	18	29	3	17	0	
JD	0	0	3	8	0	
N	100	100	100	100	100	

The western slopes contained only one Large site, accounting for eight per cent of the Large sites in the province and three per cent of the sites in the niche. A full 97 per cent of the sites in this niche ranged between 0.1 and 12.0 dunams in size. Ten of the 32 sites were Very Small (30 per cent of the Very Small sites in the province and 31 per cent of the sites in the niche). Twelve settlements were small (25 per cent of the Small sites in the province and 38 per cent of the sites in the niche), and nine were medium (29 per cent of the Medium sites in the province and 28 per cent of the sites in the niche). The central hills contained the only Very Large site of the province, and accounted for 8 of the 12 Large sites within Yehud (67 per cent of the Large sites, and 12 per cent of the sites in the niche). One-third of the remaining 59 settlements in the central hills were Medium (29 per cent of the settlements in the niche, and 65 per cent of the Medium sites in the province).

The majority of the Small sites were located in the central hills: the niche contained 22 of the 48 Small sites (46 per cent), which accounted for 32 per cent of the niche's villages and towns. Eighty-seven per cent of the desert fringe's 23 settlements were Very Small (26 per cent) or Small (61 per cent). This niche accounted for 18 per cent of the Very Small sites and 29 per cent of the Small settlements in Yehud. The desert fringe contained only one Medium sized site (4 per cent of the sites in the niche, and 3 per cent of the Medium sites in the province) and two Large sites (17 per cent of the Large sites in Yehud, and 9 per cent of the niche's settlements). The Judean desert held two settlements in the Persian II period: one Medium site, Jericho (3 per cent of the Medium-sized sites in Yehud) and one Large site, En-Gedi (8 per cent of the Large sites in the province).

An examination of the distribution of the sites by size in the individual environmental niches (Table 15) shows that the northwestern slopes (EN 1) and the central hills (EN 5) contained the highest concentration of sites (19 per cent and 29 per cent respectively). While it is expected that the central hills would contain the highest percentage of the various site sizes, an examination of the other environmental niches provides some surprising conclusions. The three niches with the highest concentration of Very Small sites are the central hills (EN 5, 30 per cent), the northwestern slopes (EN 1, 18 per cent), and the northern desert fringe (EN 3, 15 per cent). The majority of the Small sites were located in the northwestern slopes (19 per cent), the north central hills (EN 2, 17 per cent), the northern desert fringe (23 per cent) and the central hills (23 per cent). The southwestern slopes (EN 4), southern desert fringe (EN 6) and the south central hills (EN 7) each contained six per cent of the Small settlements. The Medium sites were concentrated in the central hills (35 per cent) and the northwestern slopes (26 per cent). Only the northern desert fringe did not contain any Medium sites. The other Medium sites were spread evenly over the northern and southern central hills (13 per cent and 16 per cent respectively) and the southwestern slopes, southern desert fringe and Judean desert (3 per cent each). The highest concentrations of Large sites were in the central hills (33 per cent) and southern central hills (25 per cent), accounting for nearly 60 per cent of the Large sites. The southwestern slopes did not contain any Large sites, and the remaining five environmental niches each contained one site larger than 12.1 dunams.

Table 15. *Site Size by Individual*
Environmental Niches, Persian Period II

Number	VS	S	M	L	VL	N
EN 1	6	9	8	1	0	24
EN 2	4	8	4	1	1	18
EN 3	5	11	0	1	0	17
EN 4	4	3	1	0	0	8
EN 5	10	11	11	4	0	36
EN 6	1	3	1	1	0	6
EN 7	3	3	5	3	0	14
EN 8	0	0	1	1	0	2
N	33	48	31	12	1	125
			% in EN			
EN 1	25	38	33	4	0	100
EN 2	22	44	22	6	6	100
EN 3	29	65	0	6	0	100
EN 4	50	37.5	12.5	0	0	100
EN 5	28	31	31	11	0	101
EN 6	17	50	17	17	0	101
EN 7	21	21	36	21	0	99
EN 8	0	0	50	50	0	100
			% in Yehud			
EN 1	18	19	26	8.5	0	
EN 2	12	17	13	8.5	100	
EN 3	15	23	0	8.5	0	
EN 4	12	6	3	0	0	
EN 5	30	23	35	33	0	
EN 6	3	6	3	8.5	0	
EN 7	9	6	16	25	0	
EN 8	0	0	3	8.5	0	
N	99	100	99	100.5	100	

Changes in Population and Site Distribution during the Persian Period

In the previous chapters I delineated the means by which I differentiated between Persian I and Persian II sites. While some may question
this distinction, I have attempted it in order to be able to speak more
definitively about the shifts in both site distribution and population that
inevitably occur over time in any inhabited area. Few would deny that
the population in the province of Yehud increased during the Persian

period as a whole. It was a period of relative stability, despite the growing Greek threat that may have led to an increase in fortifications and to an elevation of the status of Jerusalem among other cities in Syria-Palestine. Yet this observation is too general to allow a definitive analysis of the social structure within Yehud or the sociopolitical context in which the province existed.

Inasmuch as the two previous sections of this chapter have analyzed the relative size of the settlements in the province during the Persian I and II periods, it is now appropriate to assess the changes that occurred during the period as a whole. In the province as a whole, the number of sites increased from 86 to 125 (an increase of 45 per cent) and the population grew by 55 per cent, from 13,350 to 20,650. Within the biblical territories that comprised the province (Table 16; Chart 9), the number of sites in Benjamin increased from 41 to 59 (44 per cent), and the population grew from 5375 to 7625 (42 per cent). Similar patterns are evident in the territory of Judah, where the number of sites increased from 45 to 66 (47 per cent) and the population increased by 63 per cent, from 7975 to 13,025.

Examining the site distribution in the major environmental niches, one finds the most dramatic increase in the western slopes (Table 17; Chart 10). There, the number of settlements rose by 13, from 19 to 32 (a 68 per cent growth). While the central hill region (EN 2, 5 and 7) saw a larger increase in the number of sites (a rise of 20, from 48 to 68), the relative increase was only 42 per cent. The desert fringe saw a growth of 35 per cent, increasing from 17 to 23 settlements. An analysis of the growth in the individual environmental niches shows the following patterns (Table 18, Chart 11). The average increase in the number of sites among the eight niches was five, with a range between zero (in the Judean desert) and ten (in the central hills, EN 5). However, the relative the relative percentage of growth varied considerably. The most significant increase was in the southwestern slopes where the number of sites increased by 167 per cent, from 3 to 8 settlements. EN 1, 2 and 6 each showed a growth of 50 per cent, while the northern desert fringe and southern central hills grew by 31 per cent and 40 per cent respectively. The central hills (EN 5), which had the most site-density in both the Persian I and Persian II periods, increased by 38 per cent, from 26 to 36 settlements.

Table 16. *Increases in Site Distribution and Population
by Biblical Territory, Persian I–Persian II*

	Persian I	Persian II	% Increase
Benjamin			
Sites	41	59	44
Population	5375	7625	42
Judah			
Sites	45	66	47
Population	7975	13025	63

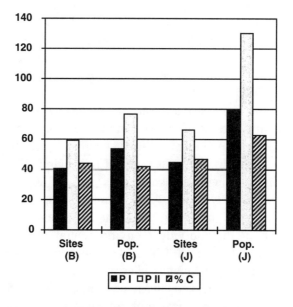

Chart 9. *Increases in Site Distribution and Population
by Biblical Territory, Persian I-Persian II*[7]

As noted above, the population of Yehud grew by 55 per cent during
the Persian period, from approximately 13,350 toward the end of the
sixth century and beginning of the fifth century, to about 20,650 by the
second half of the fourth century. The most marked growth occurred in

7.   Population figures in Charts 9, 12 and 13 are represented in multiples of
100, in order to allow a consistent graphic representation.

the western slopes (Table 19, Chart 12), which increased by 81 per cent, from 2325 to 4200. The desert fringe and central spur grew by similar percentages (50 and 52 per cent respectively), but by very different numbers. Population in the desert fringe increased from 1800 persons in the Persian I period to 2700 in the Persian II period. The population of the central spur grew from 8675 to 13,225. *Thus, in the Persian II period, the population of the central spur of the province of Yehud nearly equaled that of the entire province in the previous period.* The only niche to demonstrate a decline in population was that of the Judean desert, where a five per cent decrease occurred.

Table 17. *Increase in Site Distribution by Major Environmental Niches, Persian I–Persian II*

	Persian I	Persian II	% Increase
WS	19	32	68
CH	48	68	42
DF	17	23	35
JD	2	2	0

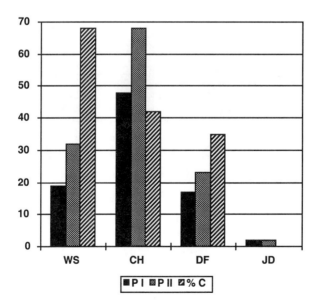

Chart 10. *Increase in Site Distribution by Major Environmental Niches, Persian I–Persian II*

Table 18. *Increase in Site Distribution by Individual*
Environmental Niches, Persian I–Persian II

	Persian I	Persian II	% Increase
EN 1	16	24	50
EN 2	12	18	50
EN 3	13	17	31
EN 4	3	8	167
EN 5	26	36	38
EN 6	4	6	50
EN 7	10	14	40
EN 8	2	2	0
TOTAL	86	125	45

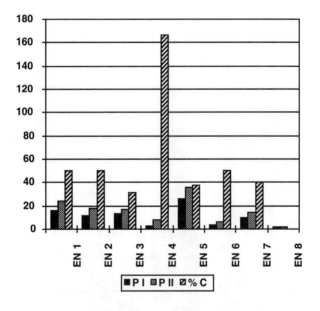

Chart 11. *Increase in Site Distribution by Individual*
Environmental Niches, Persian I–Persian II

Table 19. *Changes in Population by Major*
Environmental Niches, Persian I–Persian II

	Persian I	Persian II	% Change
WS	2325	4200	81
CH	8675	13225	52
DF	1800	2700	50
JD	550	525	-5
N	13350	20650	55

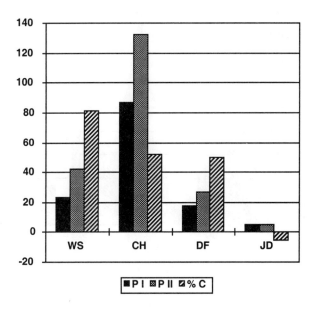

Chart 12. *Population Change by Major Environmental*
Niches, Persian I–Persian II

Table 20. *Change in Population by Individual*
Environmental Niches, Persian I–Persian II

	Persian I	*Persian II*	*% Change*
EN 1	2075	3500	69
EN 2	2600	3725	43
EN 3	1350	1700	26
EN 4	250	700	180
EN 5	4025	6150	53
EN 6	450	1000	122
EN 7	2050	3350	63
EN 8	550	525	-5
Total	13350	20650	55

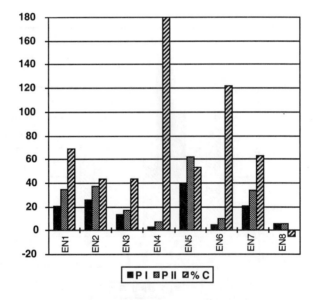

Chart 13. *Population Change by Individual*
Environmental Niches, Persian I–Persian II

Among the individual environmental niches (Table 20, Chart 13), the most marked growth was in the southwestern slopes, which increased by 180 per cent (from 250 to 700 persons). The next largest relative growth was in the southern desert fringe, which increased by 122 per cent, from approximately 450 to about 1000 persons. The northwestern slopes increased by 69 per cent, from 2075 to 3500 persons. Two niches, the central hills in the vicinity of the Jerusalem Saddle and the southern central hills around Hebron grew by more than 50 per cent. In the central hills population increased by 53 per cent, from 4025 to about 6150; population in the southern central hills grew by an even larger percentage, from 2050 to approximately 3350 (a 63 per cent rise). Growth in the other niches was more moderate, ranging from 26 per cent in the northern desert fringe to 43 per cent in the northern central hills.

The final area of comparison involves the relative site size of the settlements during the Persian period (Table 21, Chart 14). Generally speaking, one might expect a growth in the size of villages and towns that parallels the increases in both site distribution and population. What one finds does, in fact, follow the expected pattern, but with a higher rate of growth among Very Small sites and Medium sites than among Small and Large sites. Medium sites increased by 72 per cent, from 18 to 31; the number of Very Small sites grew from 21 to 33, an increase of 57 per cent. The number of small sites grew by 11, from 37 to 48, a rise of 30 per cent. What is interesting about these statistics is that in each of these categories, the number of villages increased almost equally (by 12 among Very Small sites, 13 among the Medium sized sites, and 11 among the Small sites), but by distinctively different percentages. There were only three more Large sites in the Persian II period than in the previous period. Taken together, this suggests a steady growth in the size of the sites during the two centuries of Persian rule. It is not surprising that the percentage of Medium sites grew the most throughout the period, nor that the percentage of Very Small sites showed the next most significant rise. In a period in which many new sites were established—some of which were mere farmstands and outposts—one would expect a rapid increase in the number of Very Small settlements. Similarly, one would expect that a significant number of the Small sites would increase in size from the Persian I to the Persian II period, given the relative state of continuity that imperial control imposed on the region. Within the province as a whole, the most significant growth among the Very Small sites occurred in the western slopes (Table 22). In the northern sector of that niche (EN 1), the number of Very Small sites grew from three to six (a 100 per cent rise); in the southern sector of that niche (EN 4), the number of sites grew from one to four (a 300 per cent increase). The same pattern of growth occurred in EN 2 (from one to four Very Small sites, and a 300 per cent rise).

Table 21. *Increase in Relative Site Size, Persian I–Persian II*

	Persian I	Persian II	% Increase
VS	21	33	57
S	37	48	30
M	18	31	72
L	9	12	33
VL	1	1	0

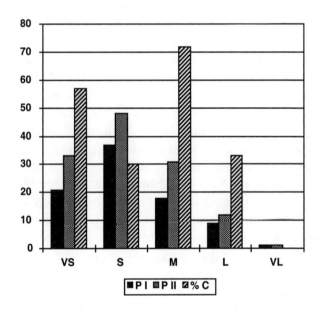

Chart 14. *Increase in Relative Site Size, Persian I–Persian II*

The most significant growth among the Small sites occurred in the north central hills (EN 2) which increased by 60 per cent, from five to eight sites and the northern desert fringe, which increased from six to eleven sites (an 83 per cent rise). In that niche, the number of Very Small sites actually decreased in the Persian II period, from six to five, a drop of 17 per cent. Among the Medium sites, the most growth occurred in the northwestern slopes, the central hills, and the southern central hills, which grew by 60 per cent, 120 per cent and 67 per cent, respectively. The number of Large sites remained relatively constant in most areas, increased from zero to one in both the northwestern slopes and the southern desert fringe. Overall, the most stable environmental

Table 22. *Changes in Relative Site Size by Individual*
Environmental Niches, Persian I–Persian II[8]

	VS			S			M			L		
	PI	PII	%	PI	PII	%	PI	PII	%	PI	PII	%
EN1	3	6	100	8	9	13	5	8	60	0	1	100
EN2	1	4	300	5	8	60	4	4	0	1	1	0
EN3	6	5	-17	6	11	83	0	0	0	1	1	0
EN4	1	4	300	2	3	50	0	1	100	0	0	0
EN5	7	10	43	10	11	10	5	11	120	4	4	0
EN6	1	1	0	2	3	50	1	1	0	0	1	100
EN7	2	3	50	3	3	0	3	5	67	2	3	50
EN8	0	0	0	1	0	-100	0	1	100	1	1	0

niche was the desert fringe, in which the number of Small sites grew by
63 per cent, and where the number of Very Small and Medium sites
remained constant.[9] The most moderate change may be observed in the
central hills in the Jerusalem Saddle region. There, the number of Large
sites remained constant and the number of Very Small and Small sites
grew at the gradual rate of 43 and 10 per cent, respectively. Only in the
number of Medium sites, which increased from 5 to 11 (a 120 per cent
increase) does this general pattern change. A similar pattern of gradual
growth may be observed in the southern central hills. The number of
Small sites remained constant, the number of Very Small and Large
sites grew from two to three, and the number of Medium sites increased
by two, from three to five.[10]

Continuity with the Iron II and Hellenistic Periods

The previous sections have concentrated on the nature of the Persian
period settlements. But Yehud did not exist in a historical vacuum.

8. This table does not contain the category of Very Large site; there was only
one Very Large site in Yehud during the Persian period (Jerusalem), located in EN
2; it was occupied in both the Persian I and Persian II periods.
9. Technically, the number of Large sites doubled (a 100 per cent increase)
from one to two. Once again, however, since the number of sites is so limited, the
results would be skewed by this increase of one site if they were applied uncritically.
10. Although the these figures represent statistical growth of between 50 and 67
per cent, the number of sites is more significant than the percentages in demonstrating the nature of the demographic shifts.

Thus, one way of testing the presentation given above is to examine the nature of continuity in Syria-Palestine from the Iron II to the Persian and the Persian to the Hellenistic periods for both site distribution and population. This is especially important when addressing the various reconstructions of the appropriate social context(s) for the province. It is important to note here that I have not completed the type of thorough investigation of the number of settlements from the Iron II period and or the early Hellenistic period that were located within the borders of the province that would be required for a full comparison. Rather, I have approximated the population within the boundaries of Persian period Yehud for the Iron II period based upon the most recent scholarly reconstructions, but have not attempted to estimate the population of the Hellenistic period.[11] One level of comparison, however, is possible—based upon the data I have presented above—namely the number of sites in Persian period Yehud that existed in the Iron II period and those that continued on to the Hellenistic period.

It is clear from the excavated sites from Yehud that considerable flux must have existed among the 125 sites I have identified as being occupied during the Persian period. Many, like Bethel and Tel el-Fûl, have settlement histories that reflect an Iron II-to-Neo-Babylonian or Persian phase, followed by a gap. After a period of abandonment of up to 150 years, there was either a Hellenistic settlement, or even a resettlement in the late Persian period that then extended into the Hellenistic period. Thus, in the following discussion, the notion of site continuity must be viewed with considerable caution. I do not claim that sites that have remains from all three periods were necessarily occupied *continuously* from the late Iron II period through the early Hellenistic period. The most the data will allow is that a given site showed evidence of being settled during any or all of the three periods from which the comparison is drawn.

The first level of comparison is based upon the hill country of Benjamin and the highland of Judah Surveys.[12] This comparison is 'global'

---

11. For the Iron Age data, I have used Broshi's and Finkelstein's estimates in 'The Population of Palestine', pp. 51-52. As of this writing, I am not aware of any studies of the population of Syria-Palestine in the Hellenistic period.

12. See Map 5: Iron Age I; Map 6: Iron Age II; Map 7: Persian Period; and Map 8: Hellenistic Period, in *ASHCB*, pp. 448-55. The summary of the Judean sites is from Ofer, 'The Highlands of Judah, I', pp. 29-30 and A. Ofer, 'Judah', *OEANE*, III, pp. 253-57 (254-56).

in nature. On the one hand, it reflects areas that extended beyond the boundaries of the province of Yehud. On the other hand, it is only possible to subdivide the respective archaeological periods (i.e. Iron IIa-c), in the territory of Judah. In the discussion that follows, I have included the Iron Age I in order to gain a broader perspective of the shifts in site distribution and population. Forty-five sites have been identified[13] in the hill country of Benjamin (Table 23) that date to the Iron Age I.

Table 23. *Settlement History in Benjamin, Iron I–Hellenistic Periods*

Period	Sites	% Change	%Change Iron I	% Change Iron II
Iron I	45			
Iron II	157	+250	+250	
Persian	39	-75	-13	-75
Hellenistic	163	+320	+260	+04

During the Iron Age II, the number of sites increased by 250 per cent to 157. The number of sites fell precipitously in the Persian period to 39 settlements, a drop of 75 per cent. Settlement recovered dramatically in the Hellenistic period, rising by 320 per cent to 163 inhabited sites. Comparing the Iron I and Persian periods, there were six fewer sites in the Persian period than in the Iron Age I (13 per cent fewer sites). In the Hellenistic period, the number of settlements surpassed that of even the Iron II period; there were six more sites during the Hellenistic period (a four per cent increase over the Iron II period).

13. *ASCHB* identifies two types of sites: sites that clearly date to the period in question, and 'possible' sites. Seven Iron I sites, 20 Iron II sites, 39 Persian period sites and 30 Hellenistic sites fall into the latter category. In the discussion that follows, I have computed the relative continuity among archaeological periods based only upon the settlements that are *definitively* dated to the respective periods. If the sites that *may* have been occupied are added, the following levels of continuity apply. The number of settlements increased by 240 per cent from the Iron I to Iron II periods. The number of sites declined from 177 to 68 from the Iron II to Persian periods, reflecting a 160 per cent drop. This was followed by an increase of 185 per cent to 193 in the Hellenistic period. Comparisons between the Iron I and Persian periods are as follows: if one includes the total number of sites, there were 68 Persian period sites as compared with 52 Iron I sites, reflecting an increase of 23 per cent. In the Hellenistic Age, there were a total of 193 sites, compared with 177 Iron II settlements. The hill country of Benjamin had roughly 8 per cent more sites in the Hellenistic period than in the Iron II period.

It is possible to present a more nuanced view of the data for the Judean highlands (Table 24).

Table 24. *Settlement History in Judean Highlands,*
Iron I–Hellenistic Period

Period	Sites	% Change	% Change, Iron I	% Change, Iron IIC
Iron I	18			
Iron IIA	33	+83		
Iron IIB	86	+160	+370	
Iron IIC	122	+42	+577	
Iron IID	113	-7	+528	-7
Persian	87	-23	+383	-29
Hellenistic	98	+13	+444	-25

In that territory there were a total of 18 sites in the Iron I age, with little settlement in the desert fringe or the area around the Hebron hills and to their south. The number of sites grew to 33 during the Iron IIA (a rise of 83 per cent), with the previously under-settled areas showing gradual development. By the Iron IIB period, there were a total of 86 sites (a 160 per cent increase), with much of this growth in the south and desert fringe areas. The apex of Iron II settlement occurred in the Iron IIC period when there were a total of 122 inhabited sites. This marks an increase of 42 per cent over the previous period, a rise of 270 per cent over the Iron IIA, and a growth of nearly 580 per cent from the Iron I period. A period of decline begins in the Iron IID period (evidently Ofer's designation of the period ending in 586, or perhaps extending to 538). During this final phase of the Iron Age, the number of highland sites declined by 7 per cent to 113. An abrupt change occurs in the Persian period, where the number of sites dropped further to 87 (a drop of 23 per cent; a decline of 29 per cent from the peak of settlement in the Iron IIC period). However, Ofer notes that in the area between Khirbet Tubeiqah, Halhul and Ras et-Tawil, 'an unprecedented enhancement of the settled area occurs'.[14] There, one finds an increase in the number of sites of 165 per cent. In the Hellenistic period, the number of sites from the Highlands, increases gradually to 98 (a 13 per cent rise).

It is clear from this brief analysis that the territories of Benjamin and Judah viewed in their entirety demonstrate distinctly different settlement histories. In Benjamin, there is a slower rate of growth from the

14. 'The Highlands of Judah, I', p. 30.

Iron I to the Iron II periods, followed by a precipitous decline from the Iron II to the Persian period. The settlement pattern rebounds during the Hellenistic period. There is a rough parallel between settlement data for the Iron I and Persian periods on the one hand, and the Iron II and Hellenistic periods on the other. In Judah, where the settlement lagged behind that of its northern neighbor, there is a decidedly lower number of villages in the Iron I period (60 per cent fewer sites). Even at its height, the highlands of Judah were less densely settled than Benjamin, with 33 per cent fewer sites. Judah experienced a somewhat less abrupt decline from the Iron II to the Persian period than did Benjamin, followed by a more gradual increase from Persian to Hellenistic periods.

With these general data about continuity in the total area that comprised the traditional territories of Benjamin and Judah, what can be said about the level of continuity among the sites within the portion of these territories that were in the province of Yehud? An interesting pattern unfolds when comparing these changes among the traditional tribal territories that comprised Yehud. Roughly 52 per cent of the sites that continued from the Iron II through the Hellenistic periods were located in Benjamin and 48 per cent in Judah (Table 25). This pattern held true for the number of Iron II sites that continued to the Persian period and those that had a Persian and Hellenistic trajectory. Nearly two-thirds of the sites that were established during the Persian period were located in Judah (62 per cent) and slightly more than one-third were located in Benjamin (38 per cent). This was true, as well, of the sites that lacked a Hellenistic phase: 65 per cent of sites that did not continue from the Persian to the Hellenistic period were located in the traditional tribal territory of Judah. Given the relative size of the territory of Judah as compared with Benjamin, this is not surprising. However, it is important to remember that the territory of Benjamin, while smaller than Judah, contained only seven fewer sites in the Persian II phase. Thus, it is evident that a somewhat higher level of flux occurred in the territory of Judah with respect to new Persian period sites and those ending in the Persian period. Statistically, the two patterns appear to be somewhat contradictory. On the one hand, an equal number of sites showed continuity in both territories. On the other hand, when change occurred, it appeared to be more marked in the territory of Judah. Together, these data appear to call into question the widely held theory that the territory of Judah was laid waste by the Babylonians, while the territory of Benjamin suffered less destruction in the fall of the Southern Kingdom in

Table 25. *Settlement Continuity among Biblical Territories*[15]

Territory	Ir2-H	Ir2-P	P-H	New P	End P
Benjamin (N)	33	43	42	13	14
Benjamin (%)	52	49	51	38	35
Judah (N)	31	45	40	21	26
Judah (%)	48	51	49	62	65

587/586. While it is true that a higher number (and percentage) of sites were settled in Judah during the Persian period than in Benjamin, factors other than the level of destruction should be sought to explain this phenomenon. These might include some of the following: economic factors, closeness to a major site, security of the province, the establishment of fortresses, or imperial policy.

How do these patterns for the territories of Benjamin and Judah as a whole compare to those sites that were part of the province of Yehud? Of the 125 sites attributed to the Persian period, roughly half were occupied in the Iron II, Persian and Hellenistic periods (64 sites, or 51 per cent of the total). Sixty-one sites (49 per cent) were occupied only in two of the three periods, either in the Iron II and Persian periods, or in the Persian and Hellenistic periods. In the Judean desert, En-Gedi and Jericho were both occupied in all three periods, and their 100 per cent level of continuity somewhat skews the statistics from the other environmental niches. Of these, the western slopes and central hills reflect a similar level of stability with 53 per cent and 51 per cent of the settlements in each respective area being occupied in Iron II, Persian and Hellenistic periods. The desert fringe shows the most volatility in settlement, with only 43 per cent of the sites occupied in all three periods (Table 26; Chart 15).

15. In Tables 25-27 and Charts 15-22, the following abbreviations are used: Ir2-H indicates settlements that were settled in the Iron II, Persian and Hellenistic Periods; Ir2-P is used for sites in which there is continuity from the Iron II to the Persian periods; P-H indicates sites that demonstrate continuity from the Persian to the Hellenistic periods. New P indicates sites that were initially settled in the Persian period or that resumed settlement after a gap of occupation in the Iron Age. End P is used for those sites where settlement did not extend into the Hellenistic period from the Persian period. In the Charts, I have included the number of sites settled in the Persian period in each environmental niche, and both the number and percentage of sites demonstrating continuity (or discontinuity) in the periods under question.

Table 26. *Settlement Continuity by Major Environmental Niches*

Number	Ir2-H	Ir2-P	P-H	New P	End P
WS	17	22	24	10	8
CH	35	44	44	21	22
DF	10	20	13	3	10
JD	2	2	2	0	0
Total	64	88	83	34	40
Percent					
WS	53	69	75	31	25
CH	51	65	64	31	32
DF	43	87	57	13	43
JD	100	100	100	0	50
Total	51	70	66	27	32

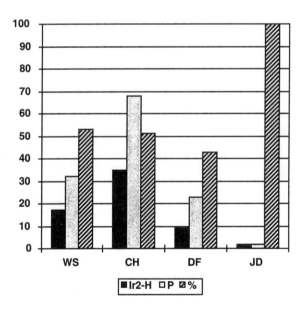

Chart 15. *Settlement Continuity in Major Environmental
Niches, Iron II–Hellenistic Periods*

Table 27. *Settlement Continuity by Individual Environmental Niches*

Number	Ir2-H	Ir2-P	P-H	New P	End P
EN 1	14	16	20	8	4
EN 2	11	11	14	4	2
EN 3	8	16	9	1	8
EN 4	3	6	4	2	4
EN 5	15	22	20	14	16
EN 6	2	4	4	2	2
EN 7	9	11	10	3	4
EN 8	2	2	2	0	0
Total	64	88	83	34	40
Percent					
EN 1	58	67	83	33	17
EN 2	61	61	78	21	11
EN 3	47	94	53	6	47
EN 4	38	75	50	25	50
EN 5	42	61	56	39	44
EN 6	33	67	67	33	33
EN 7	64	79	71	21	29
EN 8	100	100	100	0	0
Total	51	70	66	27	32

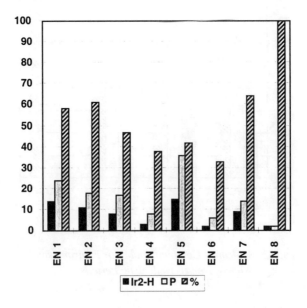

Chart 16. *Settlement Continuity in Individual*
Environmental Niches, Iron II–Hellenistic Periods

Among the eight individual niches, three showed a level of continuity of nearly 65 per cent (Table 27, Chart 16) . Fifty-eight per cent of the sites in the northwestern slopes (EN 1) were occupied from the Iron II through the Hellenistic periods. Sixty-one per cent of the settlements of the northern central hills (EN 2) and 64 per cent of the sites in the southern central hills (EN 7) reflected the same level of continuity. The central hills (EN 5), which consistently held the largest number of sites and the highest population during the Persian period showed a surprising level of flux regarding its relationship between the Persian period settlements and the preceding and succeeding periods. Only 42 per cent of the sites in the central hills were occupied in all three periods, while 61 per cent of the sites were occupied in the Iron 2 and Persian periods (Chart 17) and 56 per cent had Persian and Hellenistic phases (Chart 21). The three remaining niches reflected a level of discontinuity ranging between 53 and 66 per cent. In the southwestern slopes, 38 per cent of the sites were occupied from the Iron II through Hellenistic periods. In the northern desert fringe and the southern desert fringe, only 47 and 33 per cent of the sites respectively showed continuous occupation.

A slightly higher percentage of sites had Iron II and Persian occupation than those that were inhabited in the Persian and Hellenistic periods (Tables 26 and 27). Eighty-eight of the Persian period sites were inhabited in the Iron Age II (70 per cent), whereas only 83 of the Persian period sites continued into the Hellenistic period (66 per cent). Thirty-four sites were established in the Persian period (27 per cent of the villages of Yehud) and there were 40 whose settlement ceased in the Persian period (33 per cent). Thirteen of Yehud's settlements had only a Persian period phase; this represents 10 per cent of the province's villages and 39 per cent of the sites established in the Persian period. Of these one period sites, two were fortresses.

While these levels of continuity are significant in and of themselves, the levels of continuity from Iron II to Persian periods within the major and individual niches is equally important (Charts 17 and 18). Twenty-two of the 32 Persian period sites in the western slopes were previously settled in the Iron II period (69 per cent). Similarly, 44 of the 68 settlements of the central hill country had Iron II remains (65 per cent). What is surprising, given the low level of continuity from the Iron II through the Hellenistic periods in the desert fringe is that only three of the Persian period sites in that niche were not previously settled; 87 per cent of the Persian period sites extended from Iron II habitation.

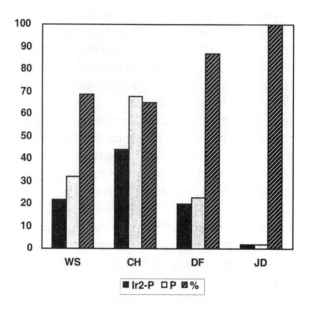

Chart 17. *Settlement Continuity in Major*
Environmental Niches, Iron II–Persian Periods

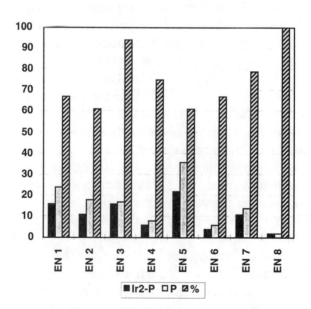

Chart 18. *Settlement Continuity in Individual*
Environmental Niches, Iron II–Persian Periods

The lowest level of Iron II-Persian continuity among the individual niches was evident in EN 2 (northern central hills) and in EN 5 (central hills) in which 61 per cent of sites were settled in both periods. The highest level of continuity was in the northern desert fringe (EN 3), in which 16 of the 17 sites were occupied in the Iron Age (a 94 per cent rate of continuity). The other niches ranged between 67 per cent and 79 per cent in their levels of continuity.

The majority of the sites that were either initially settled or re-established[16] during the Persian period were located in the western slopes and the central hills, both of which saw approximately 31 per cent of their total number of sites begin occupation in the Persian period (Chart 19). Only 13 per cent of the sites in the desert fringe originated during the Persian period. Most of the individual environmental niches saw a very modest number of sites establishes 538 and 332, usually between one and three sites (Chart 20). The northern desert fringe had the smallest percentage—6 per cent; only 1 of its 17 sites was established during the period. The other niches with small number of new sites ranged between 16 and 33 per cent. Only in EN 1 (northwestern slopes) and 5 (central hills) were there a sizable number of newly established sites. There were 8 new settlements in EN 1 (33 per cent of its sites) and 14 new settlements in EN 5 (39 per cent of its sites). These numbers reflect the sites that can be clearly identified as sites with Persian period beginning. However, one should note that seven sites from the survey in the hill country of Benjamin had pottery identified as 'Iron II/Persian'. This designation suggests that the surveyors could not clearly place the pottery exclusively in either the Iron II or the Persian period. However, it may also indicate sites that were primarily from the Neo-Babylonian period, a period in which the Iron II forms continued and began the gradual transition toward the more clearly identifiable Persian period forms. Thus, it may be that 40, rather than 33, sites should be identified as originating in the Persian period, which would increase the percentage of new sites from 27 to 32 per cent.

16. In evaluating settlement continuity for the purposes of this study, it makes no difference whether the Persian period is the first settlement of a particular site or whether it was established in an earlier period but had no Iron II remains. In either case, the site lacks continuity from the Iron Age II to the Persian period.

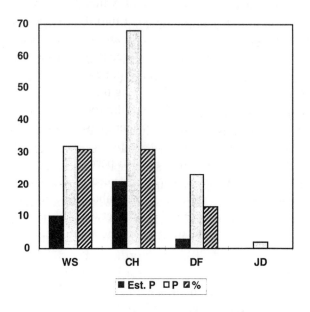

Chart 19. *Newly Settled Persian Period Sites
in Major Environmental Niches*

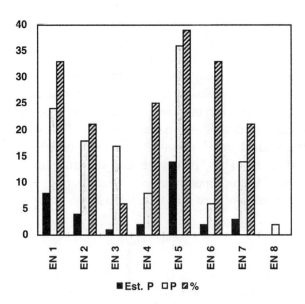

Chart 20. *Newly Settled Persian Period Sites
in Individual Environmental Niches*

One-third of the sites in the province of Yehud ended with the Persian period. Of the 83 sites that continued into the Hellenistic period, only 10 (43 per cent of the sites in EN 3 and 6) were located in the desert fringe (Chart 21). Much higher percentages of sites continued into the Hellenistic period in the western slopes (75 per cent) and the central hills (68 per cent). The areas showing the least continuity (Chart 22) were the northern desert fringe (EN 3), the southwestern slopes (EN 4) and the central hills (EN 5). In the northern desert fringe, 8 of the 17 sites (47 per cent) lacked a Hellenistic phase. In the southwestern slopes, 4 of the 8 sites ended in the Persian periods, and in the central hills (EN 5), 16 of the 36 sites (44 per cent) ceased occupation during the Persian period. In the other areas, the number of sites ending in the Persian period ranged between 2 and 4, and between 11 per cent and 33 per cent of the sites in the respective environmental niche.

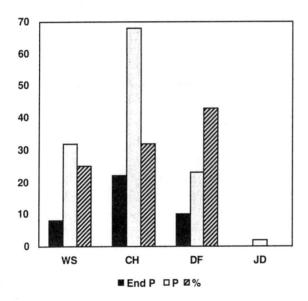

Chart 21. *Settlement Continuity among Major Environmental Niches, Persian–Hellenistic Periods*

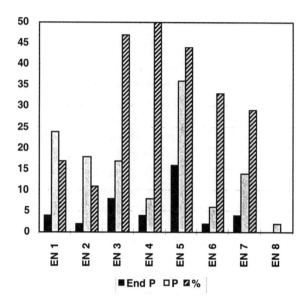

Chart 22. *Settlement Continuity among Individual*
Environmental Niches, Persian–Hellenistic Periods

Summary and Conclusions

The data presented above suggest that the province of Yehud was considerably smaller and poorer than previous estimates have allowed. Not
only was Jerusalem the only major site in the province—larger by two
to three times than its next largest town—but the majority (65 per cent)
of the sites in the province were smaller than five dunams, with populations of less than 125. By the late Persian period, only 13 (10 per cent)
of the settlements were larger than 12.0 dunams and had a population
of over 350. Other than Jerusalem, only two sites were larger than 20
dunams: Khirbet Pe'or/Khirbet Zakahdah (22 dunams) and Khirbet Ras
et-Tawil (23 dunams). Both were located in the central range, one in
EN 5 and the other in EN 7.

While these figures are surprisingly small, they do seem to fit well
with the data from the most recent archaeological studies and population estimates of the Iron Age II. Israel Finkelstein and Magen Broshi
suggest that near the end of the eighth century BCE, the population
of the Southern Kingdom was nearly 110,000.[17] If one excludes the

17. 'The Population of Palestine', pp. 51-52.

Shephelah and Coastal Plains, both of which were outside of the province of Yehud, the population was approximately 60,000. According to their estimates, 7500 people lived in Jerusalem (12.5 per cent), 22,500 (37.5 per cent) occupied the area from Jerusalem northward to Ramallah, and 30,000 (50 per cent) settled in the hill country south of Jerusalem. This figure accounts for an area somewhat larger than that of Yehud, but allows an approximate comparison. Avi Ofer estimates that there were approximately 400 hectares of settled area in Judah at the end of the Iron Age, 274 of which were comprised of the central hill regions, Jerusalem and the territory of Benjamin.[18] Using the generally accepted area-to-population ratio of 250 persons per hectare, this would allow for a population of Judah at about 100,000, and the population of the central hills, Jerusalem and the territory of Benjamin of about 68,500. If all three sets of estimates (i.e. those of Finkelstein and Broshi, Ofer, and my own estimates for Yehud) are accurate, then the population of the province in the Persian period was about one-third of that in the previous period. Jerusalem itself was approximately 20 per cent of its Iron II size, a figure that accords well with the level of destruction that can be attributed to the Babylonian conquest in 587/586 and the much smaller occupation during the Persian period. No scholar in the second half of this century has suggested that the settlement in Jerusalem extended beyond the confines of the area now known as the 'City of David' during the Achaemenid period. While the population figures I have proposed (20,650) is just over 10 per cent of the population estimates that Weinberg uses in his *Bürger-Tempel-Gemeinde* model, they are actually higher than those of W.F. Albright. His estimate of 20,000 for the province of Yehud was based on a larger geographic area I have reconstructed, one which included both the sites from the Shephelah and the Coastal Plain.

What of Hoglund's analysis discussed at the beginning of the chapter? The new data suggests an even greater drop in the number and percentages of sites in Benjamin than the earlier surveys had proposed: a drop from 155 sites to 39 settlements which reflects a 300 per cent decline. The decline was much less abrupt in the territory of Judah (a 26

---

18. Ofer, 'The Highlands of Judah, I', p. 31*. The figures he lists in 'Judah' are rounded slightly, and given in acres. For his Iron IIC-Iron III period (701–538) he lists 300 acres (= 1200 dunams, or 120 hectares) for the highlands of Judah, 225 acres (= 900 dunams, or 90 hectares) for the territory of Benjamin, and 150 acres (= 600 dunams, or 60 hectares) for Jerusalem. See 'Judah', p. 256.

per cent drop), with 26 fewer sites in the Persian period than existed in the Iron Age II. This is in contrast to Hoglund's claim that there was a 25 per cent increase in sites in Persian period Judah over the Iron II levels. Hoglund's figures are somewhat more accurate in the level of continuity from the Iron II to Persian period. The current data for the province as a whole suggest that nearly 75 per cent of the settlements had Iron II strata. However, the level of continuity from Iron II to Persian periods is markedly higher in Benjamin (81 per cent) than in Judah (69 per cent). Hoglund suggested a 65 per cent level of continuity in the traditional territory of Judah. The number of new sites in each territory, of course, follows this general pattern, with two-thirds of the sites with initial Persian period phases coming from Judah. The 33 new Persian period sites account for 26 per cent of the sites in that period, a figure just slightly higher than Hoglund's projections, based as they were on the only reliable survey that had been undertaken at the time. The newer survey data and more recent excavations suggest a higher number of sites in Yehud, and confirm his general picture of a province based on a subsistence level rural or village economy. However, there appears to be only one area within the province where there is a major increase in settlement that could be attributed to Imperial policy. This would be in the southern central hills, from Kh. Tubeiqah to Halhul, where Ofer has identified a 165 per cent increase in settlement in the Persian period compared with the Iron Age II. Continuity levels between 70 and 80 per cent call into question his conclusion that the settlement patterns in and of themselves undermine the traditional view of intra-province struggle between returnees and those who had remained on the land.

Chapter 6

YEHUD IN THE PERSIAN PERIOD: A SYNTHESIS

Given the increased scholarly interest in the Persian period, the site distribution, levels of continuity with the Iron II period, and the population
and population landscape assume a critical importance. It is only when
these are firmly established that we can begin to talk with any degree of
certainty about the social context and internal politics of Yehud. This
is especially true given the competing hypotheses about the nature of
the Jewish community within and outside of the province during this
period. Among the critical questions that can now be addressed are: To
what degree do these data allow us to reconstruct the socio-economic
setting of the province, both internally and within the larger economy of
Syria-Palestine? How closely, if at all, does Weinberg's *Bürger-Tempel-Gemeinde* model fit the data regarding site distribution and population? Do these data have any bearing on one's interpretation of social
and religious concepts of 'the true seed of Israel' and the social boundaries that the Ezra–Nehemiah traditions and the Priestly school hold
to so strongly? Can they help determine anything about the rise of
apocalyptic and its social roots? This chapter examines these important
questions from the perspective of the archaeological data presented in
Chapters 3 through 5.

Socio-Economic Indicators

Scholars have long maintained that the Persian period economy in
Yehud was predominately village based. This assertion can now be
based in part upon the large numbers of Very Small and Small settlements within the province and on the nature of the agricultural installations that both surveys and excavations have unearthed. These augment
the seal impressions, coinage and Greek pottery already discovered from
excavations to provide an unprecedented opportunity to examine the socio-economic status of the province more carefully.

Regional Agricultural Patterns

In my earlier studies of Yehud, I pointed to the apparent skewing of the data due to the lack of surveys in the Jerusalem hills. As of 1991, when I completed my initial study, Jerusalem appeared to be relatively isolated, with no smaller sites in its immediate surroundings (Figure 19).[1] Later periods (notably, the Ottoman and early British Mandatorial periods) showed at least some settlements closer to Jerusalem than those discovered in the Benjamin and Judah surveys that dated to the Persian period. I suggested that this lack of settlements did not reflect the reality of the period, and that future surveys would in fact lead to the discovery of Persian period sites closer to the provincial capital. An ongoing survey of the region, undertaken by the Israel Antiquities Authority, has in fact found a number of both settlements and agricultural installations around Jerusalem (Figure 20). These include remains of terraces, wine-presses, storage facilities, farmsteads and olive presses. The storage facilities and 16 wine-presses discovered at Kh. Er-Ras (S) in the Manahat section of Jerusalem may provide evidence of an industrial complex, intended for the production and storage of wine and perhaps grain. These presses may have provided wine for the elite of Jerusalem, for trade purposes, or even for in-kind taxation. The grain that was probably stored in the storage facilities may have been used for similar purposes, or even to provision governmental officials or Persian troops. The area around Wadi Salim contained two 2-dunam settlements with terraces and stone buildings. Nearby were several farmsteads and at least one cistern. This indicates, as well, the presence of the kind of satellite villages that would have produced goods for consumption by the inhabitants of Jerusalem.[2] While these farmsteads and their installations would have given up a certain degree of security—isolated as they were from the nearby cities or villages—they functioned as more efficient centers of cultivation and production of marketable goods.

---

1.   Carter, 'A Social and Demographic Study', pp. 345-48, figure 19.

2.   D. Hopkins suggests that 'the appearance of farmsteads is related to heightened security conditions and the burgeoning demand for specialized economic goods —that is, marketable commodities' and 'may well represent the penetration of the countryside by the managerial arm of the city-based administration' ('Farmsteads', in *OEANE*, II, pp. 306-307).

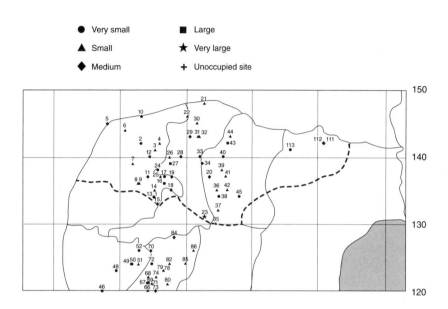

Figure 19. *Sites around Jerusalem According to 1991 Study*

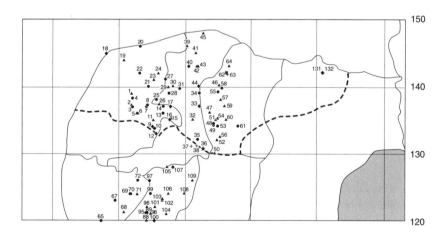

Figure 20. *Sites around Jerusalem According to 1999 Study*

In addition to these settlements that directly provisioned the Yehudite capital, the entire province was involved in the Temple and governmental economy. Both domestic and industrial installations played a part in maintaining the economy and supporting the individual households. Public grain storage areas have been discovered in Neo-Babylonian and/ or Persian period sites. El-Jîb, Tell en-Naṣbeh and Tell el-Fûl all had grain silos; major public storage facilities were also excavated at Tell en-Naṣbeh, Khirbet er-Ras (S), and Khirbet Abu et-Twein. Iron II wine-presses discovered at Tell en-Naṣbeh would most likely have been re-used for public or industrial purposes during the Persian period. A pottery kiln was also discovered at Tell en-Naṣbeh, perhaps marking it as a source for some of the local Persian period pottery from Yehud. Industrial rooms were discovered at Abu et-Twein and En-Gedi. Both contained loom weights, with the compound in En-Gedi yielding stone tools; loom weights were also discovered from the excavations in the City of David. Most likely, the rooms at Abu et-Twein and the storage facilities would have functioned primarily to produce goods to support the conscripts stationed in the fortresses. The excavators at En-Gedi have interpreted the industrial installations there as part of the perfume industry long associated with that site, but none of the implements or other discoveries there either confirm or challenge that interpretation. Whatever their function, the discoveries suggest that the settlement was more than an agricultural or trading outpost. Domestic agricultural installations were discovered at five excavated sites. Most of these were cisterns, though a tabun was discovered at the fortress at Har Adar, and terraces discovered around Wadi Salim.

Thirty of the 59 settlements documented in the Benjamin survey with Persian period remains (51 per cent) showed remains of agricultural installations, including olive-presses, wine-presses, cupmarks, threshing-floors, terraces, cisterns and lime kilns (Figure 21). Two difficulties arise from attempting to use surveys to reconstruct the economic patterns rather than using them simply to document settlement patterns. The surveys generally do *not* report the specific type of a particular installation that was discovered; nor do they attempt to date the installation or to associate it with a particular phase of settlement. Wine- and olive-presses could be included or excluded from a particular period based on their typology within a general taxonomy of each kind of press.

A   Cistern   G   Terrace/Agricultural Production

B   Terrace   H   Cistern/Terrace/Agricultural Production

C   Agricultural Production   I   Terrace/Agricultural Production/Animal Husbandry

D   Industrial Production   J   Cistern/Terrace/Industrial Production/Agricultural Production

E   Cistern/Terrace   K   Terrace/Industrial Production/Animal Husbandry

F   Cistern/AP

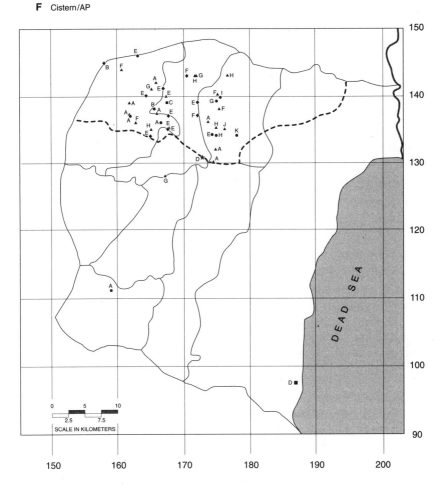

Figure 21. *Domestic, Agricultural and Industrial Installations Discovered at Sites within the Geographic Boundaries of Yehud*

The Hellenistic and Roman periods both showed marked developments in efficiency and style of both olive- and wine-presses that make
it possible to separate them from earlier types of presses.[3] At the same
time, the older presses were often re-used alongside later, more productive models when constructing the new models was not economically
viable or necessary.

Despite the problems associated with using surveys to reconstruct the
agricultural past of the province, a brief discussion of the evidence at
hand may provide the reader with a general economic framework upon
which to understand the Persian period. A more specific discussion can
only occur on the basis of the more complete excavations of these sites.[4]
Perhaps confirming the accuracy of this general portrait is the fact that
17 of the sites (57 per cent) have substantial occupations that pre-date
the Persian period, while 11 (37 per cent) have their primary occupation
in the Hellenistic, Roman and/or Byzantine periods.[5] Again, it is important to note that I am not claiming that these installations were in use in
the Persian period, but am using the data to demonstrate general patterns of economic production that *may have existed* within Yehud during this time.

Within the territory of Benjamin, 25 of the 59 sites that I have dated
to the Persian period contained one or more cisterns (42 per cent). One
suspects that this number would rise substantially when excavations
took place, though it is impossible to determine the number of these sites

---

3.   I discuss the technological developments for both wine- and olive-presses in
'A Social and Demographic Study', pp. 260-71.

4.   In including this discussion, my assumption is that the basic patterns of agricultural production remained similar over time—though certainly not constant—
from the Iron I through the late Roman periods. Although as I have noted, there
were significant developments in the technology of both olive- and wine-presses in
the Hellenistic, Roman and Byzantine periods, the presence of these units of production indicate the types of crops commonly grown in a given area. Similarly,
while terrace construction in the Persian period cannot be determined by surveys
alone, their presence at a particular site may either confirm production patterns or,
alternatively, may actually obscure the settlement patterns by covering remains
(Shimon Gibson, personal communication). See his study, 'Landscape Archaeology
and Ancient Agricultural Field Systems in Palestine' (PhD dissertation, Institute of
Archaeology, University College London).

5.   Two of the sites, making up the remaining 6.6 per cent, are impossible to
place in this schema, since the relative percentages of pottery is not given for either.
These are sites 480 (Hizma) and 524 (my 'Unnamed 11').

at which the cisterns were in use during the Persian period. Eighteen of the sites (31 per cent) showed evidence of the agricultural terracing necessary for more efficient production in the hill country of Palestine. Wine-presses were discovered at eight of the sites in Benjaminite Yehud (14 per cent), and olive oil production facilities were discovered at seven sites (12 per cent).[6] Three sites contained threshing-floors (generally considered public property of a village), two contained unidentified 'rock-cut installations' and two contained stone structures interpreted as animal pens. Two villages had lime kilns, and one had evidence of a stone industry.

These latter installations I interpret as industrial installations; the wine-presses, olive-oil presses, threshing floors and terraces may have been domestic or industrial in nature. However, given the resources required for construction and maintenance of terraces, threshing-floors and the pressing installations, it is probable that these were public in nature even if they were not industrial.[7]

The economic patterns in Yehud almost certainly remained constant with those known from the Bronze and Iron Ages: a mixed agrarian and animal husbandry economy based on the so-called 'Mediterranean Triad' of grain, wine and oil. The areas around Jerusalem—immediately to the north, south and west—have traditionally been ones in which oil production is profitable. The northwestern and southwestern hills support olive production as well as grape production, though the soil and climate in the southern central hills, near Hebron, is more

6. Five of these were oil-presses or oil-press weights, two were cup-marks. The latter are associated with domestic production of olive oil as early as the Chalcolithic period. It is unclear what type of presses were discovered at these sites. However, weights were used to provide a more efficient extraction of oil from the olives in beam presses during the Iron Age. These were in use during the Iron Age and continued to see widespread use through the Hellenistic Age. A full description of production technologies for olive oil is given in *OOIA* and R. Frankel, S. Avitsur and E. Ayalon (eds.), *History and Technology of Olive Oil in the Holy Land* (Tel Aviv: Eretz Israel Museum, 1994), pp. 28-31.

7. See D. Hopkins, 'Life on the Land: The Subsistence Struggles of Early Israel', *BA* 50 (1987), pp. 178-91, and his larger work, *The Highlands of Canaan*, for a description of the risks involved in agricultural production in the central hill country of Palestine as well as the costs involved in constructing and maintaining these 'risk-spreading' technologies. Particularly helpful in the latter work is chapter 9, 'Agricultural Objectives and Strategies: Risk Spreading and the Optimization of Labor', pp. 211-61.

suited for viticulture than for olive husbandry. Soil types, average rainfall, and elevation in the northern, northwestern and central areas of
Yehud would have been suitable for growing both wheat and barley.
The areas in the desert fringe and in the area around Hebron would be
less suitable for growing wheat but would support barley production.
The desert fringe area would be where a more mixed economy would
predominate, in which animal husbandry and limited agricultural production would complement one another. It is therefore not surprising
that the sites with architectural remains interpreted as animal pens in
the Benjamin survey are located in the desert fringe.[8] The less fertile
soil and diminished rainfall would make barley the preferred crop in
these regions.

Evidence of Trade and other Extra-Provincial Contact
Yehud was part of a larger imperial, even international economy. While
its agricultural resources supported its own population, the Yehudite
government and cultic officials, it is evident as well that goods and
other types of material culture flowed into the province from both other
provinces and other countries. While it is not clear whether or not
Yehudian produce was transported to other areas of the empire or the
world, it is probable that the flow of goods was not one-way. Throughout the history of Syria-Palestine, Palestinian wine, oil and even grain
had been the source of active international trade.[9] The presence of local
Palestinian vessels both in Yehud and along the Mediterranean coast
attests to agriculturally based trade at least within the Syro-Palestinian
provinces of the Persian empire.[10]

   Pottery, seals and jewelry reflecting Neo-Babylonian influence and/or
presence have been discovered at Tell en-Naṣbeh, Bethel, Jerusalem,
Har Adar, Horvat Zimri, 'Ain Arrub, Beth-Zur, Jericho and Tel Goren
(Figure 22). Several of the major sites in Yehud also give evidence of
active trade and contact with Greece and with areas under Achaemenid

---

   8.   Jurrat es-Saqqawi (*ASHCB*, site 482) and Unnamed 11 (*ASHCB*, site 524).
   9.   Contact between Palestine and Egypt is attested in the archeological record
as early as the Pre-Dynastic period. Palestinian vessels have been discovered in
Egyptian contexts, indicating trade between the two regions (possibly including
Palestinian wine and oil). See Mazar, *Archaeology*, pp. 105-108. Abydos Ware
indicates continued Egyptian connections in the EB II period. Mazar, *Archaeology*,
pp. 135-36.
   10.   Hoglund, 'The Achaemenid Context', pp. 60-61.

control. Greek vessels of various types were discovered at Tell en-Naṣbeh, dating from the sixth through middle of the fifth centuries.[11] Jerusalem and the tombs surrounding it have yielded the type of repertoire one would expect to find in the provincial capital. Among the finds are Greek coins (City of David, Givat Ram, Mt Zion, Ketef Hinnom); Rhodian glass vessels (City of David); various types of Greek ware (City of David, Ketef Hinnom, Mamilla)—some of which is of luxury status (Ketef Hinnom); gold jewelry styled after Achaemenid forms (Ketef Hinnom); and at least one Egyptian vessel (Mamilla).[12] While the excavation report from Tel Goren was less detailed in its discussion, Attic pottery dating to the last third of the fifth century was found both in Building 32 and in the trench dug on the northern slope of the tell. Less spectacular but incontrovertible evidence of foreign contact was discovered in Beth-Zur (coins, as discussed above) and Jericho, where Attic pottery dating to the fifth through fourth centuries was excavated. While the Persian period stratum at Bethel is minimal, some Greek pottery was recovered that has been assigned a fourth-century context.[13] Some of the cups excavated in the tomb at 'Ain Arrub may be local imitations of Achaemenid-style vessels—again, indicating foreign influence. The grave goods associated with the tomb mark its owner as a member of the social elite.

What is interesting about this distribution of foreign ware and their local imitations is the correlation of the pottery and material culture with the major centers of commerce. One expects to find sites such as En-Gedi, Jericho, Tell en-Naṣbeh and Jerusalem reflecting the most foreign influence since they were among the major sites of the province and the ones with the most pronounced percentages of the elite and the growing merchant class. This fits the pattern that Hoglund identified of an increased commercialism in Palestine during the Persian period.[14]

11. I discuss the Greek ware from Tell en-Naṣbeh above in Chapter 3, p. 131.

12. For a complete discussion of the 'foreign' finds from Jerusalem see Chapter 3, pp. 145-47. See also Barkay, 'Excavations at Ketef Hinnom', pp. 95-102, and Reich, 'The Ancient Burial Ground in the Mamilla Neighborhood', p. 116.

13. Fragments of Greek pottery have been discovered in two houses north of the Iron II city wall. See Albright and Kelso, *The Excavations of Bethel*, pp. 38, 80.

14. 'The Achaemenid Context', pp. 60-62. However, note that Hoglund draws a contrast between this broader commercial development and the pattern of ruralization he posits for Yehud.

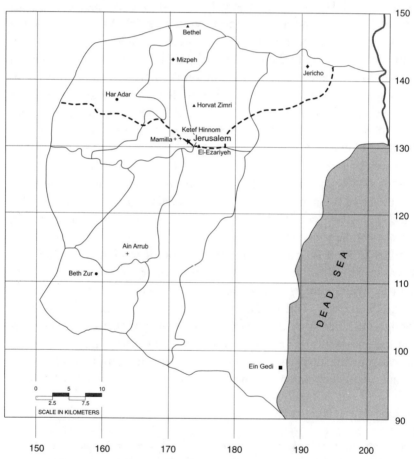

● Very small
▲ Small
◆ Medium
■ Large
★ Very large
+ Unoccupied site

Figure 22. *Distribution of Foreign Ware in the Province of Yehud*

What is unclear, however, is whether this trade and commerce was controlled by Yehud's government, fell primarily under direct Persian control or was jointly managed. It is also unclear whether the sites in Yehud that have Greek, Egyptian and/or Persian pottery received them directly from their source or whether—as is most likely—there were one or more intermediaries between Yehud and its foreign trading partners.

Seals and Coins: A Monied Economy or In-kind Tribute?
No scholars of the Persian period doubt that taxation and tribute levied upon the populace of Yehud by imperial policy contributed to Yehud's economic difficulties. The biblical texts—tendentious as they are— seem to reflect a social world marked by a subsistence level economy, social differentiation and substantial poverty. In the face of these very real conditions, it is probable that the little surplus that the people of Yehud produced quickly filled the provincial and imperial coffers. But how were these taxes collected? And how were inter- and intra-provincial trade maintained? What was the function of the seals impressed on the pottery of Yehud, and how widespread was the use of coins in the fabric of Yehud's economy? When, if at any time in the Persian period, did the use of coins replace in-kind transfers of goods and resources?

In order to evaluate the use of seals and coins, a brief review of the available evidence is necessary (Table 28; Figures 23 and 24). Two broad categories of seal impressions can be identified: anepigraphic and epigraphic. Anepigraphic impressions have been discovered at nine different sites in Yehud: Jerusalem, Bethel, Tell en-Naṣbeh, Ramat Raḥel, Jericho, En-Gedi, Ḥorvat Zimri, El-Jîb and Har Adar. These may be divided into two broad categories: those with animal representations, and those with other artistic motifs. Most prominent among those with animal motifs are the so-called lion seals. These comprise two major types: some with a representation of what may be a 'fire altar', and some simply depicting a roaring lion.[15] Another animal type depicts a bull

15. Those with the 'fire altar' are known from El-Jîb and Ramat Raḥel, and depict a lion standing on its hind legs with its two front paws outstretched toward the side of the seal. Next to the lion is an object that Stern (*Material Culture*, pp. 211-12) interprets as an 'Achaemenian fire-altar' based on typological comparisons from Ur and Persepolis. The Persepolis stamps date to the late sixth to early fifth centuries BCE, and the Ur exemplars are somewhat later, perhaps mid-to-late fifth century. Stern identifies three general sub-categories of the lion seals that lack the

with a representation of a sun-disc between its horns.[16] Other Iron Age motifs, such as the rosette pattern, may continue in use in the Neo-Babylonian or early Achaemenid period.[17] A somewhat enigmatic seal has four exemplars and depicts a human figure with upraised hands standing in front of an altar and deity. It is generally described as 'Babylonian' in style and may date to the Neo-Babylonian rather than the Persian period.[18]

The inscribed seals may be divided into three broad categories: those with the letters *m-(w)-ṣ-h*, those with a full or defective spelling of the provincial name, *Yehud*, and those with the office of governor (*p-ḥ-w-'*), some of which include the name of the governor. The *moṣah* impressions come primarily from areas associated with the tribal territory of Benjamin, which has led some to suggest that they should date to the earlier Neo-Babylonian and/or early Persian period, before Jerusalem had regained its place as the seat of the provincial government.[19]

altar: one with a lion walking; one walking, but with its mouth open in a roar and its tail raised; a third that he describes as a protome.

16. Stern, *Material Culture*, pp. 209-13, and Christoph, 'The Yehud Stamped Jar Handle Corpus', pp. 79-82.

17. J. Cahill has recently suggested that the rosette pattern is more properly dated to the Iron II and perhaps Neo-Babylonian periods. She would explain its presence in Persian period contexts at Ramat Raḥel as a result of re-use in fills, which Aharoni mentioned had mixed contents and were therefore hard to date definitively ('Rosette Stamp Seal Impressions from Ancient Judah', *IEJ* 45 [1995], pp. 230-52 [247-50]). Cahill divides exemplars of the rosette motif into five classes, of which class five is morphologically distinct.

18. This type of seal impression is known from Bethel, Har Adar and Tel Goren. The seal from Bethel is made of agate; the two from Tel Goren are made of calcedony. The Har Adar seal is on a bronze ring. See Chapter 3 for full discussion of the archaeological contexts in which these seals were discovered.

19. As proposed by both J. Zorn and C.C. McCown. The nature and dates of the *m(w)ṣh* impressions is discussed above in Chapter 3, pp. 131-32 nn. 77-81. McCown discusses the impressions in 'Inscribed Material Including Coins', in *TN*, I, pp. 156-74. Zorn's proposals may be found in 'Nasheh, Tell en-', p. 1102. Zorn has recently completed a comprehensive study of the *mwṣh* seals and restates his conviction that they reflect a Neo-Babylonian provenance and functioned administratively. See Zorn, Yellin and Hayes, 'The *m(w)ṣh* Stamp Impressions', pp. 161-83.

Table 28. *Coins and Seals in Yehud*

Seal Type	HZ	RR	BZ	Jericho	B	EJ	M	EG	BH	HA	TN	Jerusalem
lion	1	45		1		2	1	5			5	23 (CD) 6 (D)
anepigraphic animal												2 (CD)
rosette		1										
scarab					1							
yh		69		10				U			18?	22 (CD) 1 (C) U (M/D)
yhd		49		3				U			6?	10 (CD) U (M/D)2? (M/Z)
yhwd		28						U			4?	1 (CD)
yhwd (2-line)		11										3 (C) U (M/D)
yh(w)d pḥw'		6										
yhwd ḥnnh		2										2 (CD)
yhwd/yh'zr/pḥw'		4										1 (CD)
lyh'zr		8		1								
l'ḥzy/pḥw'		5?		1								9 (CD)
'urywlyhwd				1								
m(w)ṣh		1		2		5			1		30	4 (CD)
'zbq ṣdqyh		1										
b'								U				
conical					1			2				1 (CD)
gem										1		
unclassified												4 (CD)

Table 28. *Coins and Seals in Yehud* (cont.)

Coin Type	HZ	RR	BZ	Jericho	B	EJ	M	EG	BH	HA	TN	Jerusalem
yhd	1											1 (MZ), 1 (GS)
yhzqyh	1?											
Lycian			1									1 (CD)
Archaic Greek												3 (GR, MZ, KH)
Attic tetradracm			1									
imitation Attic dracm			1									
Palestinian obol			1									
Philisto-Arabian obol			2									
Tyrian hemiobol			1									
Sidonian trihemiobol			1									

This table indicates sites within Yehud at which coins and seals have been discovered in surveys or excavations. The following abbreviations are used: HZ = Ḥorvat Zimri; RR = Ramat Raḥel; BZ = Beth-Zur; B = Bethel; EJ = El-Jῑb; M = Mevaserret Zion; EG = En-Gedi; BH = Beth Ḥanina; HA = Har Adar; TN = Tell en-Naṣbeh; CD = City of David; D = Duncan; C = Crowfoot; M/D = MacAlister and Duncan; MZ = Mount Zion; GS = Givat Sarfatit; GR = Givat Ram; KH = Ketef Hinnom. Within the columns, U designates unnumbered. Bibliography for these seals and coins is provided in Chapter 3 in the discussion of the particular sites listed here, with the exception of Duncan, which refers to J.G. Duncan, *Digging up Biblical History*, II (New York: Macmillan, 1931), p. 143, as cited by Christoph, 'The Yehud Stamped Jar Handle Corpus', p. 231.

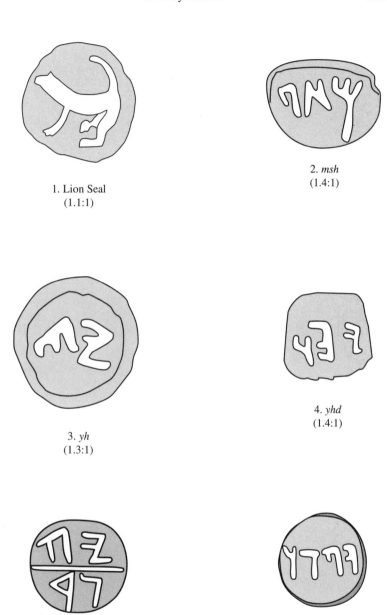

1. Lion Seal
(1.1:1)

2. *msh*
(1.4:1)

3. *yh*
(1.3:1)

4. *yhd*
(1.4:1)

5. 2-line *yhwd*
(0.9:1)

6. *yhwd*
(0.9:1)

Figure 23. *Seals and Coins Dating to the Neo-Babylonian and Persian Periods*

7. *yhwd yhw'zer pḥw'*
(1:1)

8. *yhwd ḥnnh*
(0.9:1)

9. *yhd*
Silver drachm (3:1)

10. *yḥzqyh [h]pḥh*
(4.3:1)

11. *yḥzqyh [h]pḥh yh*
(4:1)

Figure 23. (*cont.*)

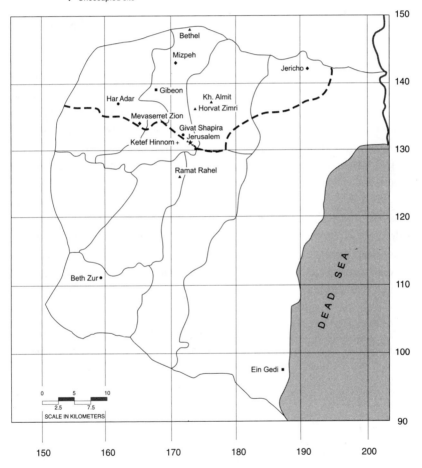

Figure 24. *Distribution of Seals and Coins from the Neo-Babylonian and Persian Periods in the Province of Yehud*

However, these impressions have also been discovered within traditional Judean territory—namely in Jerusalem and Ramat Raḥel. The
relative paucity of the *moṣah* impressions outside of the Benjaminite
territory may lend weight to the former theory; in this view, they could
simply demonstrate the existence of intra-provincial trade or taxation
and still support the notion that the seat of the government resided
within the ancient realm of Benjamin. The fact that the four impressions
from Jerusalem were found within a clear Persian period stratum may
argue against an early dating. The seals do remain somewhat enigmatic
in their own right. If they are associated with the village of Moṣah, it is
curious that none were discovered in the immediate environs of that village; if they are not, it is not clear why so many of them were discovered at Tell en-Naṣbeh. These problems could be solved by reading
m-ṣ-p for the three letter impressions, since that site is typically associated with Mizpah. However, the presence of impressions with the
plene spelling of *m-w-ṣ-h* make the former reading less likely.

The *yehud* impressions must be divided into several sub-categories
(Table 28, Figure 23).[20] The most numerous are those with the reading
of *y-h*; over 130 of these impressions have been recovered from six
sites (Ramat Raḥel, Tell en-Naṣbeh, En-Gedi, Moṣah, Jericho and Jerusalem).[21] More than 76 impressions reading *y-h-d* have been recovered
from the same six sites. The full spelling of *y-h-w-d* have been discovered in one-, two- and three-line exemplars. Some of these bear the
name of an official, some bear the title 'governor' with a proper name,

20. The coins and seals in Figure 23 are new drawings adapted either from
photographs or line drawings from the following sources: (1) *lion seal*, Aharoni,
Excavations of Ramat Raḥel: Seasons 1959 and 1960, Pl. 30: 7; (2) *mṣh*, *TN*, I, Pl.
16:16; (3) *yh*, Aharoni, *Excavations of Ramat Raḥel: Seasons 1959 and 1960*, Pl.
8:4; (4) *yhd*, Aharoni, *Excavations of Ramat Raḥel: Seasons 1959 and 1960*, Pl.
8:2; (5) (2-line *yhwd*), Avigad, *Bullae and Seals*, Fig. 17: 4; (6) *yhwd*, Aharoni,
Excavations of Ramat Raḥel: Seasons 1959 and 1960, Pl. 8:1; (7) *yhwd yhw'zer
pḥw'*, Avigad, *Bullae and Seals*, Fig. 17:7; (8) *yhwd ḥnnh*, Avigad, *Bullae and
Seals*, Fig. 17: 5; (9) *yhd* silver drachm (reverse), R. Deutsch, 'Six Unrecorded
"Yehud" Silver Coins', *INJ* 11(1990–91), pp. 4-6, Pl. 1:1 and 2; (10) *yḥzqyh [h]pḥh*,
L.Y. Rachmani, 'Silver Coins of the Fourth Century B.C. from Tell Gamma', *IEJ*
21 (1971), pp. 158-60 (160); (11) *yḥzqyh [h]pḥh yh[d* (reverse), Deutsch, 'Six
Unrecorded "Yehud" Silver Coins', Pl. 1: 11 and 12.

21. The impressions have been found in the excavations of Crowfoot and Duncan
in the Tyropean Valley, those of Duncan in the Ophel, and both the Kenyon and
Shiloh excavations in the City of David.

presumably of the one who held that office. Approximately 47 inscriptions with the simple reading of *y-h-w-d* have so-far been discovered; the majority of these were discovered at Ramat Raḥel (39), with seven coming from Jerusalem, one from Tell en-Naṣbeh, and at least one from En-Gedi. A total of 28 impressions reading *y-h-w-d* plus personal name or *y-h-w-d/p-ḥ-w-'* were discovered in Jerusalem (12), Jericho (1) and Ramat Raḥel (15). The governors named in the seals were Hananiah (*ḥ-n-n-h*), Yehoʻezer (*y-h-ʻ-z-r*), and Uriyw (*'u-r-y-w*). Fifteen impressions identify one Aḥzy as governor (reading 'belonging to Aḥzy the governors, *l'aḥzy/phw'*). Another set of impressions identify Yehoʻezer (*l-y-h-ʻ-z-r*) as the owner or authenticator of the contents of the vessel; he is presumably the same individual identified as governor in the *p-ḥ-w-'* impression discussed above. Eight of these impressions were discovered at Ramat Raḥel and one was discovered in the Jericho excavations.

This brief summary of the various types and the distribution of seal impressions dating to the Persian period shows that four sites accounted for 94 per cent of the stamps discovered to date. More than half of the impressions come from Ramat Raḥel (54 per cent), nearly one-quarter come from Jerusalem (22 per cent), and approximately one-sixth of them were discovered at Tell en-Naṣbeh (14 per cent). Jericho accounts for 19 seals, a mere 4 per cent of the total. The remaining six per cent were spread throughout the other nine sites, with En-Gedi and El-Jîb each accounting for approximately two per cent of the seals, and the other sites each having only one or two impressions.[22] Given the relative importance of these sites, it is clear that one cannot apply a simple rank-order hierarchy to them. To do so would identify Ramat Raḥel as more important than the provincial capital, Jerusalem. One could, however, argue that both Ramat Raḥel and Tell en-Naṣbeh functioned as administrative centers, perhaps for collecting of goods in-kind or other taxable items. If one accepts a relatively early date for the *m(w)ṣh* impressions, the large number of these seals discovered at Tell en-Naṣbeh —coupled with the relative infrequency of discovery at other major

22. The number of *y-h-d* impressions discovered at En-Gedi is unclear. I attempted to find more complete records of these impressions in 1990 and 1994, but in both attempts was unsuccessful. Neither the facilities at Hebrew University nor the Israel Antiquities Authority have the impressions or the full record of them. Thus, the number of impressions from Tel Goren could be substantially larger than the percentage proposed above.

centers[23]—would support the hypothesis that Tell en-Naṣbeh declined in importance as Jerusalem rebounded and became the imperial capital of the province.

The coin evidence is more meager by comparison. Only 17 coins dating to the Persian period have been discovered in excavations within the territory of Yehud. Of these, five were Yehud coins; two were inscribed with the name of Yeḥezqiyah (*yḥzqyh*) three bore the inscription *yhd* and were decorated with an Athenian owl and other common motifs. The other 12 coins were of various mints and types, including Tyrian, Sidonian, Palestinian, Philisto-Arabian, Lycian, one genuine and one imitation Attic coin, and an 'archaic' Greek type. A full eight were discovered at Beth-Zur;[24] nine were found in or around Jerusalem.

Although there is clear evidence for some use of coins in Persian period Yehud, a number of factors call into question the idea that a *full* monied economy can be dated earlier than the Hellenistic period. These include: the small number of Persian period coins along with their lateness within the period; the percentage of Persian period coins compared with those from subsequent periods in excavated sites; and textual and archaeological evidence of more traditional (i.e. non coin-based) exchange.

The Paucity and Relative Lateness of Coins
The numismatic evidence for Yehud goes far beyond those 17 coins discovered in controlled excavations. According to the catalog compiled in Y. Meshorer's work, *Ancient Jewish Coinage*,[25] a total of 41 *yehud* coins had been discovered from the early nineteenth century

23. One *mṣh* impression is known from Ramat Rahel, two have been discovered in Jericho, four in Jerusalem, five in El-Jîb and one at the 'Belmont Castle'. The latter was discovered in a wall of the castle and was mixed with remains from other periods. As a sole artifact from the Neo-Babylonian period, it is not sufficient to indicate a settlement. On the impression from Belmont Castle, see Zorn, Yellin and Hayes, 'The *m(w)ṣh* Stamp Impressions', p. 168.

24. It would not be appropriate to argue based on the presence of coins in Beth Zur that that settlement was of major economic importance at any time during the Persian period. The archaeological evidence discussed in Chapter 3 (pp. 153-57) shows Beth-Zur to have been only a small village, and raises questions as to whether it was even fortified between the Iron II and Hellenistic periods.

25. These comments are based on Volume 1, *Persian Period through Hasmonaeans*, pp. 13-34.

through 1982. These coins—which Meshorer classifies in 17 distinct types—date from the late fifth/early fourth century through the early third century BCE, from the latter period of Persian rule through the Ptolemaic period. Those dating to the Persian period tend to be inscribed in Aramiac or Paleo-Hebrew, those from the Ptolemaic period are all inscribed in Paleo-Hebrew script. Those from the Persian period generally have the defective spelling of the name of the province, that is, *y-h-d*, while those from the Ptolemaic period typically spell the name of the province as *y-h-d*, *y-h-d-h* or *y-h-w-d-h*. One may now add six previously unknown Yehud coins to the corpus.[26] These include a silver drachm, with parallels to the famous but enigmatic Yehud coin in the British Museum,[27] and five hemiobols. This drachm is decorated with a head of Athena, depicted wearing a helmet with three olive leaves. An owl with an olive spray and the inscription *y-h-d* is on the reverse. The five hemiobols have decorative motifs that are generally well known, including the owl, falcon, dove, lily and *kidaris* (Persian crown). The one unique motif, previously unknown among Yehud coins, is described as a horn, possibly from a gazelle. Two of the coins have either incomplete or transposed inscriptions of the provincial name, *y-h-d*, and two have no legend visible, and are listed as possibly 'off flan'. The final coin appears to read *yhzqyh hphh yh(d)*. The legends of all four of the six coins that are legible are inscribed in Paleo-Hebrew. Unfortunately, no information is given as to the provenance of the current location of these finds.

The discovery of several hoards of coins in Syria-Palestine with mints from important city-states and provinces may allow a more comprehensive reconstruction of the emergence of coinage than the minimal evidence from Yehud itself. Hoards of coins have been discovered in Nablus (the Samarian coins),[28] Eliachin (on the Sharon Plain)[29] and Beth-Zur (discussed above), and mints are known from Tyre, Sidon, Gaza, Ashkelon, Ashdod and the Arabian territories.[30] L. Mildenberg

26. Deutsch, 'Six Unrecorded "Yehud" Silver Coins', pp. 4-6.
27. Mershorer (*Ancient Jewish Coinage*, I, pp. 21-26), and Mildenberg, ('Yehud', pp. 185-87), discuss this coin at length.
28. Y. Meshorer and S. Qedar, *The Coinage of Samaria in the Fourth Century BCE* (Jerusalem: Numismatic Finea Arts International, 1991).
29. R. Deutsch and M. Heltzer, 'Numismatic Evidence from the Persian Period from the Sharon Plain', *Traneuphratène* 13 (1997), pp. 17-20.
30. These mints are discussed at length in Mildenberg, 'Money Circulation in

divides the Syro-Palestinian coinage into three broad categories: imperial, provincial and local. According to his reconstruction, the provincial coinage, such as the Samaria and Yehud exemplars, began to be
minted around 360 BCE; Yehud coins continued to be minted through
the early Ptolemaic period. The local coinage actually appeared before
that minted by provincial governments—sometime around 450 BCE—
and was in use through the end of the Persian period in 332.[31] The existence of both types of coins, and the paucity of imperial coinage in
Syria-Palestine suggests that Persian imperial policy tended to grant
local autonomy in preference to a centralized monetary authority.

*Percentage of Coins from Persian Period Compared with Those from
Subsequent Periods*
Two excavated sites from Yehud—Horvat Zimri and the City of David
—present a data set with which to compare the number of coins dating
to the Persian period with those from later periods. At Horvat Zimri, the
two Yehud coins represented only 3 per cent of the total 74 coins. Of
the other coins, 39 (53 per cent) were Jewish coins minted during the
Hasmonean period, 10 were Hellenistic but of foreign origin (14 per
cent), 4 were Herodian (5 per cent), and 19 were Roman-Byzantine (26
per cent). Analyzing the data according to entire historical periods,
3 per cent of the coins were Persian period, 66 per cent date to the Hellenistic period, and 31 per cent to the Roman through Byzantine periods.
    The evidence from the City of David excavations is similar.[32] Two
hundred and twenty-seven coins have been excavated from Strata 9
through 1, and date from approximately the early fifth century BCE
through the nineteenth century CE. Of these coins, 1 dates to the Persian
period (0.4 per cent), 22 to the early Hellenistic period (9.6 per cent),
113 to the Hasmonean period (49.7 per cent), 72 to the early Roman
period (31.7 per cent), 10 to the Byzantine period (4.4 per cent), and 9

Palestine', pp. 67-70. See also I. Ephal, 'Changes in Palestine during the Persian
Period in Light of the Epigraphic Sources', *IEJ* 48 (1998), pp. 106-19.
    31. According to Mildenberg, the first of the local mints was that of Tyre. The
mint at Gaza began around 420 BCE ('Money Circulation in Palestine', pp. 64 n. 5,
67-68).
    32. 'Coins, Flans, and Flan Moulds', in Ariel (ed.), *Excavations at the City of
David*, II, pp. 99-118..

(3.9 per cent) to the Islamic and later periods.[33] The numismatic evidence parallels the other archaeological data from the excavations, and reflects a continued occupation on the entire area of the City of David from the Persian through the Early Roman periods, but a more moderate occupation—probably limited to the crest of the City of David—from the third through seventh centuries CE. The Islamic period occupation was the most limited, only found in ceramic and numismatic remains in Area A1 of the City of David excavations.

The sharp increase of coins in the Hasmonean period probably reflects the centrality of Jerusalem as capital of the newly established, but short-lived, independent Jewish kingdom. While there is a decline in the number and relative percentages of coins discovered in the Roman and Byzantine periods, it would be a mistake to interpret this as a regression from a monied economy. Instead, these declines reflect a shift in settlement patterns in and around Jerusalem, as confirmed by other surveys and excavations in the Jerusalem area. Nor is it necessary to suggest that coinage entirely replaced in-kind payments of taxes or tribute. The Ottoman taxation records from Syria-Palestine indicate that in-kind payments in barley, wheat and other agricultural products was the primary means of extraction of surplus from the peasantry by the elite.[34]

Weights and Evidence of Traditional Forms of Exchange
There is now clear literary and archaeological evidence that transactions occurred without coins during the Persian period even after coins had been introduced into the economy. In some cases, contracts called for transactions to use weights of silver rather than coins, as in a marriage contract from Elephantine that dates to 420 BCE. According to that agreement, if a certain woman named Yehoyishma divorces her betrothed husband, Ananiah, she must pay '7 shekels and 2 quarters' of

---

33. In addition to the coins, three coin flans and two partial flan molds were discovered. Two of the coin flans date either to the Hasmonean or Herodian periods, and the third may date to the fourth year of the First Revolt against Rome. The flan molds come from two different areas: one was a surface find east of Area E1, the other was from the dumps in Locus 515; both have a *terminus ad quem* of approximately 70 CE ('Coins, Flans, and Flan Moulds', pp. 111-17).

34. I discuss the records from the Ottoman period and their usefulness for reconstructing a socio-economic history of Syria-Palestine in pre-Ottoman periods in 'A Social and Demographic Study', pp. 167-86, 319-44.

silver, weighed on the scales.[35] In other cases, coins were in fact cut up
into pieces for these transactions.[36]

Further evidence of traditional exchange patterns is found in a Babylonian tablet (BM74554) that dates to approximately 486 BCE. This
tablet records a transaction in which one Iddin-Bel pays 14 gur of barley
to the officials of the governor of *eber nahara*.[37] The transaction is done
in the presence of seven witnesses and documented with the seal of
a certain Ṣihā, the 'overseer of the workhouse of the "house of the
wool"', who enters the record into the 'crown ledger'. While M. Heltzer suggests that the tablet has direct import for our understanding of
Yehud's economy, I suggest a more circumspect approach. His conclusion is evidently based on some of the following features: the title of
the two recording officials, Liblut and Gadalama, as *'sipiri'*, which he
translates as '(Aramaic) scribe';[38] he suggests that the name Gadalama
is equivalent to the Yahwistic name Gedalyahu;[39] and he draws a
parallel between the recording official, Ṣihā, and the 'sons of Ṣihā' of
Ezra 2.43//Neh. 7.46. Together, these factors lead him to believe that
the transaction is related not only to *eber nahara* in general, but to
Persian period Yehud in particular.[40] While I believe it is best to avoid a
direct link between the payment to the crown recorded in this tablet and
the province of Yehud, it does show that in-kind payments to the crown
did continue to be made during the Persian period and therefore has
economic significance.

The continued use of traditional means of exchange is also supported
by the weighing stones discovered in the City of David excavations.[41]

35. This marriage contract is from Elephantine, but is relevant to the argument
in that it involves members of the Jewish community that had ties with Syria-
Palestine (Mildenberg, 'Money Circulation in Palestine', pp. 63-65).

36. Mildenberg, 'Money Circulation in Palestine', p. 64.

37. M. Heltzer, 'A Recently Published Babylonian Tablet and the Province of
Judah after 516 B.C.E.', *Transeuphratène* 5 (1992), pp. 57-61.

38. He notes that *'Si/e-pi-ru* always denotes the scribe who writes in Aramaic in
contrary to the *ṭubšarru*, the cuneiform scribe' ('A Recently Published Babylonian
Tablet', p. 58 n. 5).

39. Here, Heltzer cites R. Zadok, *The Jews in Babylonia during the Chaldean
and Achaemenian Periods (According to the Babylonian Sources)* (Haifa: University of Haifa, 1979).

40. 'A Recently Published Babylonian Tablet', p. 61.

41. A. Eran, 'Weights and Weighing in the City of David: The Early Weights

A total of 202 weights of varying denominations and standards were recovered from Strata 20 through 5. Twenty-four (12 per cent of the total) were discovered in the Persian period stratum, and the 30 weights excavated from Strata 8 through 5 date to earlier periods.[42] Of those dating to Stratum 9, 20 were 'bag and counter weights', with a mass of up to 184 grams, and 4 were 'store weights', with a mass of over 185 grams. Evidently the smaller 'bag and counter weights' were used— either individually or with other weights of similar type and mass—to weigh smaller units such as precious metals, and the 'store weights' used for larger transactions, perhaps including in-kind taxes and tribute. Several of the Persian period weights conform either to the standard Judean shekel weight (mass of 11.375 grams) or the so-called *bqʿ* weight (thought to be one-half of the shekel, or 5.70 grams).[43] One weight, found in area D2 (W 153), has a mass of two Persian karsha, and is probably not of local origin.

Taken together, these data suggest a *gradual* development of a monied economy that began in the Persian period and expanded during subsequent periods. It is almost certain that even with the emergence of coinage, in-kind taxation continued, further indicating that the use of coins took considerable time to become widely accepted and to replace the long-standing practice of using weights of precious metals in business exchanges.

Coins and Minting Authorities
Perhaps the most important of the coins for reconstructing the economic history of Persian period Yehud are the *Yeḥezqiyah* coins, of which at least ten are known.[44] One of these coins was discovered in the Beth-

from the Bronze Age to the Persian Period', in Ariel and DeGroot (eds.), *Excavations at the City of David* , IV, pp. 204-56.

42. Some of the weights from the Persian period stratum may also be intrusive and date instead to the Iron II period, although it is impossible to determine with certainty which ones pre-date the Persian period (Eran, 'Weights and Weighing in the City of David', p. 207).

43. However, the exemplars of the *bqʿ* weights are larger than this. For example, W 164 from Area G weighs 13.15 grams, and is thought to represent 'two *bqʿ* of the shekel of the sanctuary'. This, however, would make each *bqʿ* equal to 6.75 grams, and may in fact reflect an Egyptian origin to this weight (Eran, 'Weights and Weighing in the City of David', pp. 210-11, 231).

44. The exact number of the *yḥzqyh* coins is unclear from Meshorer (*Ancient Jewish Coinage*, I). Plates 2 and 3 show clear inscriptions on coins 10-12, but coins

Zur excavations and identifies *Yeḥezqiyah* as governor (*hpḥh*), and another may have been discovered in the excavations at Ḥorvat Zimri.[45] Three other types of *yḥzqyh* coins are known: those without any titular designation, those including his title (*hpḥh*) and the provincial name (*yh[d]*) and those read initially as having a blundered *hpḥh*[46] but now generally read as a coin not of *yḥzqyh hpḥh* but of *yḥn[n] hkhn*.[47] This, along with a coin attributed to another (high) priest, Yaddu'a, is taken to suggest that the institutions of governor and priest were co-equal in the late Persian period.[48] However, a note of caution on this interpretation is appropriate. The Yaddu'a coin appears to date sometime in the early fourth century, as it is inscribed in Aramaic rather than the Paleo-Hebrew that is more common as the fourth century continued. Like some of the Yehud coins that have a late-fifth/early fourth century dating, it is decorated with an owl and bears the common Greek inscription

12a and 13 appear very rough and no inscription is visible. The catalog itself is ambiguous, listing coins 12a and 13 as 'Same as No. 11 (obverse blank) but lynx to r.' and 'Same as no. 11 but on obverse different male head, to r.' (pp. 116-17). The image on coins 12a and 13 show definite parallels to coins 10 and 11, but no evidence of writing. Meshorer's catalog evidently includes the *yḥzqyh* coins from Tell-Gemma, but not the one recently published by Deutsch, 'Six Unrecorded "Yehud" Silver Coins', pp. 4-6.

45. See the discussion of that site in Chapter 3, pp. 132-33.

46. Notably, Mildenberg, 'Yehud', p. 187. Meshorer essentially followed Mildenberg's suggestion in *Ancient Jewish Coinage*, I, p. 116.

47. This reading was first proposed by D. Barag, 'A Silver Coin of Yoḥanan and the High Priest' (Heb.), *Qadmoniot* 17 (1984), pp. 59-61; 'Some Notes on a Silver Coin of Johanan the High Priest', *BA* 48 (1985), pp. 166-68; and 'A Silver Coin of Yoḥanan the High Priest and the Coinage of Judea in the Fourth Century B.C.', *INJ* 9 (1986–87), pp. 4-21, Pl. 1. This reading has been accepted by J. Betlyon and by P. Machinist ('The First Coins of Judah and Samaria: Numismatics and History in the Achaemenid and Early Hellenistic Periods', in Sancisi-Weerdenburg, Kuhrt and Cool Root [eds.], *Achaemenid History*, VIII, pp. 365-80). However, it is important to note that L. Mildenberg seems unconvinced by the reading. Betlyon quotes personal correspondence from Mildenberg as follows: 'I had noticed "careless lettering." Now, Professor D. Barag of the Hebrew University believes to read Johanan left of the owl and Hakohen right. The difference of the two *he* disturbs me very much, but it seems that Barag's reading has been approved by others' ('The Provincial Government', p. 639 n. 26).

48. A. Spaer, 'Jaddua the High Priest?', *INJ* 9 (1986-87), pp. 1-3. The exact dating of the *ydw'* coin is difficult to determine, though Spaer prefers a date in the first quarter of the fourth century.

of AΘE. Spaer suggests that the legend is not difficult, but that the *yod* is somewhat more uncertain than the other letters. What is most important, however, is that the name is not associated with a title. Spaer's attribution of the coin to Yaddu'a I (b. c. 420 BCE) is based in part on Cross's earlier reconstruction of the High Priesthood[49] and that alone. He himself admits that

> The fact that the name Jaddua does appear on this coin does not of course serve as definite proof that it was issued under the authority of Jaddua 'the High Priest'. However, since the discovery of the coin of Yohanan the Priest there seems to be proof that the high priest of Judea did issue coins in their name and although our coin bears neither title nor office of the Jaddua who issued it, this in the absence of another candidate by that name as a possible issuing authority, seems to support the conclusion that he is indeed the person referred to on the coin.[50]

This is hardly convincing logic. The argument is that (1) the Yohanan coin 'seems' to prove that the high priest issued coins during the late fourth century, (2) there is no other likely candidate for said Yaddu'a, therefore it must be Yaddu'a the high priest, and (3) this proves that high priests could and did issue coins. If, in fact, the inscription is of a priest named Yaddu'a, one must also consider the possibility that Yaddu'a II minted the coins.[51] Yaddu'a II was alive during the fall of the Persian empire to Alexander and, like Yehezqiyah, was subject to *Greek* imperial policies. The fact that at least one of the Yehezqiyah coins lacks a title would parallel the Yaddu'a coin, perhaps indicating that neither provincial economy and temple economy were as autonomous as they evidently were during the earlier Persian period. These coins would then all date from the very late Persian *or* the Macedonian period, and would represent a transitional phase of government that is typically associated with the period from 332–323.

49. Cross, 'Reconstruction', pp. 9-11, 17-18.
50. 'Jaddua the High Priest?', p. 3.
51. This proposal, entertained but apparently rejected by D. Barag, is not without its problems. Most important is that the inscription is written in Aramaic—more typical of the earlier coins—rather than the Paleo-Hebrew that is more common of the coins minted in the mid-to-late fourth century. The other factor has to do with the reliability of the accounts of this period by Josephus—typically considered problematic at best—and the accuracy of F.M. Cross's reconstruction of the High Priesthood in 'Reconstruction', pp. 5-7, 9-11. Whether the coin is of Yaddu'a I or II, one must allow for two high priests—father Yaddu'a I and son Yohanan II, or father Yohanan II and son Yaddu'a II—to have held the office at the same time.

However, as Meshorer points out, it is dangerous to attribute too much to the presence or absence of the title on the coins, since the *yḥzqyh* coins are known with and without titular designation.[52] With the coin reading *yḥzqyh hpḥh yh(d)*, we now have three types of coins associated with this governor: one that includes his name, title and the province, at least one with his name and title, and one with simply his name but without either title or provincial name.

Dating and Function of Coins and Seals

Given the variations clearly seen in the discussion above, is it possible to determine at least a provisional dating schema for the coins and the seal impressions? And if it is possible, what do these schemata tell us about the socio-economic developments within the Persian period? Finally, even with these various data, are we any closer to understanding the purpose of the seal impressions and the actual usage for the coins? Of these questions, the dating schemata are easiest to determine, even if the datings remain tentative. Stern had proposed that the impressions inscribed with *m-(w)-ṣ-h* or the enigmatic *b-'*, as well as some of the anepegraphic seals date to the late-sixth/early fifth centuries BCE. He assigned a fifth-century date to some types of lion seals that have parallels to artistic motifs from Ur.[53] He would date all of the Aramaic *y-h-(w)-d* stamps, including those with names of governors and/or the designation *p-ḥ-w-'* to the end of the fifth through the fourth century. This phasing does not, however, include the Babylonian-style impressions known from Har Adar, En-Gedi and Bethel. While Stern's assessment of the earliest impressions is essentially correct, I suggest the following reconstruction (Table 29) based in part on the tentative phasing from the City of David excavations.[54]

The dating of the coins is somewhat more difficult to establish, since so few of them have clearly demarcated archaeological contexts. Generally speaking, most of the Greek coins date to early within the Persian period, with one perhaps dating to the Neo-Babylonian period. Most of the *Yehud* coins and those from other local mints date either to the very late fifth or fourth centuries BCE.

52. *Ancient Jewish Culture*, I, p. 34.
53. Stern, *Material Culture*, pp. 211-13.
54. Chapter 3, pp. 144-45.

Table 29. *Dating of Neo-Babylonian–Persian II Seal Impressions*

Neo-Babylonian-Persian I	Persian II
Babylonian-style seals	*y-h-d*
anegpigraphic impressions	*y-h-w-d*
m-w-ṣ-h	*y-h-w-d* + personal name
b'	*p-ḥ-w-'* + personal name
y-h	*y-h-w-d p-ḥ-w-'* + personal name
y-h-w-d + personal name	
y-h-w-d p-ḥ-w-' + personal name	
p-ḥ-w-' + personal name	

This would probably indicate that the Greek coins were, by and large, 'imports', that is, a result either of foreign trade or foreign presence within Yehud rather than a substantial part of its economy. The *Yehud* and locally minted coins, however, were economically viable, though their exact use and ubiquity remain uncertain. In the table below (Table 30), I follow the general schema of L. Mildenberg, who divides the Persian period mints into the categories of imperial, local, and provincial.

The imperial mints are the least common, indicating that the Achaemenid policy was to allow considerable economic autonomy, though imperial authority is evidenced on some of the local and provincial coins. Mildenberg suggests that the local mints began in the middle of the fifth century BCE, and that the provincial mints began in about the middle of the fourth century. I am inclined to accept the proposal of Betlyon that the Yehud coinage may date as early as the beginning of the fourth century. However, I disagree with his dating of the Yehud drachms to 362–58 and the Yeḥezqiyah coins to 358–46. These datings are based upon his assumption—one widely held, but unproven—that the province of Yehud supported the revolt of Tachos in c. 370–362 BCE, and took part in the Tennes rebellion of 352–347 BCE.[55] While Betlyon points to archaeological evidence of destruction in the mid-fifth century at Hazor, Megiddo, 'Atlit, Lachish and Jericho,[56] only one of these sites was part of the province of Yehud.

55. Regarding Yehud's alleged support of the Tachos rebellion (supported by at least Abd-astart I of Sidon), Betlyon notes: 'We believe that the Judeans, always envious of their own freedom from foreign domination, participated as well and struck coinage with their own ruler's likeness upon it and in the same time period' ('The Provincial Government', p. 637).
56. 'The Provincial Government', pp. 638-39.

Table 30. *Dating of Neo-Babylonian–Persian II Coins*

Neo-Babylonian-Persian I Coins

Type	Date
Archaic Greek (inc. imitation)	Mid-sixth through mid-fifth century BCE

Persian II Coins

Type	Date
Imperial Mints	
Mazday coins[57]	c. 361–328 BCE
Tarsus	
Sidon	
Samaria	

Local Mints of Syria-Palestine	c. 450–332 BCE
Tyre	
Sidon	
Philisto-Arabian	
Gaza	
Ashkelon	
Ashdod	

Provincial Mints

Samaria	c. 350–333 BCE
šmryn	
yrb'm	
šm	
š	

Yehud	Mildenberg	Meshorer	Betlyon	Carter
Athens/Owl	360–350		400–370	400–350
Drachms	350–340	350–340	362–358	350–340
Lily/king w/kidaris	350–340	350–340	370–362	350–340
Bust/lynx	330–312	350–340	340–331	340–332

57. These include those coins bearing his name and those with one or more of his initials. Mazday, the ruler of Transuphratene and Cilicia from 345 through the end of the Persian period, was appointed satrap of Babylon from 331 until his death in approximately 328 BCE. His initials are identified on at least two of the Samarian coins (L. Mildenberg, 'Notes on the Coin Issues of Mazday', *INJ* 11 [1990–91], pp. 9-23).

Yehud	Mildenberg	Meshorer	Betlyon	Carter
Owl/no legend	332–330		345–335	340–332
Yhzqyh (hphh)	340–331	340–331	358–346	340–330
Yhzqyh	332–330	340–331		340–330
	Barag	Spaer	Betlyon	Carter
Ydw'	375–350?	375–350?		375–330?
Yhnn hkhn	350–330		335–331	335–330

And there is, in fact, no evidence of a Persian period destruction at Jericho; rather the site seems to have been gradually abandoned sometime in the late Persian period.[58] Betlyon also cites Stern's dating of a general pattern of destruction to the first quarter of the fourth century in the Benjaminite region, but gives neither a source nor a listing of sites that show this supposed destruction layer.[59] Again, of the major sites that have been excavated and are located within the traditional biblical territory of Benjamin, none shows any evidence of violent termination or the conflagration typical of military retribution.[60]

The seals and coins tell us little specifically about the development of the economy of the Persian period. However, they do confirm some of the general patterns that have been assumed over the past century of research on the Persian period. Since this and the third question raised above—relating to the purpose of both seals and coins—are interrelated, I will treat them together here. First, both seal impressions and coins make it more apparent that the province of Yehud and its economy enjoyed a significant level of autonomy *throughout* the entire Persian period. This is in contrast to the long-held theory that Yehud was subject to and part of the administrative unit of Samaria until the middle of the fifth century BCE.[61] However, one of the major weaknesses of that theory has not, to my knowledge, been identified: none of the seal impressions from Yehud that date to the Neo-Babylonian or Persian periods indicate anything but a local administrative structure,

58. See the discussion of the site in Chapter 3, pp. 160-62.

59. 'The Provincial Government', p. 639.

60. The Persian II sites that have been excavated and that were part of the Benjaminite territory are: Horvat Zimri, El-'Ezariyah, Wadi Salim, Ras el-Kharrubeh, Beitin, Tell En-Nasbeh and Kh. Er-Ras (W). Of these, only Tell En-Nasbeh shows the possibility of a dismantling in the late Persian period, and its end is *not* violent. See discussion in Chapter 3, pp. 126-32.

61. This theory, and its variations, are discussed in Chapter 1, pp. 50-52, and need not be repeated here.

emanating from Tell en-Naṣbeh in the Neo-Babylonian and early Persian period, and from Jerusalem by the end of the sixth century or beginning of the fifth century. Indeed, there are few Samarian seal impressions that parallel those from Yehud, all of which apparently date from the middle of the Persian period or the Ptolemaic period.[62] If Yehud was part of Samaria, one would expect to find at least some indication in the archaeological record of Yehud in the form of seals with Samaritan provenance. Instead, what one finds with both seal impressions and the later coins is a relatively distinct sphere of influence and economic independence. This absence, along with the presence of the various epigraphic and textual remains that allow one to reconstruct a list of governors from at least Zerubbabel through Yeḥezqiyah, would seem to deal a final death blow to Alt's theory of Yehudian subjection to the province of Samaria.[63]

If one accepts the conclusion that the archaeological record itself indicates a substantial level of autonomy in carrying out *internal* provincial affairs, one is still left with serious questions about the nature of

62. Stern notes one impression from the Wâdi ed-Dâliyeh cave that Cross read as follows: '(lyš')yhw bn (sn)'blṭ pḥt šmr(n), ['belonging to Is]aiah, son of [Sana]balat, governor of Samar[ia]'. See F.M. Cross, Jr, 'The Discovery of the Samaria Papyri', *BA* 26 (1963), pp. 110-21. This impression (WD 22) comes from a bulla attached to one of the Samarian papyri has more recently been read as '[Belonging to Yeš']yahu son of [San]ballaṭ, Governor of Samaria' and is assigned a mid-fourth century date. See M.J.W. Leith, *Wadi Daliyeh I: The Wadi Daliyeh Seal Impressions* (New York: Oxford University Press, 1997), p. 10. A second impression (WD 23) appears to name the same individual; *Wadi Daliyeh I*, pp. 184-87. Stern also reports that 16 impressions with some administrative function, probably related to product redistribution, were discovered in the Shechem excavations. These were dated to the Persian period by G.E. Wright, but to the Ptolemaic period by P. Lapp ('Ptolemaic Stamped Handles', p. 27 n. 24, as cited by Stern, *Material Culture*, pp. 214, 276). Stern notes the presence of a 'royal *ṭet* symbol', which probably parallels the symbol on the *yehud-ṭet/yehud + symbol* impressions. The *yehud + symbol* impressions should be dated to the Ptolemaic period, as argued above, and their parallel in Samaritan territory should also be assigned a post-Persian period date.

63. As P. Machinist notes, if one accepts the early dating of the term '*pḥw*' and the seal impressions that bear them—along with the association of the governor with the office it claims—then 'Alt's celebrated thesis...that Judah was originally part of the province of Samaria, separating only in the mid-fifth century after Nehemiah's arrival in Jerusalem, would have to fall' ('The First Coins of Judah and Samaria', p. 373).

that economy. It is probable that the basic economic constraints and practices known from the late Iron Age prevailed. This means that the basic economic structure of the province was tributary in nature. Taxes were extracted from the citizens of Yehud, primarily in-kind, and then passed on to the cultural elite *and* to the imperial coffers. This tributary economy was part of the cultural reality of the Iron Age in both Israel and Judah, but until the fall of both 'kingdoms', the larger portion of the tribute was consumed by national interests. What changed with the exile and the Persian period was not the exacting of tribute, but the ultimate destination of that tribute: in the Neo-Babylonian and Persian periods, the economy was based on what Gottwald calls a 'foreign tributary mode of production'.[64] As indicated above, the shift from an economic setting in which exchange was conducted in-kind to one that was primarily monied was gradual.[65]

The exact function of the seals and coins remains somewhat enigmatic, though somewhat easier to determine for coinage than for the seals. It is probable that the coins initially had two major purposes: one related to trade and the other related to the maintenance of the Persian military. Both Mildenberg and Machinist note the connection of coinage to the military, and Machinist maintains that the size and denomination of the majority of the coins 'represented very small pocket change, appropriate for day wages to soldiers and other workers'.[66] Further, he observes that both the significant military presence in Syria-Palestine and the need to promote and maintain trade to support the military further stimulated the production of coinage.[67]

64. N.K. Gottwald, 'Sociology of Ancient Israel', in *ABD*, VI, p. 84.

65. Perhaps R. Horsley makes the point most clearly: 'Now, money had indeed been "invented" or "discovered" by the sixth century, but a commodity-money economy was an early modern European development. While taxes or tribute payments were measured or accounted by monetary standards under the Achaemenids, they were usually paid in kind, and even the partial monetary economy projected by Kippenberg did not develop' ('Empire, Temple and Community—But no Bourgeoisie! A Response to Blenkinsopp and Petersen', in Davies [ed.], *Second Temple Studies 1*, pp. 163-74 (166). He is referring to Kippenberg's study, *Religion und Klassenbildung*.

66. Machinist, 'The First Coins of Judah and Samaria', p. 373. For a similar view, see Mildenberg, 'Money Circulation in Palestine', p. 64 n. 5, who notes that these coins were used for the 'daily cash' of the provinces.

67. In Machinist's words: '...there must have been numbers of soldiers moving through Palestine in the fourth and early third centuries, and the need to deal with

The use of the seals is more problematic, and is part of an extensive discussion that begins with the *lmlk* and other impressions from Iron Age Israel and Judah.[68] The various interpretations of the function of seal impressions include: (1) governmental and/or religious taxation; (2) trade; and (3) identifying the owner or authenticity of the vessel and/or its contents. Of these, the most commonly held opinion seems to be that the impressions were used primarily for civil or religious taxation. This interpretation is central to Weinberg's *Bürger-Tempel-Gemeinde* theory and forms a part of the basis for Alt's theory of Yehud's subservience to Samaria until the mission of Nehemiah. In both theories, the seal impressions that include the name and title of a governor are thought to indicate a new level of autonomy for the province. Other prominent theories concerning the use of the seals include Aharoni's proposal of a single office but dual portfolios—one civil and one religious, and Lapp's interpretation of a parallel system of taxation for temple and civil governments dating to the Ptolemaic and Hellenistic periods.

Based on a series of statistical tests and the physical distribution of the finds,[69] James Christoph concludes that the Yehud stamps that date to the Persian period were most likely used for trade purposes. In comparing the relationship of the sites with archaeological remains identified as fortresses and those designated as *'pelek'* sites in Neh. 3.2-22, he notes that too few of these sites have evidence of seal impressions, and that the majority of the impressions were from Jerusalem and Ramat Raḥel.[70]

them, and the traders and others associated with them, must have been a considerable stimulus to monetary production' ('The First Coins of Judah and Samaria', p. 373).

68. Christoph provides a useful context of the history and current state of this debate in 'The Yehud Stamped Jar Handle Corpus', pp. 37-74.

69. Christoph also discusses the import of the different language of the impressions. He concludes that the Aramaic and Hebrew are statistically distinct and cannot come from the same 'parent groupings'. Thus, the seals may point to different functions, regional difference or different sociopolitical settings. One further possibility is that—if the impressions are shown to be contemporaneous—they represented two distinct 'collection and storage systems'. If this is the case, it is impossible to determine whether the systems were civil or religious.

70. Significantly, however, Christoph does find a closer connection with the sites he designates as 'forts' than those identified as *'pelek'* sites. This may suggest that the biblical traditions and their administrative districts are more idealized than real.

Christoph contends that if the impressions did, in fact, serve a purpose in a system of collection and storage of in-kind taxes, one would expect a much wider distribution (Figure 25).[71] Since the distribution of impressions currently available through excavations and surveys would seem to leave the 'hinterland' out of the provincial system of production and taxation, Christoph concludes that the seals functioned as 'trade symbol[s]'. This explains the centralized nature of the finds since trade is more likely to 'focus on points of exchange and/or production' as demonstrated with the Rhodian jars that were used in the wine-trade throughout the Mediterranean basin.[72] Arguing against their use in trade is the fact that Yehud impressions have been found in so few places outside the boundaries of the Persian period province, with only Gezer —which some scholars believe was part of the province—and Kadesh-Barnea yielding seal impressions. If the impressions were trade symbols, then why are they not present in the archaeological record beyond the provincial sphere of influence? Further, while I agree with Christoph that the impressions and their distribution do not in and of themselves explain their function, I would expect most of the impressions to be discovered in and around central locations if they were used in taxation and storage. Taxation—either monetary or in-kind—brings resources to administrative centers where they are then redistributed to support the functioning of either political or religious elite.

Summary and Conclusions

In this section, I have analyzed socio-economic patterns and developments in Yehud that new data or new interpretations of those data have brought to light in the past two decades. In some cases, as in the discussion of seal impressions and coins, one can suggest only general economic patterns—the gradual emergence of a monied economy alongside of a traditional in-kind, taxation system; the considerable degree of autonomy enjoyed by the province in establishing its own mints; the agricultural patterns within the province; and a tributary mode of production.

---

71. He concludes: 'Were these jars to represent such practices [i.e. taxation and storage], they should have been recovered through postexilic Yehud at considerably more sites. The concentration of finds is within the capital and its immediate environs. This situation would lead us to understand that only the inhabitants of the immediate vicinity contributed to the fiscal system of Yehud (civil or religious)' (Christoph, 'The Yehud Stamped Jar Handle Corpus', pp. 197-98).

72. Christoph, 'The Yehud Stamped Jar Handle Corpus', p. 200.

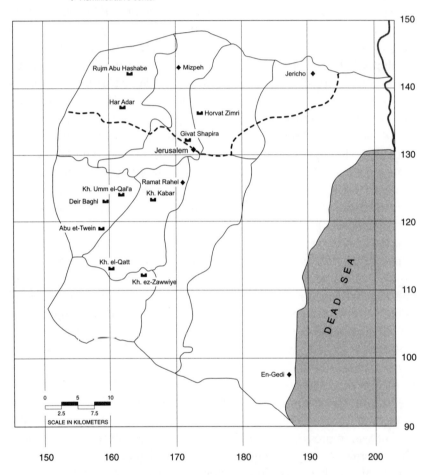

Figure 25. *Distribution of Fortresses and Administrative Centers in the Province of Yehud*

In other cases, what has long been proposed is now clearly evident in the archaeological record: trade with Greece, Egypt and Persia led not only to the exchange of goods but also to a lively local market in which imitations of foreign goods were produced. These goods—both foreign and domestically produced—are typically found in major market centers and within the context of a social elite. While this pattern is by no means new to the Persian period, what was assumed can now be rooted in a comprehensive study of the material culture. In still other cases, such as the function of seals and the implications of both seals and coins for our understanding of governmental structures, the evidence is inconclusive. There is simply not enough evidence to conclude that by the end of the Persian period, the high priesthood had eclipsed the authority of the civil government or to determine the precise function of the seal impressions. A full study of the economic patterns within Yehud is still to be written and will require new data or new methods of interpreting the existing data.

The Implications of a Small Yehud

The size and population of Yehud projected here are far lower than most previous estimates, and considerably lower than the numbers of returnees listed in Ezra 2/Nehemiah 7, both of which record approximately 42,000 exiles leaving Babylon for Yehud. Weinberg, for example, has suggested that the population of the province was about 200,000 before the advent of the *first* return in 539, a figure that is nearly 10 times greater than my projections for the *second half* of the Persian period.[73] Even if one agrees that the lists in Ezra and Nehemiah are composites, reflecting nearly 100 years of immigration to the province of Yehud, those who returned from exile joined a community of people who had remained in the land after the Babylonian conquest. If the projections presented in this study are correct, several important questions remain. If Yehud was this small and this poor, how could the social and religious elite sustain the literary activity attributed to the Persian period? What was the nature of the community that supported it? How could such a small province survive, let alone be considered significant to the security of the Persian empire? How could such a small community have built a temple and/or refortified Jerusalem?

---

73. See 'Demographic Notes', pp. 35-37.

Literary Genius in the Post-Exilic Period

Though scholars are divided as to what corpora of literature were produced in the postexilic period, there is general agreement that the period
was marked by a significant amount of literary activity. Recent suggestions have included placing the Deuteronomic School in Jerusalem in
the Persian period[74] and dating the traditions of the Yahwist to the
sixth–fifth centuries.[75] These may be added to the more traditional evi-
dences of profound literary output: the activity of an Isaian community
(Third Isaiah); the composition of Haggai and First and Second Zechariah; the books of Joel, Jonah and Malachi; the composition of Chronicles and editing of much of the writings.[76] Whether or not the biblical
claim that Ezra brought some form of 'proto-Torah' with him from
Babylon is correct,[77] these traditions attribute to him a significant role
in interpreting those writings anew to a community with different needs
and problems than their earlier audiences.[78]

74. Person, *Second Zechariah*. For the suggestion that many of the exilic works,
including the Deuteronomic History, Ezekiel, Lamentations and Second Isaiah,
were not composed in Babylon but in Jerusalem, see H.M. Barstad, 'On the History
and Archaeology of Judah during the Exilic Period: A Reminder', *OLP* 19 (1988),
pp. 25-36.

75. Van Seters suggests that the Yahwist dates not to the tenth/ninth centuries
BCE, but composed Genesis–Numbers as an introduction to the Deuteronomic His-
tory sometime during the exile. See his recent works: *Prologue to History*; and *The
Life of Moses*.

76. G. Garbini places the formative period of many of the traditions of the
Hebrew Bible squarely in the Persian period: '...under the domination of the Ache-
menids, Hebraism knew its magical moment and Hebrew Literature its golden age'
(see 'Hebrew Literature in the Persian Period', p. 188).

77. J.L. Berquist suggests that the Persian emperor Darius may have been partly
responsible for the Persian period redaction of the Torah. He holds that the later
mission of Ezra was intended to bring a Persian authorized law-code to the province
of Yehud, as both a religious and civil body of law (*Judaism in Persia's Shadow*,
pp. 137-41).

78. M. Fishbane argues that Ezra was not only a second Moses-figure, but also
that significant linguistic and symbolic images linked him to the pre-exilic prophetic community (see 'From Scribalism to Rabbinism: Perspectives on the Emergence of Classical Judaism', in J.G. Gammie and L.G. Perdue [eds.], *The Sage in
Israel and the Ancient Near East* [Winona Lake, IN: Eisenbrauns, 1990], pp. 439-
56). Fishbane draws attention to two phrases: *lidrōsh*—to seek, or in Ezra's case, to
interpret; and the idiom, the 'hand of YHWH'. Both phrases have ties to the prophetic movement and both validate Ezra as a divinely inspired interpreter of Torah.

But could a small Jerusalem support this level of literary production? This question is really one of the size and nature of urban elites. In agrarian societies urban communities accounted for a relatively small proportion of the total population, usually less than 10 per cent,[79] but were responsible for a wide variety of social, political and religious functions. In such urban communities craft specialization is ubiquitous; elites with different functions concentrated in these communities, supported in large measure by extracting surplus from agrarian peasants in the surrounding villages.[80] What type of elites were centered in Jerusalem? According to the biblical traditions, professional members of the cult were represented, including Aaronide, Zadokite and Levitical priests (Ezra 8.15-36; Neh. 7.1, 39, 43); singers (Neh. 7.1, 23, 45);

Fishbane concludes: 'The combination of these two factors ... highlights the chief *novum* of this historical record: Ezra is a priestly scribe who teaches the received, written revelation through his inspired study of it. In the process, the Torah traditions undergo a corresponding refiguration. No dead letter, the ancient divine words become the very means of new instruction through their proper inquiry and interpretation' (p. 411). If he is correct, Ezra (and more broadly, the Priestly movement) would be exonerated from the charge of Wellhausen that the legal impetus of the Priestly community led to the decline of Israelite religion. Instead, prophetic genius was mediated to the postexilic community through the person of Ezra.

79. See Lenski, *Power and Privilege*, pp. 200-204; and G. Lenski, J. Lenski and P. Nolan, *Introduction to Human Societies: A Macro-Sociological Approach* [New York: McGraw-Hill, 6th edn, 1991), pp. 163-66.

80. As Lenski, Lenski and Nolan point out, it is often the function of the religious elites to devise ideology that will support the cultus and, perhaps, the state; such ideology is generally necessary to convince the peasantry to part with surplus. He notes: '*Technological advance created the possibility of a surplus, but to transform that possibility into a reality required an ideology that motivated farmers to produce more than they needed to stay alive and productive, and persuaded them to turn that surplus over to someone else*. Although this has sometimes been accomplished by means of secular and political ideologies, a system of beliefs that defined people's obligations with reference to the supernatural worked best in most societies of the past' (*Human Societies*, p. 162 [italics in original text]). Evidently, by the mid-fifth century, that ideology was no longer entirely successful. Nehemiah 13.10 records that since they had not received their payment from the tithe, many Levitical priests and singers had 'fled to their fields'. It is possible that the tithes and 'portions' intended to support the Levitical priests had been collected, but not distributed to them due to official corruption. Nehemiah subsequently claims to have dealt with this problem, guaranteeing them payment and restoring them to their 'rightful' position. Note also that in Neh. 10.37, one function of the Levitical priests is collection of taxes.

temple servants (Neh. 3.26, 31; 7.46; 11.19); gatekeepers (Neh. 7.1, 23, 45); and a scribal class (Ezra 8.1, 9). The provincial governor would most likely have had a staff ('Solomon's servants' of Neh. 11.57-60?); with the fortification of the city under Nehemiah, conscripts would have been garrisoned there (the 'men of the guard', Neh. 4.23; 7.3). Other specialists represented include goldsmiths (Neh. 3.8, 21-22); perfumers (Neh. 3.8); and both masons and carpenters (Ezra 3.7).[81] The population of Jerusalem in the Persian II period was between 1250 and 1500, or between 6.0 and 7.3 per cent of the population of Yehud; these figures are well within the 5 to 10 per cent average of urban centers in the pre-industrial age.[82] Thus, based on historical and sociological parallels cited here, the level of literary creativity traditionally attributed to the Persian period need not be questioned on the grounds either of a small province or a small Jerusalem.

Economic Security and a Small Yehud

One could argue that a small Yehud is equivalent to an insignificant Yehud. Further, one may wonder, given the relatively modest area of the province—restricted primarily to the central hills—and its even more modest population, how Yehud could have survived economically and supported the operation of the temple complex.[83] A look at the rele-

---

81. This diversification is generally in keeping with urban elites and probably represents only a small portion of the elites of Jerusalem. G. Lenski notes: 'The cities and larger towns of agrarian societies have long been noted for *the diversity of vocations* followed by their inhabitants. Among the major occupational categories represented, the following deserve note, since, collectively, they included the great majority of the urban population: officials, priests, scholars, scribes, merchants, servants, soldiers, craftsmen, laborers, and beggars' (*Power and Privilege*, pp. 200-201). He also points out that larger cities tend to have a greater craft specialization among elites (Paris, e.g., had over 157 different crafts represented in 1313), smaller cites might typically have up to 50 craftspeople, and even small villages might have as many as 20 different specialists.

82. If anything, the population of Jerusalem was higher than normal. Lenski observes that in seventeenth- and eighteenth-century Russia, urban population accounted for no more than three per cent of the total population, and by the mid-nineteenth century was only eight per cent of the total. Likewise, in fourteenth-century England, less than 5.5 per cent of the population lived in towns of more than 3200 people (*Power and Privilege*, pp. 199-200).

83. Several scholars have raised this type of question. Among them are: J. Halligan, 'The Temple that Never Was: Zerubbabel's. A Social-Scientific Investigation', paper presented at the International meeting of the Society of Biblical Literature,

vant texts suggests that there were indeed problems with both. The prophet Haggai relates famine, blight, drought and general futility to the preoccupation of the people with their own affairs and the failure to re-build the temple (Hag. 1.3-11; 2.15-19; see also Zech. 8.9-13). If in fact the biblical traditions are correct in according success to the ministries of Haggai and Zechariah—that is, if in fact a temple was constructed in the late sixth century—Jerusalem was still apparently not fully restored. Nehemiah evidently came to Jerusalem some 70 years later to find its walls still in disrepair (Neh. 1-2) and the Levitical priesthood dispersed throughout the province because their base of economic support had been severely eroded (Neh. 13.10-13). The people are also character-ized as suffering from the effects of heavy (imperial?) taxation and (internal Yehudite?) administrative abuses (Neh. 5.1-19). The long-term effect of the latter was the increase of debt slavery, the breakdown of the family structure, and general economic malaise. These kinds of problems, even though exaggerated for rhetorical or other purposes, reflect the kind of conditions one would expect in a relatively small and poor province.

If these texts and the archaeological data do correspond to one another, as they appear to, how could this struggling community have survived? It is here that the wider social, geographic and economic contexts must be brought to bear. For if one focuses solely on one component part of the empire, that is, the province of Yehud, one's conclusions concerning the nature of that part may become skewed. But Yehud did not exist in a vacuum; other important social, political and religious developments took place outside of the province within Syria-Palestine. Yehud was part of a larger administrative district, *eber nahara*, which was in turn part of the Persian empire. The temple-building program claimed for Yehud in Ezra–Nehemiah seems to have

Dublin, 1996); Carroll, 'So What Do We *Know* about the Temple?', pp. 34-51; and D.J.A. Clines, 'Haggai's Temple Constructed, Deconstructed and Reconstructed', in Eskenazi and Richards (eds.), *Second Temple Studies 2*, pp. 60-87 (a revised ver-sion of this article was published in *Interested Parties: The Ideology of Writers and Readers of the Hebrew Bible* [JSOTSup, 205; Sheffield: Sheffield Academic Press, 1995], pp. 46-75); P. Marinkovic, 'What Does Zechariah 1–8 Tell Us about the Second Temple', in Eskenazi and Richards (eds.), *Second Temple Studies 2*, pp. 88-103. Halligan's approach is more socio-economic, whereas the latter studies are more literary in nature. All agree that the temple, whatever else it might have been, was a cultural and/or ideological construct.

been consistent with the Persian imperial policy of restoring cults and temples of peoples and religions that had previously been subjugated by the Neo-Babylonians.[84] If the project was financed at least in part by the empire, then the total weight of fiscal responsibility did not fall on the *gôlāh* community. Further, there is ample textual witness to returnees settling outside the border of the province. For as both Rainey and Ackroyd have pointed out, '*Jewry is larger than Judah*'.[85] The loyalty of these returnees was not only financial,[86] but may also be seen in their providing work details for the rebuilding of the walls of Jerusalem (Neh. 3).

One of the chief criticisms that could be leveled against a small Yehud is its alleged instability without the economic surplus that the Shephelah and Coastal Plain would have provided. If these two geographic entities were not part of Yehud, to what province should they be attached? The situation on the coastal plain is relatively clear (Figure 26). According to L. Stager, it was under Phoenician control, with specific authority over the major cities of the plain alternating between Tyre and Sidon.[87] Dor may have been the capital city of the province named after itself,[88] as was Ashdod.[89]

---

84. See the extended discussion of J. Blenkinsopp in 'Temple and Society', pp. 22-26.

85. Ackroyd, 'Archaeology, Politics and Religion', p. 5 (emphasis added); Rainey, 'The Biblical Shephelah', p. 18.

86. In this regard, see Blenkinsopp and his discussion of the wider temple economy (the so-called *Bürger-Tempel-Gemeinde*, or 'civic–temple community') of Yehud. He maintains that 'the community, therefore, shared with the imperial government the expenses of construction and maintenance. By means of this partial underwriting, and by reserving to themselves responsibility for the actual rebuilding to the exclusion of the native population (Ezra 4.1-5), the *gôlāh* community in effect claimed control of the Jerusalem cult under the supervision and protection of the imperial authorities' (Blenkinsopp, 'Temple and Society', pp. 39-40).

87. 'Why Were Hundreds of Dogs Buried at Ashkelon?', *BARev* 17 (1991), pp. 26-42 (28). This arrangement evidently was in force as far south as Ashkelon, which was itself under Tyrian control. This view is supported by the Eshmun'ezer inscriptions which claims control the Sharon Plain. See Chapter 2 above, pp. 96-97.

88. E. Stern, 'The Dor Province in the Persian Period in the Light of the Recent Excavations at Tel Dor', *Transeuphratène* 2 (1990), pp. 147-55; *idem*, 'New Evidence on the Administrative Division of Palestine in the Persian Period', in Sancisi-Weerdenburg and Kuhrt (eds.), *Achaemenid History*, IV, pp. 221-26.

89. Bennett, Jr, and Blakely (eds.), *Tell el-Ḥesi*, pp. 335-39.

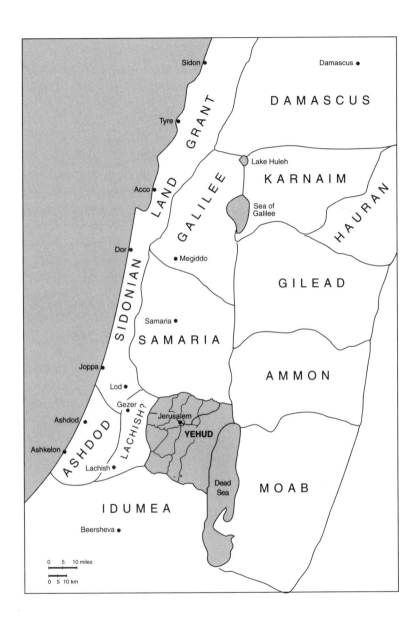

Figure 26. *The Province of Yehud in Syria-Palestine during the Persian Period*

Lachish was probably the seat of another province, perhaps Idumea.[90] Gaza remained an independent city-state, but may have been linked to the provinces of Arabia.[91] Control of the Shephelah itself evidently alternated between Egypt and Persia; when controlled by the Persians, it is somewhat unclear to which province it was attached, although it would have fallen most naturally under the jurisdiction of Lachish.

How did Yehud relate to other provinces? Once again it is important to remember that according to my reconstruction loyal Judeans lived outside the borders of Yehud. Presumably, that loyalty would have been shown, in part, financially, just as during the later Second Temple period Jews from the diaspora contributed to the upkeep of the Temple.[92] Thus, former exiles who had returned to their homeland would have continued to offer sacrifices in Jerusalem and to celebrate the major pilgrim festivals there. The sacrifices themselves were a form of taxation and designed to underwrite the priesthood and other temple officials. This income from the periodic influx of pilgrims would also have had wider effects on the economy of Jerusalem. And, if Nehemiah's claim to have imposed a one-third shekel temple-tax on the inhabitants of the province is accepted (Neh. 10.33-34), that tax would have further supported temple operations.[93]

Just as economic support for the temple and its operations may have flowed into Yehud from beyond its borders, it is evident that other, non-cultic exchanges occurred as well. Perhaps exchanges between provinces were similar to those in effect in the late Iron II period. It is likely, for example, that by the late seventh century BCE, Tel Miqne-Ekron

90. Bennett, Jr, and Blakely (eds.), *Tell el-Hesi,* p. 337. At Lachish a monumental building, called 'The Residency', dating to the Persian period, was excavated; Bennett and Blakely suggest that it may have been the governor's residence.

91. Bennett, Jr, and Blakely (eds.), *Tell el-Hesi*; p. 337; see also Stager, 'Hundreds of Dogs', p. 28.

92. As argued by M. Broshi, 'The Role of the Temple in the Herodian Economy', *JJS* 38 (1987), pp. 31-37.

93. It is unclear how extensive this tax was collected; it is certainly possible that if Jews from the diaspora paid it, as they did during the Herodian period. Broshi suggests that about 500,000 Jews lived in Palestine and paid the tax during that later period, and that as many as 2,000,000 diaspora Jews contributed to the temple in this manner. We also know that during the Persian period the *gôlāh* community had offers from other communities to assist in rebuilding the temple. Although their offers were rebuffed, it is possible that Jewish communities existed in Galilee and perhaps the Transjordan during this time.

produced up to 80 per cent of the olive oil of all of Palestine. Although Tel Miqne-Ekron was destroyed by the Babylonians (perhaps as early as 603 BCE), the principle of regional production centers was probably maintained by the Neo-Babylonian and Persian empires.[94] These kinds of interrelationships with other provinces in Palestine would have been vital to the security of Yehud, and may explain, the large granaries at Tell el-Hesi and, perhaps, El-Jîb, the public storage areas such as those in Tell en-Naṣbeh, and the production centers such as those in Kh. Er-Ras (S). These kinds of interrelationships with other areas of Palestine would have been vital to the security of Yehud (Figure 26).

At issue, then, is not only the survival of a small province in the central hill country in Palestine in the sixth through fourth centuries BCE. Larger imperial policy dictated, to a certain degree, events in and around Yehud.[95] Thus, as K. Hoglund maintains, the refortification of Jerusalem was not merely an act of largesse on the part of the Persian emperor, designed to gain the loyalty of a small but important ethnic group in western Palestine. Rather, it was evidently intended to secure western Palestine, Yehud, Samaria and the southern coastal plain for the empire in the face of growing threats from Greece and Egypt, threats in which the city of Dor may have been involved. In this regard, Hoglund has argued that the economic stability of Yehud was in the best interests of the empire;[96] even a small Yehud would have been guaranteed adequate resources from other provinces, including the Shephelah (when in Persian hands) and coastal plain sites. This does not mean that the interrelationships among the provinces would have been

94. On the importance of and evidence for regional interrelationships in the seventh century BCE see S. Gitin, 'Tel Miqne-Ekron: A Type Site for the Inner Coastal Plain in the Iron Age II Period', in S. Gitin and W.G. Dever (eds.), *Recent Excavations in Israel: Studies in Iron Age Archaeology* (AASOR, 49; Winona Lake, IN: Eisenbrauns, 1989), pp. 23-58 (48-51).

95. Hoglund, *Achaemenid Imperial Policy*, and Berquist, *Judaism in Persia's Shadow*, both develop this very point extensively. Yet, Ackroyd's caveat that too much can be made of the concept of 'imperial policy' is well taken. He observes that such policy 'is not necessarily always consistent. Pragmatic decisions may be at different levels, responding to different needs as they are perceived. Politicians, as we all know, can make mistakes of judgment, and they can show themselves inept...We must not look for a greater coherence and intelligibility in political action in the past than we should expect to find in our own time' ('Archaeology, Politics, and Religion', p. 17).

96. *Achaemenid Imperial Administration*, pp. 207-40.

free from the petty rivalries that traditionally existed among city-states in earlier periods of Palestine's history. Rather, the apparent shift in imperial policy signified by the increased status of Jerusalem in the mid-fifth century led to just such rivalries between Yehud and representatives from Samaria, Ashdod and the Arab provinces.[97] These observations suggest that a distinction should be drawn between a small Yehud and an unstable Yehud. Yes, Yehud was probably smaller and poorer than many earlier reconstructions of the province have suggested.[98] This would in turn explain the relatively minimal messianic expectations of the early Persian period and would suggest that little if any hope for independence existed at that time.[99] But small and relatively poor does not mean insignificant or isolated. The archaeological witness and textual data seem to agree that as the Persian period progressed, the size and status of the province increased.

The Bürger-Tempel-Gemeinde *and a Small Yehud*

Joel P. Weinberg's theory of a collective of communities he calls a *Bürger-Tempel-Gemeinde* has influenced many of the recent reconstructions of the social structure of the province of Yehud in the Persian

97. On both the political and religious implications of the tensions between Samaria and Yehud, see Ackroyd, 'Archaeology, Politics, and Religion', pp. 13-15. He suggests a linkage in rule of the two areas, at least early in the Persian period, due in part to the the correspondence from Elephantine addressed to both cities. Berquist suggests that the Persian rulers took advantage of the petty rivalries between the various provinces in Syria-Palestine by using them to keep regional coalitions from forming and thus threatening Persian interests in the region. See *Judaism in Persia's Shadow*, pp. 116-19.

98. Contrast, e.g., the figures of J.P. Weinberg and N.P. Lemche. As noted, Weinberg suggests that even before the return from exile, the population of Yehud was approximately 200,000, more than 10 times that of my reconstructed province. See Weinberg, 'Demographic Notes', pp. 43-48. Lemche estimates that the pre-exilic population was between 50,000 and 100,000, and envisions a rather extensive defeat of Judah at the hands of the Babylonians. Given that destruction, he asks why Jews who had been in exile would have chosen to return and what would they have found upon returning? (*Ancient Israel*, pp. 189-90).

99. Contra Hanson, *The Dawn of Apocalyptic* (pp. 240-63), who sees a heated conflict within the postexilic community between the so-called hierocratic party, represented by the dyarchy of Zerubbabel ben Shealtiel and Yehoshua ben Yehozadak, and the visionary party, represented in the prophecies of Third Isaiah. On the role and place of Zerubbabel, see below.

period. While Weinberg's work contributes to the scholarly discourse concerning Yehud and is a testimony to his courage and creativity,[100] it is nonetheless surprising that it has been accepted so uncritically. This may be due in part to the relative lack of accessibility to the work that he cites; much of his own previous work and some of the research upon which he bases his model is available only in Russian. Whatever the reasons for the widespread appeal of his work, it is appropriate to begin a preliminary evaluation of his model in light of the much smaller province that this study presents.

As pointed out in Chapter 1, Weinberg's model assumes that Yehud in the Achaemenid period is best understood in the context of a general pattern of urbanization[101] and economic growth that he refers to as 'pre-Hellenism'.[102] This pattern normally includes an economic setting centered in a temple economy in which the social, political and economic power is seated in the temple of the major deity of the major cities of these emerging communities. Membership in the *Bürger-Tempel-Gemeinde* (hereafter, *BTG*) is typically limited to the priesthood and temple functionaries of the deity and members of agnatic collectives that are loyal to the deity and economically related to the temple/deity. Weinberg identifies postexilic Yehud as an emergent *BTG*. In its earliest history, Weinberg believes that Yehud was composed of two entities: a politically/geographically defined province; and the members of the *BTG*, whom he identifies with the *gôlāh* community that had returned to

100. As noted by Smith-Christopher in 'Translator's Foreword', pp. 15-16.

101. Weinberg repeats this assertion in 'Transmitter and Recipient in the Process of Acculturation: The Experience of the Judean Citizen–Temple Community', *Transeuphtratène* 13 (1997), pp. 91-105 (93-96). Here, Weinberg is most certainly incorrect, at least for Yehud, where there are only 2 villages over 20 dunams in the Persian II period. These villages are less than half the size of the provincial capital, Jerusalem. Further, I am uncomfortable with using a term like 'urbanization', for it seems somewhat anachronistic. It brings to mind social developments that are more correctly place in pre-industrial age Western culture. While major urban centers existed in both horticultural and agrarian cultures as early as the Early Bronze Age, this is quite different from 'urbanization' in the modern sense. As Robert McC. Adams notes: '...these first steps in urban growth lead to a distinctive constellation of features that cannot be regarded simply as progressively approximating contemporary urbanism more and more closely' (*The Evolution of Urban Society: Early Mesopotamia and Prehispanic Mexico* [Hawthorne, NY: Aldine Publishing Co., 1966], p. 10).

102. 'Comments on the Problem', pp. 17-33.

the province from Babylon. These two entities often had competing interests. A major shift took place in the middle of the fifth century BCE, with the missions of Ezra and particularly Nehemiah, after which the entire province of Yehud became a more fully developed and more fully franchised *BTG*.

Areas of Agreement with Weinberg

At this point it may be helpful to see the areas in which I am in agreement with Weinberg's assessment of the exilic and postexilic periods in Palestine. We agree that there is a need to address the sociology and socio-economic structure of the exile and the Persian period. We concur that the exile was perhaps more psychologically and sociologically devastating both to the deportees and those who remained in Judah than has often been maintained. It is also necessary to consider the different strategies for survival that developed in Babylon and Judah in any reconstruction of the period.[103] We agree that it is impossible to understand the period without addressing the sociology of empires in general and the needs and motivations of the Persian empire in particular.[104] We agree that there was a change in imperial policy and the fortunes of the postexilic community in the mid-fifth century BCE, and that change is reflected both in biblical texts and archaeological context. We further agree that textual data and archaeological remains must be consulted in tandem to reach a more accurate picture of Achaemenid Yehud. Moreover, we agree that there is a clear demarcation between the returnees and the people left behind, and a definite attempt on the part of the returnees to be the power-brokers in both religious and socio-economic matters for the larger community. It is also quite possible that Weinberg is correct in identifying the *bêt 'abôt* as one of the basic social units of the Persian period. These lines of agreement are significant, and I highlight them so that the objections I am about to raise to Weinberg's work will not obscure my respect for his work.

103. As noted in Chapter 1, this notion is developed in its most complete form by Smith, in *The Religion of the Landless.*

104. The studies of Hoglund (*Achaemenid Imperial Administration*) and Berquist (*Judaism in Persia's Shadow*) both demonstrate the importance of understanding wider Persian imperial policy in any discussion of Yehud's history.

Crucial Areas of Disagreement

Much of Weinberg's reconstruction stands or falls on his uncritical use of three sets of texts: the list of returnees in Ezra 2/Nehemiah 7; other lists of cities in which people settled (particularly Neh. 3 and Neh. 11.25-35); and the account of a tax remission for the temple functionaries of Yehud (Ezra 7.13-26, esp. v. 24). According to Weinberg, the list of Ezra 2/Nehemiah 7[105] represents an accurate picture of the returning *gôlāh* community as it was constituted from 538 through 458/457 BCE. He uses this list to form the basis of his sociology of the first half of the Persian period, including the make-up of the *BTG*.

Weinberg considers the lists of Nehemiah 3 and Nehemiah 11 as authentic documents that reflect accurately the changes within the *BTG* in Yehud that occurred with and subsequent to the missions of Ezra and Nehemiah. He rejects the more common views that Neh. 11.25-36 is patterned after the boundary lists of Joshua 15 and 18, reflects the Judean monarchy in the late seventh/early sixth century, or is an idealized portrait of the province.[106] Instead, he suggests that both lists indicate that the *BTG* had grown substantially. He maintains that whereas the *BTG* had 42,000 members, 19 communities in 3 geographic regions before 458/457, after that point (based on the lists of Neh. 3, 11), the community had 150,000 members, 50 communities, in up to six regions.[107] The *BTG*, even at that point, did not represent the entire

105. He views the Neh. 7 version as the original, and as reflective of the social context for the list of returnees. See 'Demographic Notes', pp. 41-42.

106. 'Demographic Notes', pp. 44-45. He cites the following scholars for the first two of these views on p. 45 nn. 1-2: G. von Rad, *Das Geschichtsbild des chronistischen Werkes* (BWANT, 4.3; Stuttgart: W. Kohlhammer), 1930), pp. 21-24, and E. Meyer, *Die Entstehung des Judentums: Eine historische Untersuchung* (Halle: Niemeyer, 1896), pp. 105-107, note the parallel between the Nehemiah list and those of Josh. 15 and 18. U. Kellerman, 'Die Listen in Nehemia 11: Eine Dokumentation aus den letzten Jahren des Reiches Juda?', *ZDPV* 82 (1966), pp. 209-27, argues that Neh. 11.25-36 reflects the social setting at the end of the Judean monarchy. To these we may add Stern, 'The Province of Yehud', pp. 9-21. While Stern himself tends to attribute a significant level of veracity to the lists of villages within Ezra–Nehemiah texts, he does argue that the Neh. 11 text presents an idealized portrait of the province, one modeled after the Judean monarchy.

107. 'Demographic Notes', pp. 44-47, see esp. Table 5, p. 47. Here, Weinberg's math is incorrect. He cites the growth in the community, the number of villages/cities, and regions as 3.6 per cent, 2.6 per cent, and 2 per cent respectively. According to his own figures, the *BTG* was 3.54 times larger at the end of the Persian period than at its beginning, comprised of 2.6 times more communities, and twice

province, but only 50-60 per cent of the total population.[108] This would make the population range for the entire province somewhere between 250,000 and 300,000. Even allowing for a community settled in a larger geographic area including the Negev, the Judean highlands, the coastal plain and the Judean desert, these figures lack credibility.

Here, two major problems emerge. On the one hand, Weinberg's approach is not sufficiently nuanced or sensitive to the textual histories or their use within Ezra–Nehemiah. It is notoriously difficult to date the lists in Ezra 2//Nehemiah 7, Nehemiah 3 and 11 to a particular point within the Persian period.[109] While they purport to reflect the status of the community during the mission of Nehemiah, Weinberg does not take into consideration the role of the final redactor of these lists and their placement within Nehemiah. Simply put, even if they *are* accurate, there is no evidence, biblical or otherwise, that they relate specifically to the *BTG* that Weinberg assumes existed. As I have indicated in my discussion of Nehemiah 11 as it relates to the boundaries of the province, it is best interpreted not as an enumeration of localities that were part of the province of Yehud, but as representing an *idealized* portrait of the province.[110] Weinberg is alone in taking the texts of Ezra 2// Nehemiah 7, Nehemiah 3, and Nehemiah 11 at face value and assigning them the level of historical accuracy that his hypothesis requires, and he is alone in proposing that they reflect substantial growth in the size or social setting of Yehud. Thus, in two crucial areas, Weinberg relies too heavily on these texts and draws conclusions from them that are questionable at best.

Weinberg's use of population figures is also seriously flawed. This begins with his use of the numbers in the lists of deportees from 2 Kings and Jeremiah as a basis for establishing the population of Yehud in the postexilic period. He estimates that 20,000 persons were exiled from Judah and Jerusalem in 597 and 586, and that the population of the Southern Kingdom was approximately 240,000 at that time.[111] He then assumes a total number of those that remained on the land was

as many regions. The level of growth was 254 per cent, 163 per cent, and 100 per cent respectively.

108. 'The Postexilic Citizen–Temple Community', pp. 132-33.

109. Grabbe summarizes the difficulties in *Judaism from Cyrus to Hadrian*, pp. 38-41, 79-80.

110. See Chapter 2, pp. 80-81.

111. 'Demographic Notes', pp. 34-37.

220,000, and uses this figure as the basis of all of his computations on the population of Persian period Yehud and the make-up of the *BTG*. Recent estimates of the population of the Kingdom of Judah at the end of the eighth century BCE are less than half that amount.[112] Finkelstein and Broshi estimate that the population of Judah in the central hills, Benjamin and Jerusalem was approximately 110,000.[113] Even allowing for the expansion of Judah after the destruction of Israel, 240,000 as a population of Judah 100 years later would be too high. Estimates of the population of Judah at the end of the Judean monarchy (in the late seventh, early sixth century) based on Ofer's survey suggest that approximately 100,000 lived in the kingdom, with the population of the central hills, Jerusalem and Benjamin about 69,000.[114] Thus, recent archaeological studies provide additional support for what biblical scholars have already suggested: Weinberg's figures, both as a starting point for the exile and as an estimate for the population of Yehud at any time during the Achaemenid period, are far too high.[115]

H. Williamson has recently pointed out a further problem—one perhaps more damaging than his use of these lists—centering around Weinberg's interpretation of Ezra 7.24-26.[116] These verses are part of the putative letter in which Artaxerxes commissions Ezra to take people and resources to Yehud, and to establish the 'law of your God' in the province. According to this document, cultic functionaries—including priests, Levites, singers, gatekeepers, (cultic) servants or ministers—are

112. Broshi and Finkelstein, 'The Population of Palestine', pp. 51-52.

113. According to their estimates, the population for all of Palestine at the end of the eighth century BCE was approximately 400,000.

114. Figures of settled area and population are given above in Chapter 5, pp. 246-48 and nn. 17-18.

115. This is compounded by Weinberg's use of a population coefficient of 1000 persons per hectare (= 100 persons per dunam) in 'Demographic Notes', p. 35. While this figure was appropriate in the early use of ethnographic data for population estimates—those in use when Weinberg wrote this article in 1972—they are now fourfold higher than the number used in current population estimates. Weinberg does not address this issue in his retrospective article in *The Citizen–Temple Community* ('The Postexilic Citizen–Temple Community'), but still assumes a population in the range noted above.

116. H. Williamson, 'Judah and the Jews', in M. Brosious and A. Kuhrt (eds.), *Achaemenid History. XI. Studies in Persian History: Essays in Memory of David M. Lewis* (Leiden: Nederlands Instituut voor Het Nabije Oosten, 1998), pp. 145-63 (154-56).

exempt from any form of taxation (Ezra 7.24). While in its current context, the tax exemption refers only to temple functionaries with widely divergent duties, Weinberg maintains that the exemption was extended to the entire *BTG*. Further, he contends that this exemption served to distinguish the *BTG* from the rest of the Jewish community in Palestine, which was required to pay taxes.[117] How does Weinberg reach the conclusion that lay and cultic members of the province were included in this exemption? He identifies the *nᵉtînîm* with non-cultic artisans, and the enigmatic פלחי בית אלהא דנה with unspecified lay functionaries. As Williamson observes, this interpretation is neither supported in the context—which includes only cultic officials—nor is it in harmony with other traditions from the Ezra–Nehemiah traditions. In particular, he notes that it conflicts with the basic sense of Neh. 5.4, a text in which the people of the province complain that imperial taxes (מדת המלך) levied upon the populace are both impoverishing the community and undermining social cohesion. The מדה is one of the types of taxes from which the members of the clergy are exempt according to Ezra 7.24. Williamson asks how this type of tax can be levied in this way if all members of the *BTG*, not just the clergy, were exempted. In his view, Neh. 5.4 undermines Weinberg's conclusion that all members of the *BTG* were exempt from taxation, this further weakens his contention that there were in fact two entities in Persian period Yehud: a political province and a religious community centered around the temple.

Weinberg also uses a wealth of archaeological and epigraphic data to support his claim that after Nehemiah's mission, the sociopolitical province of Yehud merged with the *BTG*. To support the latter argument, he presses the seal impressions and coins into service. Notably, he dates virtually all of the impressions to the late-fifth/early fourth centuries, including the *yodh-he*, *yhd*, *yhwd*, *yhwd-pḥw'*, *yhwd-pḥw'-PN*, *yhd-ṭet* and *yršlm* seals to the Persian period. He also suggests that the *yḥzqyh* coin from Beth Zur refers to the High Priest, and, following Cross, argues that this coin demonstrates that the High Priest functioned

---

117. 'Central and Local Administration', p. 117, as cited by Williamson, 'Judah and the Jews', pp. 154-56. Here, Weinberg is following I.D. Amusin, 'The People of the Land' (Russian), *Vestnik drevnjej istorii* 2 (1955), pp. 14-36 (32), as cited by Weinberg, '*Nᵉtînîm* and "Sons of the Slaves of Solomon" in the Sixth to Fourth Centuries BCE', in *idem, The Citizen–Temple Community*, p. 88 n. 2.

as governor and had authority to mint coins;[118] thus, both the *BTG* and the province were at that time fully under the control of the priesthood.

Once again we must ask whether or not these data support his reconstruction. Since Weinberg's initial work[119] excavations in the City of David and the cache of bullae from Jerusalem[120] have allowed a more careful nuancing of the impressions, as discussed above. It is now possible to exclude two types of impressions from the Persian period corpus (the *yršlm* and *yhd-ṭet* seals), and it is possible that at least some of the *yhwd-pḥw'* impressions may date to the middle to late fifth century (or even earlier[121]). In this case, they are earlier than Weinberg contends, and would discount his claim that they demonstrate a high-priestly governorship. Using these data, Avigad and Eric Meyers and Carol Meyers have used the various *yhwd-pḥw'* seals to fill in the so-called 'governor-gap' between Zerubbabel and Nehemiah.[122] While these reconstructions should probably be considered provisional, the weight of evidence seems to suggest a much earlier date for some of the *yhwd* seals than Weinberg has allowed. This again calls into question his suggestion that the major change in status of Yehud in the mid-fifth century was from a political entity distinct from the *BTG* to a socio-economic and political unity.

Part of this difference in interpretation centers on our very different reconstruction of the autonomy of Yehud and the meaning of the term

118. 'Central and Local Administration', pp. 124-25. Weinberg incorrectly identifies the inscription on the Beth Zur coin as *ḥzkyw*.

119. His major treatment of the seal impressions is in 'Central and Local Administration', pp. 123-26.

120. Avigad, *Bullae and Seals*.

121. Avigad proposes a pre-458/457 for the Aramaic impressions (*yhd*, *yhwd-pḥw'*). He would date the mixed Aramaic/paleo-Hebrew and paleo-Hebrew seals are later in the period, probably fourth century (*Bullae and Seals*, pp. 26-28, 32). Weinberg is aware of Avigad's mongraph, and cites it in 'The Postexilic Citizen–Temple Community', p. 135 n. 2. However, he does not discuss its impact for the *BTG* in any depth.

122. Avigad reconstructs the governors from Sheshbazzar to Yeḥezqiyah as follows: Sheshbazzar, Zerubbabel, Elnathan, Yeho'ezer, Aḥzai, Nehemiah, Bagohi, Yeḥezqiyah (*Bullae and Seals*, p. 35). He would Elnathan to the late sixth century, and both Yeho'ezer and Aḥzai to the early fifth century. For another extended discussion of the evidence and similar reconstruction, see Meyers and Meyers, *Haggai, Zechariah 1–8*, pp. 9-16. Especially note Chart 12, 'Governors, Davidides, and High Priests of Yehud in the Persian Period (538–433 BCE)', p. 14.

phw'. Weinberg follows Alt's theory that Yehud was annexed to Samaria upon the destruction of 587/586, and that it only became a fully independent province after the work of Nehemiah.[123] Prior to that time, according to Weinberg, the term 'governor' referred not to the ruler of a fully independent province, Yehud, but to the ruler of the *BTG*. Thus there were, for all intents and purposes, two leaders functioning in the province: a political leader, whose seat of authority was in Samaria, and the 'prince' or 'governor' of the *gôlāh* group, who are to be identified as the *BTG*. It is only after 458/457, the missions of Ezra and Nehemiah, when more and more settlements and people joined the *BTG*, that the lines of demarcation between the political and religious centers of power became less distinct. In his view, it is only at this point that the term 'governor' really means leader of an independent province. And even Nehemiah, when he arrived in Jerusalem, was the governor *only* of the *BTG*, not of the entire province. After the governorship of Nehemiah, the control of the priesthood on the affairs of the province outstripped that of the political leader, with the priesthood in effect taking over the office of governor.

While Weinberg is certainly correct that the province of Yehud became more secure and more economically viable in the second half of the Persian period, the two-governors theory he has proposed seems both unnecessary and impractical from the perspective of Persian imperial concerns. P. Bedford and H. Williamson have raised serious questions about Weinberg's theory on just this point.[124] While, as we have noted, the traditions of Ezra and Nehemiah are distinctly tendentious, the texts themselves suggest the opposite situation[125]—Nehemiah claims

123. He continues to support the Altian hypothesis, despite the difficulties that many others have enumerated, in 'The Postexilic Citizen–Temple Community', p. 135.

124. P.R. Bedford, 'On Models and Texts: A Response to Blenkinsopp and Peterson', in Davies (ed.), *Second Temple Studies* 1, pp. 154-62. H. Williamson, 'Judah and the Jews', pp. 156-58.

125. D.J.A. Clines has duly noted the problems involved in using the Nehemiah materials as a basis for historical reconstructions. To be sure, the materials are ideological and propogandistic, and must be used carefully. I deal in the following comments with what Nehemiah claims, being fully cognizant of the fact that the historical situation might have been quite different. See 'The Nehemiah Memoir: The Perils of Autobiography', in *idem*, *What Does Eve Do to Help? And Other Readerly Questions to the Old Testament* (JSOTSup, 94; Sheffield: Sheffield Academic Press, 1990), pp. 124-64.

to have governor over all of the members of the province of Yehud. As such, Nehemiah claims to have intervened in the affairs of groups that were both inside and without Weinberg's hypothetical *BTG*.[126] Williamson also raises these objections to the two-governors theory:

1. The opposition that the fortification of Jerusalem caused among Yehud's neighbors would have certainly brought about official intervention from a political governor of the province if such a position existed. The texts instead show Nehemiah dealing with the situation without recourse to a higher authority.[127]

2. Nehemiah requests a letter of safe-conduct and cooperation to be addressed to other provinces within *eber nahara*. If there were a separate governor for Yehud, one would have expected a letter to be addressed to him.

3. Weinberg assumes that the refortification of Jerusalem was a project that involved only the *BTG* members and not the entire province. Williamson asks, 'Are we to suppose that the province had a separate capital?'

4. Weinberg is incorrect in his reading of Neh. 5.14-18, on two counts. Nehemiah 5.14 identifies Nehemiah as 'governor in the land of Judah', which Weinberg assumes means not the entire province but governor of the members of the *BTG*. Williamson suggests that this is an over-reading of the text. Further, Nehemiah's claim to have refrained from accepting the wages due a governor, implies 'the level of jurisdiction we should associate with a provincial governor'.

5. Nehemiah acts independently and without the constraints one would have expected if he were subject to a secular governor when corresponding with the king or leaders of the provinces around Yehud.

Based on these caveats, Williamson concludes that there is 'no justification for the assumption that he was not the provincial governor' and

---

126. Bedford, 'On Models and Texts', p. 158.
127. However, given the self-interest that the Nehemiah material exhibits, one should not be too surprised that the texts show him operating independently.

'it becomes impossible to isolate a separate citizen-temple community within Judah at that time'.[128]

In addition to the issues raised above, one major—and fundamental—problem with Weinberg's hypothesis remains: his understanding of the socio-economic setting of the temple-economy. In 'Comments on the Problem of "Pre-Hellenism in the Near East"', Weinberg proposes that the *BTG* in Yehud is the best documented type in which the temple neither owns lands nor maintained its own economy.[129] Yet, he characterizes the temple as the 'main collecting and unifying epicenter of the emergent community'.[130] I agree that we cannot, on the basis of the texts, determine whether or not the temple itself controlled or owned land. The biblical texts were not interested in providing us with the type of economic data that the temple-archives of Babylon provide; rather they are texts that seek to validate the missions of their protagonists. This makes them all the more intractable for those of us who would use them, even provisionally, to reconstruct the social history of the era.[131] However, if the temple is indeed a central point for the collection and distribution of resources, then there is *by definition* a 'temple economy'. Indeed, several texts in Ezra–Nehemiah are suggestive of some type of direct economic function for the temple. These include:

1. Collection of various types of 'offerings', including 'free-will' (נדבה, Ezra. 1.1-6), 'firstfruits' (בכורים, Neh. 10.35-37, 12.44-47; 13.31); 'tithes' (מעשר, Neh. 10.38; 13.12); Many of the latter two are collected in-kind as contributions of grain, wine and oil.

128. Williamson, 'Judah and the Jews', pp. 157-58.
129. In his typology of *BTG*s, Group A has two sub-types. A1 is comprised of those communities whose temples owned lands, and in which the community managed the economy. Group A2 is characterized by communities whose temples owned lands, but did not manage the economy. Notably, Yehud is the only example that Weinberg offers of a *BTG* that neither owns lands nor manages its economy ('Comments on the Problem', p. 29).
130. 'The Postexilic Citizen–Temple Community', p. 135.
131. As argued effectively by Clines, 'The Nehemiah Memoir'. Clines shows in a remarkable fashion the degree to which critical commentators have uncritically used the Nehemiah materials in their reconstructions, and have even, at times, unwittingly embellished them. See in particular his treatment of the alleged plot against Nehemiah (pp. 144-50).

2. The putative establishment of a one-third shekel temple tax that is intended to support the workings (lit. the 'service') of the temple (Neh. 10.33).

3. Storage of these resources in the temple treasury or store-rooms (אוצר or לשכות; Ezra 8.29; Neh. 10.38-40, 12.44-47, 13.4-14).[132]

4. Identification of the Levites as those who collect the tithe (Neh. 10.38).

5. Indication of neglect that has subverted the effective working of the temple system (Neh. 13.4-9, 10-14).

It is, of course, not possible at this point to reconstruct the exact nature of the temple economy in Persian period Yehud, but I do believe that these texts demonstrate its existence. Further, whatever the size and population of the province, this economy seems to have been co-extensive with the economy of the province as a whole. This leads to two final objections to Weinberg's model, raised by P. Bedford and R. Horsley. Bedford turns to Nehemiah's account of the disrepair of the walls and city of Jerusalem (Neh. 1–3), the relatively underpopulated state of the city (Neh. 11.1-3)[133] and the breakdown of the temple economy (Neh. 13), and asks how this state of neglect of both temple and city could be possible if both were so central to the emergent *BTG*. If a *BTG* existed as early as the first returns under Sheshbazar and Zerubbabel, what caused its radical decline in the time between the construction of the temple and the mission of Nehemiah?[134] The following

132. Note also that Clines interprets Haggai's primary understanding of the temple as a divine store-house for the riches that the nations will bring, and thereby restore its 'glory' ('Haggai's Temple', pp. 49-57).
133. Bedford, 'On Models and Texts', p. 159, notes: 'If the city of Jerusalem remained largely unpopulated until the time of Nehemiah, then the correctness of the *Gemeinde* hypothesis is in any case suspect'. While Bedford is entirely correct, I would caution against taking Nehemiah's account here at face value. While the archaeological evidence from Jerusalem makes it difficult to determine the city's size with precision, it is highly unlikely that the city was unpopulated in the mid-fifth century. Here, Nehemiah appears to be promulgating what R.P. Carroll calls 'Biblical facts' ('So What Do We *Know* about the Temple?', pp. 45-51) and what D.J.A. Clines calls 'lies' or 'acts of deception' ('The Nehemiah Memoir', pp. 125-29).
134. Bedford, 'On Models and Texts', p. 157.

questions are, in fact, difficult to answer if one holds the *BTG* model:

> The temple was not of great significance to the Judean population. If it
> were, why would there have been a need for an agreement to financially
> support it as late as the time of Nehemiah? Does not the Levites' aban-
> donment of the temple to return to their own lands (Neh. 13.10ff) denote
> lack of funding? Why would the temple have been neglected (Neh.
> 10.40c)? How strong could the *Gemeinde* structure have been if temple
> funding had been so low?[135]

Horsley points to an even more telling weakness of the theory: the centering of a temple economy around a major city, such as Jerusalem, is
not at all a new development in the ancient Near East, as Weinberg
maintains. If anything, it is simply the continuation of a pattern of
socio-economic organization that existed in the pre-587/586 state of
Judah.[136] In this respect, the social division within Yehud was not
between members of a *BTG* and the populace, but between the social
and political elite on the one hand and the 'peasantry' on the other. In
all probability, Horsley notes, the biblical texts present

> a situation in which the descendants of the exiles are simply re-establish-
> ing their traditional position as a 'community' of the powerful—the domi-
> nant lineages together with their retainers—for the priestly-temple appa-
> ratus which ruled under Persian mandate. The role of the temple as,
> among other things, symbol of social order is resumed and authenticates
> the system.[137]

Conclusions

In an early review of Weinberg's hypothesis of the *BTG*, H. Kreissig
raised the question whether the hypothesis was a necessary or even helpful notion to apply to the history of the Persian period in Yehud.[138]
Given the problems adduced in the discussion above, the widespread
acceptance of Weinberg's *BTG* model for the province of Yehud appears to have been somewhat premature. On several key points, particu-

---

135. Bedford, 'On Models and Texts', p. 158.

136. Horsley, 'Empire, Temple, and Community', pp. 169-70.

137. Horsley, 'Empire, Temple, and Community', p. 170.

138. This question is raised by H. Kreissig, 'Eine beachtenswerte Theorie zur
Organisation alt vorderorientalischer Templegemeinden im Achamenidenreich: Zu
J.P. Weinberg's "Bürger-Tempel-Gemeinde" in Juda', *Klio* 66 (1984), pp. 35-39,
as cited by Weinberg, 'The Postexilic Citizen–Temple Community', p. 127 n. 2.
Kreissig's answer is negative.

larly his tendency to take texts with ideological interests as self-evident indications of social make-up, his use of the archaeological data and his estimates of the size of the population in and around Yehud, he appears to be off the mark. Weinberg is, of course, correct in recognizing the need for a heuristic model to apply to the data of the Persian period, given its limited nature. However, when models are applied to a set of data, one must take adequate care to determine the levels in which they correspond to that data-set. If the Hebrew evidence is relatively inconsistent with the source of a model's parallels, then that model does not apply. Thus, if the presumed *BTG* of Palestine is the *only* example of a citizen–temple community that has neither land holdings nor a temple economy—both features of what Weinberg associates with the more normal *BTG*—then it is probable that the model upon which the theory is based is inappropriate. In retrospect, the judgment of Kreissig on Weinberg's hypothesis seems to be warranted: the existence of a *BTG* in Yehud remains 'unproven' and is not 'historically necessary'.

Establishing Social Boundaries: The Emergent 'True Seed' of Israel

One of the corollaries of the recent interest in Yehud has been a renewed attention to the concept of Israel and its placement in the history of the literary traditions contained in the Hebrew Bible. Indeed, this has been one of the central issues for those defined (unfortunately) as minimalist and maximalist in their approach both to biblical texts and the archaeological record. Many scholars have maintained traditional views of the notion of Israel—that an entity known as Israel emerged in the thirteenth or twelfth century BCE in central Palestine, had become a monarchic state by the tenth century, and split into two petty kingdoms at the end of that century. From the 'united' monarchy of Israel came two states, Israel and Judah. Both would later fall at the hands of the more powerful Assyrians and Babylonians, respectively. Others, such as T.L. Thompson, P.R. Davies, G. Ahlström and N.P. Lemche have sought a more nuanced interpretation of the data.[139] They have instead suggested that Israel is more of a theological construct—a biblical image that was imposed on an earlier period by the writers and redactors

---

139. For the relevant bibliography on their works, see Chapter 1, p. 37 nn. 17-19.

of what we now call the Hebrew Bible.[140] Davies, in particular, has championed the notion that the concept of Israel is best explained as a Persian period invention.[141] While he does hold to the existence of an Israel that the biblical traditions call the Northern Kingdom, he suggests that Judah was at most a minor, rump state, perhaps created by the Assyrians as an administrative district in the ninth century BCE.[142] It identified itself with Israel's history only later, perhaps as it accepted refugees from its larger neighbor when that kingdom fell in 722.[143] Like Torrey before him, Davies downplays the importance of the exile and refers to it instead as a deportation. The 'exile' as contained in the various biblical traditions is a theological construct.[144] For while deportations seek to sever cultural, religious and ethnic ties, the construct of the 'exile' and 'return' in fact reinforced or, perhaps, created these ties.[145] Even the Moses traditions may date to the Persian period and could reflect a migration of members of the garrisons in Elephantine to Jerusalem.[146]

While many scholars have already rejected Davies's theories—some without adequately understanding the force of his argument, but instead vilifying him for challenging the scholarly establishment[147]—he has

140. One of the first to raise the issue of the nature of 'Israel' was G. Ahlström in his work, *Who Were the Israelites?* (Winona Lake, IN: Eisenbrauns, 1986).

141. He develops this notion in chapter 5, 'The Social Context of the Biblical Israel', in *In Search of 'Ancient Israel'*, pp. 75-93.

142. *In Search of 'Ancient Israel'*, pp. 67-69.

143. *In Search of 'Ancient Israel'*, pp. 69-70.

144. This understanding is reflected in the Holiness Code, which viewed the exile as a complete emptying of the land for 70 years (Lev. 26.27-35). This conception is also evident in the Chronicler's account of the fall of Judah (2 Chron. 20.21). The reference to the destruction of both Israel and Judah in the Deuteronomic history and in Jeremiah present a different historical picture, but a theological ideology, nonetheless, namely, that the kingdoms of Israel and Judah had been removed from the land for having broken the Deuteronomic covenant.

145. *In Search of 'Ancient Israel'*, pp. 41-44, 57-59 and 75-93.

146. Davies cites Hecataeus's account of an Egyptian story that 'the Jewish priesthood was established by a certain Moses who was an Egyptian and left to found Jerusalem'. He wonders: 'Is this a garbled version of the exodus story or does it relate the same more recent historical event' (*In Search of 'Ancient Israel'*, p. 119)?

147. The most notable of these responses is I. Provan's 'Ideologies', pp. 585-606.

raised several fundamentally important issues.[148] He has drawn attention
to the various meanings of the term 'Israel' within the biblical traditions
and shown that this term functioned as an ideological/theological
construct. He has demonstrated the degree to which biblical scholars
have followed the biblical ideology relatively uncritically.[149] He has
drawn attention to the need for a far more nuanced and integrative
approach to the biblical texts. He has highlighted the need to assess the
material culture of the central highlands of Palestine *apart from*, not
just *alongside*, the biblical traditions. And he has underscored the growing conviction among scholars that the Persian period was a period of
intense creativity within emergent Judaism.[150] It is to this latter point
that the following paragraphs will turn.

Even if one accepts Davies' critique of the exile—that it is an ideological construct that allowed the 'returnees' to impose their power and
worldview on the native population in Yehud—one must still allow for
a significant level of crisis and upheaval in the lives of both those who
were deported and those who remained on the land. Both communities
were without the social and religious institutions that had determined so
much of their identity. It is true, of course, that those who remained in
Palestine had less interruption of their daily lives. Not all members of
the elite were deported; nor was there a total vacuum of political or religious leadership. The new Babylonian overlords swiftly established

148. My own response to Davies' critique is mixed. As I have noted, I believe
he has raised a number of points that biblical scholarship must take seriously. His
reconstruction of the Persian period is fundamentally in keeping with the presentation in this study, and I am certain that much, if not most, of the final editing of
the biblical traditions will have taken place in this period. However, I am not yet
ready to agree that the prophetic tradition that is usually considered pre-exilic, for
example, dates primarily to the Persian period and makes little sense in an Iron Age
context. Nor do I yet agree that his proposal obviates as much of traditional
criticism as he believes. Doubtless, some scholars will fault me for 'giving too much
away' or 'going too far' in my assessment (becoming a minimalist?), while others
will fault me for not going far enough (being a traditionalist or maximalist?). My
concern, rather, is to be fair and accurate in my presentation, and to note the points
at which I believe the data support or challenge his positions.

149. For a similar critique, see Oden, *The Bible without Theology*.

150. Though Davies does not make this connection, this perspective should
stand as a corrective to much Christian scholarship that had characterized the period
as one marked by theological decline and moribund legalism.

their own order, with Gedeliah appointed as governor in the new provincial seat of Tell en-Naṣbeh, biblical Mizpeh. And though the central place of Jerusalem was destroyed, so that the temple no longer stood, it is possible that some of the priests who remained in the former kingdom plied their trade and conducted some form of worship.[151] Thus, although the monarchy was no longer in place, the socio-economic situation was in some respects similar to that which existed before the destruction of Jerusalem. Peasants had their surplus—as minimal as it may have been—extracted by the elite; some of that surplus went as well to the Babylonian imperial coffers. Now, rather than a state-based system of taxation—a 'native tributary mode of production'—an imperial system of taxation exists—a 'foreign tributary mode of production'.[152] When the Persians conquered the Neo-Babylonian empire, only the final destination of the taxes changed.

In Babylon, a different situation evolved, one that required a greater level of creativity to keep any ancestral religious, ethnic and historical memories alive (or, if one follows Davies, to create them). To this end, Ezekiel's fantastic visions sought to comfort the exiles—however many there were and wherever they were located—with the promise that YHWH would deliver and restore them (e.g. Ezek. 40–48). Similarly, Second Isaiah[153] sought to provide the exiles with a level of hope rather than the despair that could have overtaken them. This anonymous prophet called their attention to the actions of a 'Servant of YHWH' who would bring comfort and whose suffering would in some way bring atonement to the people. Restoration was on the way; a remnant would return to Jerusalem, once the divinely appointed Cyrus—YHWH's anointed messiah—conquered Babylon and assumed the throne. Some members of the Jewish community who were deported to Babylon evidently attained positions of some status within the Babylonian elite, as

---

151. J. Blenkinsopp argues that worship in Jerusalem before the rebuilding of the temple would not have included animal sacrifice, but would have been limited to agricultural produce. He suggests that such worship may have taken place in or around Tell en-Naṣbeh, at least in the Neo-Babylonian period ('The Judean Priesthood during the Neo-Babylonian and Achaemenid Periods: A Hypothetical Reconstruction', *CBQ* 60 (1998), pp. 25-43).

152. Gottwald, 'Sociology of Ancient Israel', p. 84.

153. Davies considers Deutero-Isaiah to be a product of the elite of Yehud in the fifth century, one that underlines the concept of 'exile' and 'return' so central to the documents of the period (*In Search of 'Ancient Israel'*, pp. 118-19).

witnessed by the banking firm known as the Murašu household. These deportees found other ways to maintain their heritage and sense of community. One such means, one that was evidently developed within the Judean community that had been deported and which they maintained after their return to Yehud, was the development of new ritual impulses intended to sharpen the boundaries of social and religious identity.[154]

Thus, many of the texts that originate from the Persian period make a sharp distinction between the *gôlāh* community and those who remained in Palestine. This, according to Davies, is something of an ideological necessity. New power brokers, new elite, are rarely welcomed without response, even opposition. While many scholars have sought to identify the exact nature of the opposition—some would read intense internal conflict—a precise identification has remained elusive. However, it seems that the *gôlāh* community and its viewpoint had not won the day by the time of the putative missions of Ezra and Nehemiah. Both of these mid-fifth century 'reformers' sought to establish boundaries that were both religious and legal in nature and carried with them a binding imperial imprimatur and Priestly blessing.[155] These boundaries provided ethnic and religious demarcation between the 'true seed of Israel' and either 'the people of the land' or other foreign peoples. Indeed, it is this need that Davies suggests led to a development of a theological concept of 'Israel'—not as a group of former Canaanites who had become a petty state along with the other peoples of Syria-Palestine—but as a group of divinely called people with a divine right to a 'promised land'.

The Hebrew root בדל, 'to make a distinction', is commonly used to carry this meaning both in texts that purportedly predate and post-date the Ezra–Nehemiah traditions[156]. Its three major usages include:

154. This is one of the four methods for survival that Daniel Smith identifies in his work, *The Religion of the Landless*.

155. Even if one rejects the veracity of the texts as historical documents, they do tell us what was important to at least one part of the Yehudite community. Thus, they can legitimately be used to determine something of the ideology of the writers and, in so doing, inform us that ideology was not universally accepted.

156. For a complete discussion, see my unpublished paper delivered in the 1993 annual meetings of the Society of Biblical Literature, Washington, DC, 'Purity and Distinction in Leviticus 20: 22-26'.

1. 'To designate or separate for a specific purpose', such as military service (1 Chron. 12.9), or the cities of refuge (Deut. 4.41; 19.2, 7). When applied to the cultus, this usage of the word refers to the selection of people or tribes for particular cultic duties. In this usage, the Levites were designated to carry the Ark of the Covenant and separated from the rest of Israel to perform other cultic functions (Deut. 10.8; Num. 8.14); in Num. 8.14, the Levites are separated from the rest of Israel to belong to Israel. In the Chronicler's work the word describes both Yahweh's choice of the Levites for the sacrificial cult and David's choice of the household of Asaph as Temple singers (1 Chron. 23.13; 25.1).

2. 'To separate physically'. God separates the celestial and terrestrial waters, light and darkness, and day from night (Gen. 1). Israel is warned to separate itself from the rebellious followers of Korah, Dathan and Abiram, whom YHWH is about to consume with fire (Num. 16.21). YHWH will separate out (for punishment) anyone who refuses to obey the covenant (Deut. 29.20). Physical separation from foreign wives is mandated in the Ezra–Nehemiah traditions. Applied to the cultus, this sense often relates to the designation of sacred space (Exod. 26.33, where a curtain separates the Holy Place from the Holy of Holies; Ezek. 42.20, where the temple wall separates the sacred precinct from the profane).

3. 'To separate or to sever'. A technical, cultic term for sacrificial practices. In Lev. 1.17, priests are instructed to rip open a sacrificial bird without separating the two sides and in Lev. 5.8 they are instructed to wring the victim's neck without severing its head from its body.

Although many of the nuances of בדל discussed above are present in Ezra–Nehemiah, the idea of physical separation is most common and is developed in two ways. This separation is always from some type of uncleanness, usually related to foreigners; sometimes the emphasis is placed on the act of separation itself, while in other cases one separates oneself *from* the impurity of the nations *to* or *for* obedience to YHWH and/or the Torah.

Separation to YHWH/Torah

Ezra 6 and Nehemiah 10 recount two different events, separated in time
but related in ideology. Ezra 6 is an account of a Passover celebration
ostensibly held in Jerusalem after completing and dedicating the Second Temple. The returned exiles were joined in the celebration by those
who had separated themselves from the ritual uncleanness of the
nations around them (וכל הנבדל מטמאת גויי־הארץ אלהם) in order to seek
YHWH, the God of Israel (לדרש ליהוה אלהי ישראל).

Nehemiah 10 presents a portrait of a covenant renewal ceremony led
by the Levitical priests. After rehearsing the history of Israel and admit-
ting that YHWH was justified in punishing the nation with exile,[157] the
people gather together in order to bind themselves by oath and curse to
follow YHWH. The assembly includes the cultic officials along with
'everyone who had separated themselves from the people of the land to
the Torah of God' (וכל־הנבדל מעמי הארצות אל־תורת האלהים). These
distinct people, who 'understand wisdom', then bound themselves 'to
follow the Torah of God which was given by Moses, the servant of
God' and promised to 'observe and to do all of the commandments of
YHWH our God'. The terms of the covenant are recorded in vv. 31-40
of the chapter; significantly, the first stipulation involves ethnic purity
—the people promise neither to give their daughters to the people of the
land nor to take foreign wives for their sons.

Physical Separation from Foreign Influence

The most significant usages of בדל related to physical separation occur
in Ezra 9 and 10. According to these traditions, shortly after Ezra's arrival in Jerusalem, officials inform him that neither the people of Israel
nor the cultic officials (both priests and Levites are included) had
'separated themselves from the people of the land' (לא־נבדלו העם ישראל
והכהנים והלוים מעמי הארצות) whose abominations (כתועבתיהם) are like
the various archetypical Canaanites and their abominations.[158] The re-

---

157. Again, this is part of the 'theology of exile' that runs throughout the Pentateuch and the Deutereonomic history, part of the ideology that the traditions of
Ezra–Nehemiah use to support the privileged place of the *gôlāh* community.

158. Notably, these people are categorized as 'the Canaanites, the Hittites, the
Perrizites, the Jebusites, the Ammonites, the Moabites, the Egyptians, and the Amorites', many of whom were traditional enemies of Israel, but no longer existed in any
real sense at the time of the writing of the text (e.g. Hittites, Perrizites, Jebusites and
Amorites). D. Smith-Christopher views the characterization of the partners in these

sult of this lack of separation was that 'the holy seed has been mixed with the people of the land'.

In response, Ezra issues a proclamation commanding the entire *gôlāh* community to gather in Jerusalem; refusal to do so would result in the exclusion from that community (יבדל מקהל הגולה). At the appointed time, the people gather; Ezra condemns them for the sin of intermarriage, commands them to confess their sins, to 'do his (God's) will' (ועשו רצונו) and to 'separate yourselves from the people of the land and from the foreign wives' (והבדלו מעמי הארץ ומן־הנשים הנכריות).[159] In this case, physical separation amounts to divinely sanctioned divorce. According to the text, the people agree to his demands and Ezra designates leaders to oversee this separation.[160]

This connection between purity and distinction that concerns the redactors of the Ezra and Nehemiah traditions comes into sharper focus when we look at the relative size of Yehud and its relationship with its neighbors. In this regard, it appears that the materialist model of Harris *and* the ideological model of Douglas explain the need for 'distinguishing between clean and unclean' and 'separating from the people of the land', that is, for establishing categories for both ethnic and ritual purity. As Douglas has demonstrated, social boundaries function not only to determine who or what activities are outside and therefore bring uncleanness, but to determine who or what practices are accepted, and

mixed marriages as veiled references to early sectarian differences. See his extended discussion in 'The Mixed Marriage Crisis', pp. 243-65. In my translation, I follow the JPS Tanakh, as proposed by Eskenazi and Judd, 'Marriage to a Stranger', pp. 266-85. As they note, the practices of the 'people of the land' are likened to those of the Canaanites, but the people themselves appear to be Judeans who are not part of the *gôlāh* group.

159. Eskenazi and Judd point out that the women in question were probably not foreign, but women who had once been considered full members of the Jewish community; because of the nature of the redefinition of Ezra's mission, they were now cast as outsiders, impure, and thus foreign ('Marriage to a Stranger', pp. 268-72, 284-85).

160. Texts from Lev. 10 and 11, and 20.22-26 in the Holiness Code provide interesting parallels. Lev. 10 and 11 are concerned primarily with discerning, establishing, maintaining and teaching ritual purity. Lev. 20.22-26 links ritual and ethnic purity. In this text, the rationale for keeping the commandments regarding dietary and ritual purity (for distinguishing between clean and unclean) is that YHWH has separated the Israelites from the nations around them.

therefore that establish 'cleanness' and normative being/behavior.[161] While it may possible to present the concern for ethnic and ritual boundaries as purely ideological, the perspectives of Marvin Harris are also instructive. Harris seeks material answers for what he calls 'riddles of culture', that is, ideologies whose rationale are not readily apparent to an external observer.[162] He explains, for example, the pig taboo in Israelite culture and the provisions for protecting cows in Hindu culture on the basis of material realities and socio-economic necessities.[163] In both cases, societal choices were reinforced through ritual law and practice, and ideology served to solve social dilemmas and thereby to promote social survival.

If Yehud was as small and as poor as the archaeological data suggest, and if members of the *gôlāh* community found themselves in some cases residing within other provinces of the Persian empire, then the need for both ritual purity and ethnic boundaries became all the more imperative. The texts of the Priestly source/editor, the Holiness Code, and Ezra–Nehemiah reflect a reality of survival by self-definition, or what D. Smith calls 'a self-conscious community that is occupied with self-preservation, both as a pure community in a religious sense, and also in a material sense'.[164] That is, if 'Israel' was to continue as more than a historical memory or ideological construct, new markers needed to be established or, alternatively, traditional markers needed to be

161. As argued by Douglas, *Purity and Danger*. D. Smith draws a similar parallel between the Ezra–Nehemiah traditions and the perspectives of Douglas in 'The Politics of Ezra', pp. 73-97. He understands the distinctions drawn on both ethnic and cultic purity to be part of a 'Priestly theology of a "culture of resistance" (or a "spirituality of resistance") which uses a religious term to accomplish social ends, namely the avoidance of social "pollution"' (p. 86).

162. *Cows, Pigs, Wars, and Witches* and *The Sacred Cow and the Abominable Pig: Riddles of Food and Culture* (New York: Touchstone, 1987).

163. In the case of Israelite dietary restrictions, Harris points to a complex of environmental, economic and other material constraints. Pigs, unlike ruminants such as sheep, goats and cattle, do not consume agricultural waste such as hay, stubble or straw, but require a diet high in maize, wheat and tubers for ultimate growth. Thus, while ruminants transform waste and products that are inedible to humans into other products, pigs actually compete with humans for resources. And, unlike cows, sheep and goats, they add little to the domestic economy aside from their meat. Since raising pigs was more costly than raising ruminants, and since they inevitably competed with humans for needed resources, the benefits of raising pigs did not justify the cost.

164. 'The Politics of Ezra', p. 97.

reaffirmed. One of the major ways that those markers could be established was through the exact combination of religious and political mechanisms that the Ezra–Nehemiah traditions reflect. Indeed, religion and its symbolism have a power that often transcends that of the state, and remains one of the most potent forces for social stability (and even for promoting social change).[165] One can view the theological concerns in Ezra–Nehemiah as a means of promoting Persian imperial policy, as K. Hoglund does. In this view, Ezra and Nehemiah hoped to prod the members of the Yehudite community to retain rights to their ancestral properties and so to ensure the survival of the province.[166] One may view their missions as simply furthering the ideology of the *gôlāh* group and its claims to the land. But increasingly, it appears that their concerns were related to the material realities of a small, poor Yehud and the need to maintain a more basic sense of community and identity. Thus, the relationship between a small Yehud and an ideology of purity and distinction appears to prove Gottwald's oft-quoted dictum: 'only as the full *materiality* of Israel is more securely grasped will we be able to make proper sense of its *spirituality*'.[167]

The Rise of Apocalyptic Communities and Literature

A final area that a small Yehud may impact is the rise of apocalyptic. The theories of Otto Plöger and Paul Hanson were among the first to seek a social location for apocalyptic.[168] Both proposed that the genre emerged from conflict between two distinct groups with competing visions and bases of power. Plöger traces this conflict back from the

165. On the power of religion to promote ideologies and influence human behavior within a social order, see Lenski, Lenski and Nolan, *Human Societies*, pp. 160-62. Berquist also includes a helpful section on 'The Construction and Maintenance of Society' which brings the insights of C. Geertz on the role of religion in human society to bear on the social science study of the Hebrew Bible. See Berquist, *Judaism in Persia's Shadow*, pp. 247-48.

166. *Achaemenid Imperial Policy*, pp. 207-40.

167. *The Tribes of Yahweh*, p. xxv.

168. The relevant works are Otto Plöger, *Theocracy and Eschatology* (trans. S. Rudman; Richmond, VA: John Knox Press, 1968); and Hanson, *The Dawn of Apocalyptic*. See the discussion of their work in Stephen L. Cook, *Prophecy and Apocalypticism: The Postexilic Social Setting* (Minneapolis: Fortress Press, 1995), pp. 1-9. Jon Berquist also critiques both Plöger and Hanson in *Judaism in Persia's Shadow*, pp. 7-9, 182-84.

Hellenistic period to the postexilic period and identifies two major interest groups: a Priestly, or 'theocratic' group, and an anti-establishment 'prophetic' group. Hanson agrees that the basic conflict was between a Priestly group (whom he identifies as 'hierocrats') and those with a 'visionary' perspective. He specifically identifies Third Isaiah and Second Zechariah as texts that reflect this conflict. In both theories, the conflict is between the privileged power-brokers and those deprived of power who view both the power and the institution that validates it as corrupt. In response to this corruption, they envision a world in which YHWH will intervene to remove the priestly establishment and vindicate the visionaries.

This theory of 'cognitive dissonance' or 'deprivation' as the origin of apocalyptic has increasingly come under scrutiny. Two new proposals have recently been put forward, both of which are more sensitive to the social context of Yehud. Both criticize Plöger and Hanson for oversimplifying the texts and the sociological contexts of apocalyptic groups. Jon Berquist roots the rise of the genre in a scribal or bureaucratic class who are members of the establishment but who are 'middle-management', that is, outside of the true elite who set social and religious policy.[169] This explains the intellectual and international focus of apocalyptic texts as well as the expectation of a divine retribution that may even destroy them. Jerusalem has become corrupted by an elite who are not accountable to the needs of the apocalyticists. According to Berquist, their concerns are less with the truly disenfranchised—who would be represented by the peasantry—and more with their own inability to attain the social prowess and powers of their rulers. While Berquist has moved from the dualistic conflict between priestly and visionary groups, he puts in its place a conflict between the true elite and those who aspire to become full members of the ruling class. He therefore maintains a conflict-based, even a deprivation-based theory, though he criticizes Hanson and Plöger on this very point.

More satisfying is the theory of Stephen Cook, who identifies the rise of apocalypse in the context of millenarian groups. These groups are formed in a variety of social contexts, many of which are not related to a palpable sense of deprivation. Cook identifies a series of 'family' characteristics within such groups and suggests that simply to root all apocalyptic literature and groups into the straightjacket of deprivation

---

169. *Judaism in Persia's Shadow*, pp. 177-92.

theory is to fall into the scholarly trap of reductionism. Millennial apocalyptic groups typically share some of the following concepts: a 'linear view of history', a 'futuristic eschatology' that expects 'imminent' and 'radical' change of the world order. Often this change is supernaturally induced, and often it punishes those whom the group views as outsiders and/or opponents. It is characteristic for such groups to be ethically dualistic in nature and therefore to see their adherents as 'good' and their opponents as 'evil'.[170] Many of these characteristics are evident regardless of the social location of the apocalpytic group. What Cook suggests, however, is that social deprivation alone is not enough to explain the growth of apocalyptic fervor. Instead, he gives evidence of many apocalyptic groups that *held* places of social power and that used that power to further their expectations and worldviews. His examination divides groups into two major categories, endogamous and exogamous. These are subdivided further into six areas: those native groups that are central or peripheral in their own society; those dominating/ colonizing groups that are central and peripheral in their society; and those dominated/colonized groups that are central or peripheral in their wider society. He suggests that many proto-apocalyptic texts[171] of the Neo-Babylonian and early Persian period—namely Ezekiel 38–39, Zechariah 1–8 and Joel—show evidence of the activity of priests located who are centrally rather than peripherally located.

At first glance, it would appear that the views of Hanson that are dependent on a deprivation model would fit the social context of Yehud as constructed above. It would be easy to posit that a small Yehud with an upper class that has recently wrested control from the traditional rural leadership would be in direct conflict with the latter. It could futher follow that this conflict might appear in such texts as Isaiah 56–66 and Haggai–Zechariah 1–8, which he maintains support the position of the oppressed over against the oppressors. However, both Berquist and Cook raise important issues with Hanson's reconstruction, issues that in no way conflict with a small, poor Yehud.

---

170. *Prophecy and Apocalypticism*, pp. 26-27.

171. It is important to note that Cook uses the term 'proto-apocalyptic' differently than Hanson. While Hanson sees a relatively unbroken trajectory from prophecy to apocalyptic, Cook sees other influences in apocalyptic's 'prehistory'. However, he employs the term 'proto-apocalyptic' to distinguish the Persian period texts from the more fully developed apocalypses of the Hellenistic and Roman periods (*Prophecy and Apocalypticism*, pp. 34-35).

One of the key areas in which the archaeological data can make a contribution in understanding the relationship between apocalyptic worldviews and material culture relates to the role and place of Zerubbabel, the shadowy figure who has evoked much controversy in reconstructions of the province of Yehud. Hanson suggests that the texts surrounding this governor of Yehud—namely those from Haggai and First Zechariah—reflect an expectation that Zerubbabel would deliver Yehud to independence from Persia. This messianic expectation, he claims, explains why Zerubbabel falls so quickly from historical view.

It is true that Zerubbabel is a Davidide who bore the title 'governor of Yehuda' (יהדה פחת; Hag. 1.1). He is identified in messianic terms, as the evocative symbols of servant of YHWH and becoming YHWH's 'signet ring' indicate (Hag. 2.20-23). This latter passage is strongly apocalyptic, promising YHWH's imminent intervention on behalf of both Yehud and its governor. Yet this same Davidic scion is nearly absent from First Zechariah, which together with the book of Haggai probably formed a literary unit.[172] The one passage that mentions him by name (Zech. 4.6-9) is often treated as a late intrusion.[173] Furthermore, one must account for Zerubbabel's absence in the vision recorded in Zech. 6.9-14, which also employs typical messianic language (i.e. the Branch) but does not name the governor, only Yehoshua the priest.

The common explanation of the difference in tone of Haggai and First Zechariah is that Zerubbabel, caught up in messianic fervor, attempted to take advantage of the alleged instability in the empire at the death of Cambyses.[174] In this view, he did so by fomenting or joining revolt, and was subsequently removed from office by the Persians when Darius I had consolidated his hold on the empire.[175] Several scholars

172. After Meyers and Meyers, *Haggai, Zechariah 1–8*, pp. xliv-lxiii.
173. Ackroyd, 'Archaeology, Politics, and Religion', pp. 19-20.
174. See, for example, Hanson, *The Dawn of Apocalyptic*, pp. 245-62.
175. Another explanation for the absence of Zerubbabel in Zech. 1–8, and one inherent in the text of First Zechariah, is that as the Persian period progressed, the power and authority of the priest increased. Thus, as E. Meyers points out, 'A concomitant of a strong high priest was the diminution, at least by First Zechariah, of the role of the Davidic scion, who is relegated to an eschatological status (Zech 3.3; 4.6b-10a; 6.12). The attitude of the prophet is that the Davidic line will be reestablished at a future time of God's choosing, but for the meantime a Davidic governor—possibly groomed for the job in the court of Darius I—was thought to be sufficient evidence of Persian goodwill and Yehudite aspirations.' See 'The Persian Period and the Judean Restoration', p. 512.

have recently challenged this assumption as conjectural, pointing out
that candidates for the position of governor would be chosen based in
part on their loyalty to the Persian throne.[176] Thus, it would be in the
best interests of Yehud and Zerubbabel to remain loyal to Persia rather
than to attempt an uprising. Both the governor and the *gôlāh* would
have recognized that their autonomy came from the crown. Therefore,
'official relations with the Persian administration would be viewed as a
means *towards* the aspirations of the community', and Yehudites would
not be likely to be hostile toward Imperial policies.[177]

The likelihood of a rebellion diminishes strikingly when one applies
the demographic data for Yehud presented in the previous chapters.
While a small community alone does not obviate the possibility of messianic fervor—history is full of revolts that had little opportunity to suc-
ceed—Yehud's size, relative poverty, and dependence on Persia must
be given due consideration when evaluating this theory. The province
of Yehud could not hope to mount a serious attack upon the Persian
forces in the period of Haggai and Zechariah due in large part to the
lack of human and financial resources necessary to support a military.
The resources of the province were either diverted to the project of
building the temple, supporting the Yehudite elite, or paying taxes in-
kind to an increasingly rapacious imperial appetite. Even when Jerusalem was re-fortified in the mid-fifth century and several new fortresses
built and placed in service, the presence of imperial forces in Yehud
and its proximity would have made any resistance unlikely. What is
more, there is no substantial archaeological evidence of conflagration or
destruction in the excavated Persian period sites that would be expected
if a rebellion were to have been mounted.

If the archaeological data call into question Hanson's reconstruction
of the Haggai–Zechariah 1–8 texts, do they shed any further light on the
social setting of apocaplyptic literature and its concomitant worldviews? Do they make either Cook's or Berquist's reconstructions more
or less likely? At first glance the answer would appear to be negative.
Both interpretations are based on specific readings of specific texts and
neither consults the archaeological data. However, in that both purport
to be social-scientific in nature, it may be possible to judge both in light

176. Kessler, 'The Second Year of Darius', pp. 63-84. Throughout his work,
Kessler notes the need for Yehud and its officials to be supportive of and subject to
Imperial laws and interests. See in particular pp. 69-75 and 83-84.

177. Kessler, 'The Second Year of Darius', p. 74.

of their use of social-science methodology in relationship to both textual and archaeological interpretations.

Berquist's understanding of Yehud is based in large part on the nature
of imperial structure and the notion of 'core' and 'periphery'.[178] While
his attention to the history of the Persian empire and its socio-political
and socio-economic setting is laudible, it is unfortunate that he has so
little concern with issues such the size of the province, its site distribution or its population. These data would, I believe, inform and often
support his general interpretations of the data. But when one simply
reports the various estimates that have been proposed for the province
—from Albright's to Weinberg's—rather than presenting a critical analysis of these estimates, the resulting force of one's historical reconstruction is weakened.[179] Indeed, without consulting such information,
how can one assess the social structure of a sociopolitical or socio-
economic unit? For example, his proposal for a social setting of apocalyptic within the 'middle-management' of Yehudite bureaucracy would
make more sense if the population of Jerusalem were the 10,000 to
15,000[180] he proposes rather than the 1500 of my reconstruction. The
difference is, of course, considerable. Berquist cites an early study by
M. Broshi as a basis for his population figures. However, what Berquist
failed to take into account is that Broshi's estimates were no longer accurate when he (Berquist) completed his work; that the number of people per dunam that Broshi uses in his current estimates of population
are about 33 per cent of those he was using in the former article.[181] This

178. His appendix, 'Methods for Studying Postexilic Society' is particularly
helpful and presents an insightful, if brief, summary of issues related to the use of
the social sciences in interpretation of the Hebrew Bible (*Judaism in Persia's Shadow*, pp. 241-55).

179. Preliminary data were readily available in Hoglund's study, 'The Achaemenid Context', pp. 54-72. However, my 'A Social and Demographic Study' and
'The Province of Yehud in the Post-Exilic Period: Soundings in Site Distribution
and Demography', in Eskenazi and Richards (eds.), *Second Temple Studies 2*, pp.
106-45, may have been completed too late for his consideration.

180. It is unclear exactly what territory Berquist includes in his population estimate for Jerusalem 'and its environs' (*Judaism in Persia's Shadow*, p. 83 n. 43). Is
he including sites around Jerusalem, such as Tell en-Naṣbeh and Ramat Raḥel, or
considering Jerusalem proper?

181. See above, Chapter 3, pp. 147-48. As I point out in Chapter 4, pp. 200-202,
Broshi's and my own estimates of the amount of occupied space in Jerusalem are
similar. Broshi's earlier work on populations used the coefficient of 375 people per

serves to confirm the concerns of Dever, who calls on biblical scholars and archaeologists to show greater sensitivity to one another's work in order to avoid under- or over-reading of either texts or archaeological data.[182]

Cook's proposal of the social location of apocalypticism in the central Zadokite priesthood is likewise sociological and literary in nature, and fails to consider archaeological, socio-economic or socio-political information. One is left, therefore, questioning the degree to which either study can speak to social location of apocalyptic literature and groups without first assessing the larger internal and external social setting that obtained within Yehud as it related both to its surrounding provinces and the Persian empire. Each work has its strong points:

Berquist's study is more socio-historical and broadly based in its concerns, while Cook's is more focused on a particular type of social group and its application to the specific genre and worldview of apocalyptic. Each make important contributions to the discussion and understanding of Yehud and its social, political and religious world. Yet, each is incomplete to the extent that it was written without due consideration of the data available at the time of publication that would have set the study within a broader social context.

Having raised these methodological issues, is one assessment of the origins of the apocalyptic worldview more convincing or more likely given the small, poor Yehud that existed during the Persian period? It is my judgment that Cook's suggestion of the social location of the apocalyptic worldview within the Zadokite priesthood rather than either a visionary group that opposed the ruling priesthood (Hanson's hierocrat vs. visionary conflict) or in a disgruntled group of middle-managment bureaucrats (Berquist's proposal) would fit best in the social setting I have proposed above. Berquist is quite correct in recognizing the level of international awareness and education that is required to produce the apocalyptic literature of the Persian period. As he points out, literature of this type could not have been produced by a rural populace in an environment where illiteracy was still widespread. Yet, it is more likely

---

hectare, rather than the figure of 250 people per hectare (= 25 people per metric dunam) that is now more generally accepted.

182. Dever, 'Biblical Archaeology', p. 719.

that in a small Jerusalem, there would most likely be a significant overlap between Priestly and scribal groups, especially given the long-standing link between the 'academy' and the temple. It is important to point out here that my judgment is based not on the archaeological data alone—for they cannot speak authoritatively concerning issues of the size and nature of the priesthood or a scribal class. Rather it is based on the overall data set: social science theory, archaeological witness and textual traditions.

Conclusions

These programmatic comments highlight the difficulties involved in any socio-economic or historical reconstruction. Even if the historian gives priority to 'what the evidence makes it reasonable for us to believe' rather than 'what the evidence obliges us to believe',[183] responsible reconstructions require extreme care. The problem is exacerbated by the limited data of the Persian period and widely divergent opinions on what is 'reasonable'. Given these concerns, what are the implications of this study for future research?

While this study has made considerable progress in examining the archaeological data and presenting a coherent portrait of the province of Yehud, several issues remain to be examined. I have presented a Yehud based in the central hills of Palestine, excluding sites in the Shephelah and Coastal Plain. Since this limited reconstruction is not universally accepted, one of the next issues to consider is what the population and site distribution would be for the province if it extended into these areas. This would give an extended range of population and site distribution, based upon a more inclusive and more exclusive reconstruction of Yehud's boundaries. A related project would turn to the socio-economic setting of the entire province, an issue that deserves careful study. An important aspect of this, and of the larger socioeconomic setting, remains the temple economy. If Weinberg's *Bürger-Tempel-Gemeinde* model of the temple economy is not appropriate for Jerusalem and Yehud in the early Second Temple period, as the discussion above suggests, what model should replace it? What was the relationship among the various political and relgious centers of power, and how did they shift during the Persian period? Related to the question of the temple is the degree to which any kind of religious purity was

183. Jacobsen, 'Early Political Development', p. 95.

maintained. Stern has claimed, on the basis of a lack of cultic figurines within the boundaries of the province, that the exile led to a new adherence to the aniconic commandment.[184] In this view, the predilection in pre-exilic Israelite and Judean religion towards idolatry was curbed in the exilic period. But does this square with the textual traditions from the period? How does one account for continued problems of idolatry and heterdoxy (see, e.g., Zech. 5.5-11) and a perceived 'decline' in religion (Mal. 1.12-13; 2.8-9, etc.)? This is an old problem, but could profit from new approaches.

One of the problems involved in making large-scale reconstructions on the basis of surface surveys is that of properly nuancing the site distribution within the period. This is especially true for Persian period Yehud. The site list that Ofer provided me treated the period as a whole, rather than breaking it into either the more generic early and late or the more specific Persian I and II. Even more problematic is that for the purpose of his survey he initially collapsed the Neo-Babylonian and Persian periods. Thus, it is possible that some of the sites listed in Chapter 3 were occupied for only a small portion of the Persian period, or were not Persian but Neo-Babylonian. Once his survey is published, it may be possible to provide a more nuanced and accurate view of the period from 586–332 (the Neo-Babylonian, Persian I and Persian II periods).[185]

A final prospect for future research on the Persian period is a study of the site distribution and population of all of Palestine along the model of the studies by Broshi, Broshi and Gophna, and Finkelstein and Broshi of Palestine for earlier periods. Such a study would take advantage of the recently completed surveys of Judah, Benjamin, Ephraim and Manassah, but might require new surveys as well. It would allow a clearer understanding of the relationships of the various Persian provinces and could perhaps lead to fruitful socio economic reconstruction of the various segments of Syria-Palestine and to a more comprehensive understanding of the place of Syria-Palestine in the Persian imperial world and the wider world that eventually caused the end of Persian control and the rise of Hellenism.

184. 'What Happened to the Cult Figurines? Israelite Religion Purified after the Exile', *BARev* 15 (1989), pp. 22-29, 53-54.

185. In his interpretation of the data in 'Judah' (*OEANE*, III, pp. 253-67), Ofer ends the Iron Age in 539 BCE, but this division is not reflected in the site list upon which the present work is based.

Appendix

EXCAVATED AND SURVEYED SITES IN THE PROVINCE OF YEHUD[1]

1. Kh. Ras El-Mughar
Israel Grid: 1619.1387
Environmental Niche: 1
Maximal Size: 24 dunams
Pottery: Iron II/P, H; R

ח' רס אל־מע'ר
Elevation: 780 m.
Estimated Population: 200
Size, Persian Period: 8 dunams
Established: Iron II/Persian Period

Bibliography: *ASHCB*, site 268 (16-13/18/1), p. 41*; p. 212; *JSG*, site 131, p. 184.

2. Kh. el-Kafira
Israel Grid: 1620.1375
Environmental Niche: 1
Maximal Size: 15 dunams
Pottery: Iron I, Iron II, P, H/R

ח' אל־כפירה
Elevation: 600 m.
Estimated Population: 125
Size, Persian Period: 5.1 dunams
Established: Iron I

Bibliography: *ASHCB*, site 263 (16-13/07/1), p. 41*; pp. 209-11.

1.   I have made every effort to provide complete information on the sites that were located within the boundaries of Yehud as I have reconstructed them. Where possible, I have included elevation, maximal size of the site, size in the Persian period, estimated population of the site in Persian Period II, pottery represented in the periods around the Persian period, and limited bibliographic resources. The latter generally focus on the surveys and major excavation reports related to particular sites. Where either the maximal size or elevation was not available to me, I have listed them as NG (= not given). Most sites that were located within the traditional biblical territory of Benjamin have locations listed in meters above or below sea level, as listed in *ASHCB* or *JSG*. Listing of sites in the biblical territory of Judah are in meters above/below sea level and are correct within 25 meters. The latter elevations are taken from *Map of Palestine, Scale 1:20,000* (Jaffa: Department of Lands and Surveys, 1927). The following abbreviations are used: C = Chalcolithic Period; EB = Early Bronze Age; MB = Middle Bronze Age; LB = Late Bronze Age; P = Persian Period; H = Hellenistic Period; R = Roman Period, Byz. = Byzantine Period; M = Medieval. When pottery is either mixed between two periods, or it is difficult to determine whether it comes from one period or the next, the two periods are listed with a slash separating them (i.e. P/H = Persian/Hellenistic).

3. Kh. Nijam (Har Adar)
Israel Grid: 1623.1372
Environmental Niche: 1
Maximal Size: NG
Pottery: P; H

ח׳ נג׳ם
Elevation: 600 m.
Estimated Population: 37.5
Size, Persian Period: VS
Established: Persian

Bibliography: Dadon, 'Har Adar', *ESI* 14 (1994), pp. 87-88.

4. Kh. Judeida
Israel Grid: 1623.1381
Environmental Niche: 1
Maximal Size: 7 dunams
Pottery: Iron II?/H; P/H; R; Byz.

ח׳ ג׳דידה
Elevation: 790 m.
Estimated Population: 75
Size, Persian Period: 3 dunams
Established: Iron II?

Bibliography: *ASHCB*, site 276 (16-13/28/1), p. 42*; pp. 215-16.

5. Kh. el-Murran
Israel Grid: 1627.1359
Environmental Niche: 1
Maximal Size: 20 dunams
Pottery: Iron II/P; H; R; Byz.

ח׳ אל-מרן
Elevation: 837 m.
Estimated Population: 200
Size, Persian Period: 8 dunams
Established: Iron II/Period

Bibliography: *ASHCB*, site 272 (16-13/18/1), p. 41*; p. 214 (= Iron II/P).

6. Kh. el-Bawaya
Israel Grid: 1629.1364
Environmental Niche: 1
Maximal Size: 9 dunams
Pottery: P; H/R; Byz.

ח׳ אל-בויה
Elevation: 820 m.
Estimated Population: 75
Size, Persian Period: 3 dunams
Established: Persian Period

Bibliography: *ASHCB*, site 274 (16-13/26/1), p. 42*; p. 215.

7. Beit Surik
Israel Grid: 1642.1367
Environmental Niche: 1
Maximal Size: 25 dunams
Pottery: P, H; R; Byz.

בית סוריך
Elevation: 830 m.
Estimated Population: 225
Size, Persian Period: 9 dunams
Established: Persian Period.

Bibliography: *ASHCB*, site 284 (16-13/46/1), p. 43*; pp. 218-19.

8. Kh. 'Ein el-Keniseh
Israel Grid: 1646.1369
Environmental Niche: 1
Maximal Size: 5.5 dunams
Pottery: MB; Iron I & II; Iron II/P; H; R. Byz.

ח׳ עין אל-כנסה
Elevation: 740 m.
Estimated Population: 50
Size, Persian Period: 2 dunams
Established: Iron I

Bibliography: *ASHCB*, site 286 (16-13/46/3), p. 43*; p. 219.

9. Unnamed 1
Israel Grid: 1650.1341
Environmental Niche: 1
Maximal Size: 23 dunams
Pottery: Iron II; Iron II/P; P/H

Elevation: 700 m.
Estimated Population: 275
Size, Persian Period: 11 dunams
Established: Iron II

Bibliography: *ASHCB*, site 294 (16-13/54/2), p. 44*; pp. 222-23.

10. Mevasseret Zion
Israel Grid: 1652.1339
Environmental Niche: 1
Maximal Size: NG
Pottery: Iron II; P

מוצרת ציון
Elevation: 650 m.
Estimated Population: 87.5
Unknown Size, Persian Period: S
Established: Iron II

Bibliography: Stern, *Material Culture*, pp. 34-35.

11. Kh. Beit Mizza
Israel Grid: 1652.1349
Environmental Niche: 1
Maximal Size: 10 dunams
Pottery: MB; Iron II; P; P/H; H/ R/ Byz.

ח׳ בית מצה
Elevation: 740 m.
Estimated Population: 100
Size, Persian Period: 4 dunams
Established: MB

Bibliography: *ASHCB*, site 293 (16-13/54/1), p. 44*; p. 222.

12. Qaluniya
Israel Grid: 1656.1333
Environmental Niche: 1
Maximal Size: 30 dunams
Pottery: Iron II, P/H

קלוניה
Elevation: 580 m.
Estimated Population: 275
Size, Persian Period: 11 dunams
Established: Iron II

Bibliography: *ASHCB*, site 291 (16-13/53/1), p. 44*; p. 221.

13. Unnamed 2
Israel Grid: 1667.1361
Environmental Niche: 1
Maximal Size: 5 dunams
Pottery: Iron II; P; P/H; Byz.

Elevation: 800 m.
Estimated Population: 50
Size, Persian Period: 2 dunams
Established: Iron II

Bibliography: *ASHCB*, site 305 (16-13/66/2), p. 45*; p. 228.

14. Unnamed 3
Israel Grid: 1667.1368
Environmental Niche: 1
Maximal Size: 4 dunams
Pottery: MB; Iron II; Iron II/P; P/H

Elevation: 780 m.
Estimated Population: 75
Size, Persian Period: 3 dunams
Established: MB

Bibliography: *ASHCB*, site 304 (16-13/66/1), p. 45*; p. 228.

15. Kh. El-'Alawina
Israel Grid: 1675.1354
Environmental Niche: 1
Maximal Size: 7 dunams
Pottery: Iron II; P: H; R; Byz

ח' אל־עלוינא
Elevation: 700 m.
Estimated Population: 75
Size, Persian Period: 3 dunams
Established: Iron II.

Bibliography: *ASHCB*, site 309 (16-13/75/1), p. 46*; p. 230; Milevski, 'Settlement Patterns', pp. 15-18 .

16. Unnamed 4
Israel Grid: 1677.1351
Environmental Niche: 1
Maximal Size: 30 dunams
Pottery: MB; Iron II; P

Elevation: 630 m.
Estimated Population: 275
Size, Persian Period: 11 dunams
Established: MB

Bibliography: *ASHCB*, site 310 (16-13/75/2), p. 46*; p. 231.

17. Kh. el-Burj
Israel Grid: 1678.1367
Environmental Niche: 1
Maximal Size: 30 dunams
Pottery: Iron I & II; P, P/H; H; R

ח' אל־ברג'
Elevation: 830 m.
Estimated Population: 300
Size, Persian Period: 12 dunams
Established, Iron I

Bibliography: *ASHCB*, site 311 (16-13/76/2), p. 46*; pp. 231-33; *JSG*, site 150, pp. 186-87.

18. Beit 'Ur et-Tahta
Israel Grid:1582.1446
Environmental Niche: 1
Maximal Size: 30 dunams
Pottery: Iron I & II, P; H; R; Byz.

בית עור א־תחתא
Elevation: 390 m.
Estimated Population: 250
Size, Persian Period:10 dunams
Established: Iron I?

Bibliography: *ASHCB*, p. 15*; pp. 43-46. Site 22 (15-14/84/1).

19. Beit 'Ur el-Fauqa
Israel Grid: 1608.1436
Environmental Niche: 1
Maximal Size: 15 dunams
Pottery: Iron I & II; P; H; Byz.

בית עור אל־פוקא
Elevation: 590 m.
Estimated Population: 125
Size, Persian Period:5 dunams
Established: Iron I

Bibliography: *ASHCB,* site 28 (16-14/03/1), p. 16*; pp. 49-50; see also site 143 (16-14/03/1), p. 28*; p. 142.

20. Kh. el-Hafi
Israel Grid: 1633.1455
Environmental Niche: 1

ח' אל־חפי
Elevation 670 m.
Estimated Population: 50

Maximal Size: 3 dunams
Pottery: Late Persian/H; H; R; Byz.

Size, Persian Period: 2 dunams
Established: Persian

Bibliography: *ASHCB*, site 47 (16-14/38/1), p. 18*; pp. 61-62.

21. Kh. Badd Abu-Mu'ammar
Israel Grid: 1645.1403
Environmental Niche: 1
Maximal Size: 2.4 dunams
Pottery: Iron I & II; Persian; H; R; Byz.

ח' בד אבו־מעמר
Elevation: 791 m.
Estimated Population: 25
Size, Persian Period: 1 dunam
Established: Iron I

Bibliography: *ASHCB*, site 150 (16-14/40/1), p. 29*; pp. 145-46.

22. Rujm Abu Ḥashabe
Israel Grid: 1632.1419
Environmental Niche: 1
Maximal Size: NG
Pottery: P; R; Byz.

רוג'ם אבו ח'שבה
Elevation: 635 m.
Estimated Population: 37.5
Size, Persian Period: VS
Established: Persian

Bibliography: *JSG*, p. 181. Site 105 (16-14/31/1); *ASHCB*, site 43 (16-14/31/1), pp. 147-48, p. 29*.

23. Kh. el-Jufeir
Israel Grid: 1653.1411
Environmental Niche: 1
Maximal Size: 5 dunams
Pottery: P; H; Byz.

ח' אל־ג'ופיר
Elevation: 760 m.
Estimated Population: 87.5
Size, Persian Period: S
Established: Persian

Bibliography: *JSG*, p. 181. Site 111 (16-14/51/1); *ASHCB*, site 153 (16-14/15/1), pp. 147-48, p. 29*.

24. Kh. el-Latatin
Israel Grid: 1660.1418
Environmental Niche: 1
Maximal Size: 4 dunams
Pottery: Persian; Roman, Byz.

ח' א־לטטין
Elevation: 775 m.
Estimated Population: 87.5
Size, Persian Period: S
Established: Persian

Bibliography: *JSG*, p. 181. Site 112 (16-14/61/1); *ASHCB*, site 60 (16-14/61/1), p. 19*; p. 69.

25. Unnamed 5
Israel Grid: 1657.1378
Environmental Niche: 2
Maximal Size: 4 dunams
Pottery: Iron II; Persian, H; Byz.

Elevation: 820 m.
Estimated Population: 50
Size, Persian Period: 2 dunams
Established: Iron II

Bibliography: *ASHCB*, site 298 (16-13/57/1), p. 44*; p. 224.

26. Kh. Abu Leimun
Israel Grid: 1661.1370
Environmental Niche: 2
Maximal Size: 11 dunams
Pottery: P; H; R; Byz.

ח׳ אבו לימון
Elevation: 800 m.
Estimated Population: 150
Size, Persian Period: 6 dunams
Established: Persian

Bibliography: *ASHCB*, site 306 (16-13/67/1) p. 45*; pp. 228-29; *JSG*, site 141, p. 185.

27. Unnamed 6
Israel Grid: 1666.1416
Environmental Niche: 2
Maximal Size: 18 dunams
Pottery: MB; Iron II; Persian; Byz.

Elevation: 800 m.
Estimated Population: 150
Size, Persian Period: 6 dunams
Established: MB

Bibliography: *ASHCB*, site 158 (16-14/61/2) p. 30*; pp. 149-50.

28. El Jîb
Israel Grid: 1676.1394
Environmental Niche: 2
Maximal Size: 60 dunams
Pottery: EB; MB; Iron I & II; P; H; R; Byz.

אל־ג׳יב
Elevation: 779 m.
Estimated Population: 0
Size, Persian Period: Unknown
Established: EB

Bibliography: *ASHCB*, site 315 (16-13/79/1), p. 46*; p. 235; Pritchard, 'El Jîb', *NEAEHL*, II, pp. 511-14.

29. Kh. 'Id
Israel Grid: 1675.1402
Environmental Niche: 2
Maximal Size: 16 dunams
Pottery: P; H.; R.; Byz.

ח׳ עיד
Elevation: 760 m.
Estimated Population: 150
Size, Persian Period: 6 dunams
Established: Persian

Bibliography: *ASHCB*, site 160 (16-14/70/1), p. 30*; p. 151.

30. Judeira
Israel Grid: 1688.1406
Environmental Niche: 2
Maximal Size: 5 dunams
Pottery: Iron II?; P?; H

ג׳דירה
Elevation: 760 m.
Estimated Population: 87.5
Size, Persian Period: S
Established: Iron II

Bibliography: *ASHCB*, site 163 (16-14/80/3), p. 30*; pp. 153-54.

31. Kh. el-Ballut el-Khalis
Israel Grid: 1692.1395
Environmental Niche: 2
Maximal Size: 5 dunams
Pottery: MB; P/H; H

ח׳ אל־בלוט אל־ח׳לץ
Elevation: 790 m.
Estimated Population: 50
Size, Persian Period: 2
Established: MB (No Iron II)

Bibliography: *ASHCB*, site 321 (16-13/99/1), p. 47*; p. 237.

32. Kh. er-Ras (W)   ח׳ א־רס
Israel Grid: 1709.1354   Elevation: 790 m.
Environmental Niche: 2   Estimated Population: 87.5
Maximal Size: NG   Size, Persian Period: S
Pottery: Iron II; P; H   Established: Iron II

Bibliography: Onn and Rapuano, 'Jerusalem, Kh. er-Ras', p. 71.

33. Tell el-Fûl   תל אל־פול
Israel Grid: 1719.1367   Elevation: 838 m.
Environmental Niche: 2   Estimated Population: 0
Maximal Size: NG   Size, Persian Period: Not occupied
Pottery: Iron IIC/Neo-Babylonian; H   Established: Iron II?

Bibliography: Kloner, *Archaeological Survey of Jerusalem*, site 117; Lapp, *The Third Campaign*; Lapp, 'Fûl, tell el-', p. 448.

34. Kh. Irha   ח׳ ארהא
Israel Grid: 1724.1394   Elevation: 760 m.
Environmental Niche: 2   Estimated Population: 100
Size: 10 dunams   Size, Persian Period: 4 dunams
Pottery: Iron I & II, P/H: Byz.   Established: Iron I

Biblography: *ASHCB*, site 430 (17-13/29/1), p. 58*; p. 348.

35. French Hill   גבעת צרפתית
Israel Grid: 1725.1343   Elevation: 823 m.
Environmental Niche: 2   Estimated Population: 37.5
Maximal Size: NG   Size, Persian Period: VS
Pottery: Established:

Bibliography: O. Negbi, 'Remains of a Fortress next to French Hill' (Heb.), *HA* 30–31 (1969), p. 18; Kloner, *Archaeological Survey of Jerusalem*, site 284 (17-13/24/32).

36. Jerusalem (City of David)   ירשלים
Israel Grid: 1728.1313   Elevation: 750 m.
Environmental Niche: 2   Estimated Population: 1500
Maximal Size: NG   Size, Persian Period: 60 dunams
Pottery: Chal; EB; MB; LB;
Ir I/II; P; H; R; Byz.   Established: Chal.

Bibliography: Shiloh, *Excavations at the City of David*, I; Ariel (ed.), *Excavations at the City of David*, II; Ariel and DeGroot (eds.), *Excavations at the City of David*, III and IV.

37. Ketef Hinnom   כתף חנום
Israel Grid: 1714.1307   Elevation: 750 m.
Environmental Niche: 2   Estimated Population: 0

Maximal Size: Tomb
Pottery: Iron II, P, H, R, Byz.

Size Persian Period: Tomb
Established: Iron II

Bibliography: *AJR*, pp. 85-106.

38. Mamilla
Israel Grid: 1716.1316
Environmental Niche: 2
Maximal Size: Tomb
Pottery: Iron II, P, H, R, Byz.

ממלא
Elevation: 775 m.
Estimated Population: 0
Size Persian Period: Tomb
Established: Iron II

Bibliography: *AJR*, pp. 111-18; Reich and Shukron, 'Jerusalem, Mamilla', *ESI* 14, pp. 92-6.

39. Ras eṭ-Ṭaḥune (S)
Israel Grid: 1702.1462
Environmental Niche: 2
Maximal Size:
Pottery: C; EB; MB; Iron I & II; P.

רס אט־טחונה
Elevation: 875 m.
Estimated Population: 87.5
Size, Persian Period: S
Established: Chalcolithic

Bibliography: *JSG* site 94 (17-14/06/1), p. 178.

40. Tell en-Naṣbeh
Israel Grid: 1706.1436
Environmental Niche: 2
Maximal Size: 25 dunams[2]
Pottery: C; EB; Iron I & II; P; H; R.

תל א־נצבה
Elevation: 848 m.
Estimated Population: 425
Size, Persian Period: 17 dunams
Established: Chalcolithic

Bibliography: *ASHCB*, site 175 (17-14/03/2), p. 31*; p. 161; *TN*, I; Zorn, 'Nashbeh, Tell en-', pp. 1098-1102; McClellan, 'Town Planning'.

41. Kh. Nisieh
Israel Grid: 1717.1449
Environmental Niche: 2
Maximal Size: 15 dunams
Pottery: MB; Iron I & II; Persian; H; R; Byz.

ח׳ ניסיה
Elevation: 850 m.
Estimated Population: 125
Size, Persian Period: 5 dunams
Established: MB

Bibliography: *ASHCB*, site 184 (17-14/14/1), p. 32*; pp. 166-67.

42. Unnamed 7
Israel Grid: 1718.1434
Environmental Niche: 2
Maximal Size: 3 dunams
Pottery: Iron II; P; P/H; R; Byz.

Elevation: 820 m.
Estimated Population: 25
Size, Persian Period: 1 dunam
Established: Iron II

Bibliography: *ASHCB*, site 183 (17-14/13/2), p. 32*, p. 166.

2.   McCown gives size as 34 Dunams. See *EAEHL*, McCown, 'Nashbeh, Tell-en', pp. 912-18.

43. Unnamed 8
Israel Grid 1720.1429
Environmental Niche: 2
Maximal Size: 13 dunams
Pottery: Iron I; Persian; H; R; Byz.

Elevation: 810 m.
Estimated Population: 25
Size, Persian Period 1 dunam
Established: Iron I (No Iron II)

Bibliography: *ASHCB*, site 190 (17-14/22/1), p. 33*; pp. 169-70.

44. Er-Ram
Israel Grid: 1721.1402
Environmental Niche: 2
Maximal Size: 30 dunams
Pottery: Iron I & II; Persian; H; R; Byz.

א־רם
Elevation: 880 m.
Estimated Population: 250
Size, Persian Period: 10 dunams
Established: Iron I

Bibliography: *ASHCB*, site 188 (17-14/20/1), p. 33*, pp. 168-69.

45. Beitin
Israel Grid: 1728.1481
Environmental Niche: 2
Maximal Size: 20 Dunams
Pottery: C; EB; MB; LB; Iron I/II; P; H; R; Byz.

ביתין
Elevation: 900 m.
Estimated Population: 87.5
Size, Persian Period: S
Established: Chalcolithic

Bibliography: *ASHCB*, site 82 (17-14/28/1), pp. 19*-20*; p. 80; Albright and Kelso, *The Excavations of Bethel*; Kelso, 'Bethel', *NEAEHL*, I, p. 192.

46. Jaba'
Israel Grid: 1749.1405
Environmental Niche: 2
Maximal Size: 20 dunams
Pottery: Iron I & II; Persian; H; R, Byz.

ג'בע
Elevation: 690 m.
Estimated Population: 87.5
Size, Persian Period: S
Established, Iron I

Bibliography: *ASCHB*, site 206 (17-14/40/1) p. 35*; pp. 177-79; *JSG*, site 125, p. 183.

47. Horvat Zimri
Israel Grid: 1738.1363
Environmental Niche: 3
Maximal Size: NG
Pottery: Iron II; Persian

הרות זמרי
Elevation: 675 m.
Estimated Population: 87.5
Size, Persian Period: S
Established: Iron II

Bibliography: Nadelman, 'Jerusalem—Pisgat Ze'ev "D"', pp. 49-51; 'Jerusalem, Pisgat Ze'ev D (H. Zimri)', pp. 54-56; Kloner, *Archaeological Survey of Jerusalem*.

48. Unnamed 9
Israel Grid: 1743.1343
Environmental Niche: 3
Maximal Size: NG
Pottery: Iron II; Persian

Elevation: 650 m.
Estimated Population: 37.5
Size, Persian Period: VS
Established: Iron II

49. Wadi Salim
Israel Grid: 1743.1344
Environmental Niche: 3
Maximal Size: 4 dunams
Pottery: Iron II, Persian, H

ודי שלים
Elevation: 650 m.
Estimated Population: 100
Size, Persian Period: 4 dunams
Established: Iron II

Bibliography: Kloner, site 307 (17-13/44/3); Pommerantz (ed.), ' "Isawiye"—Survey of New Road', pp. 54-55.

50. El 'Eizariya
Israel Grid: 1744.1309
Environmental Niche: 3
Maximal Size: NG
Pottery: Iron II; Persian; H; Byz.

אל־עיזריה
Elevation: 660 m.
Estimated Population: 87.5
Size, Persian Period: S
Established: Iron II

Bibliography: *ASHCB*, site 436 (17-13/40/5), p. 58*; p. 351.

51. Ras el Kharubeh
Israel Grid: 1746.1350
Environmental Niche: 3
Maximal Size: 10 dunams
Pottery: Iron II, Persian; H; R; Byz.

ראס אל־חרובה
Elevation: 748 m.
Estimated Population: 87.5
Size, Persian Period: S
Established: Iron II

Bibliography: *ASHCB*, site 450 (17-13/45/1), p. 60*; p. 358; Biran, 'On the Problem of the Identification of Anathoth', pp. 209-14.

52. Ras Abu Subeitan
Israel Grid: 1748.1321
Environmental Niche: 3
Maximal Size: 10 dunams
Pottery: Iron II/Persian; Byz.

ראס אבו סביתן
Elevation: 660 m.
Estimated Population: 100
Size, Persian Period: 4 dunams
Established: Iron II/Persian

Bibliography: *ASHCB*, site 444 (17-13/42/1), p. 59*; p. 354.

53. Kh. Harabat 'Audeh
Israel Grid: 1749.1340
Environmental Niche: 3
Maximal Size: 10 dunams
Pottery: MB; Iron II; Persian; Byz.

ח׳ הראבת עודה
Elevation: 660 m.
Estimated Population: 75
Size, Persian Period: 3 dunams
Established: Iron II

Bibliography: *ASHCB*, site 448 (17-13/44/1), p. 60*; p. 357.

54. 'Anata
Israel Grid: 1749.1356
Environmental Niche: 3
Maximal Size: NG
Pottery: LB?; Iron I/ II; Persian; H., R; Byz.

ענתא
Elevation: 680 m.
Estimated Population: 87.5
Size, Persian Period: S
Established: LB?

Bibliography: *ASHCB*, site 452 (17-13/45/3), p. 60*; pp. 359-60.

55. Unnamed 10
Israel Grid: 1750.1389
Environmental Niche: 3
Maximal Size: NG
Pottery: Iron II; Persian

Elevation: 570 m.
Estimated Population: 37.5
Size, Persian Period: VS
Established: Iron II

Bibliography: *ASHCB*, site 481 (17-13/58/3), p. 63*; pp. 373-74.

56. Ras Tumeim
Israel Grid: 1754.1332[3]
Environmental Niche: 3
Maximal Size: 5 dunams
Pottery: Iron I, Perisan, H, Rom/Byz.

רס תומים
Elevation: 851 m.
Estimated Population: 87.5
Size, Persian period: S
Established: Iron I

Bibliography: U. Dinur, 'Jerusalem Region, Survey of Map 102', *ESI* 6 (1987/88), pp. 62-65.

57. Hizma
Israel Grid: 1754.1382
Environmental Niche: 3
Maximal Size: NG
Pottery: MB; Iron II; Persian; R; Byz.

חזמא
Elevation: 630 m.
Estimated Population: 87.5
Size, Persian Period: S
Established: MB

Bibliography: *ASHCB*, site 480 (17-13/58/2), p. 63*; pp. 372-73.

58. Jurrat es-Saqqawi
Israel Grid: 1756.1398
Environmental Niche: 3
Maximal Size: NG
Pottery: Iron II; Persian

ג׳ורת א־סקאוי
Elevation: 661 m.
Estimated Population: 37.5
Size, Persian Period: VS
Established: Iron II

Bibliography: *ASHCB*, site 482 (17-13/59/1), p. 63*; p. 374.

59. Kh. 'Almith
Israel Grid: 1760.1369
Environmental Niche: 3
Maximal Size: 70 dunams
Pottery: MB; Iron I & II; Persian; H/R; Byz.

ח׳ עלמית
Elevation: 638 m.
Estimated Population: 87.5
Size, Persian Period: S
Established: MB

Bibliography: *ASHCB,* site 496 (17-13/66/1), p. 65*; pp. 380-81; Dinur, 'Khirbet 'Almit'.

60. Kh. Deir es-Sid
Israel Grid: 1762.1353
Environmental Niche: 3

ח׳ דאיר א־סד
Elevation: 610 m.
Estimated Population: 87.5

3.   Coordinates on map are listed as 1744.1332.

Maximal Size: 30 dunams   Size, Persian Period: S
Pottery: Iron II, P; H; R; Byz.   Established: Iron II

Bibliography: *ASHCB*, site 493 (17-13/65/1), p. 65*; p. 379; Biran, 'On the Problem of the Identification of Anathoth', pp. 209-14.

61. Unnamed 11
Israel Grid: 1780.1344   Elevation: 380 m.
Environmental Niche: 3   Estimated Population: 25
Maximal Size: NG   Size, Persian Period: 1 dunam
Pottery: EBI; Iron II; Persian; Byz.   Established: EB I; Iron II

Bibliography: *ASHCB,* site. 524 (17-13/84/1), p. 68*; p. 399.

62. Kh. el-Ḥara el-Fauqa, and Mukhmas   ח׳ אל־חרה אל־פוקא ומחמס
Israel Grid: 1763.1424   Elevation: 620 m.
Environmental Niche: 3   Estimated Population: 400
Maximal Size: 40 dunams   Size, Persian Period: 16 dunams
Pottery: MB; Iron I & II; Persian; H; R; Byz.   Established, MB.

Bibliography: *ASHCB*, site 223 (17-14/62/2), p. 36*; pp. 185-86.

63. Unnamed 12
Israel Grid: 1767.1422   Elevation: 560 m.
Environmental Niche: 3   Estimated Population: 0
Maximal Size: Tomb   Size, Persian Period: 0
Pottery: MB, Iron I & II, Persian, H, R, Byz.   Established, MB.

Bibliography: *ASCHCB*, site 222 (17-14/62/1), p. 36*, p. 184.

64. Kh. Tell el-Askar   ח׳ תל אל־עסכר
Israel Grid: 1767.1430   Elevation: 640 M.
Environmental Niche: 3   Estimated Population: 100
Maximal Size: 12 dunams   Size, Persian Period: 4
Pottery: MB; Iron I & II; Persian; R; Byz.   Established: MB

Bibliography: *ASHCB*, site 227 (17-14/63/1), p. 37*; pp. 187-88.

65. el-Jab'a   אל־ג׳ בעה
Israel Grid: 1573.1203   Elevation: 663 m.
Environmental Niche: 4   Estimated Population: 37.5
Maximal Size: NG   Size, Persian Period: VS
Pottery: Persian (small amount), H, R, Byz., O. Established: Persian

Bibliography: Kokhavi, site 36, (15-12/70/1), pp. 42-43.

66. Abu-et-Twein
Israel Grid: 1587.1192
Environmental Niche: 4
Maximal Size: NG
Pottery: Iron II, P

אבו א־תוין
Elevation: 700 m.
Estimated Population: 87.5
Persian Period: S
Established: Iron II

Bibliography: Mazar, 'Iron Age Fortresses', pp. 86-109; Mazar, 'Abu Tuwein, Khirbet', pp. 15-16; Hoglund, *Achaemenid Imperial Administration*, pp. 191-96.

67. Deir Bagl
Israel Grid: 1594.1228
Environmental Niche: 4
Maximal Size: 1 dunam
Pottery: Iron I & II, R

דיר בע׳ל
Elevation: 718 m.
Estimated Population: 25
Persian Period: 1 dunam
Established: Iron I

Bibliography: *JSG*, Site 28 (15-12/92/1); Hoglund, *Achaemenid Imperial Administration*, pp. 195-96.

68. Kh. El-Kabarah
Israel Grid: 1607.1215
Environmental Niche: 4
Maximal Size: NG
Pottery: Iron II, P. Byz.

ח׳ אל־כברה
Elevation: 625 m.
Estimated Population: 87.5
Size, Persian Period: S
Established: Iron II.

Bibliography: *JSG*, site 32 (16-12/01/1), p. 42.

69. Kh. Jrish
Israel Grid: 1616.1241
Environmental Niche: 4
Maximal Size: 3 dunams
Pottery: P, R

ח׳ ג׳ריש
Elevation: 775 m.
Estimated Population: 75
Size, Persian Period: 3 dunams
Established: Persian

Bibliography: *JSG*, Site 14 (16-12/14/3).

70. Kh. Umm el-Qal‘a
Israel Grid: 1617.1243
Environmental Niche: 4
Maximal Size: NG
Pottery: Iron Age, P; H; R, Byz., M.

ח׳ אם אל־קלעה
Elevation: 800 m.
Estimated Population: 37.5
Size, Persian Period: VS
Established: Iron Age.

Biblography: *JSG*, site 13 (16-12/14/1), pp. 37-38.

71. Ḥusan
Israel Grid: 1627.1244
Environmental Niche: 4
Maximal Size: NG
Pottery: Iron II; P; H; R I & II; Byz.; M; O.

חוסן
Elevation: 801 m.
Estimated Population: 87.5
Size, Persian Period: S
Established: Iron II

Bibliography: *JSG*, site 17 (16-12/24/3), p. 39.

72. Kh. el-Yahudi   ח׳ אל־יהודי
Kh. el-Yahud   ח׳ אל־יהוד
Israel Grid: 1628.1264:   Elevation: 680 m.
Environmental Niche: 4   Estimated Population: 37.5
Maximal Size: NG   Size, Persian Period: VS
Pottery: Iron I & II; P, H, R   Established: Iron I

Bibliography: *JSG*, site 4 (16/12/28/1), p. 36.

73. Kh. Judur   ח׳ ג׳דור
Israel Grid: 1588.1156   Elevation: 922 m.
Environmental Niche: 5   Estimated Population: 350
Size: 24 dunams   Size, Persian Period: 14 dunams
Pottery: MB; LB; Iron I/II; P; H, R, Byz. Established: MB II?

Bibliography: *JSG*, site 60 (15-11/75/1), pp. 46-7. Ofer, 'The Highlands of Judah, I', Map 108 (15-11), site 108/85/1, p. 12*.

74. Beit Ummar   בית אומר
Israel Grid: 1598.1143   Elevation: 970 m.
Environmental Niche: 5   Estimated Population: 325
Maximal Size:28 dunams   Size, Persian Period: 13 dunams
Pottery: P; H; R; Byz; Med; LA   Established: Persian

Bibliography: Ofer, 'The Highlands of Judah, I', map 108 (15-11), site 108/94/1. p. 12*.

75. Kh. el-Qaṭṭ   ח׳ אל־קט
Israel Grid: 1602.1127   Elevation: 980 m.
Environmental Niche: 5   Estimated Population: 25
Maximal Size: 1 dunam   Size, Persian Period: 1 dunam
Pottery: (Iron II, few sherds); P, H; R   Established: Iron II?

Bibliography: *JSG*, site 79 (16-11/02/1), p. 50; Ofer, 'The Highlands of Judah, I', map 307 (16/11), site 307/02/1, p. 12*.

76. Kh. Hubeilah   ח׳ חובילה
Israel Grid: 1602.1157   Elevation: 950 m.
Environmental Niche: 5   Estimated Population: 225
Maximal Size: 20 dunams   Size, Persian Period: 9 dunams
Pottery: Iron II; P; H; Byz   Established: Iron II

Bibliography: Ofer, 'The Highlands of Judah, I', map 307 (16-11), site 307/08/2, p. 12*.

77. Kh. Umm ed-Durj   אום א׳דרג׳
Israel Grid: 1608.1124   Elevation: 950 m.
Environmental Niche: 5   Estimated Population: 50

Maximal Size: 2 dunams
Pottery: P; Byz.

Size, Persian Period: 2 dunams
Established: Persian

Bibliography: Ofer, 'The Highlands of Judah, I', map 307 (16-11), site 307/02/2.

78. Kh. Kufin
Israel Grid: 1609.1143
Environmental Niche: 5
Maximal Size: 6 dunams
Pottery: MBII; P; H; R; Byz

ח׳ כופין
Elevation: 925 m.
Estimated Population: 150
Size, Persian Period: 6 dunams
Established: MB; (No Iron Age)

Bibliography: Ofer, 'The Highlands of Judah, I', map 307 (16-11), site 307/04/1,
p. 12*.

79. Kh. Beit Zakariyeh
Israel Grid: 1617.1189
Environmental Niche: 5
Maximal Size: 10.4 dunams
Pottery: Iron II; P; H; Byz.

ח ב בת־זכריא
Elevation: 950 m.
Estimated Population: 260
Size, Persian Period: 10.4 dunams
Established: Iron II

Bibliography: Ofer, 'The Highlands of Judah, I', map 307 (16-11), site 307/18/1,
p. 12*.

80. Deir Sha'ar
Israel Grid: 1619.1170
Environmental Niche: 5
Maximal Size: 10 dunams
Pottery: Iron II; P; H; R; Byz.

דיר שער
Elevation: 950 m.
Estimated Population: 175
Size, Persian Period: 7 dunams
Established: Iron II

Bibliography: Ofer, 'The Highlands of Judah, I', map 307 (16-11), site 307/17/1,
p. 12*.

81. Kh. el-Qarn
Israel Grid: 1620.1140
Environmental Niche: 5
Maximal Size:8 dunams
Pottery: P; H; R; Byz.

ח׳ אל־קרן
Elevation: 954 m.
Estimated Population: 150
Size, Persian Period: 6 dunams
Established: Persian

Bibliography: Ofer, 'The Highlands of Judah, I', map 307 (16-11), site 307/24/1,
p. 12*.

82. Suwir
Israel Grid: 1625.1172
Environmental Niche: 5
Maximal Size: 1 dunam
Pottery: Iron II; P; H; R

סוויר
Elevation: 971 m.
Estimated Population: 25
Size, Persian Period: 1 dunam
Established: Iron II

Bibliography: Ofer, 'The Highlands of Judah, I', map 307 (16-11), site 307/28/1,
p. 12*.

83. Kh. Umm eṭ-Ṭalʿah[4]
Israel Grid: 1630.1160
Environmental Niche: 5
Maximal Size: 6 dunams
Pottery: Iron I; P

אום א־טלעה
Elevation: 976 m.
Estimated Population: 145
Size, Persian Period: 5.8 dunams
Established: Iron I (no Iron II)

Bibliography: Ofer, 'The Highlands of Judah, I', map 307 (16-11), site 307/36/1, p. 13*.

84. Rujm es-Sabit
Israel Grid: 1636.1178
Environmental Niche: 5
Maximal Size: 5 dunams
Pottery: Iron I & II; P

רוג׳ם א־סבית
Elevation: 925 m.
Estimated Population: 125
Size, Persian Period: 5 dunams
Established: Iron I

Bibliography: Ofer, 'The Highlands of Judah, I', map 307 (16-11), site 307/37/1, p. 13*.

85. Ain Arrub
Israel Grid: 1637.1139
Environmental Niche: 5
Maximal Size: Tomb
Pottery:

עין ערוב
Elevation: 839 m.
Estimated Population: 0
Size, Persian Period: Tomb
Established:

Bibliography: Stern, 'A Burial of the Persian Period', pp. 25-30.

86. Kh. Baricuth
Israel Grid: 1637.1168
Environmental Niche: 5
Maximal Size: 25 dunams
Pottery: P; R; Byz

בריכות
Elevation: 950 m.
Estimated Population: 375
Size, Persian Period: 15 dunams
Established: Persian

Bibliography: Ofer, 'The Highlands of Judah, I', map 307 (16-11), site 307/47/1, p. 13*.

87. Kh. Peʿor
Kh. Zakahdah
Israel Grid: 1640.1193
Environmental Niche: 5
Maximal Size: 15 dunams
Pottery: Iron I & II; P; H; R; Byz

ח׳ פעור
ח׳ זכנדה
Elevation: 924 m.
Estimated Population: 375
Size, Persian Period: 15 dunams
Established: Iron I

Bibliography: Ofer, 'The Highlands of Judah, I', map 307 (16-11), site 307/49/2, p. 13*; *JSG*, site 46 (16-11/49-2), p. 44.

---

4.   Adjacent to the site are two installations, each of 0.4 dunams, one a well and wine-press; the other spring. Persian period remains are found at each.

88. Kh. Humeidiyah   ח׳ חומידיה
Israel Grid: 1641.1197   Elevation: 927 m.
Environmental Niche: 5   Estimated Population: 125
Maximal Size: 12 dunams   Size, Persian Period: 5 dunams
Pottery: Iron II; P; H; R; Byz.   Established: Iron II

Bibliography: Ofer, 'The Highlands of Judah, I', map 307 (16-11), site 307/39/2, p. 13*.

89. Kh. Shanah   ח׳ שנה
Israel Grid: 1642.1144   Elevation: 900 m.
Environmental Niche: 5   Estimated Population: 50
Maximal Size: 2 dunams   Size, Persian Period: 2 dunams
Pottery: P; H; Byz.   Established: Persian

Bibliography: Ofer, 'The Highlands of Judah, I', map 307 (16-11), site 307/44/2, p. 13*.

90. Salmuneh   סלמונה
Israel Grid: 1655.1172   Elevation: 954 m.
Environmental Niche: 5   Estimated Population: 25
Maximal Size: 1 dunam   Size, Persian Period: 1 dunam
Pottery: Iron II; P; R   Established: Iron II

Bibliography: Ofer, 'The Highlands of Judah, I', map 307 (16-11), site 307/57/1, p. 13*.

91. Marsiya‘   מרסיע
Israel Grid: 1661.1187[5]   Elevation: 900 m.
Environmental Niche: 5   Estimated Population: 25
Maximal Size: 1 dunam   Size, Persian Period: 1 dunam
Pottery: P; Byz   Established: Persian

Bibliography: Ofer, 'The Highlands of Judah, I', map 307 (16-11), site 307/58/1, p. 13*.

92. Shem‘ah   שמעה
Israel Grid: 1665.1181   Elevation: 900 m.
Environmental Niche: 5   Estimated Population: 25
Maximal Size: 2 dunams   Size, Persian Period: 1 dunam
Pottery: MB; P   Established: MB (No Iron II)

Bibliography: Ofer, 'The Highlands of Judah, I', map 307 (16-11), site 307/68/2.

---

5. Coordinates on map are listed as 1655.1187.

93. Khalil 'Isma'il
Israel Grid: 1674.1175[6]
Environmental Niche: 5
Maximal Size: 5 dunams
Pottery: Iron II; P; Byz.

חליל איסמעיל
Elevation: 900 m.
Estimated Population: 75
Size, Persian Period: 3 dunams
Established: Iron II

Bibliography: Ofer, 'The Highlands of Judah, I', map 307 (16-11), site 307/77/2.

94. Wadi Arrub
Israel Grid: 1675.1135
Environmental Niche: 5
Maximal Size: 4 dunams
Pottery: MB; Iron II; P; M;

ודי ערוב
Elevation: 725 m.
Estimated Population: 60
Size, Persian Period: 2.4 dunams?
Established: MB

Bibliography: Ofer, 'The Highlands of Judah, I', map 307 (16-11), site 307/63/1, p. 13*.

95. Kh. Jumi'a
Israel Grid: 1641.1214
Environmental Niche: 5
Maximal Size: 12 dunams
Pottery: Iron II; P; Byz.

ח׳ ג׳ומיע
Elevation: 975 m.
Estimated Population: 150
Size, Persian Period: 6 dunams
Established: Iron II

Bibliography: Ofer, 'The Highlands of Judah, I', map 105 (16-12), site 105/41/3, p. 12*.

96. Kh. Merah ej-Jumi'a
Israel Grid: 1642.1217
Environmental Niche: 5
Maximal Size: 5 dunams
Pottery: Iron II; P; H; R; Byz.

ח׳ מרח א־ג׳ומיע
Elevation: 975 m.
Estimated Population: 75
Size, Persian Period: 3 dunams
Established: Iron II

Bibliography: Ofer, 'The Highlands of Judah, I', map 105 (16-12), site 105/41/1, p. 12*.

97. Kh. Abu Shawan
Israel Grid: 1646.1263
Environmental Niche: 5
Maximal Size: 25 dunams
Pottery: P; R

ח׳ אבו־שון
Elevation: 797 m.
Estimated Population: 225
Size, Persian Period: 9 dunams
Established: Persian

Bibliography: Ofer, 'The Highlands of Judah, I', map 105 (16-12), site 105/46/1, p. 12*.

---

6. Coordinates on map are listed as 1664.1175.

98. Kh. Gharib
Israel Grid: 1647.1212
Environmental Niche: 5
Maximal Size: 4 dunams
Pottery: Iron II; P; H; R; Byz.

ח׳ ע׳רב
Elevation: 925 m.
Estimated Population: 100
Size, Persian Period: 4 dunams
Established: Iron II

Bibliography: Ofer, 'The Highlands of Judah, I', map 105 (16-12), site 105/41/1, p. 12*.

99. Rujm el-Khadar
Israel Grid: 1647.1235
Environmental Niche: 5
Maximal Size: 1 dunam
Pottery: P, H; R

ר׳גם אל־ח׳דר
Elevation: 909 m.
Estimated Population: 25
Size, Persian Period: 1 dunam
Established: Persian

Bibliography: *JSG*, site 24 (16-12/43/1); p. 40; Ofer, 'The Highlands of Judah, I', map 105 (16-12), site 105/43/1).

100. Kh. Umm el-Qiṭa'
Israel Grid: 1653.1202
Environmental Niche: 5
Maximal Size: 15 dunams
Pottery: Iron II, Persian; R; Byz.

ח׳ אם אל־קטע
Elevation: 860 m.
Estimated Population: 150
Size, Persian Period: 6 dunams
Established: Iron II

Bibliography: *JSG*, site 39, (16-12/50/1), p. 43; Ofer, 'The Highlands of Judah, I', map 105 (16-12), site 105/50/1, p. 12*.

101. Kh. 'Aliya'
Israel Grid: 1654.1224
Environmental Niche: 5
Maximal Size: 5 dunams
Pottery: P, Roman, Byz.

ח׳ עליא
Elevation: 875 m.
Estimated Population: 100
Size, Persian Period: 4 dunams
Established: Persian

Bibliography: Ofer, 'The Highlands of Judah, I', map 105 (16-12), site 105/51/1, p. 12*.

102. Nimer
Israel Grid: 1665.1229
Environmental Niche: 5
Maximal Size: 3 dunams
Pottery: Iron II; P

נימר
Elevation: 875 m.
Estimated Population: 75
Size, Persian Period: 3 dunams
Established: Iron II

Bibliography: Ofer, 'The Highlands of Judah, I', map 105 (16-12), site 105/62/1, p. 12*.

103. Kh. Kabar
Israel Grid: 1665.1231
Environmental Niche: 5

ח׳ כבר
Elevation: 888 m.
Estimated Population: 100

Maximal Size: 5 dunams   Size, Persian Period: 4 dunams
Pottery: P, R.   Established; Persian

Bibliography: *JSG*, site 26 (16-12/63/1), pp. 40-1; Ofer, 'The Highlands of Judah, I', map 105 (16-12), site 105/63/1, p. 12*.

104. Kh. el-Khwakh   ח' אל־ח'וח'
Israel Grid: 1671.1214   Elevation: 700 m.
Environmental Niche: 5   Estimated Population: 125
Maximal Size: 10 dunams   Size, Persian Period: 5 dunams
Pottery: Iron I & II; P; H, R, Byz   Established: Iron I

Bibliography: *JSG*, site 35 (16-12/71/1), p. 42; Ofer, 'The Highlands of Judah, I', map 105 (16-12), site 105/71/1, p. 12*.

105. Kh. er-Ras (S)   ח' א־רס
Israel Grid: 1671.1282   Elevation: 750 m.
Environmental Niche: 5   Estimated Population 75
Maximal Size: 3 dunams   Size, Persian Period: 3 dunams
Pottery: MB; Iron II; P; H; R.   Established: MB.

Bibliography: Kloner, *Archaeological Survey of Jerusalem*, site 1034 (16-13/); Zehavi, 'Jerusalem, Manahat', pp. 66-67.

106. Ras el-Kabir   רס אל־כביר
Israel Grid: 1674.1237   Elevation: 840 m.
Environmental Niche: 5   Estimated Population: 125
Maximal Size: 5 dunams   Size, Persian Period: 5 dunams
Pottery: Iron II; P, H   Established, Iron II

Bibliography: *JSG*, site 27 (16-12/73/1), p. 41; Ofer, 'The Highlands of Judah, I', map 105 (16-12), site 105/73/1, p. 12*.

107. Sharafat   שרפת
Israel Grid: 1681.1278   Elevation: 765 m.
Environmental Niche: 5   Estimated Population: 275
Maximal Size: 12 dunams   Size, Persian Period: 11 dunams
Pottery: P; R;   Established: Persian

Bibliography: Ofer, 'The Highlands of Judah, I', map 105 (16-12), site 105/87/1, p. 12*.

108. Bethlehem   בת־לחם
Israel Grid: 1698.1235   Elevation: 700 m.
Environmental Niche: 5   Estimated Population: 100

Maximal Size: 12 dunams
Pottery: Iron I & II; P; H; R; Byz

Size, Persian Period: 4 dunams
Established: Iron I

Bibliography: Ofer, 'The Highlands of Judah, I', map 105 (16-12), site 105/93/1, p. 12*.

109. Ramat Raḥel
Israel Grid: 1706.1274
Environmental Niche: 5
Maximal Size: 10 dunams
Pottery: Iron II, P, H

רמת רחל
Elevation: 803 m.
Estimated Population: 212.5
Size, Persian Period: M
Established: Iron II

Bibliography: Aharoni, *Excavations of Ramat Raḥel: Seasons 1959 and 1960*; *Excavations of Ramat Raḥel: Seasons 1961 and 1962*; 'Ramat Raḥel', pp. 1261-65.

110. Kh. 'Arbiyeh
Israel Grid: 1658.1042
Environmental Niche: 6
Maximal Size: 4 dunams
Pottery: P; H; Byz

ח׳ ערביה
Elevation: 925 m.
Estimated Population: 50
Size, Persian Period: 2 dunams
Established: Persian

Bibliography: Ofer, 'The Highlands of Judah, I', map 310 (16-10), site 310/54/1, p. 12*.

111. Kh. el-Seimar
Israel Grid: 1664.1080
Environmental Niche: 6
Maximal Size: 6 Dunams
Pottery: P; H

ח׳ אל־סימר
Elevation: 916 m.
Estimated Population: 75
Size, Persian Period: 3 Dunams
Established: Persian

Bibliography: Ofer, 'The Highlands of Judah, I', map 310 (16-10), site 310/68/1.

112. Kh. Za'afran
Israel Grid: 1672.1102
Environmental Niche: 6
Maximal Size: 10 Dunams
Pottery: Iron II; P; H; Byz

ח׳ זעפרן
Elevation: 910 m.
Estimated Population: 100
Size, Persian Period: 4 Dunams
Established: Iron II

Bibliography: Ofer, 'The Highlands of Judah, I', map 307 (16-11), site 307/70/1, p. 13*.

113. Beideh
Israel Grid: 1683.1194
Environmental Niche: 6
Maximal Size: 3 dunams
Pottery: Iron II; P

בידה
Elevation: 850 m.
Estimated Population: 75
Size, Persian Period: 3 dunams
Established: Iron II

Bibliography: Ofer, 'The Highlands of Judah, I', map 307 (16-11), site 307/89/3.

114. Kh. Sib'ah
Israel Grid: 1695.1185
Environmental Niche: 6
Maximal Size: 12 dunams
Pottery: Iron I & II; P; H; R; Byz

סיבעה
Elevation: 750 m.
Estimated Population: 150
Size, Persian Period: 6 dunams
Established: Iron II

Bibliography: Ofer, 'The Highlands of Judah, I', map 307 (16-11), site 307/98/1.

115. Kh. et-Tuqu'
Israel Grid: 1700.1157
Environmental Niche: 6
Maximal Size: 25 dunams
Pottery: Iron I & II; P (on E. slope);
R, Byz.

ח׳ א־תקוע
Elevation 825 m.
Estimated Population: 375
Size, Persian Period: 15 dunams

Established: Iron I

Bibliography: *JSG*, site 62 (17-11/05/1), p. 47; Ofer, 'The Highlands of Judah, I', map 308 (17-11), site 308/05/1, p. 13*.

116. Kh. et-Tayyibe
Israel Grid: 1531.1072[7]
Environmental Niche: 7
Maximal Size: 30 Dunams
Pottery: MB II, Iron I & II; P, H, R, Byz.

ח׳ א־תייבה
Elevation: 784 m.
Estimated Population: 450
Size, Persian Period: 18 Dunams
Established: MB II

Bibliography: *JSG*, site 115 (15-10/37/1), p. 57; Ofer, 'The Highlands of Judah, I', map 309 (15-10), site 309/37/2, p. 13*.

117. Tafuḥ
Israel Grid: 1545.1052
Environmental Niche: 7
Maximal Size: 30 dunams
Pottery: Iron II, P, H, R, Byz,

תפוח
Elevation: 800 m.
Estimated Population: 300
Size, Persian Period: 12 dunams
Established: Iron II

Bibliography: *JSG*, site 133 (15-10/45/1), pp. 59-60; Ofer, 'The Highlands of Judah, I', map 309 (15-10), site 309/45/1, p. 13*.

118. Kh. Daḥdaḥ
Israel Grid: 1590.1074
Environmental Niche: 7
Maximal Size: 4 dunams
Pottery: P; H; Byz.

ח׳ דחדח
Elevation: 1000 m.
Estimated Population: 100
Size, Persian Period: 4 dunams
Established: Persian

Bibliography: Ofer, 'The Highlands of Judah, I', map 309 (15-10), site 309/97/2.

---

7.   Kokhavi lists grid reference as 1531/1702, an obvious typographical error (*JSG*, p. 57).

119. Gebel Namra'
Israel Grid: 1598.1048
Environmental Niche: 7
Maximal Size: 3 dunams
Pottery: P

ג׳בל נמרא
Elevation: 950 m.
Estimated Population: 75
Size, Persian Period: 3 dunams
Established: Persian

Bibliography: Ofer, 'The Highlands of Judah, I', map 309 (15-10), site 309/94/1.

120. 'Kh. Arnav
Israel Grid: 1557.1108
Environmental Niche: 7

ח׳ ארנב
Elevation: 800 m.
Estimated Population: 150

Maximal Size: 8 dunams
Pottery: Iron II; P; R

Size, Persian Period: 6 dunams
Established: Iron II

Bibliography: Ofer, 'The Highlands of Judah, I', map 108 (15-11), site 108/50/5.

121. Kh. Ṭubeiqah (Bet-Zur)
Israel Grid: 1590.1108
Environmental Niche: 7
Maximal Size: 12 dunams
Pottery: MB II; LB; Iron II; Persian; H; R

ח׳ טביקה
Elevation: 950 m.
Estimated Population: 50
Size, Persian Period: 2 dunams
Established: MB II

Bibliography: *CBZ*; Lapp and Lapp, 'Iron II-Hellenistic Pottery Groups'; Reich, 'The Beth-Zur Citidel II'; Ofer, 'The Highlands of Judah, I', map 108 (15-11), site 108/90/3, p. 12*.

122. Ḥalḥul
Israel Grid: 1603.1095
Environmental Niche: 7
Maximal Size: 18 dunams
Pottery: Iron I & II; P; H; Byz.

חלחול
Elevation: 1000 m.
Estimated Population: 285
Size, Persian Period: 11.4 dunams
Established: Iron I

Bibliography: Ofer, 'The Highlands of Judah, I', map 310 (16-10), site 310/09/1, p. 13*.

123. Kh. Beit 'Anun
Israel Grid: 1621.1078
Environmental Niche: 7
Maximal Size: 6 dunams
Pottery: Iron II; P; R; Byz.

ח׳ בת ענון
Elevation: 950 m.
Estimated Population: 100
Size, Persian Period: 4 dunams
Established: Iron II

Bibliography: Ofer, 'The Highlands of Judah, I', map 310 (16-10), site 310/27/3, p. 13*.

124. Kh. el-'Udeise
Israel Grid: 1632.1064
Environmental Niche: 7

ח׳ אל-עדיסה
Elevation: 1010 m.
Estimated Population: 225

Maximal Size: 25 dunams
Pottery: Iron II; P, H, R, Byz.

Size, Persian Period: 13 dunams
Established: Iron II

Bibliography: *JSG*, site 123 (16-10/36/1), p. 58; Ofer, 'The Highlands of Judah, I', map 310 (16-10), site 310/36/1, p. 13*.

125. Rujm el-Qaṣr
Israel Grid: 1664.1092
Environmental Niche: 7
Maximal Size: 1 dunam
Pottery: Iron II; P; H; Byz.

רג׳ם אל־קצר
Elevation: 900 m.
Estimated Population: 25
Size, Persian Period: 1 dunam
Established: Iron II

Bibliography: Ofer, 'The Highlands of Judah, I', map 310 (16-10), site 310/69/1, p. 13*.

126. Kh. Ras eṭ-Ṭawil
Israel Grid: 1636.1083
Environmental Niche: 7
Maximal Size: 45 dunams
Pottery: Iron I & II; P; H; Byz.

ח׳ רס א־טויל
Elevation: 1013 m.
Estimated Population: 575
Size, Persian Period: 23 dunams
Established: Iron I

Bibliography: Ofer, 'The Highlands of Judah, I', map 310 (16-10), site 310/38/1, p. 13*; *JSG*, site 111 (16-10/38/1), p. 56.

127. Si'ir
Israel Grid: 1637.1101
Environmental Niche: 7
Maximal Size: 17 dunams
Pottery: Iron II; Persian; H; R; Byz.

סעיר
Elevation: 850 m.
Estimated Population: 150
Size, Persian Period: 6 dunams
Established: Iron II

Bibliography: *JSG*, site100 (16-11/30/1), p. 54; Ofer map 307 (16-11), site 307/30/1, *HJBP*, p. 12*.

128. Kh. Ez-Zawiye
Israel Grid: 1651.1121
Environmental Niche: 7
Maximal Size: 1 dunam
Pottery: P

"אבו זויה" ;"ח׳ מזע" א־זויה
Elevation: 934 m.
Estimated Population: 25
Size, Persian Period: 1 dunam
Established: Persian.

Bibliography: *JSG*, site 85 (16-11/52/1), pp. 51-2; Ofer, 'The Highlands of Judah, I', site map 307 (16-11), site 307/52/1, p. 13*.

129. Kh. Zawiyye
Israel Grid: 1652.1122
Environmental Niche: 7
Maximal Size: 18 dunams
Pottery: Iron I & II; P; H; Byz.

ח׳ זויה
Elevation: 934 m.
Estimated Population: 200
Size, Persian Period: 8 dunams
Established: Iron I

Bibliography: Ofer, 'The Highlands of Judah, I', map 307 (16-11), site 307/52/3, p. 13*.

130. Tel Goren (Ein Gedi)   תל גורן
Israel Grid: 1863.0965   Elevation: 336 m.
Environmental Niche: 8   Estimated Population: 462.5
Maximal Size: NG   Size, Persian Period: L
Pottery: Iron II; Persian; H; R; Byz.   Established: Iron II

Bibliography: Mazar, Dothan and Dunayevsky, *En-Gedi*; Mazar and Dunayevsky, 'En-Gedi: The Third Season'; Mazar and Dunayevsky, 'En-Gedi: Fourth and Fifth Seasons'; Mazar, 'En-Gedi', *NEAEHL*, II, pp. 399-405.

131. Jericho   יריחו
Israel Grid: 1908.1424   Elevation: -224 m.
Environmental Niche: 8   Estimated Population: 212.5
Maximal Size: NG   Size, Persian Period: M
Pottery: Iron II, Persian, H.   Established: PPN

Bibliography: Kenyon, 'Jericho, Tell es-Sultan', *NEAEHL*, II, pp. 680-81; Netzer, 'Jericho', *NEAEHL*, II, p. 681; Sellin and Watzinger, *Jericho*; Hammond, 'A Note on Two Seal Impressions'; Bartlett, 'Iron Age and Hellenistic Stamped Jar Handles'.

132. Ketef Yeriho   כתף יריחו
Israel Grid: 1908.1424   Elevation: -224 m.
Environmental Niche: 8   Estimated Population: 0
Maximal Size: Cave   Size, Persian Period: 0
Pottery: Persian, H, R   Established: Persian

Bibliography: Eshel, 'Ketef Yeriho'; Eshel and Misgav, *ESI*, 1986; 'A Fourth Century B.C.E. Document from Ketef Yeriho'.

BIBLIOGRAPHY

Ackroyd, P.R., 'Two Old Testament Historical Problems of the Early Persian Period', *JNES* 17 (1958), pp. 13-27.
—*Exile and Restoration: A History of Hebrew Thought in the Sixth Century B.C.* (Philadelphia: Westminster Press, 1968).
—*Israel under Babylon and Persia* (London: Oxford University Press, 1970).
—'The History of Israel in the Exilic and Post-exilic Periods', in G.W. Anderson (ed.), *Tradition and Interpretation: Essays by Members of the Society for Old Testament Study* (Oxford: Clarendon Press, 1979), pp. 320-50.
—'Archaeology, Politics, and Religion: The Persian Period', *The Iliff Review* 39 (1982), pp. 5-24.
Adams, R.McC., *Land behind Baghdad: A History of Settlement on the Diyala Plains* (Chicago: University of Chicago Press, 1965).
—*The Evolution of Urban Society: Early Mesopotamia and Prehispanic Mexico* (Hawthorne, NY: Aldine Publishing Co., 1966).
—*Heartland of Cities: Surveys of Ancient Settlement and Land Use on the Central Floodplain of the Euphrates* (Chicago: University of Chicago Press, 1981).
Adams, R.McC., and H.J. Nissen, *The Uruk Countryside: The Natural Setting of Urban Societies* (Chicago: University of Chicago Press, 1972).
Aharoni, Y., *The Settlement of the Israelite Tribes in the Upper Galilee* (Jerusalem: Hebrew University, 1957 [Heb.]).
—*Excavations of Ramat Raḥel: Seasons 1959 and 1960* (Serie Archaeologica, 2; Rome: Centro di Studi Semitici, 1962).
—*Excavations of Ramat Raḥel: Seasons 1961 and 1962* (Serie Archaeologica, 6; Rome: Centro di Studi Semitici, 1964).
—*The Land of the Bible: A Historical Geography* (trans. A. Rainey; London: Burns & Oates, 2nd rev. edn, 1979).
—*The Archaeology of the Land of Israel* (Philadelphia: Westminster Press, 1982).
—'Ramat Raḥel', in *NEAEHL*, IV, pp. 1261-67.
Aharoni, Y., and M. Avi-Yonah, *The Macmillan Bible Atlas* (ed. A. Rainey and Z. Saphrai; New York: Macmillan, 3rd rev. edn, 1993).
Ahlström, G., *Who Were the Israelites?* (Winona Lake, IN: Eisenbrauns, 1986).
—*The History of Ancient Palestine from the Paleolithic Period to Alexander's Conquest* (Sheffield: Sheffield Academic Press, 1993).
Albright, W.F., *Excavations and Results at Tell el-Fûl (Gibeah of Saul)* (AASOR, 4; New Haven: American Schools of Oriental Research, 1924).
—'The Kyle Memorial Excavation at Bethel', *BASOR* 56 (1934), pp. 1-14.
—'Archaeology and the Date of the Hebrew Conquest of Palestine', *BASOR* 58 (1935), pp. 10-18.

—'Additional Note', *BASOR* 62 (1936), pp. 25-26.

—'The Israelite Conquest of Canaan in the Light of Archaeology', *BASOR* 74 (1939), pp. 11-23.

—'The Seal Impression from Jericho and the Treasurers of the Second Temple', *BASOR* 148 (1957), pp. 28-30.

—'Reports on Excavations in the Near and Middle East (Continued)', *BASOR* 159 (1960), pp. 37-39.

—*The Archaeology of Palestine and the Bible* (New York: Fleming H. Revell, 1932).

Albright, W.F., and J.L. Kelso, *The Excavations of Bethel (1934–1960)* (AASOR, 39; Cambridge, MA: American Schools of Oriental Research, 1968).

Albright, W.F., and O.R. Sellers, 'The First Campaign of Excavation at Beth-Zur', *BASOR* 43 (1931), pp. 2-13.

Alt, A., 'Die Rolle Samarias bei der Entstehung des Judentums', in A. Alt *et al.*, *Festschrift Otto Procksch zum sechzigsten Geburtstag* (Leipzig: J.C. Hinrichs, 1934), pp. 5-28; = *Kleine Schriften zur Geschichte des Volkes Israel*, II (Munich: Beck, 1953), pp. 316-37.

—'Judas Nachbarn zur Zeit Nehemias', *Palästinajahrbuch des deutschen evangelischen Institut für Altertumswissenschaft* 27 (1931), pp. 66-74.

—'Zur Geschichte der Grenze zwischen Judäa und Samaria', *Palästinajahrbuch des deutschen evangelischen Institut für Altertumswissenschaft* 31 (1935), pp. 94-111.

—'Die Landnahme der Israeliten in Palästina', in *idem, Kleine Schriften zur Geschichte des Volkes Israel*, I (Munich: Beck, 1953), pp. 89-125; ET 'The Settlement of the Israelites in Palestine', in *idem, Essays on Old Testament History and Religion* (Oxford: Basil Blackwell, 1966), pp. 135-69.

Amiran, D.H.K., and D. Nir, 'Geomorphology II/1, Geomorphology', in *Atlas of Israel Cartography, Physical Geography, Human and Economic Geography, History* (Jerusalem: Survey of Israel, Ministry of Labor; Amsterdam: Elsevier Publishing Co., 2nd edn, 1970).

Ammerman, A.J., 'Surveys and Archaeological Research', *ARA* 10 (1981), pp. 63-88.

Amusin, J.D., 'The People of the Land' (Russian), *Vestnik drevnjej istorii* 52 (1955), pp. 14-36.

Anderson, G., *Sacrifice and Offerings in Ancient Israel: Studies in their Social and Political Importance* (Atlanta: Scholars Press, 1987).

Ariel, D.T., 'A Survey of Coin Finds in Jerusalem (Until the End of the Byzantine Period)', *Studium Biblicum Franciscanum* 32 (1982), pp. 273-326.

Ariel, D.T. (ed.), *Excavations at the City of David.* II. *1978–1985, Directed by Yigal Shiloh, Imported Stamped Amphora, Handles, Coins, Worked Bone and Ivory, and Glass* (Qedem, 30; Monographs of the Institute of Archaeology; Jerusalem: The Hebrew University, 1990).

Ariel, D.T., and A. DeGroot (eds.), *Excavations in the City of David.* III. *1978–1985, Directed by Yigal Shiloh. Stratigraphical, Environmental, and Other Reports* (Qedem, 33; Jerusalem: Institute of Archaeology, The Hebrew University of Jerusalem, 1992).

—*Excavations at the City of David.* IV. *1978–1985, Directed by Yigal Shiloh* (Qedem, 35; Jerusalem: Institute of Archaeology, The Hebrew University of Jerusalem, 1996).

Ariel, D.T., and Y. Shoham, 'Locally Stamped Handles and Associated Body Fragments of the Persian and Hellenistic Periods' (forthcoming).

Atlas of Israel (Jerusalem: Survey of Israel, 2nd edn, 1970).

Avigad, N., 'A New Class of Yehud Stamps', *IEJ* 7 (1951), pp. 146-53.

—'Some Notes on the Hebrew Inscriptions from Gibeon', *IEJ* 9 (1959), pp. 130-33.

—*Bullae and Seals from a Post-Exilic Judan Archive* (Qedem, 4; Hebrew University Institute of Archaeology Monograph Series; Jerusalem: Hebrew University, 1976).

Avi-Yonah, M., 'The Walls of Nehemiah: A Minimalist View', *IEJ* 4 (1954), pp. 239-48.

—*The Holy Land* (Grand Rapids: Baker Book House, 1966).

—'The Newly Found Wall of Jerusalem and its Topographical Significance', *IEJ* 21 (1971), pp. 168-69.

Bahat, D., *The Illustrated Atlas of Jerusalem* (trans. S. Ketko; New York: Simon & Schuster, 1990).

Baly, D., *The Geography of the Bible* (New York: Harper & Row, rev. edn, 1974).

Barag, D., 'A Silver Coin of Yoḥanan and the High Priest' [Heb.], *Qadmoniot* 17 (1984), pp. 59-61.

—'Some Notes on a Silver Coin of Johanan the High Priest', *BA* 48 (1985), pp. 166-68.

—'A Silver Coin of Yoḥanan the High Priest and the Coinage of Judea in the Fourth Century B.C.', *INJ* 9 (1986–87), pp. 4-21.

Barkay, G., 'The Redefining of Archaeological Periods: Does the Date 588/586 B.C.E. Indeed Mark the End of the Iron Age Culture?', *BAT* (1990), pp. 106-109.

—'Excavations at Ketef Hinnom in Jerusalem', in *AJR*, pp. 85-106.

Barkay, R., 'An Archaic Greek Coin from the "Shoulder of Hinnom" Excavations in Jerusalem', *INJ* 8 (1984–85), pp. 1-5.

Barr, D.L., *New Testament Story: An Introduction* (Belmont, CA: Wadsworth, 2nd edn, 1995).

Barstad, H.M., 'On the History and Archaeology of Judah during the Exilic Period: A Reminder', *OLP* 19 (1988), pp. 25-36.

Bartlett, J.R., 'Appendix A: Iron Age and Hellenistic Stamped Jar Handles from Tell es-Sultan', in K.M. Kenyon and T.A. Holland (eds.), *Excavations at Jericho. IV. The Pottery Type Series and Other Finds* (Jerusalem and Oxford: British School of Archaeology and Oxford University Press, 1982), pp. 537-45.

Beach, E., 'Cultural Relations in the Shephelah in the Persian Period: Preliminary Observations from the Tell Halif Figurines', paper presented in the Literature and History of the Persian Period Group of the Society of Biblical Literature, Philadelphia, 20 November 1995.

Bedford, P.R., 'On Models and Texts: A Response to Blenkinsopp and Peterson', in P.R. Davies (ed.), *Second Temple Studies 1: Persian Period* (JSOTSup, 117; Sheffield: Sheffield Academic Press, 1991), pp. 154-62.

Beidelman, T., *W. Robertson Smith and the Sociological Study of Religion* (Chicago: University of Chicago Press, 1974).

Beit-Arieh, I., 'New Light on the Edomites', *BARev* 14 (1988), pp. 28-41.

Beit-Arieh, I. (ed.), *Ḥorvat Qitmit: An Edomite Shrine in the Biblical Negev* (Tel Aviv: Institute of Archaeology of Tel Aviv University, 1995).

Bennett, W.J., Jr, and J.A. Blakely (eds.), *Tell el-Hesi: The Persian Period (Stratum V)* (Winona Lake, IN: Eisenbrauns, 1989).

Ben-Sasson, H.H. (ed.), *A History of the Jewish People* (Cambridge, MA: Harvard University Press, 1976).

Bergman, A., 'Soundings at the Supposed Site of Anathoth', *BASOR* 62 (1936), pp. 22-25.

Berquist, J.L., *Judaism in Persia's Shadow: A Social and Historical Approach* (Minneapolis: Fortress Press, 1995).

Betlyon, J.W., *The Coinage and Mints of Phoenicia* (HSM, 26; Chico, CA: Scholars Press, 1982).

—'The Provincial Government of Persian Period Judea and the Yehud Coins', *JBL* 105 (1986), pp. 633-42.

—'Archaeological Evidence of Military Operations in Southern Judah during the Early Hellenistic Period', *BA* 54 (1991), pp. 36-43.

Bickerman, E., *From Ezra to the Last of the Maccabees* (New York: Schocken Books, 1962).

Biran, A., 'Anathoth?', *BASOR* 63 (1936), pp. 22-23.

— 'Ras el-Kharubbe (Anathoth)', *ESI* 2 (1983), p. 89.

— 'On the Problem of the Identification of Anathoth' [Heb.], *EI* 18 (1985), pp. 209-14.

Blakely, J.A., 'Site Survey', in *OEANE*, V, pp. 49-51.

Blenkinsopp, J., *A History of Prophecy in Israel from the Settlement in the Land to the Hellenistic Period* (Philadelphia: Westminster Press, 1983).

—*Ezra–Nehemiah* (OTL; Philadelphia: Fortress Press, 1988).

—'Temple and Society in Achaemenid Judah', in P.R. Davies (ed.), *Second Temple Studies 1: Persian Period* (JSOTSup, 117; Sheffield: Sheffield Academic Press, 1991), pp. 22-53.

—'The Judean Priesthood during the Neo-Babylonian and Achaemenid Periods: A Hypothetical Reconstruction', *CBQ* 60 (1998), pp. 25-43.

Bliss, F., 'Narrative of an Expedition of Moab and Gilead in March 1895', *PEFQS* (1895), pp. 203-204.

—*Excavations at Jerusalem 1894–1897* (London: Palestine Exploration Fund, 1898).

Bliss, F.J., and R.A.S. Macalister, *Excavations in Palestine during the Years 1898–1900* (London: Committee of the Palestine Exploration Fund, 1902).

Bothmer, D. von., 'Greek Pottery', in *TN*, I, pp. 175-78.

Briant, P., *Achaemenid History. X. Histoire de l'Empire perse de Cyrus à Alexandre* (Leiden: Nederlands Instituut voor het Nabije Oosten, 1996).

Bright, J., *A History of Israel* (Philadelphia: Westminster Press, 3rd edn, 1981).

Broshi, M., 'Excavations on Mount Zion, 1971–1972', *IEJ* 26 (1976), pp. 81-88.

—'Estimating the Population of Ancient Jerusalem', *BARev* 4 (1978), pp. 10-15.

—'The Population of Western Palestine in the Roman-Byzantine Period', *BASOR* 236 (1980), pp. 1-10.

—'The Diet of Palestine in the Roman Period: Introductory Notes', *Israel Museum Journal* 5 (1986), pp. 41-56.

—'The Role of the Temple in the Herodian Economy', *JJS* 38 (1987), pp. 31-37.

— 'Agriculture and Economy in Roman Palestine: Seven Notes on the Babatha Archive', *IEJ* 42 (1992), pp. 230-40.

—'Methodology of Population Estimates: The Roman-Byzantine Period as a Case Study', in *BAT 1990*, pp. 420-25.

Broshi, M., and I. Finkelstein, 'The Population of Palestine in Iron Age II', *BASOR* 287 (1992), pp. 47-60.

Broshi, M., and R. Gophna, 'The Settlements and Population of Palestine during the Early Bronze Age II-III', *BASOR* 253 (1984), pp. 41-53.

—'Middle Bronze Age II Palestine: Its Settlements and Population', *BASOR* 261 (1986), pp. 73-90.

Buss, Martin, review of *The Tribes of Yahweh: A Sociology of the Religion of Liberated Israel 1250–1050 B.C.E.* (Maryknoll, NY: Orbis Books, 1979), by N.K. Gottwald, in *RSR* 6 (1980), pp. 271-75.
Cahill, J., 'Chalk Vessel Assemblages of the Persian/Hellenistic and Early Roman Periods', in A. DeGroot and D.T. Ariel (eds.), *Excavations in the City of David.* II. *1978–1985, Directed by Yigal Shiloh. Stratigraphical, Environmental, and Other Reports* (Qedem, 33; Jerusalem: Institute of Archaeology, The Hebrew University of Jerusalem, 1992), pp. 190-278.
—'Rosette Stamp Seal Impressions from Ancient Judah', *IEJ* 45 (1995), pp. 230-52.
—'Stratum 9: Stratigraphy and Pottery' (forthcoming).
Cahill, J.M., and D. Tarler, 'Excavations Directed by Yigal Shiloh at the City of David, 1978–1985', *AJR*, pp. 35-40.
Campbell, E.F., 'Jewish Shrines in the Hellenistic and Persian Periods', in F.M. Cross (ed.), *Symposia Celebrating the 75th Anniversary of the Founding of the American Schools of Oriental Research (1900–1975)* (Cambridge, MA: American Schools of Oriental Research, 1979), pp. 159-67.
Carroll, R.P., 'Textual Strategies and Ideology in the Second Temple Period', in P.R. Davies (ed.), *Second Temple Studies 1: Persian Period* (JSOTSup, 117; Sheffield: Sheffield Academic Press, 1991), pp. 108-24.
—'So What Do We *Know* about the Temple? The Temple in the Prophets', in T.C. Eskenazi and K.H. Richards (eds.), *Second Temple Studies 2: Temple and Community in the Persian Period* (JSOTSup, 175; Sheffield: Sheffield Academic Press, 1994), pp. 34-51.
Carter, C.E., 'The Emerging Frontier in the Highlands of Canaan: New Models for an Old Problem', unpublished manuscript (1988).
—'Reconstructing the Past with Analogies from the Present: Establishing the Appropriate Limits for Ethnoarchaeological Approaches to Biblical Archaeology', paper presented at the Southeast regional SBL/AAR/ASOR meetings, March 1991.
—'A Social and Demographic Study of Post-Exilic Judah' (PhD dissertation, Duke University, 1991).
—'The Province of Yehud in the Post-Exilic Period: Soundings in Site Distribution and Demography', in T.C. Eskenazi and K.H. Richards (eds.), *Second Temple Studies 2: Temple and Community in the Persian Period* (JSOTSup, 175; Sheffield: Sheffield Academic Press, 1994), pp. 106-45.
—'A Discipline in Transition: The Contributions of the Social Sciences to the Study of the Hebrew Bible', in C.E. Carter and C.L. Meyers (eds.), *Community, Identity and Ideology: Social Science Approaches to the Hebrew Bible* (Winona Lake, IN: Eisenbrauns, 1996), pp. 3-36.
Casselberry, S.E., 'Further Refinement of Formulae for Determining Population from Floor Area', *WA* 6 (1974), pp. 117-22.
Causse, A., *Du groupe ethnique à la communauté religieuse: Le problème sociologique de la religion d'Israël* (Etudes d'histoire et de philosophie religieuses, 33; Paris: Alcan, 1937).
—*Les 'pauvres' d'Israël: Prophètes, psalmistes, messianistes* (Strasbourg: Librairie Istra, 1922).
—*Les dispersés d'Israël: Les origines de la diaspora et son rôle dans la formation du Judaïsme* (Paris: Alcan, 1929).

—'Du groupe ethnique à la communauté religieuse: Le problème sociologique du judaïsme', *RHPR* 14 (1934), pp. 285-335; ET 'From an Ethnic Group to a Religious Community: The Sociological Problem of Judaism' (trans. D.W. Baker; ed. C.E. Carter), in C.E. Carter and C.L. Meyers (eds.), *Community, Identity, and Ideology: Social Science Approaches to the Hebrew Bible* (Winona Lake, IN: Eisenbrauns, 1996), pp. 95-118.

Christaller, W., *Die zentralen Orte in Süddeutschland: Eine ökonomisch-geographische Untersuchung über die Gesetzmässigkeit der Verbreitung und Entwicklung der Siedlungen mit städtischen Funktionen* (Jena: Gustave Fischer, 1933).

Christoph, J., 'The Yehud Stamped Jar Handle Corpus: Implications for the History of Postexilic Palestine' (PhD dissertation, Duke University, 1993).

Clines, D.J.A., 'The Nehemiah Memoir: The Perils of Autobiography', in *idem, What Does Eve Do to Help? And Other Readerly Questions to the Old Testament* (JSOTSup, 205; Sheffield: Sheffield Academic Press, 1990), pp. 124-64.

—Haggai's Temple Constructed, Deconstructed and Reconstructed', in T.C. Eskenazi and K.H. Richards (eds.), *Second Temple Studies 2. Temple and Community in the Persian Period* (JSOTSup, 175; Sheffield: Sheffield Academic Press, 1994), pp. 60-87.

—*Interested Parties: The Ideology of Writers and Readers of the Hebrew Bible* (JSOTSup, 205; Sheffield: Sheffield Academic Press, 1995).

Cohen, R., 'Solomon's Negev Defense Line Contained Three Fewer Fortresses', *BARev* 12 (1986), pp. 40-45.

—'Salvage Excavations: Salvage Excavation in Israel', *OEANE*, IV, pp. 461-63.

—'Survey of Israel', *OEANE*, V, pp. 104-106.

Cohen, S.J.D., *From the Maccabees to the Mishnah* (Philadelphia: Westminster Press, 1987).

Collins, R., 'Some Principles of Long-Term Social Change: The Territorial Power of States', in L. Kriesberg (ed.), *Research in Social Movements, Conflicts, and Change*, I (Greenwich, CT: JAI Press, 1978), pp. 1-34.

—'Does Modern Technology Change the Rules of Geopolitics?', *JPMS* 9 (1981), pp. 163-77.

Computer Applications and Quantitative Methods in Archaeology (British Archaeological Reports, International Series, 548; Oxford: British Archaeological Reports, 1989–).

Conder, C.R., *Heth and Moab* (London: A.P. Watt, 1889).

—*Survey of Eastern Palestine* (London: The Committee of the Palestine Exploration Fund, 1889).

Cook, S.L., *Prophecy and Apocalypticism: The Postexilic Social Setting* (Minneapolis: Fortress Press, 1995).

Cross, F.M., Jr, *Canaanite Myth and Hebrew Epic: Essays in the History of the Religion of Israel* (Cambridge, MA: Harvard University Press, 1973).

—'The Cultus of the Israelite League', in *idem, Canaanite Myth and Hebrew Epic*, pp. 77-144.

—'The Discovery of the Samaria Papyri', *BA* 26 (1963), pp. 110-21.

—'The Divine Warrior', in *idem, Canaanite Myth and Hebrew Epic*, pp. 91-111.

—'Epigraphical Notes on the Hebrew Documents of the Eighth Centuries B.C. III. The Inscribed Jar Handles from Gibeon', *BASOR* 168 (1962), pp. 18-23.

—'A Reconstruction of the Judean Restoration', *JBL* 94 (1975), pp. 4-18.

Crowfoot, J.W., and G.M. Fitzgerald, *Excavations in the Tyropean Valley, Jerusalem 1927* *PEFA* 5 (1927).

Dadon, M., 'Har Adar', *ESI* 14 (1994), pp. 87-88.

Dalman, G., *Arbeit und Sitte in Pälestina* (Gütersloh: C. Bertelsmann, 1928–39).

Dandamaev, M.A., *Slavery in Babylonia: From Nabopolassar to Alexander the Great (626–331)* (trans. V.A. Powell; Dekalb, IL: Northern Illinois University Press, 1984).

—'State and Temple in Babylonia in the First Millennium B.C', in E. Lipínski (ed.), *State and Temple Economy in the Ancient Near East*, II (Leuven: Departement Oriëntalistiek, 1979), pp. 589-96.

Dandamaev, M.A., and V. Lukonin, *The Culture and Social Institutions of Ancient Iran* (Cambridge: Cambridge University Press, 1989).

Dar, S., *Landscape and Pattern: An Archaeological Survey of Samaria 800 B.C.E.—636 B.C.E.* (British Archaeological Reports International Series, 308.1; Oxford: British Archaeological Reports, 1986).

Davies, P.R., *In Search of 'Ancient Israel'* (JSOTSup, 148; Sheffield: Sheffield Academic Press, 1992).

—'The Society of Biblical Israel', in T.C. Eskenazi and K.H. Richards (eds.), *Second Temple Studies 2: Temple and Community in the Persian Period* (JSOTSup, 175; Sheffield: Sheffield Academic Press, 1994), pp. 22-33.

—'Method and Madness: Some Remarks on Doing History with the Bible', *JBL* 114 (1995), pp. 699-705.

Davies, P.R. (ed.), *Second Temple Studies 1: Persian Period* (JSOTSup, 117; Sheffield: Sheffield Academic Press, 1991).

De Geus, C.H.J., 'The Importance of Archaeological Research into the Palestinian Agricultural Terraces, with an Excursus on the Hebrew Word *gbi**', *PEQ* 107 (1975), pp. 65-74.

Demsky, A., 'The Genealogy of Gibeon (I Chronicles 9:35-44): Biblical and Epigraphic Considerations', *BASOR* 202 (1971), pp. 16-23.

—'*Pelekh* in Nehemiah 3', *IEJ* 33 (1983), pp. 242-44.

Deutsch, R., 'Six Unrecorded "Yehud" Silver Coins', *INJ* 11 (1990–91), pp. 4-6.

Deutsch, R., and M. Heltzer, 'Numismatic Evidence from the Persian Period from the Sharon Plain', *Transeuphratène* 13 (1997), pp. 17-20.

Dever, W., 'Material Remains and the Cult in Ancient Israel: An Essay in Archaeological Systemics', in C.L. Meyers and M. O'Connor (eds.), *The Word of the Lord Shall Go Forth: Essays in Honor of David Noel Freedman in Celebration of his Sixtieth Birthday* (Winona Lake, IN: Eisenbrauns, 1983), pp. 571-87.

—'The Impact of the "New Archaeology" on Syro-Palestinian Archaeology', *BASOR* 242 (1981), pp. 15-29.

—'Syro-Palestinian and Biblical Archaeology', in D. Knight and G. Tucker (eds.), *The Hebrew Bible and its Modern Interpreters* (Chico, CA: Scholars Press, 1985), pp. 31-74.

—'The Impact of the "New Archaeology"', in J.F. Drinkard, G.L. Mattingly and J.M. Miller (eds.), *Benchmarks in Time and Culture: An Introduction to Biblical Archaeology* (Atlanta: Scholars Press, 1988), pp. 337-57.

—'Yigal Yadin: Prototypical Biblical Archaeologist', *EI* 20 (1989), pp. 44*-51*.

—'Biblical Archaeology: Death and Rebirth', in *BAT 1990*, pp. 706-22.

Dion, P., 'The Civic-and-Temple Community of Persian Period Judaea: Neglected Insights from Eastern Europe', *JNES* 50 (1991), pp. 281-87.

Dinur, U., 'Khirbet 'Almit', *ESI* 5 (1986), p. 1.

—'Jerusalem Region, Survey of Map 102', *ESI* 6 (1987–88), pp. 62-65.

Dorsey, D., *The Roads and Highways of Israel* (Baltimore: The Johns Hopkins University Press, 1991).

Douglas, M., *Purity and Danger: An Analysis of the Concepts of Pollution and Taboo* (London: Routledge & Kegan Paul, 1966).

Duling, D., and N. Perrin, *The New Testament: Proclamation and Parenesis, Myth and History* (New York: Harcourt Brace Jovanovich, 1994).

Duncan, J.G., *Digging up Biblical History*, II (New York: Macmillan, 1931).

Edelman, D., *King Saul in the Historiography of Judah* (JSOTSup, 121; Sheffield: Sheffield Academic Press, 1991).

Edelstein, G., and S. Gibson, 'Ancient Jerusalem's Rural Food Basket: The "New" Archaeology Looks for an Urban Center's Agricultural Base', *BARev* 8 (1982), pp. 46-54.

Eitam, D., 'Olive Oil Production during the Biblical Period', in *OOIA*, pp. 16-36.

—'Olive Presses of the Israelite Period', *TA* 6 (1979), pp. 146-55.

Elgavish, J., *Archaeological Excavations at Shikmona, Field Report No. 1: The Levels of the Persian Period. Seasons 1963–1965* (Haifa: Museum of Ancient Art, 1968).

Elayi, J., and J. Sapin, *Beyond the River: New Perspectives on Transeuphratenè* (JSOTSup, 250; trans. J.E. Crowley; Sheffield: Sheffield Academic Press, 1998).

Engnell, I., *Gamla Testamentet: En traditionshistorisk inledning*, I (Stockholm: Svenska Kyrkans Diakonistyrelses Bokförlag, 1945).

—'Mosesböckerna', in I. Engnell and Fridrichsen (eds.), *Svenskt Bibliskt Upplagsverk* (Gävle: Skolförlaget, 1948), pp. 324-42.

Ephal, I., 'Changes in Palestine during the Persian Period in Light of the Epigraphic Sources', *IEJ* 48 (1998), pp. 106-19.

Eran, A., 'Weights and Weighing in the City of David: The Early Weights from the Bronze Age to the Persian Period', in D.T. Ariel and A. DeGroot (eds.), *Excavations at the City of David. IV. 1978–1985, Directed by Yigal Shiloh* (Qedem, 35; Jerusalem: Institute of Archaeology, The Hebrew University of Jerusalem, 1996), pp. 204-56.

Eshel, H., 'Ketef Yeriḥo', *ESI* 5 (1986), pp. 58-59.

Eshel, H., and H. Misgav, 'A Fourth Century B.C.E. Document from Ketef Yeriḥo', *IEJ* 38 (1988), pp. 158-76.

Eskenazi, T., *In an Age of Prose: A Literary Approach to Ezra–Nehemiah* (Atlanta: Scholars Press, 1988).

Eskenazi, T.C., and E.P. Judd, 'Marriage to a Stranger in Ezra 9–10', in T.C. Eskenazi and K.H. Richards (eds.), *Second Temple Studies 2. Temple and Community in the Persian Period* (JSOTSup, 175; Sheffield: Sheffield Academic Press, 1994), pp. 266-85.

Eskenazi, T.C., and K.H. Richards (eds.), *Second Temple Studies 2: Temple and Community in the Persian Period* (JSOTSup, 175; Sheffield: Sheffield Academic Press, 1994).

Finkelstein, I., *'Izbet Sarṭah: An Early Iron Age Site near Rosh Ha'ayin, Israel* (British Archaeological Reports International Series, 299; Oxford: British Archaeological Reports, 1986).

—'The Value of Demographic Data from Recent Generations for Environmental Archaeology and Historical Research', paper presented at the Society for Biblical Literature International Meeting (Sheffield, England, 1988).

—*The Archaeology of the Israelite Settlement* (Jerusalem: Israel Exploration Society, 1988).

—'The Land of Ephraim Survey 1980–1987: Preliminary Report', *TA* 15–16 (1988–89), pp. 117-83.

—'Environmental Archaeology and Social History: Demographic and Economic Aspects of the Monarchic Period', paper presented at the Second International Congress on Biblical Archaeology (Jerusalem, Israel, 1990).

Finkelstein, I., and I. Magen, *Archaeological Survey of the Hill Country of Benjamin* (Jerusalem: Israel Antiquities Authority, 1993).

Finkelstein, I., and N. Na'aman (eds.), *From Nomadism to Monarchy: Archaeological and Historical Aspects of Early Israel* (Jerusalem: Yad Izhak Ben-Zvi and The Israel Exploration Society, 1990).

Fishbane, M., 'From Scribalism to Rabbinism: Perspectives on the Emergence of Classical Judaism', in J.G. Gammie and L.G. Perdue (eds.), *The Sage in Israel and the Ancient Near East* (Winona Lake, IN: Eisenbrauns, 1990), pp. 439-56.

Flannagan, J., *David's Social Drama: A Hologram of Israel's Early Iron Age* (Sheffield: Almond Press, 1988).

Frankel, R., S. Avitsur and E. Ayalon (eds.), *History and Technology of Olive Oil in the Holy Land* (Tel Aviv: Eretz Israel Museum, 1994).

Franken, H.J., 'The Problem of Identification in Biblical Archaeology', *PEQ* 108 (1976), pp. 3-11.

Frick, F., *The Formation of the State in Ancient Israel: A Survey of Models and Theories* (The Social World of Biblical Antiquity Series, 4; Decatur, GA: Almond Press, 1985).

Freedman, D.N., and D.F. Graf (eds.), *Palestine in Transition: The Emergence of Ancient Israel* (The Social World of Biblical Antiquity, 2; Sheffield: Almond Press, 1983).

Fritz, V., 'Conquest or Settlement? The Early Iron Age in Palestine', *BA* 50 (1987), pp. 84-100.

Funk, R.W., 'The History of Beth-Zur with Reference to its Defenses', in O.R. Sellers (ed.), *The 1957 Excavation at Beth-Zur* (AASOR, 38; Cambridge, MA: American Schools of Oriental Research, 1968), pp. 4-17.

—'Beth-Zur', in *NEAEHL*, I, pp. 259-61.

Gal, Z., 'Khirbet Roš Zayit—Biblical Cabul: A Historical-Geographical Case', *BA* 53 (1990), pp. 88-97.

—'Regional Survey Projects: Revealing the Settlement Map of Ancient Israel', in *BAT 1990*, pp. 453-58.

Galling, K., 'The "Gōlā-List" According to Ezra 2//Nehemiah 7', *JBL* 70 (1951), pp. 149-58.

Garbini, G., 'Hebrew Literature in the Persian Period', in T.C. Eskenazi and K.H. Richards (eds.), *Second Temple Studies 2: Temple and Community in the Persian Period* (JSOTSup, 175; Sheffield: Sheffield Academic Press, 1994), pp. 180-88.

Garrison, M.B., and M. Cool Root (eds.), *Achaemenid History. IX. Persepolis seal studies: An Introduction with Provisional Concordances of Seal Numbers and Associated Documents on Fortification Tablets 1–2087* (Leiden: Nederlands Instituut voor het Nabije Oosten, 1996).

Gibson, S., 'Landscape Archaeology and Ancient Agricultural Field Systems in Palestine' (PhD dissertation, Institute of Archaeology, University College London).

Gibson, S., and G. Edelstein, 'Investigating Jerusalem's Rural Landscape', *Levant* 17 (1985), pp. 139-55.

Gitay, Y. (ed.), *Prophecy and Prophets: The Diversity of Contemporary Issues in Scholarship* (Atlanta: Scholars Press, 1997).

Gitin, S., 'Tel Miqne-Ekron: A Type Site for the Inner Coastal Plain in the Iron Age II Period', in S. Gitin and W.G. Dever (eds.), *Recent Excavations in Israel: Studies in Iron Age Archaeology* (AASOR, 49; Winona Lake, IN: Eisenbrauns, 1989), pp. 23-58.

—'Glueck, Nelson', in *OEANE*, II, pp. 415-16.

Gitin, S., and T. Dothan, 'The Rise and Fall of Ekron of the Philistines: Recent Excavations at an Urban Border Site', *BA* 50 (1987), pp. 197-222.

Glueck, N., *Exploration in Eastern Palestine* (AASOR, 14, 15, 18/19 and 25–28; New Haven: American Schools of Oriental Research, 1934–51).

—*Rivers in the Desert: A History of the Negev* (New York: W.W. Norton, 1968).

—*The Other Side of the Jordan* (Cambridge, MA: American Schools of Oriental Research, rev. edn, 1970).

Gordon, R.P. (ed.), *The Place Is Too Small for Us: The Israelite Prophets in Recent Scholarship* (Sources for Biblical and Theological Study; Winona Lake, IN: Eisenbrauns, 1995).

Gottwald, N.K., 'Domain Assumptions and Societal Models in the Study of Pre-Monarchic Israel', in G.W. Anderson *et al.* (eds.), *Congress Volume: Edinburgh, 1974* (VTSup, 28; Leiden: E.J. Brill, 1974), pp. 89-100.

—*The Tribes of Yahweh: A Sociology of the Religion of Liberated Israel 1250–1050 B.C.E.* (Maryknoll, NY: Orbis Books, 1979).

—'Part X. The Religion of the New Egalitarian Society: Idealist, Structural Functional, and Historical-Materialist Models', in *idem*, *The Tribes of Yahweh*, pp. 591-103.

—'The Pastoral Nomadic Model for Early Israel: Critique and Radical Revision', in *idem*, *The Tribes of Yahweh*, pp. 435-63.

—*The Hebrew Bible: A Socio-Literary Introduction* (Philadelphia: Fortress Press, 1985).

—'Sociology of Ancient Israel', in *ABD*, VI, pp. 79-89.

—'Reconstructing the Social History of Early Israel', *EI* 24 (1993), pp. 77*-82*.

Grabbe, L., 'Reconstructing History from the Book of Ezra', in P.R. Davies (ed.), *Second Temple Studies 1: Persian Period* (JSOTSup, 117; Sheffield: Sheffield Academic Press, 1991), pp. 98-106.

—*Judaism from Cyrus to Hadrian*. I. *The Persian and Greek Periods* (Minneapolis: Fortress Press, 1992).

—'What Was Ezra's Mission?', in T.C. Eskenazi and K.H. Richards (eds.), *Second Temple Studies 2: Temple and Community in the Persian Period* (JSOTSup, 175; Sheffield: Sheffield Academic Press, 1994), pp. 286-99.

Grabbe, L. (ed.), *Can a 'History of Israel' Be Written?* (JSOTSup, 145; Sheffield: Sheffield Academic Press, 1997).

—*Leading Captivity Captive: 'The Exile' as History and Ideology* (JSOTSup, 278; Sheffield: Sheffield Academic Press, 1998).

Graham, J.A., 'Previous Excavations at Tell el-Fûl: A Survey of Research and Exploration', in N. Lapp (ed.), *The Third Campaign at Tel el-Fûl: The Excavations of 1964* (AASOR, 45; Cambridge, MA: American Schools of Oriental Research, 1981), pp. 1-17.

Halligan, J., 'The Temple that Never Was: Zerubbabel's. A Social-Scientific Investigation', paper presented at the International meeting of the Society of Biblical Literature, Dublin, 1996).

Halpern, B., *The First Historians: The Hebrew Bible and History* (New York: Harper & Row, 1988).
Hammond, P.C., 'A Note on Two Seal Impressions from Tell es-Sultan', *PEQ* 89 (1957), pp. 68-69.
—'A Note on a Seal Impression from Tell es-Sultan', *BASOR* 147 (1957), pp. 37-39.
Hanson, P., *The Dawn of Apocalyptic: The Historical and Sociological Roots of Jewish Apocalyptic Eschatology* (Philadelphia: Fortress Press, rev. edn, 1979).
Harris, M., *The Rise of Anthropological Theory: A History of Theories of Culture* (New York: Columbia University Press, 1968).
— *Cows, Pigs, Wars, and Witches: The Riddles of Human Culture* (New York: Random House, 1979).
—*Cultural Materialism: The Struggle for a Science of Culture* (New York: Vintage Books, 1979).
—*The Sacred Cow and the Abominable Pig: Riddles of Food and Culture* (New York: Touchstone, 1987).
Harris, S.L., *The New Testament: A Student's Introduction* (MountainView, CA: Mayfield, 1988).
Hassan, F.A., 'Demography and Archaeology', *ARA* 8 (1979), pp. 137-60.
Heltzer, M., 'A Recently Published Babylonian Tablet and the Province of Judah after 516 B.C.E.', *Transeuphratène* 5 (1992), pp. 57-61.
Hengel, M., *Judaism and Hellenism* (Philadelphia: Fortress Press, 2nd edn, 1981).
Herion, G., 'The Impact of Modern and Social Science Assumptions on the Reconstruction of Israelite History', *JSOT* 34 (1986), pp. 3-33.
Herzog, Z., 'Persian Period Stratigraphy and Architecture', in Z. Herzog, G. Rapp, Jr, and O. Negbi (eds.), *Excavations at Tel Michal, Israel* (Minneapolis and Tel Aviv: The University of Minnesota Press and The Sonia and Marco Nadler Institute of Archaeology, 1989), pp. 88-114.
Heschel, A.J., *The Prophets* (New York: Harper & Row, 1962).
Hodder, I., 'The Identification and Interpretation of Ranking in Prehistory: A Contextual Perspective', in C. Renfrew and S. Shennan (eds.), *Ranking, Resource and Exchange: Aspects of the Archaeology of Early European Society* (Cambridge: Cambridge University Press, 1982), pp. 150-54.
—*Reading the Past: Current Approaches to Interpretation* (Cambridge: Cambridge University Press, 1986).
Hodder, I. (ed.), 'The Contribution of the Long Term', in *idem* (ed.), *Archaeology as Long-Term History* (Cambridge: Cambridge University Press, 1987), pp. 1-8.
Hoglund, K., 'The Establishment of a Rural Economy in the Judean Hill Country during the Late Sixth Century BCE', paper presented at the Southeastern Regional Meeting of the Society of Biblical Literature, American Association of Religion, and American Schools of Oriental Research, Charlotte, NC, 16–18 March 1989.
—'The Achaemenid Context', in P.R. Davies (ed.), *Second Temple Studies 1: Persian Period* (JSOTSup, 117; Sheffield: Sheffield Academic Press, 1991), pp. 54-68.
—*Achaemenid Imperial Administration in Syria-Palestine and the Missions of Ezra and Nehemiah* (Atlanta: Scholars Press, 1992).
Hölscher, G., *Geschichte der israelitischen und jüdischen Religion* (Giessen: Alfred Töpelmann, 1922).
— 'Die Bücher Esra und Nehemia', in E. Kautzsch (ed.), *Die Heilige Schrift des Alten Testaments*, II (Tübingen: J.C.B. Mohr, 4th edn, 1923), pp. 491-562.

—'Les origines de la communauté juive à l'époque perse', *RHPR* 6 (1926), pp. 105-26.

Holland, T.A., 'Jericho', in *OEANE*, III, pp. 221-24.

Hopkins, D., *The Highlands of Canaan: Agricultural Life in the Early Iron Age* (The Social World of Biblical Antiquity series, 3; Decatur, GA: Almond Press, 1985).

—'Life on the Land: The Subsistence Struggles of Early Israel', *BA* 50 (1987), pp. 178-91.

—'Farmsteads', in *OEANE*, II, pp. 306-307.

Horsley, R., 'Empire, Temple and Community—But no Bourgeoisie! A Response to Blenkinsopp and Petersen', in P.R. Davies (ed.), *Second Temple Studies 1: Persian Period* (JSOTSup, 117; Sheffield: Sheffield Academic Press, 1991), pp. 163-74.

Hurvitz, Avi, *A Linguistic Study of the Relationship between the Priestly Source and the Book of Ezekiel: A New Approach to an Old Problem* (Cahiers de la Révue Biblique, 20; Paris: J. Gabalda, 1982).

—'The Evidence of Language in Dating the Priestly Code: A Linguistic Study in Technical Idioms and Terminology', *RB* 81 (1984), pp. 25-46.

Ibach, R.D., Jr, *Archaeological Survey of the Hesban Region: Catalogue of Sites and Characterizations of Periods* (Hesban, 5; Berrien Springs, MI: Andrews University, 1987).

Ibn Khaldûn, *The Muqaddimah: An Introduction to History* (3 vols.; trans. F. Rosenthal; Princeton, NJ: Princeton University Press, 1968; abridged edn, ed. N.J. Dagwood; Princeton, NJ: Princeton University Press, 1969).

Ishida, T., *The Royal Dynasties in Ancient Israel: A Study on the Formation and Development of Royal-Dynastic Ideology* (Berlin: W. de Gruyter, 1977).

—*Studies in the Period of David and Solomon and Other Essays* (Winona Lake, IN: Eisenbrauns, 1982).

Jacobsen, T., 'Early Political Development in Mesopotamia', *ZA* 52 (1957), pp. 91-140.

Jamieson-Drake, D., *Scribes and Schools in Monarchic Judah: A Socio-Archaeological Approach* (Social World of Biblical Antiquity Series, 9; Sheffield: Almond Press, 1991).

Japhet, S., 'The Supposed Common Authorship of Chronicles and Ezra–Nehemiah Investigated Anew', *VT* 18 (1968), pp. 330-71.

—'Sheshbazzar and Zerubbabel: Against the Background of the Historical and Religious Tendencies of Ezra–Nehemiah', *ZAW* 94 (1982), pp. 66-98.

Johnson, G.A., 'A Test of the Utility of the Central Place Theory in Archaeology', in P.J. Ucko, R. Tringham and G.W. Dimbleby (eds.), *Man, Settlement and Urbanism* (Cambridge, MA: Shenkman Publishing Co., 1972), pp. 769-85.

Kallai, Z., *The Northern Boundaries of Judah from the Settlement of the Tribes until the Beginning of the Hasmonean Period* (Jerusalem: Magnes Press, 1960 [Heb.]).

Kaufman, Y., *The Religion of Israel: From its Beginnings to the Babylonian Exile* (trans. and abridged M. Greenberg.; New York: Schocken Books, 1938–56 [Heb.]).

Kee, H.C., *Understanding the New Testament* (Englewood Cliffs, NJ: Prentice–Hall, 4th edn, 1983).

Kellerman, U., 'Die Listen in Nehemia 11: Eine Dokumentation aus den letzten Jahren des Reiches Juda?', *ZDPV* 82 (1966), pp. 209-27.

Kelso, J., 'Bethel', in *NEAEHL*, I, pp. 192-94.

Kenyon, K., 'Excavations in Jerusalem, 1962', *PEQ* 95 (1963), pp. 7-21.

—'Excavations in Jerusalem, 1965', *PEQ* 98 (1966), pp. 73-88.

—'Excavations in Jerusalem, 1966', *PEQ* 99 (1967), pp. 65-71.

—'Excavations in Jerusalem, 1967', *PEQ* 100 (1968), pp. 97-109.

—'Jericho, Tell es-Sultan', *NEAEHL*, II, pp. 680-81.

Kessler, J., 'The Second Year of Darius and the Prophet Haggai', *Transeuphratène* 5 (1992), pp. 63-84.

Kimbrough, S.T., 'A Non-Weberian Approach to Israelite Religion', *JNES* 31 (1972), pp. 197-202.

King, P., *American Archaeology in the Mideast: A History of the American Schools of Oriental Research* (Philadelphia: American Schools of Oriental Research, 1983).

—*Amos, Hosea, Micah: An Archaeological Commentary* (Philadelphia: Westminster Press, 1988).

—*Jeremiah: An Archaeological Companion* (Louisville, KY: Westminster/John Knox Press, 1993).

Kippenberg, H.G., *Religion und Klassenbildung im antiken Judäa* (SUNT, 14; Göttingen: Vandenhoeck & Ruprecht, 1978).

Kloner, A. (ed.), *Archaeological Survey of Jerusalem* (Jerusalem: Israel Antiquities Authority, forthcoming).

Knoppers, G.N., *Two Nations under God: The Deuteronomistic History of Solomon and the Dual Monarchies*. I. *The Reign of Solomon and the Rise of Jeroboam* (HSM, 52; Cambridge, MA: Harvard University Press, 1993).

—*Two Nations under God: The Deuteronomistic History of Solomon and the Dual Monarchies*. II. *The Reign of Jeroboam, the Fall of Israel, and the Reign of Josiah* (HSM, 53; Cambridge, MA: Harvard University Press, 1994).

Koch, K., *The Prophets*. I. *The Assyrian Period* (Philadelphia: Fortress Press, 1982).

—*The Prophets*. II. *The Babylonian and Persian Periods* (Philadelphia: Fortress Press, 1984).

Kochman, M., 'Status and Extent of Judah in the Persian Period' (PhD dissertation, The Hebrew University of Jerusalem, 1980).

Kramer, C., *Ethnoarchaeology: Implications of Ethnography to Archaeology* (New York: Columbia University Press, 1979).

Kreissig, H., 'Eine beachtenswerte Theorie zur Organisation altvorderorientalischer Templegemeinden im Achamenidenreich: Zu J.P. Weinberg's "Bürger-Tempel-Gemeinde" in Juda', *Klio* 66 (1984), pp. 35-39.

Kuhrt, A., and H. Sancisi-Weerdenburg (eds.), *Achaemenid History*. III. *Method and Theory* (Leiden: Nederlands Instituut voor Nabije Oosten, 1988).

Lapp, N.L., 'Fûl, tell el-', in *NEAEHL*, II, pp. 444-48.

Lapp, N.L. (ed.), *The Third Campaign at Tell el-Fûl: The Excavations of 1964* (AASOR, 45; Cambridge, MA: American Schools of Oriental Research, 1981).

—'Casemate Walls in Palestine and the Late Iron II Casemate at Tell el-Fûl (Gibeah)', *BASOR* 223 (1976), pp. 25-42.

Lapp, P.W., 'Ptolemaic Stamped Handles from Judah', *BASOR* 172 (1963), pp. 22-35.

—'Tell el-Fûl', *BA* 28 (1965), pp. 2-10.

—review of *Winery, Defenses, and Soundings at Gibeon* (Philadelphia: The University Museum, 1964), by J.B. Pritchard, in *AJA* 72 (1968), pp. 391-93.

—'The Pottery of Palestine in the Persian Period', in A. Kuschke and E. Kutsch (eds.), *Archäologie und Altes Testament: Festschrift für Kurt Galling* (Tübingen: J.C.B. Mohr, 1970), pp. 179-97.

Lapp, P., and N. Lapp, 'Iron II-Hellenistic Pottery Groups', in O.R. Sellers (ed.), *The 1957 Excavation at Beth-Zur* (AASOR, 38; Cambridge, MA: The American Schools of Oriental Research, 1968), pp. 54-79.

Leith, M.J.W., *Wadi Daliyeh I: The Wadi Daliyeh Seal Impressions* (New York: Oxford University Press, 1997).

Lemche, N.P., *Early Israel: Anthropological and Historical Studies on the Israelite Society before the Monarchy* (VTSup, 37; Leiden: E.J. Brill, 1985).

—'The Revolution Hypothesis: Its Formulation and Presuppositions', in idem, *Early Israel*, pp. 1-79.

—*Ancient Israel: A New History of Israelite Society* (The Biblical Seminar; 5; Sheffield: Sheffield Academic Press, 1988).

—'On the Use of "System Theory", "Macro-Theories", and "Evolutionistic Thinking" in Modern Old Testament Research and Biblical Archaeology', *SJOT* 2 (1990), pp. 73-88.

Lenski, G., J. Lenski and P. Nolan, *Introduction to Human Societies: A Macro-Sociological Approach* (New York: McGraw-Hill, 6th edn, 1991).

Lenski, G., *Power and Privilege: A Theory of Social Stratification* (New York: McGraw-Hill, 1966).

—Review of *The Tribes of Yahweh: A Sociology of the Religion of Liberated Israel 1250–1050 B.C.E.* (Maryknoll, NY: Orbis Books, 1979), by N.K. Gottwald, in *RSR* 6 (1980), pp. 275-78.

Levy, T.E., 'Survey, Archaeological', in *OEANE*, V, pp. 101-104.

Lowery, R., *The Reforming Kings: Cult and Society in First Temple Judah* (JSOTSup, 120; Sheffield: JSOT Press, 1991).

MacAlister, R.A.S., and J.G. Duncan, *Excavations on the Hill of Ophel, Jerusalem, 1923–1925* (*PEFA* 4 [1923–25]).

MacDonald, B., *The Wadi el Hasa Archaeological Survey 1979–1983* (Waterloo, Ontario: Wilfrid Laurier University, 1988).

—*The Southern Ghors and Northeast Arabah Archaeological Survey* (Sheffield Archaeological Monographs, 5; Sheffield: University of Sheffield, 1992).

MacDonald, B., G. Rollefson and D.W. Roller, 'The Wadi el-Hasa Survey 1981: A Preliminary Report', *ADAJ* 26 (1982), pp. 117-31.

Machinist, P., 'The First Coins of Judah and Samaria: Numismatics and History in the Achaemenid and Early Hellenistic Periods', in A. Kuhrt and M. Cool Root (eds.), *Achaemenid History. VIII. Continuity and Change* (Leiden: Nederlands Instituut voor Nabije Oosten, 1994), pp. 365-80.

Malamat, A., 'Charismatic Leadership in the Book of Judges', in F.M. Cross, W.E. Lemke and P.D. Miller (eds.), *Magnalia Dei: The Mighty Acts of God. Essays on the Bible and Archaeology in Memory of G. Ernest Wright* (Garden City, NY: Doubleday, 1976), pp. 152-68.

Malina, B., 'The Social Sciences and Biblical Interpretation', *Int* 37 (1982), pp. 229-42.

Map of Palestine, Scale 1: 20,000 (Jaffa: Department of Lands and Survey, 1927).

Marinkovic, P., 'What Does Zechariah 1–8 Tell Us about the Second Temple', in T.C. Eskenazi and K.H. Richards (eds.), *Second Temple Studies 2: Temple and Community in the Persian Period* (JSOTSup, 175; Sheffield: Sheffield Academic Press, 1994), pp. 88-103.

Mayes, A.D.H., *The Old Testament in Sociological Perspective* (London: Pickering, 1989).

Mazar, A., 'Iron Age Fortresses in the Judean Hills', *PEQ* 114 (1982), pp. 86-109.

—*Archaeology of the land of the Bible 10,000–586 B.C.E.* (New York: Doubleday, 1990).

—'Abu Tuwein, Khirbet', in *NEAEHL*, I, pp. 15-16.

Mazar, B., *The Mountain of the Lord* (New York: Doubleday, 1975).

— 'En-Gedi', in *NEAEHL*, II, pp. 399-405.

Mazar, B., T. Dothan and I. Dunayevsky, *En-Gedi: The First and Second Seasons of Excavations, 1961–1962* ('Atiqot, 5; Jerusalem: The Department of Antiquities and Museums, 1966).

Mazar, B., and I. Dunayevsky, 'En-Gedi: The Third Season of Excavation', *IEJ* 14 (1964), pp. 121-30.

—'En-Gedi: Fourth and Fifth Seasons of Excavations'. *IEJ* 17 (1967), pp. 133-43.

McClellan, T.L., 'Town Planning at Tell en-Naṣbeh', *ZDPV* 100 (1984), pp. 53-69.

McCown, C.C. 'Inscribed Material Including Coins', in *TN*, I, pp. 175-78.

—'Nashbeh, Tell en-', *EAEHL*, III, pp. 912-18.

McCown, C.C. (ed.), 'Palestine, Geography of', in *IDB*, III, pp. 626-39.

McEvenue, S., 'The Political Structure in Judah from Cyrus to Nehemiah', *CBQ* 43 (1981), pp. 353-64.

McGovern, P.E., *The Late Bronze/Early Iron Age of Central Transjordan: The Baq'ah Valley Project, 1977–1981* (Philadelphia: University of Pennsylvania Museum, 1986).

Mendenhall, G., 'Covenant Forms in Israelite Tradition', *BA* 17 (1954), pp. 50-76.

—'The Hebrew Conquest of Palestine', *BA* 25 (1962), pp. 66-87.

—*The Tenth Generation: The Origins of the Biblical Tradition* (Baltimore: The Johns Hopkins University Press, 1973).

—'Ancient Israel's Hyphenated History', in D.N. Freedman and D.F. Graf (eds.), *Palestine in Transition: The Emergence of Ancient Israel* (The Social World of Biblical Antiquity, 2; Sheffield: Almond Press, 1983), pp. 91-103.

Meshorer, Y., *Ancient Jewish Coinage. I. Persian Period through Hasmonaeans* (Dix Hills, NY: Amphora Books).

Meshorer, Y., and S. Qedar, *The Coinage of Samaria in the Fourth Century BCE* (Jerusalem: Numismatic Fine Arts International, 1991).

Mettinger, T.N.D., *Solomonic State Officials: A Study of the Civil Government Officials of the Israelite Monarchy* (Lund: C.W.K. Gleerup, 1971).

Meyer, E., *Die Entstehung des Judentums: Eine historische Untersuchung* (Halle: Niemeyer, 1896).

Meyers, C.L., 'The Roots of Restriction: Women in Early Israel', *BA* 41 (1978), pp. 91-103.

—'Of Seasons and Soldiers: A Topological Appraisal of the Pre-Monarchic Tribes of Galilee', *BASOR* 252 (1983), pp. 47-59.

—'Procreation, Production, and Protection: Male-Female Balance in Early Israel', *JAAR* 51 (1983), pp. 569-73.

—*Discovering Eve: Ancient Israelite Women in Context* (New York: Oxford University Press, 1988).

—'David as Temple Builder', in P.D. Miller, P.D. Hanson and S.D. McBride (eds.), *Ancient Israelite Religion: Essays in Honor of Frank Moore Cross* (Philadelphia: Fortress Press, 1987), pp. 357-76.

Meyers, C.L., and E.M. Meyers, *Haggai, Zechariah 1–8* (AB, 25B; Garden City, NY: Doubleday, 1987).

—'Expanding the Frontiers of Biblical Archaeology', *EI* 20 (1989), pp. 140*-47*.

—*Zechariah 9–14* (AB, 25C; Garden City, NY: Doubleday, 1993).

Meyers, E.M., 'The Persian Period and the Judean Restoration: From Zerubbabel to Nehemiah', in P.D. Miller, P. Hanson, and D. McBride (eds.), *Ancient Israelite*

Religion: Essays in Honor of Frank Moore Cross (Philadelphia: Fortress Press, 1987), pp. 509-21.

—'The Shelomith Seal and the Judean Restoration: Some Additional Considerations', *EI* 18 (1985), pp. 33*-38*.

Mildenberg, L., 'Yehud: A Preliminary Study of the Provincial Coinage of Judea', in O. Markholm and N.M. Waggoner (eds.), *Greek Numismatics and Archaeology: Essays in Honor of Margaret Thompson* (Belgium: Wettern, 1979), pp. 183-96.

—'Notes on the Coin Issues of Mazday', *INJ* 11 (1990–91), pp. 9-23.

—'On the Money Circulation in Palestine from Artaxerxes II till Ptolemy I: Preliminary Studies of Local Coinage in the Fifth Persian Satrapy. Part 5', *Transeuphratène* 7 (1994), pp. 63-71.

Milevski, I., 'Settlement Patterns in Northern Judah during the Achaemenid Period, According to the Hill Country of Benjamin and Jerusalem Surveys', *BAIAS* 15 (1996–97), pp. 7-29.

Miller, J.M., 'Archaeological Survey South of Wadi Mujib: Glueck's Sites Revisited', *ADAJ* 23 (1979), pp. 79-81.

—'Site Identification: A Problem Area in Contemporary Biblical Scholarship', *ZDPV* 99 (1983), pp. 119-29.

—'Introduction', in *idem* (ed.), *Archaeological Survey of the Kerak Plateau*, pp. 16-17.

Miller, J.M. (ed.), *Archaeological Survey of the Kerak Plateau* (Atlanta: Scholars Press, 1991).

Muilenburg, J. 'Survey of the Literature on Tell en-Naṣbeh', in *TN*, I, pp. 13-22.

—'The Literary Sources Bearing on the Question of Identification', in *TN*, I, pp. 23-45.

Myers, J., *II Chronicles* (AB, 13; Garden City, NY: Doubleday, 1983).

—*Ezra, Nehemiah: Introduction, Translation and Notes* (AB, 14; Garden City, NY: Doubleday, 1983).

Nadelman, Y., 'Jerusalem—Pisgat Ze'ev "D" ', *HA* 99 (1993), pp. 49-51.

—'Jerusalem, Pisgat Ze'ev D (H. Zimri)', *ESI* 12 (1993), pp. 54-56.

Narrol, R. 'Floor Area and Settlement Population', *AA* 27 (1962), pp. 587-89.

Negbi, O., 'Remains of a Fortress next to French Hill' (Heb.), *HA* 31–32 (1969), p. 18.

Negev, A. (ed.), *The Archaeological Encyclopedia of the Holy Land* (New York: Prentice-Hall, 3rd edn, 1990).

—'The Archaeological Periods in Palestine', in *idem* (ed.), *The Archaeological Encyclopedia of the Holy Land*, p. 416.

Netzer, E., 'Jericho: Hellenistic to Early Arab Periods', in *NEAEHL*, II, pp. 681-91.

O'Brien, J., *Priest and Levite in Malachi* (Atlanta: Scholars Press, 1990).

Oden, R., *The Bible without Theology: The Theological Tradition and Alternatives to It* (San Francisco: Harper & Row, 1987).

Ofer, A., 'The Judean Hill Country: From Nomadism to National Monarchy', in I. Finkelstein and N. Naaman (eds.), *From Nomadism to Monarchy: Archaeological and Historical Aspects of Early Israel* (Jerusalem: Yad Izhak Ben Zvi and the Israel Exploration Society, 1990), pp. 92-121.

—'All the Hill Country of Judah? From a Settlement Fringe to a Prosperous Monarchy', in I. Finklestein and N. Naaman (eds.), *From Nomadism to Monarchy: Archaeological and Historical Aspects of Early Israel* (Jerusalem: Yad Izhak Ben-Zvi, Israel Exploration Society and Biblical Archaeological Society, 1994).

—'The Highlands of Judah during the Biblical Period, I' (PhD dissertation, Tel Aviv University, 1993).

—'Judah', *OEANE*, III, pp. 253-57.
Olmstead, A.T., *History of the Persian Empire* (Chicago: University of Chicago Press, 1948).
Onn, A., and Y. Rapuano, 'Jerusalem, Kh. er- Ras', *ESI* 13 (1993), p. 71.
Orni, E., and E. Ephrat, *Geography of Israel* (Jerusalem: Israel Program for Scientific Translations, 1964).
Overholt, T., 'Prophecy: The Problem of Cross-Cultural Comparison', *Semeia* 21 (1982), pp. 55-78.
—'Seeing Is Believing: The Social Setting of Prophetic Acts of Power', *JSOT* 23 (1982), pp. 3-31.
Parker, S.T. (ed.), *The Roman Frontier in Central Jordan: Interim Report on the Limes Arabicus Proejct, 1980–1985* (British Archaeological Reports International Series, 340; Oxford: British Archaeological Reports, 1987).
Paar, P.J., review of *Winery, Defenses, and Soundings at Gibeon* (Philadelphia: The University Museum, 1964), by J.B. Pritchard., in *PEQ* 98 (1966), pp. 114-118.
Peckham, B., *History and Prophecy: The Development of the Late Judean Literary Traditions* (Garden City, NY: Doubleday, 1993).
Person, R., *Second Zechariah and the Deuteronomic School* (JSOTSup, 167; Sheffield: Sheffield Academic Press, 1993).
Petersen, D., *Late Israelite Prophecy: Studies in Deutero-Prophetic Literature and in Chronicles* (Missoula, MT: Scholars Press, 1977).
—'Zerubbabel and Jerusalem Temple Reconstruction', *CBQ* 36 (1974), pp. 366-72.
Picard, C.Y., and V. Golani, 'Geological Map of Israel' (Jerusalem: Survey of Israel, 1965, repr. 1987).
Plöger, Otto, *Theocracy and Eschatology* (trans. S. Rudman; Richmond, VA: John Knox Press, 1968).
Polzin, R., *Samuel and the Deuteronomist* (Bloomington: Indiana University Press, 1993).
—*David and the Deuteronomist: 2 Samuel* (Bloomington: Indiana University Press, 1993).
Porath, J., 'A Persian Period Fortress at the Beach of Ashdod' (Heb.), *'Atiqot* 7 (1974), pp. 43-55.
Porten, B., *Archives from Elephantine* (Berkeley: University of California Press, 1968).
Pommerantz, I. (ed.), ' "Isawiye"—Survey of New Road', *ESI* 1 (1982), pp. 54-55.
Pritchard, J.B., *Hebrew Inscriptions and Stamps from Gibeon* (Philadelphia: University of Pennsylvania Press, 1959).
—'The Bible Reports on Gibeon', *Expedition* 3 (1960), pp. 2-9.
—'Discovery of the Biblical Gibeon', *University Museum Bulletin* 21 (1957), pp. 3-26.
—'Gibeon's History in Light of Excavation', in G.W. Anderson *et al.* (eds.), *Congress Volume: Oxford, 1959* (VTSup, 7; Leiden: E.J. Brill, 1960), pp. 1-12.
—'Gibeon', in *EAEHL*, II, pp. 446-50.
—'El Jîb', in *NEAEHL*, II, pp. 511-14.
—'Industry and Trade at Biblical Gibeon', *BA* 23 (1960), pp. 23-29.
—'A Second Excavation at Gibeon', *University Museum Bulletin* 22 (1958), pp. 13-24.
—'The Water System at Gibeon', *BA* 19 (1956), pp. 66-75.
—'The Wine Industry at Gibeon: 1959 Discoveries', *Expedition* 2 (1959), pp. 17-25.
—*Winery, Defenses, and Soundings at Gibeon* (Philadelphia: The University Museum, 1964).
Provan, I.W., 'Ideologies, Literary and Critical: Reflections on Recent Writing on the History of Israel', *JBL* 114 (1995), pp. 585-606.

Rachmani, L.Y., 'Silver Coins of the Fourth Century B.C. from Tell Gamma', *IEJ* 21
    (1971), pp. 158-60.
Rad, G. von, *Das Geschichtsbild des chronistischen Werkes* (BWANT, 4.3; Stuttgart:
    W. Kohlhammer, 1930).
Rader, M., *Marx's Interpretation of History* (New York: Oxford University Press, 1979).
Rainey, A., 'The Satrapy "Beyond the River"', *AJBA* 1 (1969), pp. 51-78.
—'Historical Geography: The Link between Historical and Archaeological Interpretation',
    BA 45 (1982), pp. 217-23.
—'The Biblical Shephelah of Judah', *BASOR* 251 (1983), pp. 1-22.
—'Tel Gerisah and the Inheritance of the Danite Tribe' (Heb.), *Annual of the Eretz Israel
    Museum* 23–24 (1987–89), pp. 59-72.
—review of *The Tribes of Yahweh: A Sociology of the Religion of Liberated Israel 1250–
    1050 B.C.E* (Maryknoll, NY: Orbis Books, 1979), by N.K. Gottwald, in *JAOS* 107
    (1987), pp. 541-43.
Ravikovitch, S., 'Geomorphology II/3, Soil Map', in *Atlas of Israel: Cartography, Physical
    Geography, Human and Economic Geography, History* (Jerusalem: Survey of Israel,
    Ministry of Labor; Amsterdam: Elsevier Publishing Co., 2nd edn, 1970).
Redman, C.L., *The Rise of Civilization: From Early Farmers to Urban Society in the
    Ancient Near East* (San Francisco: W.H. Freeman and Company, 1978).
—*Archaeological Explanation: The Scientific Method in Archaeology* (New York:
    Columbia University Press, 1984).
Redman, C.L. (ed.), *Social Archaeology* (New York: Academic Press, 1978).
Reich, R., 'Tombs in the Mamilla Street Area, Jerusalem', in A. Drori (ed.), *Highlights of
    Recent Excavations* (Jerusalem: The Israel Antiquities Authority, 1990), pp. 16-17.
—'The Ancient Burial Ground in the Mamilla Neighborhood, Jerusalem', in *AJR*, pp. 111-
    18.
—'The Beth-Zur Citadel II: A Persian Residency?', *TA* 19 (1992), pp. 113-23.
Reich, R., and E. Shukron, 'Jerusalem, Mamilla', *ESI* 14 (1994), pp. 92-96.
Reich, R., E. Shukrun and Y. Bilig, 'Jerusalem, Mamilla Area', *ESI* 10 (1991), pp. 24-25.
Reifenberg, A., *The Soils of Palestine: Studies in Soil Formation and Land Utilization in
    the Mediterranean* (London: Thomas Murby & Co., 2nd rev. edn, 1947).
Renfrew, C., *Approaches to Social Archaeology* (Cambridge, MA: Harvard University
    Press, 1984).
Richards, K., 'Reshaping Chronicles and Ezra–Nehemiah Research', in J.L. Mays, D.L.
    Petersen and K.H. Richards (eds.), *The Old Testament Interpretation: Past, Present,
    and Future: Essays in Honor of Gene M. Tucker* (Nashville: Abingdon Press, 1995),
    pp. 211-24.
Rim, M., 'Interpretation of Polymorphic Profiles in Soils of the Eastern Mediterranean: An
    Analysis of the Geophysical Factor in Soil Genesis', *IEJ* 4 (1954), pp. 266-77.
Roberts, J.J.M., 'In Defense of the Monarchy: The Contribution of Israelite Kingship to
    Biblical Theology', in P.D. Miller, P.D. Hanson and S.D. McBride (eds.), *Ancient
    Israelite Religion: Essays in Honor of Frank Moore Cross* (Philadelphia: Fortress
    Press, 1987), pp. 377-96.
Robinson, E., *Biblical Researches in Palestine, Mount Sinai and Arabia Petraea* (London:
    J. Murray, 1856).
Rogerson, J.W., *Anthropology and the Old Testament* (Atlanta: John Knox Press, 1979).
—'The Use of Sociology in Old Testament Studies', in J.A. Emerton (ed.), *Congress
    Volume: Salamanca, 1983* (VTSup, 36; Leiden: E.J. Brill, 1985), pp. 245-56.

Rosen, B., 'Subsistence Economy of Stratum II', in I. Finkelstein, *'Izbet Ṣarṭah: An Early Iron Age Site near Rosh Ha'ayin, Israel* (British Archaeological Reports International Series, 299; Oxford: British Archaeological Reports, 1986), pp. 156-85.

Roseman, N., 'Climate, IV/2: Rainfall', in *Atlas of Israel: Cartography, Physical Geography, Human and Economic Geography, History* (Jerusalem: Survey of Israel, Ministry of Labor; Amsterdam: Elsevier Publishing Co., 2nd edn, 1970).

Ruppé, R.J., 'The Archaeological Survey: A Defence', *AA* 31 (1966), pp. 313-33.

Saller, S.J., *Excavations at Bethany (1949–1953)* (Publications of the Studium Biblicum Franciscanum, 12; Jerusalem: Franciscan Press, 1957).

Sancisi-Weerdenburg, H. (ed.), *Achaemenid History. I. Sources, Structures, Synthesis* (Leiden: Nederlands Instituut voor Nabije Oosten, 1987).

Sancisi-Weerdenburg, H., and J.W. Drijvers (eds.), *Achaemenid History. V. The Roots of the European Tradition* (Leiden: Nederlands Instituut voor Nabije Oosten, 1990).

—*Achaemenid History. VII. Through Travellers' Eyes* (Leiden: Nederlands Instituut voor Nabije Oosten, 1991).

Sancisi-Weerdenburg, H., and A. Kuhrt (eds.), *Achaemenid History. II. The Greek Sources* (Leiden: Nederlands Instituut voor Nabije Oosten, 1987).

—*Achaemenid History. IV. Centre and Periphery* (Leiden: Nederlands Instituut voor Nabije Oosten, 1990).

—*Achaemenid History. VI. Asia Minor and Egypt* (Leiden: Nederlands Instituut voor Nabije Oosten, 1991).

Sancisi-Weerdenburg, H., A. Kuhrt and M. Cool Root (eds.), *Achaemenid History. VIII. Continuity and Change* (Leiden: Nederlands Instituut voor Nabije Oosten, 1994).

Sandel, G., 'Am Toten Meer', *ZDPV* 30 (1907), pp. 79-106.

Sasson, J.M., 'On Choosing Models for Recreating Israelite Pre-Monarchic History', *JSOT* 21 (1981), pp. 3-24.

Saulcy, F. de, *Voyage autour de la Mer Morte et dans les terres bibliques: Exécuté de décembre 1850 à avril 1851* (2 vols.; Paris: Gide & J. Baudry, 1853).

Schacht, R.M., 'Estimating Past Population Trends', *ARA* 10 (1981), pp. 119-40.

Schäffer, P., 'The Hellenistic and Maccabeaean Periods', in J.H. Hayes and J.M. Miller (eds.), *Israelite and Judaean History* (Philadelphia: Westminster Press, 1977), pp. 556-57.

Schiffer, M.B., T.C. Klinger and A.P. Sullivan, 'The Design of Archaeological Surveys', *WA* 10 (1978), pp. 1-28.

Schultz, C., 'The Political Tensions Reflected in Ezra–Nehemiah', in W.W. Hallo, C.D. Evans and J.B. White (eds.), *Scripture in Context: Essays on the Comparative Method* (PTMS, 34; Pittsburgh: Pipwick Press, 1980), pp. 221-44.

Schürer, E., *The History of the Jewish People in the Age of Jesus Christ* (3 vols.; ed. G. Vermes, F. Millar and M. Black; Edinburgh: T. & T. Clark, 1973).

Schwartz, G., 'Salvage Excavations: An Overview', in *OEANE*, IV, pp. 159-61.

Seetzen, U., *A Brief Account of Countries Adjoining the Lake Tiberias, the Jordan and the Dead Sea* (London: Palestine Association of London, 1810).

Sellers, O.R., 'Catalog of the Coins', in *CBZ*, pp. 71-73.

—'The 1957 Campaign at Beth-Zur', *BA* 21 (1958), pp. 71-76.

—'Echoes of the 1931 Campaign', in *idem* (ed.), *The 1957 Excavation at Beth-Zur* (AASOR, 38; Cambridge, MA: The American Schools of Oriental Research, 1968), pp. 1-3.

Sellers, O.R. (ed.), *The 1957 Excavation at Beth-Zur* (AASOR, 38; Cambridge, MA: The American Schools of Oriental Research, 1968).

Sellin, E., and C. Watzinger, *Jericho: Die Ergebnisse der Ausgrabungen* (Wissenschaftliche Veröffentlichung der deutschen Orient-gesellschaft, 22; Leipzig: J.C. Hinrichs, 1913).

Sharer, R.J., and W. Ashmore, *Archaeology: Discovering our Past* (Mountain View, CA: Mayfield, 2nd edn, 1993).

Shiloh, Y., 'Tables of Major Archaeological Activities in Jerusalem since 1863', in Yigal Yadin (ed.), *Jerusalem Revealed: Archaeology in the Holy City 1968–1974* (Jerusalem: Israel Exploration Society, 1976), pp. 131-35.

—*Excavations at the City of David. I. 1978–1982, Interim Report of the First Five Seasons* (Qedem, 19; Jerusalem: Institute of Archaeology, The Hebrew University of Jerusalem, 1984).

—'News and Notes: Jerusalem, City of David, 1984', *IEJ* 35 (1985), pp. 65-67.

—'News and Notes: Jerusalem, City of David, 1985', *IEJ* 35 (1985), pp. 301-303.

—'A Group of Hebrew Bullae from the City of David', *IEJ* 36 (1986), pp. 16-38.

—'Stratigraphical Introduction to Parts I and II', in Ariel (ed.), *Excavations at the City of David,* II.

—'The Population of Iron Age Palestine in the Light of a Sample Analysis of Urban Plans, Areas and Population Density', *BASOR* 239 (1980), pp. 25-35.

—'Jerusalem: The Early Periods and the First Temple. Excavation Results', in *NEAEHL,* II, pp. 701-712.

Silberman, N., *Digging for God and Country: Exploration in the Holy Land, 1799–1917* (New York: Doubleday, 1991).

Sinclair, L.A., *An Archaeological Study of Gibeah (Tell el-Fûl)* (AASOR, 34–35; New Haven: American Schools of Oriental Research, 1960).

—'An Archaeological Study of Gibeah (Tell el-Fûl)', *BA* 27 (1964), pp. 52-64.

—'Bethel Pottery of the Sixth Century B.C.', in W.F. Albright and J.L. Kelso (eds.), *The Excavations of Bethel (1934–1960)* (AASOR, 39; Cambridge, MA: American Schools of Oriental Research, 1968), pp. 70-76.

Smith, D., *The Religion of the Landless: A Sociology of the Babylonian Exile* (Bloomington: Meyer-Stone, 1989).

— 'The Politics of Ezra: Sociological Indicators of Postexilic Judaean Society', in P.R. Davies (ed.), *Second Temple Studies 1: Persian Period* (JSOTSup, 117; Sheffield: Sheffield Academic Press, 1991), pp. 73-97.

Smith, G.A., *The Historical Geography of the Holy Land* (London: Hodder & Stoughton, 25th edn, 1931; repr.; Gloucester, MA: Peter Smith, 1972).

Smith, M., *Palestinian Parties and Politics that Shaped the Old Testament* (London: SCM Press, 2nd edn, 1987).

Smith, W. Robertson, *Lectures on the Religion of the Semites: First Series. The Fundamental Institutions* (Edinburgh: A. & C. Black, 1889).

—*Kinship and Marriage in Early Arabia* (Cambridge: Cambridge University Press, 1885).

—*Lectures on the Religion of the Semites: Second and Third Series* (ed. J. Day; JSOTSup, 183; Sheffield: Sheffield Academic Press, 1995).

Smith-Christopher, D., 'The Mixed Marriage Crisis in Ezra 9–10 and Nehemiah 13: A Study of the Sociology of the Post-Exilic Judaean Community', in T.C. Eskenazi and K.H. Richards (eds.), *Second Temple Studies 2: Temple and Community in the*

Persian Period (JSOTSup, 175; Sheffield: Sheffield Academic Press, 1994), pp. 242-65.

—'Translators Foreword', in Weinberg, *The Citizen–Temple Community*, pp. 10-16.

Spaer, A., 'Jaddua the High Priest?', *INJ* 9 (1986–87), pp. 1-3.

Stager, L.E. 'Climatic Conditions and Grain Storage in the Persian Period', *BA* 34 (1971), pp. 86-88.

—'The Archaeology of the Family', *BASOR* 260 (1985), pp. 1-35.

—'Why Were Hundreds of Dogs Buried at Ashkelon?' *BARev* 17 (1991), pp. 26-42.

Stern, E. 'A Burial of the Persian Period near Hebron', *IEJ* 21 (1971), pp. 25-30.

—'Yehud in Vision and Reality', *Cathedra* 4 (1977), pp. 13-25 (Heb.).

—'Archaemenid Clay Rhyta from Palestine', *IEJ* 32 (1982), pp. 36-43.

—*Material Culture of the Land of the Bible in the Persian Period 538–332 B.C.* (Warminster, England: Aris & Phillips Ltd, 1982).

—'The Province of Yehud in Vision and Reality', in L. Levine (ed.), *The Jerusalem Cathedra: Studies in the History, Archaeology, Geography, and Ethnography of the Land of Israel*, I (Jerusalem: Yad Izhak Ben-Zvi Institute, 1981), pp. 9-21.

—'The Persian Empire and the Political and Social History of Palestine in the Persian Period', in *CHJ*, I, pp. 70-87.

—'What Happened to the Cult Figurines? Israelite Religion Purified after the Exile', *BARev* 15 (1989), pp. 22-29, 53-54.

—'The Dor Province in the Persian Period in the Light of the Recent Excavations at Tel Dor', *Transeuphratène* 2 (1990), pp. 147-55.

—'New Evidence on the Administrative Division of Palestine in the Persian Period', in H. Sancisi-Weerdenburg and A. Kuhrt (eds.), *Achaemenid History. IV. Centre and Periphery* (Leiden: Nederlands Instituut voor Nabije Oosten, 1990), pp. 221-26.

Stinespring, W.F., 'Prolegomenon: C.C. Torrey's Contribution to Ezra Studies', in C.C. Torrey, *Ezra Studies* (New York: Ktav, 1970), pp. xi-xxviii.

Sukenik, E.L., 'Paralipomena Palestinensia', *JPOS* 14 (1935), pp. 178-84.

—'More about the Oldest Coins of Judaea', *JPOS* 15 (1936), pp. 341-43.

Summer, W.M., 'Estimating Population by Analogy', in C. Kramer (ed.), *Ethnoarchaeology: The Implications of Ethnography for Archeology* (New York: Academic Press, Inc., 1977), pp. 164-74.

Talmon, S., *King, Cult and Calendar in Ancient Israel* (Jerusalem: Magnes Press, 1986).

Thompson, T.L., *Early History of the Israelite People: From the Written and Archaeological Sources* (Leiden: E.J. Brill, 1992).

—'A Neo-Albrightean School in History and Biblical Scholarship?', *JBL* 114 (1995), pp. 683-98.

Torrey, C.C., 'The Chronicler as Editor and as Independent Narrator', in *idem, Ezra Studies* (New York: Ktav, 1970), pp. 208-251.

—'The Exile and Restoration', in *idem, Ezra Studies* (New York: Ktav, 1970), pp. 285-335.

Tsafrir, Y., 'The Walls of Jerusalem in the Period of Nehemiah' (Heb.), *Cathedra* 4 (1977), pp. 31-42.

Turner, J., *The Structure of Sociological Theory* (Chicago: Dorsey Press, 4th edn, 1986).

Tushingham, A.D., *Excavations in Jerusalem 1961–1967*, I (Toronto: Royal Ontario Museum, 1985).

Tyson, J.B., *The New Testament and Early Christianity* (New York: Macmillan, 1984).

Van Seters, J., *Prologue to History: The Yahwist as Historian in Genesis* (Louisville, KY: Westminster/John Knox Press, 1992).

—*The Life of Moses: The Yahwist as Historian in Exodus–Numbers* (Louisville, KY: Westminster/John Knox Press, 1994).

—'The Pentateuch (Genesis, Exodus, Leviticus, Numbers, Deuteronomy)', in Steven L. McKenzie and M. Patrick Graham (eds.), *The Hebrew Bible Today: An Introduction to Critical Issues* (Louisville, KY: Westminster/John Knox Press, 1998), pp. 3-49.

Vogel, E.K., 'Bibliography of Holy Land Sites', *HUCA* 42 (1971), pp. 1-96.

—'Bibliography of Holy Land Sites, Part II', *HUCA* 52 (1981), pp. 1-92.

—'Bibliography of Holy Land Sites, Part III', *HUCA* 58 (1987), pp. 1-67.

Wacquant, L., 'Heuristic Models in Marxian Theory', *Social Forces* 64 (1985), pp. 17-45.

Wampler, J.C., 'The Stratification of Tell en-Naṣbeh', in *TN*, I, pp. 179-86, 221.

Watson, P.J., 'The Idea of Ethnoarchaeology: Notes and Comments', in C. Kramer (ed.), *Ethnoarchaeology: The Implications of Ethnography for Archaeology* (New York: Academic Press, Inc., 1977), pp. 277-87.

—*Archaeological Ethnography in Western Iran* (Tucson, AZ: University of Arizona Press, 1979).

—'Ethnoarchaeology in the Near East, Lettre d'Information', *AO* 5 (1982), pp. 72-79.

Weber, M., *Ancient Judaism* (trans. H. Gerth and D. Martindale; New York: The Free Press, 1952).

—'Part II. The Covenant and the Confederacy', in *idem*, *Ancient Judaism*, pp. 61-77.

—*The Agrarian Sociology of Ancient Civilization* (trans. R.I. Frank; London: NLB, 1976).

Weinberg, Joel, *The Citizen–Temple Community* (trans. D. Smith-Christopher; JSOTSup, 151; Sheffield: Sheffield Academic Press, 1992).

Weinberg, J.P., 'Demographische Notizen zur Geschichte der nachexilischen Gemeinde in Juda', *Klio* 54 (1972), pp. 45-59 (ET 'Demographic Notes on the History of the Postexilic Community in Judah', in *idem*, *The Citizen–Temple Community*, pp. 34-48).

—'Das *Bēit ʾAḇōt* im 6.–4. Jh. v.u.Z.', *VT* 23 (1973), pp. 400-14 (ET 'The *Bêt Āḇôt* in the Sixth to Fourth Centuries BCE', in *idem*, *The Citizen–Temple Community*, pp. 49-61).

—'Der *ʿammē hāʾāreṣ* des 6.–4. Jh. V.u.Z.', *Klio* 56 (1974), pp. 325-35 (ET The *ʿAm Hāʾāreṣ* of the Sixth to Fourth Centuries BCE', in *idem*, *The Citizen–Temple Community*, pp. 62-74).

—'Die Agrarverhältnisse in der Bürger-Tempel-Gemeinde der Achämenidenzeit', *AAASH* 12 (1974), Fasc, pp. 1-4 (ET 'The Agricultural Relations of the Citizen–Temple Community in the Achaemenid Period', in *idem*, *The Citizen–Temple Community*, pp. 92-104).

—'Nᵉtînîm und Söhne der Sklaven Salomos" im 6.–4 Jh. v.u.Z.', *ZAW* 87 (1975), pp. 355-71 (ET 'Nᵉtînîm and "Sons of the Slaves of Solomon" in the Sixth to Fourth Centuries BCE', in *idem*, *The Citizen–Temple Community*, pp. 75-91).

—'Bemerkungen zum Problem, "Der Vorhellenismus im Vorden Orient"', *Klio* 58 (1976), pp. 5-20 (ET 'Comments on the Problem of "Pre-Hellenism in the Near East"', in *idem*, *The Citizen–Temple Community*, pp. 17-33).

—'Zentral- und Partikulargewalt im achämenidischen Reich', *Klio* 59 (1977), pp. 25-43 (ET 'Central and Local Administration in the Achaemenid Empire', in *idem*, *The Citizen–Temple Community*, pp. 105-26).

—'The Postexilic Citizen–Temple Community: Theory and Reality', in *idem*, *The Citizen–Temple Community*, pp. 127-38).
—'Transmitter and Recipient in the Process of Acculturation: The Experience of the Judean Citizen–Temple Community', *Transeuphratène* 13 (1997), pp. 91-105.
Weippert, M., *The Settlement of the Israelite Tribes in Palestine: A Critical Survey of the Recent Debate* (London: SCM Press, 1971).
Wellhausen, J., *Prolegomena to the History of Ancient Israel* (Gloucester, MA: Peter Smith, 1983).
Westermann, C., *Basic Forms of Prophetic Speech* (Philadelphia: Westminster Press, 1967).
Widengren, G., 'The Persian Period', in J.H. Hayes and J.M. Miller (eds.), *Israelite and Judean History* (Philadelphia: Westminster Press, 1977), pp. 489-538.
Wightman, G.J., *The Walls of Jerusalem from the Canaanites to the Mamluks* (Mediterranean Archaeology Supplement, 4; Sydney: Meditarch, 1993).
Wilkinson, J., 'Ancient Jerusalem: Its Water Supply and Population', *PEQ* 106 (1974), pp. 33-51.
Williamson, H.G.M., 'Nehemiah's Walls Revisited', *PEQ* 116 (1984), pp. 81-88.
—*Ezra, Nehemiah* (WBC, 16; Waco, TX: Word Books, 1988).
—'Exile and After: Historical Study', forthcoming in D.W. Baker and B.T. Arnold (eds.), *Faces of Old Testament Study* (Grand Rapids: Baker Book House, 1999).
—'Judah and the Jews', in M. Brosious and A. Kuhrt (eds.), *Achaemenid History*. XI. *Studies in Persian History: Essays in Memory of David M. Lewis* (Leiden: Nederlands Instituut von Het Nabije Oosten, 1998), pp. 145-63.
Wilson, C., *The Ordnance Survey of Jerusalem* (London: HMSO, 1865; Jerusalem: Ariel House Publishers, 1980).
Wilson, R.R., *Prophecy and Society in Ancient Israel* (Philadelphia: Fortress Press, 1980).
—*Sociological Approaches to the Old Testament* (Philadelphia: Fortress Press, 1984).
Wright, G.E., review of 'The Water System of Gibeon' (*BA* 19 [1956], pp. 66-75), by J.B. Pritchard, in *JNES* 22 (1963), pp. 210-11.
Wright, G.E., 'The Provinces of Solomon (I Kings 4:7-9)', *EI* 8 (1967), pp. 58*-68*.
Yaalon, D.H., 'Calcareous Soils of Israel: The Amount and Particle-size Distribution of the Calcareous Material', *IEJ* 4 (1954), pp. 278-85.
Zadok, R., *The Jews in Babylonia during the Chaldean and Achaemenian Periods (According to the Babylonian Sources)* (Haifa: University of Haifa, 1979).
Zehavi, A., 'Jerusalem, Manahat', *ESI* 12 (1993), pp. 66-67.
Zorn, J., 'Tell en-Naṣbeh: A Re-evaluation of the Architecture and Stratigraphy of the Early Bronze Age, Iron Age and Later Periods' (PhD dissertation, University of California, Berkeley, 1993).
—'Estimating the Population Size of Ancient Settlements: Methods, Problems, Solutions, and a Case Study', *BASOR* 295 (1995), pp. 31-48.
—'Naṣbeh, Tell en-', in *NEAEHL*, III, pp. 1098-1102.
—'Mizpah: Newly Discovered Stratum Reveals Judah's Other Capital', *BARev* 23.5 (1997), pp. 28-37, 66.
Zorn, J., J. Yellin and J. Hayes, 'The *m(w)ṣh* Stamp Impressions and the Neo-Babylonian Period', *IEJ* 44 (1994), pp. 161-83.

INDEXES

INDEX OF REFERENCES

OLD TESTAMENT

INDEX OF AUTHORS

INDEX OF SUBJECTS

Samaritan 38, 50, 77, 82

seal impressions 47, 57, 58, 88, 89, 116,
119, 125, 132, 144, 151, 152, 161,
166, 169, 170, 249, 256, 259, 260,
262, 266, 276, 279-83, 285, 300,
301
anepigraphic 23, 56, 144, 151, 159,
259, 261, 276, 277
animal 142
b' 261, 276, 277
conical 125, 160, 261, 263
cruciform 170
epigraphic 56, 259
l'hzy/phw 144, 145, 151, 261
Latin-F 145
Lion 144, 159, 259, 261, 266, 276
m(w)sh/msp 132, 144, 145, 151, 161,
162, 260, 262, 266, 268, 276,
277
rosette 133, 151, 194, 195, 233, 235,
260, 261
taw 151, 170, 260
'uryw/sgnd 161
'uryw/yhwd 261
yh 88, 132, 137, 144, 151, 162, 261,
277
yhd 88-90, 132, 137, 142, 144, 151,
152, 161, 261, 262, 266, 277
yhd plus symbol 152, 166
yhd-tet 57, 145, 300, 301
yhwd 132, 137, 144, 145, 151, 162,
261, 266, 267, 276, 277
yhwd hnnh 144, 151, 261, 266, 267
yhwd plus personal name 277
yhwd phw' 261, 267, 277
yhwd yhw 'zr phw' 144, 145, 151, 261
yrslm 54, 57, 88-90, 132, 137, 152,
166, 170, 300, 301

Second Isaiah 39, 286, 310

Second Temple 22, 33, 34, 37, 42, 150,
292, 302, 313, 323

Second Zechariah 317

segmentary society 61

settlement 27, 28, 55, 93, 102, 119, 146,
157, 160, 174, 175, 180-82, 190,
222, 237, 238, 240-42, 245-48, 250,
251, 268

history 29, 171, 175-78, 183, 235,
236
map 176
patterns 172, 173, 179, 182, 183,
214, 237, 271

Shephelah 29, 79-81, 83, 88, 91-94, 98,
100, 102, 111, 247, 290, 292, 293,
323

Sheshbazzar 36, 39, 51, 52, 148, 301, 305

Sidon 97, 98, 269, 277, 290

site(s) 36, 47, 93, 98, 113, 117, 172, 176,
178, 180, 181, 183, 190, 200, 216,
225-28, 235, 238, 241, 245, 247,
248, 252, 254

site distribution 26, 27, 29, 38, 55, 114,
171, 173, 176, 178, 179, 182, 185,
188, 189, 198, 202, 204, 206, 211-
13, 215, 220, 224, 226, 231, 234,
249, 323

social science(s) 24, 38, 39, 60-65, 68-70,
101, 316, 321

social structures 183

socio-archaeology 71, 74

socioeconomic 21-23, 26, 27, 29, 38, 45,
46, 48, 56, 58, 76, 93, 102, 176,
185, 249, 276, 283, 289, 296, 301,
304, 306, 310, 315, 321-23

sociohistorical 322

sociopolitical 21, 27, 29, 44, 47, 83, 91,
176, 225, 282, 321, 322

socio-religious 27, 76, 317

soil type 100-104, 112, 185, 256

south central hills 103, 111, 241, 248,
255

southern desert fringe 111, 186, 205, 220,
241

southwestern hills 103, 110, 205, 255

southwestern slopes 186, 223, 225, 230,
241, 245

structural-functional approach 64

subsistence strategy 100, 104, 177, 183,
248

survey(s) 22, 26, 29, 37, 53-55, 58, 59,
76, 78, 79, 113, 114, 172, 174-79,
182, 183, 199, 214, 215, 248-50,
252, 254, 271, 283
non-probabilistic 178, 179

JOURNAL FOR THE STUDY OF THE OLD TESTAMENT
SUPPLEMENT SERIES